WITHDRAWN

D1342098

WP 2173584 0

Scotland and Wales: Nations Again?

Scotland and Wales: Nations Again?

Edited by

Bridget Taylor and Katarina Thomson

UNIVERSITY OF WOLVERHAMPTON
LIBRARY

Acc No. 2173584   CLASS 141

CONTROL 0708315062   320.

DATE 19. MAY 1999   SITE WV   9411

SCO

ae 320.9429

UNIVERSITY OF WALES PRESS • CARDIFF • 1999

© The Contributors, 1999

British Library Cataloguing-in-Publication Data.
A catalogue record for this book is available from the British Library.

ISBN 0–7083–1506–2

All rights reserved. No part of this book may be reproduced, stored in a retrieval system, or transmitted, in any form or by any means, electronic, mechanical, photocopying, recording or otherwise, without clearance from the University of Wales Press, 6 Gwennyth Street, Cardiff, CF2 4YD.

Published by the University of Wales Press
in association with

CENTRE FOR RESEARCH INTO
ELECTIONS AND SOCIAL TRENDS

Typeset at the Centre for Research into Elections and Social Trends
Printed in Great Britain by Bookcraft, Midsomer Norton, Avon

Contents

Notes on contributors.. viii

List of tables and figures ix

Foreword... xi

Preface xv

Acknowledgements... xxi

Introduction and Conclusions.. xxiii

1   Referendums.. 1
    David Butler and Iain McLean

    The history of referendums..1
    Referendums in the UK..4
    The future of referendums in the UK....................................9
    Notes 14
    References...14

2   The Scottish and Welsh referendum campaigns..................17
    David McCrone and Bethan Lewis

    The Scottish referendum campaign 19
    The Welsh referendum campaign...27
    Conclusion..36
    Notes 39
    References...39

3   The 1997 Scottish referendum vote...................................41
    Paula Surridge and David McCrone

    From 1979 to 1997...42
    Rational voting and the referendum result..........................45
    Democratic effectiveness...47
    National identity 49

Debating the future 52
Political parties 55
The Scottish parliamentary elections.............................. 59
Conclusion.. 62
Notes 63
References... 63

4   The 1997 Welsh referendum vote.................................... 65
Richard Wyn Jones and Dafydd Trystan

Partisan alignment and referendum vote...................... 66
National identity and referendum vote 73
The mutual implication of partisan alignment
and national identity... 83
Conclusion 88
Notes.. 91
References... 92

5   Why was 1997 different? 95
Geoffrey Evans and Dafydd Trystan

The changing political context.. 96
Social change... 98
An emerging national identity 99
The politics of national identity 100
The Welsh referendums as second-order elections.................. 102
Party cues and electoral change 105
Further considerations: timing and turnout.................. 108
Why was there differential turnout between pro- and anti-
devolution voters in 1997? 110
Conclusion.. 113
Notes 114
References.. 117

6   Is Scotland a nation and Wales not? 119
John Curtice

Explaining the difference 122
National identity in Scotland and Wales...................... 124
National identity and referendum voting 128
Non-voting 130
Voting yes or no?.. 133
Grievances and expectations 137
Conclusion 142
Notes.. 143
References.. 146

7   **Were the Welsh and Scottish referendums second-order elections?**.. 149
Anthony Heath

The concept of second-order elections..150
Turnout and how much was at stake...152
The first-order context...158
The second-order context...160
Conclusion...167
Notes...168
References...168

8   **Does civil society drive constitutional change?**......................169
Lindsay Paterson and Richard Wyn Jones

What is civil society?..169
Civil society in Wales and Scotland..171
Civil society mobilisation in Scotland and Wales.......................178
The meaning of national identity in Wales and Scotland..........183
The referendum votes..187
Conclusion...193
Notes...194
References...194

9   **Welsh devolution: the past and the future**............................. 199
Kenneth O Morgan

Note.. 218
References.. 218

10 **The Scottish political system revisited**..................................... 221
James G Kellas

Conclusion.. 232
Notes...234
References...235

Appendix I   Technical appendix...237

Appendix II The questionnaires...245

Subject index...303

The Centre for Research into Elections and Social Trends (CREST) is an ESRC Research Centre linking Social and Community Planning Research (SCPR) in London and Nuffield College Oxford. Its purpose is to measure and analyse trends in social and political attitudes at an individual, national and international level, and in particular to investigate why people vote as they do, and why they change their allegiances.

The cornerstone of CREST's work are the British Election Panel Studies (BEPS), which follow a panel of voters - interviewing them at least once a year - throughout the course of a parliament. The first BEPS panel was interviewed during the period 1992 to 1997. The second BEPS panel started in 1997 and will run until the next general election. CREST also carried out the 1997 British Election Study, the 1997 Scottish and Welsh Referendum Studies and the 1998 Northern Ireland Referendum and Assembly Election Study.

The contributors

David Butler, FBA, is Emeritus Fellow, and former Professor of Politics, Nuffield College Oxford.

John Curtice is Professor of Politics and Director of the Social Statistics Laboratory at the University of Strathclyde, and Deputy Director of CREST.

Ron Davies is MP for Caerphilly, and was secretary of state for Wales from May 1997 to October 1998.

Geoffrey Evans is Faculty Fellow, Nuffield College Oxford.

Anthony Heath FBA, is Official Fellow of Nuffield College and Professor of Sociology at the University of Oxford, and Co-Director of CREST.

James Kellas is Professor of Politics at the University of Glasgow.

Bethan Lewis is a University of Wales Board of Celtic Studies Research Assistant based in the Institute of Welsh Politics at the Department of International Politics, University of Wales Aberystwyth.

David McCrone is Convenor of the Unit for the Study of Government in Scotland, Professor of Sociology, and co-director of the Governance of Scotland Forum at the University of Edinburgh.

Iain McLean is Professor of Politics

and Official Fellow of Nuffield College Oxford.

Kenneth O Morgan, FBA, is Honorary Fellow of The Queen's College Oxford and Research Professor and former Vice-Chancellor of University of Wales Aberystwyth.

Lindsay Paterson is Professor of Educational Policy and Vice-Convener of the Unit for the Study of Government in Scotland at the University of Edinburgh.

Steve Smith is Professor of Politics and Head of the Department of International Politics at the University of Wales Aberystwyth.

Paula Surridge is Lecturer in Sociology at the University of Salford.

Bridget Taylor is Research Officer in CREST at Nuffield College, Oxford.

Katarina Thomson is Research Director at Social and Community Planning Research, co-director of the British Social Attitudes survey series, and member of CREST.

Dafydd Trystan is Tutor in the Department of International Politics at the University of Wales Aberystwyth.

Richard Wyn Jones is Lecturer in the Department of International Politics and Director of the Institute of Welsh Politics at the University of Wales Aberystwyth.

List of tables and figures

I.1	The 1997 referendum results	xxii
2.1	Opinion polls of Scottish referendum vote intention	25
2.2	Opinion polls of Welsh referendum vote intention	36
3.1	Scottish referendum vote and social characteristics, 1979 and 1997	43
3.2	Expectations of Scottish parliament in policy areas	46
3.3	Number of expected benefits of Scottish (excluding taxation)	47
3.4	Expected democratic effectiveness of Scottish parliament	48
3.5	National identity and Scottish referendum vote	50
3.6	Expected democratic effectiveness of Scottish parliament and national identity	51
3.7	Expectations of Scottish independence	52
3.8	Proportion expecting Scottish independence by expected effects of Scottish parliament	54
3.9	Policy preferences by pools of party support, Scotland	56
3.10	Intended vote in elections to Scottish parliament by vote in 1997 general election	58
3.11	Logistic regression model of intended vote at elections to Scottish parliament	60
3.12	Trust in each party to work in Scotland's interests	61
4.1	Party identification and Welsh referendum vote	66
4.2	Strength of party identification and Welsh referendum vote	68
4.3	Perceived party recommendations in the Welsh referendum	69
4.4	Perceived party divisions in the Welsh referendum	69
4.5a	National identity and Welsh referendum vote: singular categories	75
4.5b	National identity and Welsh referendum vote: Moreno scale	75
4.6	Place of birth and national identity, Wales	76
4.7	Place of birth and Welsh referendum vote	76
4.8	Age and national identity, Wales	77
4.9	Age and Wales referendum vote	77
4.10	Welsh linguistic competence and national identity	78
4.11	Welsh linguistic competence and referendum vote	79
4.12	Logistic regression model of exclusive Welsh identity	79
4.13	National identity and Welsh devolution knowledge quiz	81
4.14a	Expectations in Wales and national identity about the: health service	82
4.14b	Expectations in Wales and national identity about the: economy	82
4.15	Party identification and national identity, Wales	84
4.16	Logistic regression model of partisan identification	85
4.17	Party identification, national identity and Welsh referendum vote	87
4.18	Logistic regression model of Welsh referendum vote	89
5.1	The changing social character of Wales 1979 and 1997	98
5.2	Changing patterns of identity in Wales 1979 and 1997	100
5.3a	National identity and Welsh referendum vote 1979 and 1997	101
5.3b	Place of birth and Welsh referendum vote 1979 and 1997	101

5.3c   Welsh linguistic competence and referendum vote 1979 and 1997 101
5.4   Attitudes in Wales towards the parties 1979 and 1997 103
5.5   General election vote in Wales 1979 and 1997 104
5.6a   Perceptions of parties' support for devolution in Wales 1979 104
5.6b   Perceived party recommendations on Welsh devolution 1997 105
5.7   Party identification and Welsh referendum vote 1979 and 1997 106
5.8   Subjective class identification and Welsh referendum vote 1979 and 1997 107
5.9   Region and Welsh referendum vote 1979 and 1997 107
5.10a   Welsh referendum vote by time of decision 1979 108
5.10b   Welsh referendum vote by time of decision 1997 108
5.11   Preferences for Welsh devolution of different groups 1979 and 1997 109
5.12   Levels of involvement by Welsh devolution preference in 1997 110
5.13   Logistic regressions of turnout in the Welsh referendum in 1997 111
5.14   Logistic regression of the decision to turn out among pro- and
        anti-devolution groups, Wales, 1997 112
6.1   Scottish, Welsh and English national identity 125
6.2   Alternative measure of Scottish, Welsh and English national identity 126
6.3   Sources of national pride in Scotland and Wales 127
6.4   Scottish and Welsh national identity and referendum vote 129
6.5   The referendum prferences of non-voters in Scotland Wales 131
6.6   Scottish and Welsh national identity and perceived impact of the referendum 133
6.7   Logistic model of Scottish and Welsh national identity and referendum vote 134
6.8   Scottish and Welsh national identity, Welsh speaking and referendum vote 135
6.9   Scottish and Welsh party identification and referendum vote 136
6.10   Scottish and Welsh national identity and ideological differences 138
6.11   Expectations of devolution in Scotland and Wales 140
6.12   Expanded model of referendum vote in Scotland and Wales 141
6.13   Alternative measure of Scottish and Welsh national identity and
        referendum vote 144
7.1   How much difference will the general election/referendum make? 153
7.2   Turnout by difference the referendum will make, Scotland and Wales 154
7.3   Logistic regressions of turnout in Scottish and Welsh referendums 155
7.4   Scottish and Welsh national identity and perceived perceptions of how
        much was at stake 157
7.5   Yes vote and current party preference 159
7.6   Yes vote among respondents who correctly perceived their current party's
        recommendation, Scotland and Wales 160
7.7   Value priorities in Scotland and Wales 162
7.8   Logistic regression of yes vote and value priorities, Scotland and Wales 164
7.9   Logistic regression of yes vote, issues and current party, Scotland and Wales 165
8.1   Attitudes to definitions of Welsh identity 184
8.2   Attitudes to definitions of Scottish identity 187
8.3   Referendum vote by broad preference for the government of Scotland 188
8.4   Knowledge of proposals for Welsh assembly/Scottish parliament 189
8.5   Knowledge of proposals for Welsh assembly/Scottish parliament - summary 190
8.6   Referendum vote by broad preference for the government of Wales 191
A.1   Response summary, Scottish and Welsh Referendum Studies 242

Figures

I.1   1997 Scottish and Welsh Referendum results by local authority districts xxiii
4.1   Understanding the Welsh referendum vote 88

Foreword

Steve Smith [*]

The conference at which seven of the ten chapters in this book were originally presented as papers took place at the National Museum of Wales in Cardiff on 18 September 1998, the first anniversary of the Welsh devolution referendum, as the Annual Conference of the Centre for Research into Elections and Social Trends (CREST), a Research Centre funded by the Economic and Social Research Council (ESRC).

The conference represented the first opportunity to present findings from detailed surveys of the Welsh and Scottish electorates conducted immediately following the two devolution referendums. These surveys were undertaken by CREST in conjunction with teams at the University of Wales, Aberystwyth and the University of Edinburgh. They were funded by the ESRC, and I should like to acknowledge publicly how grateful we are to the ESRC for having had the foresight to support these studies. The amount of interest in the work - both public and academic - evidenced by the interest in the conference and subsequently, certainly justifies their decision to provide the funding.

The conference was organised by CREST in conjunction with the Department of International Politics at Aberystwyth. We at Aberystwyth have been delighted to have developed such a good working relationship with CREST and to have collaborated with them both on the Welsh Referendum Study and in the organisation of the conference. I am sure that this is merely the start of many years of equally fruitful collaborative work between us.

---

[*] Steve Smith is Professor of Politics and Head of the Department of International Politics, University of Wales, Aberystwyth.

Conferences do not organise themselves. I therefore want to take this opportunity to thank all those who worked so hard to make the event possible. The person who deserves greatest thanks is undoubtedly Bethan Lewis, who works in the department as the University of Wales, Board of Celtic Studies, research assistant on our devolution project. She carried out the lion's share of the work on the conference as part of a team at Aberystwyth led by Richard Wyn Jones and also including Dafydd Trystan. In addition, Katarina Thomson and Catherine Bromley at Social and Community Planning Research (SCPR) in London, and Mandy Roberts and particularly Bridget Taylor at Nuffield College Oxford, contributed greatly in terms of their time and expertise. We are also grateful to Sara Williams and Eli Stamnes for their assistance on the day.

I want to pay special tribute to the sponsors of the conference. BBC Wales, and in particular Aled Eurig, the Head of News and Current Affairs in Wales, have been very supportive of the research project in general, and were particularly generous in their sponsorship of this conference. I want to thank also Welsh Context, and in particular Andrew Davies and Leighton Andrews, who sponsored the reception which ended our day's deliberations. I should also like to thank the Institute of Welsh Affairs who supported the organisation of the conference, and, of course, the staff of the National Museum in Cardiff.

This was the second year running where the CREST conference was the occasion for the British Academy Annual Lecture. We were delighted that one of our most eminent Welsh historians, and former Vice-Chancellor of Aberystwyth, Professor Kenneth O Morgan accepted the invitation to deliver the lecture. Fittingly, the lecture was chaired by Professor Morgan's successor as Vice-Chancellor, Professor Derec Llwyd Morgan. We would like to thank the British Academy for their co-operation and support. We were fortunate in having Ron Davies, arguably the principal architect of devolution in Wales, and then secretary of state, give the opening address to the conference and write the Preface to this book. Finally I want to thank Huw Edwards from the BBC for being so ready to agree to chair the conference, and keeping all of us under control.

For many years Welsh politics has been under-studied at the academic level. While scholars have done important work, they have largely done so as isolated individuals without the benefits that accrue from the support of a wider research community and - it must be said - without much recognition from funding bodies. This cannot, and will not, continue in post-referendum Wales. At Aberystwyth we are determined to play our part in ensuring that all those involved in, and affected by, the new political structures in Wales - in the policy community and in civil society at large - benefit from well-informed academic analyses of contemporary developments. To this end, in early 1997 the Department of International Politics decided to establish and fund an Institute of Welsh Politics to act as a focus for its research activities in this area. The Institute now has a complement of four staff led by Richard Wyn Jones and is already developing a reputation in Wales and beyond. With its further planned studies into the first Assembly election and the political parties in Wales, we are determined that the Institute of Welsh Politics will become a significant authoritative and non-partisan voice in the coming years. The great success of the referendum research project and conference from which this book has emerged gives me confidence that the work of the Institute will find an attentive audience.

Preface

The Rt Hon Ron Davies, MP *

Thursday 18 September 1997 is a day that will go down in history. In a referendum on St David's Day 1979 the people of Wales had rejected the option of a devolved tier of government by a majority of four to one. Just eighteen and a half years later we achieved a remarkable turn-around. The 1997 referendum saw a massive 30% shift in public attitude from the vote on 1 March 1979. The result, however narrow, marked a decisive break with the stagnant political structures of the past and a significant milestone in the Labour government's mission to modernise the United Kingdom.

Less than one year after the endorsement of our plans for devolution the Government of Wales Act reached the statue books on 31 July 1998. The first elections to the Scottish parliament and the National Assembly for Wales on 6 May 1999 mark the opening of a new chapter in British history.

Devolution is not, nor was it ever, an optional 'add on' extra. The decentralisation of power is an essential part of transforming the way we govern ourselves, with fundamental and far-reaching consequences for society at large and the political process itself.

Throughout my time as the Labour Party's spokesman for Wales (1992-98), I made it my task to dispel the myth that progressive politics requires centralisation. It has been my mission over the last six years to demonstrate that the achievement of a just and equal society depends on devolving power from the centre to local communities.

---

* Ron Davies is MP for Caerphilly and was secretary of state for Wales from May 1997 to October 1998.

The brand of socialism that sought to help people by doing things for them is dead. Modern socialism must empower people: we must give them the tools to improve their own lives. Devolution is central to this vision and it represents a key part of the modern Labour Party's philosophy. At the heart of the party's aims and values is the commitment to put power in the hands of the many and not the few by creating an open democracy, in which the government is held to account by the people and decisions are taken by the communities they affect.

A democratically elected assembly will provide the people of Wales with a platform to articulate their aspirations for the first time. Not only will Wales have a voice, but the people of Wales will have greater power to shape their own lives.

Let no one think that now the devolution genie is out of his bottle he can be forced back in or that he will not want to stretch his muscles. I have stressed at every stage of the battle to create an assembly for Wales that devolution is a process and not an event. As Huw T Edwards, the north Wales trade union leader appointed to chair the advisory Council for Wales and Monmouth in 1949, wrote

> It would be foolish in the extreme for us to disparage today these short steps forward because without any doubt at all they are leading us along the path we want to travel. The words of the old Welsh proverb 'Bach hedyn pob mawredd' (Mighty oaks from little acorns grow) are perfectly true … once a start is made on this path of devolution there is no possibility of turning back. (Edwards 1967: 131)

No doubt our new democratic settlement will have many imperfections but it will change and adapt over the years; it will grow in confidence and stature; its powers will increase and it will become the respected forum and authoritative voice of our country. Our preoccupation now, however, must not be to complain about the powers currently devolved to Wales, but to make the assembly work to bring benefits to the people. Only then can the question of further powers be addressed. After all the purpose of devolution is not to exercise the minds of academics, nor is it to satisfy dreams of national destiny, but to deliver real improvements to the lives of ordinary people.

We stand at the dawn of a new democracy and a new era for Wales. I have been privileged to have played a central role between 1992 and 1998 in the process which delivered this important constitutional change. It has been a difficult and demanding journey to get to this point and there are important lessons to be learned that are relevant to the choices we now face.

In the last six years we have successfully worked towards the creation of a new style of government, the challenge now is to develop a new style of politics.

Only Labour had the strength and organisation to deliver change in Wales, but with that power should have come the recognition that we do not have a monopoly of wisdom. The experience of opposition, both in local government and at Westminster, taught me that the maintenance of a healthy democracy relies upon building consensus and accommodating dissent rather than demanding acquiescence. In formulating its policy on devolution, however, the Labour Party in Wales resisted pressure to be inclusive and as a consequence failed to broaden its support among other parties and broader Welsh society. Ingrained in the mindset of the party establishment was the orthodox view that 'any kind of devolution required in Wales can be discussed within the confines of the Labour movement'.[1] However, we should have had the confidence to work more closely with others to seek wider agreement and to identify common ground where such ground existed.

The structure of the assembly and its status as a body corporate will require (indeed, it will force) parties to become more collaborative. That approach does not weaken the political process, it strengthens it; politics will be more mature and the electors will have a more informed choice as the process moves forward from the rhetoric and posturing.

The failure of the Labour Party in Wales to involve other political parties and wider civil society in the formation of its devolution policy was made all the more significant when Tony Blair decided to hold a pre-legislative referendum on our proposals. Those groups Labour excluded in its policy-making process were essential to the wider task of winning endorsement in a referendum. By failing to mobilise support for the concept of an assembly beyond the circles of Labour politics in Wales, we failed to broaden support for it among the population at large and the decision to hold a referendum cruelly exposed that fact (see also the chapter by Lindsay Paterson and Richard Wyn Jones in this book).

A further reason for our failure to win widespread support for an assembly was the British party's reluctance to campaign on the issue. Neither before, nor during, the 1997 general election did we take our case to the people. New Labour's advisors and apparatchiks were cool to say the least about devolution, seeing it as irrelevant to 'the project' and a potential vote-loser, in England at least. As a result we held just one press conference in Wales on our plans for an assembly, at the start of the six-week long general election campaign. Although it was officially one of the party's key election pledges, as far as Labour's national campaign was concerned Welsh devolution was a non-issue.

As a result of this basic failure in political education, we failed to develop a coherent intellectual case for devolution and consequently we failed to develop a campaign to win the hearts and minds of the people of Wales. This nearly cost us dear in the referendum.

This is an exciting time to be involved in Welsh politics. It is a time of hope. However, if we are to meet the challenge of developing a new style of politics in Wales based on a culture of openness and inclusivity, we shall all have to learn from these mistakes. For the feeling of hope to be fulfilled, there will need to be profound change in the way we conduct the business of politics. It is incumbent upon all those involved in the political process to adapt to the new Welsh context.

The Labour Party is responsible for delivering important change for Wales. We now have to face up to the consequences of the changes in our own party. We must learn to apply ourselves now in the Welsh context and use our energies to apply Welsh solutions to Welsh problems through the Welsh government.

The organisation and status of the Labour Party in Wales must now change to reflect the new reality. It would be an unacceptable contradiction for us as a political party to have facilitated the transfer of power to people in Wales, but not to allow our own members to exercise parallel decision-making in respect of our own party. In all matters relating to devolved functions, therefore, the decision-making authority should rest with the Labour Party in Wales. On matters that have been devolved there can be no policy over-ride by London over Cardiff.

As Labour comes to terms with the consequences and implications of a Welsh tier of government, it is also time for it, at last, to come to terms with the issue of national identity. For many in the party notions of 'Welshness' are sectarian, and to address such questions would be to give in to the agenda of the nationalists. It is a tension that James Griffiths, the first ever secretary of state for Wales, described as the "contrary pulls of country and cause" (Griffiths 1967: 1).

It is vital that we do not just accept the current conceptions of what it is to be Welsh. We must re-brand notions of Welshness to reflect the real, living, modern Wales. We must turn our backs on the Wales of myth and legend, and instead project a vibrant, diverse and tolerant Wales. Not a parochial Wales which looks inward upon itself, but an outward-looking Wales with an internationalist spirit. A Welsh national identity based on civic values and not ethnic criteria (see also the chapter by Richard Wyn Jones and Dafydd Trystan in this book). That is the agenda which the Labour Party must embrace, rather than avoiding any debate on identity for fear of 'responding to the hidden agenda of the nationalists'.

Devolution is not a response to dreams of national destiny, rather it is a recognition that in the complex modern world the notion of identity is an important one for people and their communities. Devolved government is an acknowledgement that regional diversity and decentralisation are effective promoters of social and economic progress, and that democracy works best when it is closest to the people.

Devolution is, therefore, a central part of the Labour Party's agenda for change and modernisation. The decentralisation of decision-making is motivated not by a secret nationalist (small 'n') agenda but by the need to improve accountability and the desire to make government more representative of society. The establishment of a democratic assembly is the start of a process of opening up politics and government in Wales.

I believe that in my time as secretary of state for Wales we laid the foundations to ensure that our new assembly will be a successful institution, capable of responding effectively to the needs of communities across Wales. It is however an ongoing challenge.

Politics and government in Wales have changed forever. The new structure of government that we have created demands that we develop a new style of politics and all those involved in the political process must adjust their point of orientation to reflect the changes that we have made.

The academic community has a lot to offer in terms of knowledge and understanding, in dealing with the problems of building a more inclusive politics in Wales. However, the fact that the 1997 Welsh Referendum Survey is the first piece of large-scale research to be conducted in Wales since 1979 is a matter of concern. Comparatively little is known from academic research about the attitudes and values of people in Wales. I hope that the funding bodies will react positively to the new political context in innovative ways. I am also hopeful that those responsible for the organisation of higher education in Wales will address the need for research and the generation of ideas about how we can take the Welsh agenda forward.

Our devolved settlement represents a new partnership between Wales and the United Kingdom. Wales is just as much a part the United Kingdom as it ever was. In the future, however, we will have to take responsibility for our own actions. We can no longer justifiably look to London to cast blame. Equally the government in Westminster and Whitehall must recognise that Wales has a right to diverge and to innovate. This new partnership demands a different approach to politics which replaces polarised and dogmatic confrontation with a more consensual style; it will require maturity and tolerance.

Nobody could claim that the road to the establishment of the National Assembly for Wales has been easy. No radical change is ever easy. But the coming of the assembly represents a great opportunity. For devolution is not an end in itself but a means to an end. Through the National Assembly for Wales we have the opportunity to create a country that more fully embodies the values of social justice and equality which have long animated the people of Wales.

December 1998

Note

1. This was the response of Cliff Prothero, the secretary of the then Regional Council of Labour, in his report to its conference in 1955 (Prothero 1982: 68). He was responding to calls for the party to join the cross-party Parliament for Wales campaign.

References

Edwards H T (1967) *Hewn from the Rock*, Cardiff: Western Mail and TWW Ltd.

Griffiths J (1967) 'Introduction: The Political Career of Huw T Edwards', in Edwards H T, *Hewn from the Rock*, Cardiff: Western Mail and TWW Ltd.

Prothero C (1982) *Recount*, Ormskirk, Lancashire and Northridge, CA: G W and A Hesketh.

Acknowledgements

This book represents the first publication of findings from the 1997 Scottish and Welsh Referendum Studies, conducted by the Centre for Research into Elections and Social Trends (CREST). CREST is a research centre funded by the Economic and Social Research Council (ESRC) and based jointly at Social and Community Planning Research, London and Nuffield College Oxford. We are grateful to the ESRC for their support for CREST and, in particular, for the additional funding that made the referendum studies possible.

Our thanks go to our chapter authors, both those who gave papers at the CREST conference in Cardiff in September 1998 and those who have contributed chapters since, particularly for helping us to meet the tight timetable for publication. We are grateful to the British Academy for allowing us to publish here their annual lecture, given by Kenneth O Morgan on the occasion of the conference. We owe a huge debt of gratitude to Sheila Vioche who single-handedly prepared the camera-ready copy with endless care, patience and goodwill. Thanks also to Mandy Roberts, Martin Range, Ann Mair, Sarinder Hunjan and Catherine Bromley; to our colleagues in CREST, in the Scottish team in Edinburgh and Aberdeen, and in the Welsh team in Aberystwyth; and last but not least to the respondents to the Referendum Studies.

Introduction and Conclusions

Bridget Taylor, John Curtice and Katarina Thomson [*]

The 1997 devolution referendums

On 1 March 1979, a dying Labour government, internally divided and crippled by the so-called 'winter of discontent', suffered what proved to be a fatal blow from the people of Scotland and Wales. Forced against its will to hold referendums[1] on the merits of devolution proposals it had laboured for two years to enact, the government crashed to defeat. In Wales the 'no' camp had a majority of no less than four to one while in Scotland the 'yes' camp failed to meet the hurdle imposed by the legislation that no less than 40% of the electorate should vote in favour. Within days the government was faced with a vote of no confidence in parliament. Lacking a majority, Labour needed the support of at least one of the opposition parties to stay afloat. But after the defeat of devolution in the referendums, Labour's allies decided to desert the sinking ship, and the government was defeated by one vote. The resulting general election in May 1979 heralded the beginning of 18 long years in the wilderness for Labour.

The 1979 referendums are then an unhappy memory for the Labour Party (Bochel *et al* 1981; Foulkes *et al* 1983). They were certainly marked down as an experience never to be repeated. Yet within four months of at last securing the reins of power again in the May 1997

[*] Bridget Taylor is a Research Officer in CREST at Nuffield College Oxford. John Curtice is Professor of Politics at the University of Strathclyde and Deputy Director of CREST. Katarina Thomson is Research Director at SCPR, co-director of the British Social Attitudes survey series and a member of CREST.

general election, Labour voluntarily held another test of public opinion in both Scotland and Wales on the merits of new and in many respects more sweeping proposals for devolution than those that had failed to secure sufficient support in 1979. This time, however, devolution was approved. In Scotland no less than 44.7% of the electorate actively supported the government's proposal for a new devolved parliament. And although the 'yes' majority in Wales was just 6,721 out of over one million votes cast, in the absence of any 40% rule it was enough for the government to proceed. By the following autumn the Government of Wales Act 1998 and the Scotland Act 1998 were safely on the parliamentary statute book.

This book examines why devolution finally received public approval in Scotland and Wales in 1997, and what the implications of that approval might be for the future of the United Kingdom. Why was public opinion so different in 1997 from 1979? Do the votes for devolution reflect a reawakening of a sense of nationhood among England's two neighbours? If so, why has this happened? And are the new devolved institutions likely to prove sufficient to satisfy that sense of nationhood? Or does support for devolution reflect different concerns? Perhaps it simply reflects a wish for more opportunity to be involved in government? Or a reaction to 18 years of Conservative rule for which neither Scotland nor Wales ever voted? Maybe it is just the difference between a referendum held in the early months of a popular government rather than the dying days of an unpopular one?

Referendums are of course rarely used devices in the United Kingdom (for a review see Balsom 1996). Only one UK-wide referendum has ever been held, in 1975 on Britain's membership of what was then known as the Common Market. Yet it now seems as though they may become a somewhat more frequent occurrence. Indeed, the current Labour government has already held two further referendums: one in Northern Ireland, seeking public approval for the new constitutional arrangements proposed for the province in the Good Friday agreement, and one in London on the proposal for an elected mayor and a new strategic authority for the capital. Now two further UK-wide referendums may be in the offing, one on whether Britain should join the European single currency, the other on changing the electoral system for the House of Commons.

If referendums are to become a more regular feature of British constitutional practice, we may well want to ask what referendums can be expected to achieve (Butler and Ranney 1994). Are they satisfactory devices for settling important issues of public policy? In part at least the answer to this question depends on what motivates people to vote in a referendum. Do they make a judgement on the merits of the issue at stake? Are they sufficiently well informed to make such a judgement? Or do they simply follow the advice of the party they normally support, or use the referendum as a chance to express their view about the merits of the government of the day?

Why the 1997 referendums were held

One important question clearly arises out of the discussion so far. Given Labour's unhappy experience in 1979, and given that questions might be raised about what referendums achieve anyway, what did the new Labour government hope to achieve by holding the Scottish and Welsh referendums? Why, with a majority of 179 in the House of Commons, did it think it worth taking the risk?

One crucial point, of course, is that the decision to hold the referendums was made, not in government, but in opposition, in the summer of 1996, nearly 12 months before Labour was elected. At that time the party leadership had two concerns. The first was that the devolution legislation might have a difficult passage through parliament. This after all had been the experience with the previous devolution proposals in the 1970s (Bogdanor 1979). Despite the message of the opinion polls, few in the Labour leadership anticipated winning a Commons majority of the size that was obtained the following May, making backbench rebellions of the kind that tripped up devolution in the 1970s irrelevant, let alone the possibility that the Conservatives would lose all their MPs in both Scotland and Wales (Gould 1998). And they knew for certain that the legislation would be scrutinised by a House of Lords where of course Labour was in a minority.

Labour's second concern was that it wished to ensure that it no longer had the image of 'tax and spend' that it believed had been heavily responsible for 18 years in the wilderness. Yet its proposals for Scotland included giving the new parliament the ability to vary the basic rate of income tax by up to three pence in the pound. Although this meant the parliament would be able to lower as well as increase tax, it was the latter ability that attracted most attention, including not least from Conservative spokespersons who labelled it the 'tartan tax'.

The decision to hold a referendum addressed both these concerns. Note that in contrast to 1979, the 1997 referendums were held before the substantive legislation was presented to parliament and not after the bills had received legislative approval. This meant that, assuming a favourable result, they would demonstrate both to any potential backbench rebels and to their lordships clear public support for the proposals, and undermine the legitimacy of any attempts to filibuster.

Meanwhile, in Scotland Labour proposed to ask not one question, but two, seeking approval not only for the creation of a Scottish parliament in principle, but also separately for the tax-varying power in particular. By giving the public the chance to vote on the tax powers, it was hoped that any claims that a Labour election victory would mean a 'tartan tax' would be defused.

Holding the referendums also had one further advantage. One of the criticisms made of devolution by those of a nationalist persuasion was that what Westminster gave away, Westminster could take back again. In other words, there could be no guarantee that a future UK government would not decide to abolish the Scottish parliament or the Welsh assembly in much the same way that Stormont, the Northern Ireland parliament, was prorogued in 1973. Only independence, it was suggested, could provide that guarantee. By holding a referendum before establishing the new devolved institutions, however, it could be suggested that no future UK government would feel able to abolish the Scottish parliament or the Welsh assembly without securing the assent of the people in an equivalent referendum (Brown *et al* 1999). In other words, the new institutions would indeed be safe at least for as long as the populations that they served wanted them.

These arguments were far from uncontroversial, as shown in the chapter by David McCrone and Bethan Lewis in this volume. For some supporters of devolution, they suggested a weakening of the commitment of Tony Blair, the Labour leader, to devolution and a willingness on his part to scrap the Scottish parliament's tax-varying powers, as he focused his efforts on winning votes in 'middle England'. There was serious opposition to the referendum idea in the Scottish Labour Party in particular. But the proposal reflected the fact that party spokespersons had found it difficult to argue that a general election would represent clear and sufficient evidence of a demand in Scotland and Wales for devolution. After all, polls in Scotland had long indicated that voters did not simply vote for the party whose views on devolution accorded with their own (Brown *et al* 1999). So, the idea of the Scottish and Welsh referendums was born.

The outcomes

Once installed in power after its success in the May 1997 election, the new Labour government made the implementation of its devolution promises an early priority. The necessary legislation to hold the referendums was among the earliest to be presented to parliament. After an intense and reportedly not always harmonious series of discussions in Cabinet committee, in July the government published

White Papers giving details of the proposals for which they sought public approval (Scottish Office 1997; Welsh Office 1997). In contrast to 1979, Scotland and Wales were each to have their own separate polling day, with Scotland casting its judgement first on 11 September, with Wales following a week later on 18 September. With the opinion polls suggesting that the current in favour of devolution ran more swiftly in Scotland than in Wales, it was hoped that Wales would be swept along by a wish not to be left behind by Scotland.

Less apparent was the logic behind the questions that were posed in the referendums. Although the choice open to the voters was widely referred to in the media as being between 'yes' and 'no', this was not the choice actually printed on the ballot papers. Instead, as detailed in table I.1, voters were presented with two long-winded statements that were only differentiated from each other by the presence or absence of the word, 'not'. The inevitable result was that when some voters then wrote the word 'no' on their ballot paper against the negatively phrased option, the resulting double negative led to some dispute about whether their intention was clear and thus whether their vote should be counted. It was a mistake that was not repeated in the Northern Ireland referendum the following year.

The two campaigns proved to be rather muted affairs. Not least of the reasons for this was the death of Diana, Princess of Wales, in Paris on 31 August. As a result campaigning was suspended for a week, halting the Welsh campaign just as it was getting into gear, and leaving Scottish campaigners with just four days in which to mobilise the electorate and get their message across. Yet in the event, as table I.1 shows, no less than 60% of the registered Scottish electorate turned out to vote, just 11 points down on the general election, and well above the levels normally recorded in local elections.

In Scotland the verdict of those who turned out to vote was clear. Nearly three votes were cast in favour of a Scottish parliament for every one against. And although less popular, the tax-varying powers secured close to a two to one majority as well. While opposition to devolution was, at it was in 1979, stronger in the northern isles and along the border with England, and indeed generally in those areas where the Conservatives could still command some strength, none the less every single one of Scotland's local authority districts produced a majority in favour of the parliament. Only on the second question on the tax-varying powers did any district cast a majority against, with 51% voting against in Dumfries and Galloway and 53% on Orkney, the two areas which recorded the lowest 'yes' vote on the first question. Faced with such a decisive outcome even Conservative spokespersons who had campaigned for a 'no' vote conceded that devolution's day had come.

Table I.1 The 1997 referendum results

Scotland	'Yes' vote	
(a) on principle of a Scottish parliament		
I agree that there should be a Scottish parliament	1,775,045	(74.3%)
I do not agree that there should be a Scottish parliament	614,000	(25.7%)
(b) on tax-varying powers		
I agree that a Scottish parliament should have tax-varying powers	1,512,889	(63.5%)
I do not agree that a Scottish parliament should have tax-varying powers	870,263	(36.5%)
Turnout 60.4%		
Wales		
I agree that there should be a Welsh assembly	559,419	(50.3%)
I do not agree that there should be a Welsh assembly	552,698	(49.7%)
Turnout 50.1%		

Source: BBC Political Research Unit (1998)

But in Wales, the result was far less satisfactory from the government's point of view. Only just over half the electorate turned out to vote. And only just over half of those who did so supported devolution. Indeed, 'no' votes outnumbered 'yes' votes until the very last result from Carmarthenshire was declared, with a 65% vote in favour. Indeed, that Wales appeared to be split down the middle on the issue of devolution was graphically illustrated by the geography of the result. As the map shows, 'no' votes outnumbered 'yes' votes all along the border with England. Even the capital, Cardiff voted against. Only in the western, less anglicised half of the country did a majority vote in favour. In short while 'Welsh' Wales may have backed devolution, 'British' Wales still appeared to want to retain its links with Westminster. Far from giving the new assembly the legitimacy that would have derived from a clear popular vote, the referendum simply exposed a fault line at the heart of Welsh society.

Figure I.1
1997 Scottish and Welsh Referendum results
by local authority districts[2]

■ =	Scotland: 'yes' to parliament, 'yes' to tax-raising powers. Wales: 'yes' to assembly
▩ =	Scotland: 'yes' to parliament, 'no' to tax-raising powers.
▢ =	Wales: 'no' to assembly.

The devolution proposals

Not only were the outcomes of the two referendums rather different from each other, but so also were the proposals on which the two countries were invited to vote. Reflecting the apparently more insistent demand for devolution in Scotland (and, doubtless, the greater significance of the nationalist threat to Labour's electoral base), the powers proposed for the Scottish parliament were substantially more extensive than those proposed for Wales (Scottish Office 1997; Welsh Office 1997; see also Constitution Unit 1996a; Constitution Unit 1996b).

In Scotland, the government's proposals closely followed the scheme that had been developed by the Scottish Constitutional Convention, a body that included not only included Labour and the Liberal Democrats but also a wide section of Scottish civil society (Scottish Constitutional Convention 1990; Scottish Constitutional Convention 1994). For the most part this meant that the new parliament should have primary legislative power in those areas of government activity that were currently run by the Scottish Office. Most notably this included health and education, law and order, transport and the environment, local government and housing, together with economic development. The only major matters left in Westminster's hands were to be defence and foreign policy, and social security and fiscal matters. Moreover, the legislation was to be written in such a way that the bill specified those matters that were to be reserved to Westminster rather than those to be devolved to the Scottish parliament, making it more likely that the latter's role would grow as the functions of government changed.

But while the new parliament was to be granted substantial legislative powers, its financial powers were much more limited. For the most part the government proposed that the parliament's budget should be determined in just the same way as the Scottish Office's budget was already, that is through a block grant determined by the Treasury and adjusted in response to changes in spending in England through the so-called Barnett formula. The one discretionary power the parliament would have was, as we have seen, to vary the basic rate of income tax by up to three pence a pound, a tax whose yield would constitute only a small proportion of the existing Scottish Office budget.

Two other features of the proposal are of note. First, the new parliament of 129 members would be elected by a variant of the Additional Member System of proportional representation. Given that Labour had never won half of the vote in Scotland, this appeared to be a major concession, although it had the advantage that it would also make it more difficult for the Scottish National Party to secure an overall majority (Curtice 1996). In fact the particular system chosen is one that is still likely to give Labour some advantage over its opponents. Second, the devolution bill also included measures designed to eliminate Scotland's over-representation relative to population at Westminster. This was at least in part an attempt to respond to the so-called West Lothian question in which it was asked why, after devolution, Scottish MPs at Westminster should continue to have the right to vote on exclusively English legislation, when English MPs would no longer be able to influence Scottish legislation. Once the number of Scottish MPs at Westminster had been reduced, at least it would no longer be possible to argue that Scotland was overly influencing English legislation.

The proposals for Wales matched those for Scotland in only one respect, that is in the electoral system, where again the assembly's 60 MPs would be elected by a variant of the Additional Member System. But with Labour capable of winning over 50% of the vote in Wales, and with the proportion of additional to directly elected members lower than in Scotland, this was a proposal that could still allow Labour to control the assembly on its own. Meanwhile, there were no proposals to reduce the number of Welsh MPs at Westminster, even though the average Welsh constituency is also smaller in population than its English counterpart.

Doubtless, the failure to reduce the number of Welsh MPs reflected the fact that, in contrast to Scotland, primary legislation for Wales is still to be made at Westminster. In effect the government was proposing a form of administrative devolution for Wales, giving to the assembly the powers and responsibilities currently exercised by the Secretary of State for Wales. This includes the disbursement of the budget of the Welsh Office together with the ability to pass secondary legislation, that is legislation giving detailed effect to primary legislation passed by Westminster. So while this means that the Welsh assembly would, like its Scottish counterpart, have responsibility for the day-to-day running of services like health and education, it would not have the ability to change the major structures or objectives of those services. Moreover, unlike the Scottish parliament, the assembly would have to work entirely within a budget determined by the UK government.

The contents and coverage of the book

The 1998 conference of the Centre for Research into Elections and Social Trends (CREST), at which many of the chapters in this book were first presented, was opened by the Rt. Hon. Ron Davies, then Secretary of State for Wales. (For more details about the conference, see the Foreword to this volume.) From his unique vantage point, Ron Davies emphasises in the Preface that devolution is not only a way of giving Wales a voice, but an essential part of the project of extending democracy. His analysis foreshadows many of the other findings in the book, in particular identifying the failure of the Labour Party in the run-up to the referendum either to involve other political parties and wider civil society in building a coherent intellectual case for devolution in Wales or to mobilise popular support. In common with the other authors, he sees this as the cause of the closeness of the result in Wales. He identifies the challenge now as being to develop a forward-looking Wales, based on civic values not ethnic criteria, and to replace polarised and dogmatic confrontation with a more consensual style of politics.

But to start at the beginning: what sort of beast is a referendum? In chapter 1, David Butler and Iain McLean chart the use of referendums around the world and discuss the prospects for future referendums in the UK. They point to the risk of political manipulation and call for a principled debate on the rules for calling and conducting referendums in the UK so that these risks can be minimised. They conclude that the use of referendums should be embedded in the constitution and that the calling of referendums on non-constitutional issues should be taken out of the hands of the government and made subject to popular initiative. Meanwhile, the fairness of the Scottish and Welsh referendum campaigns themselves is addressed in chapter 2, where David McCrone and Bethan Lewis compare and contrast the progress of the 'long' and 'short' referendum campaigns in Scotland and Wales. They show that in both countries, the 'yes' campaign was better organised and more successful than the 'no' campaign, but that the Scottish 'yes' campaign had deeper roots than its Welsh equivalent.

There then follows a sequence of chapters that put the attitudes and behaviour of Scottish and Welsh voters in the referendums under the microscope. In chapter 3, Paula Surridge and David McCrone find that the Scottish people voted 'yes' primarily for the instrumental reason that they believed a Scottish parliament would improve the quality of public welfare in Scotland, especially health and education, as well as democratic effectiveness. The authors argue that a 'yes' vote was not in the main an affective affirmation of Scottish national identity, nor was it particularly dependent on socio-economic factors. This underlying instrumental basis for support for the Scottish parliament, combined with the fact that some of the areas where Scots are hoping for change will still largely be determined at Westminster, leads the authors to predict strong pressures for an extension of the powers of the parliament. If the parliament makes a success of its areas of competence, it will seem logical to extend its powers; if it does not make a success of them, it will seem logical to blame this on its lack of powers and try to extend them.

In chapter 4, Richard Wyn Jones and Dafydd Trystan examine the importance of the cues given to voters by political parties in Wales given that devolution was less clearly the 'settled will' of the people of Wales. They find that these cues were overlaid by the issue of national identity, which had both a direct impact on referendum vote and an indirect impact via party identification. Exploring the concerns mentioned by Ron Davies, the authors argue that, since the vote in Wales was split so clearly along lines of national identity, the challenge for the National Assembly will be to find a way of striking a chord with all those who live in Wales, not just those who voted for devolution.

One of the intriguing issues of these referendums is, of course, that although Scotland **did** vote for devolution in 1979 (albeit not by the required proportion of the electorate), Wales did **not**. In chapter 5, Geoffrey Evans and Dafydd Trystan use the 1979 Welsh Election Study, together with the 1997 Welsh Referendum Study, to explore why Wales changed its mind. The authors consider - and reject - the possibility of social changes being the cause. They then pick up the argument from the previous chapter and identify both a pro-devolution shift among those with Welsh national identity and born in Wales, and a party cue effect: the Labour Party was not only more popular in 1997, but its message was also much clearer. As a result there was a dramatic increase in 'yes' voting among Labour voters (despite the weakness of the 'yes' campaign identified elsewhere). However, their most intriguing finding comes when considering non-voters: in both the 1979 and 1997 Welsh referendums, non-voters were disproportionately opposed to devolution. In 1979, this differential turnout between supporters and opponents did not affect the outcome of the referendum - in 1997 it did. The authors show that in 1997 even if only those non-voters who cared a great deal about the result had voted, this would have reversed the result. Their failure to do so must be interpreted as the result of the failure to mount an effective 'no' campaign in Wales and of both campaigns to engage the mass of the population on the issue of devolution, as outlined in chapter 2.

Another key question is why the outcomes were so different in Scotland and Wales, and this is addressed explicitly in chapter 6 by John Curtice. He finds that part of the answer lies in national identity: the Scots are more likely than the Welsh to think of themselves as a separate nation. But this is insufficient to explain all of the difference in the outcome. Echoing the conclusions of chapter 3, that the expectations that people held of a Scottish parliament were crucial to the referendum vote, John Curtice is able to show that expectations of devolution were much lower in Wales (where the powers on offer to the assembly are also much fewer and weaker).

Anthony Heath and Bridget Taylor approach the contrasting results in Scotland and Wales from a different angle in chapter 7: they examine the extent to which the theory of second-order elections can be applied to referendums. This theory predicts that secondary elections (such as local and European elections) will be regarded by the voters as having 'less at stake' and therefore, first, will have lower turnout, and, second, voting decisions will be based, at least in part, on issues from the first-order (in this case: British) arena. The authors find the results to be somewhat contradictory: voters in Wales did tend to think there was less at stake in the referendum than in general elections, while this was not the case in Scotland. This suggests good grounds for expecting the Welsh referendum to exhibit the characteristics of a second-order election while the Scottish referendum resembles more a first-order election. This prediction fits well for the differences in referendum turnout in the two countries, but when the authors examine whether it is first-order or second-order issues that are linked to voting, they find no real differences between Scotland and Wales. This suggests that the theory may not be directly applicable to constitutional referendums. But, as the authors note, it will be interesting to repeat the analysis for the 1999 elections to the Scottish parliament and Welsh assembly.

A theme running through the book is the differences between Scotland and Wales in the institutional background to and public debate about devolution - in short, differences in civil society. In chapter 8, Lindsay Paterson and Richard Wyn Jones chart the rather different histories of civil society in Scotland and Wales, examining along the way the extent to which nationality is conceived in civic or ethnic terms. They find, not surprisingly given the findings presented in earlier chapters, that civil society is stronger in Scotland and that this was probably crucial in the campaign for home rule. Meanwhile, not only was civil society weaker in Wales but it was also unable to take on the same leadership role. Their predictions for the future are intriguing. As we have seen, several authors have identified that the challenge that now lies before the National Assembly is to build a consensus around devolution in Wales. Lindsay Paterson and Richard Wyn Jones predict that the stronger civil society in Scotland may actually come to act as a break on the new parliament, while the Welsh assembly, with no alternative power base with which to contend, may have the freedom to be more radical.

The book finishes with two discursive essays by Kenneth O Morgan and James Kellas, on Wales and Scotland respectively. These essays set the referendums in their historical and political contexts. The chapter by Kenneth O Morgan was delivered as the 1998 British Academy lecture at the 1998 CREST conference.

Much of the evidence in this book comes from the 1997 Scottish and Welsh Referendum Studies which were conducted by CREST in conjunction with teams led by David McCrone at the University of Edinburgh and Richard Wyn Jones at the University of Wales, Aberystwyth. The fieldwork was conducted by Social and Community Planning Research (SCPR) and financial support was provided by the Economic and Social Research Council (ESRC). The technical details are set out in the Appendix to this book.

As also outlined in that Appendix, the 1997 Scottish and Welsh Referendum Studies formed part of a wider programme of election studies conducted in Britain since 1964. This adds substantially to the value of the studies since the results can be compared both with the results of earlier surveys undertaken in Scotland and Wales, and with recent survey work in England. One or more of the chapters in this book draw in particular on the 1997 British Election Study and Scottish Election Study, the 1979 Scottish Election Study and the 1979 Welsh Election Study.

The 1997 British Election Study was funded by the ESRC[3] and the Gatsby Charitable Foundation and was conducted by CREST in conjunction with Pippa Norris of Harvard University. The sample size for this study was boosted in Scotland and respondents there were also asked an extra module of questions; the resulting Scottish data are referred to as the 1997 Scottish Election Study. The Scottish Election Study was also funded by the ESRC[4] and conducted by CREST in conjunction with David McCrone and Alice Brown of the University of Edinburgh and Paula Surridge, then of the University of Aberdeen. The fieldwork for both the British and the Scottish studies was conducted by SCPR.

The 1979 Welsh Election Study was sponsored by the ESRC's forerunner, the Social Science Research Council, and directed by Denis Balsom and Peter Madgwick of the University of Wales, Aberystwyth. The fieldwork was conducted by Social Surveys (Gallup Poll) Ltd. The

1979 Scottish Election Study was also funded by the Social Science Research Council and was directed by William Miller and Jack Brand of the University of Strathclyde. The fieldwork was undertaken by Research Services Ltd.

Further information about major publications based on these earlier surveys can be found in the Appendix. The data from the studies can be obtained at the Data Archive at the University of Essex.

Conclusions

What broad messages can we discern from the various chapters? What do they tell us about the value of referendums? Are they an experience to be repeated or avoided? And why did Scotland and Wales vote for devolution? Does their decision demonstrate that Scotland and Wales are nations once again, and as a result set on a path towards independence from the rest of the UK?

The role of referendums in the UK

In the UK referendums there are no rules to determine when referendums should be held. Equally there are no clear rules about how they should be conducted. Hitherto they have been held either for the convenience of the government or, as in the case of the 1979 Scottish and Welsh Referendums, the government's parliamentary opponents. Rather than a constitutionally obligated attempt to ascertain public opinion, the 1997 Scottish and Welsh Referendums were held because to do so appeared politically advantageous for the Labour government. And their timing and the rules about campaigning were devised with an eye to maximising the chances of the 'yes' vote that the government desired.

Despite all this, the government nearly lost the vote in Wales, and if more people had actually turned out to vote, it would probably have done so. On the one hand this suggests that governments cannot always manipulate public opinion to their own advantage even when they have considerable discretion about how referendums are conducted. On the other hand, the fact that a higher turnout might have produced a 'no' vote together with the fact that in both countries the 'yes' campaign was better funded than the 'no' campaign, raises questions about the fairness of the rules under which campaigning was conducted. Concern has indeed already been expressed by the Neill Committee on Standards in Public Life (Neill of Bladen 1998). 'Fairness' is after all one of the essential characteristics of the electoral process in any democracy. For it to be seen to be achieved so far as referendums in Britain are concerned, greater codification of their use is clearly necessary. The work undertaken by the Nairne Commission gives an indication of how this might be done (Constitution Unit 1996c).

Still, a strong case can be made that the referendums should have been held. Many countries require that major constitutional changes can only happen with the expressed consent of the people. And by securing a 'yes' vote, the government has helped to ensure that future changes to the constitutional status of the devolved bodies cannot be made without equivalent public endorsement. But of course referendums only succeed in entrenching and legitimising new institutions if they produce a clear result. In Scotland that happened. But one of the persistent messages of the chapters in this book is that the close result and low turnout in Wales meant that the referendum result failed to enhance the legitimacy of the new institution. Rather, it exposed the fact that the new National Assembly for Wales faces a substantial task in winning over the hearts and minds of people in Wales if it is to become an authoritative 'voice for Wales'.

Of course not even a clear referendum result demonstrates the existence of public support for new institutions if people are not voting on the basis of the issue before them. If, for example, they are simply following the advice of their favoured party, a referendum cannot tell us any more about people's views on a subject than a general election. Our evidence on this is somewhat equivocal. It can be shown, most notably in the chapter by Richard Wyn Jones and Dafydd Trystan, that voters were influenced by the position of their parties. On the other hand more than one chapter also demonstrates that voters' views about the merits and demerits of devolution also made a difference to how they voted independently of their partisan sympathies. Indeed, if this were not the case the result in Wales could not have been as close as it was. In short, while voters clearly are influenced by political parties when deciding how to vote in a referendum, they can reveal evidence about public opinion that cannot be discerned from a general election.

Devolution and national identity: are Scotland and Wales nations again?

Why, though, did that public opinion opt to back devolution? Why did both Scotland, decisively, and Wales, narrowly, vote to loosen their political ties with the rest of the United Kingdom? Does it reflect a resurgence of a Scottish and Welsh national identity, and a decline in a sense of Britishness? Should we as a result conclude that Scotland and Wales are nations again?

Of course to address such questions we need to be clear what a nation is. A nation is commonly defined as a group of people with a common ancestry, history and culture (and thus most likely, though not necessarily, language), who exhibit a positive affective attachment to a common set of symbols that express and reflect that ancestry, history and culture, and who recognise each other as equal members of their society (see, for example, Bogdanor 1987). Membership of a nation is not a question of legal rights but of subjective feeling; those who belong to the same nation thus share a common national identity.

Two important points follow. The first is that a nation is not in the first instance a political entity. It is a social phenomenon that may be expressed in the establishment of institutions of civil society rather than institutions of a state. The second is that national identities are not necessarily exclusive, but rather may overlap. Someone may feel Scottish and British, or Catalan and Spanish (Heath and Kellas 1998). The United Kingdom has indeed never been a simple nation-state. For example, since the Act of Union in 1707 Scotland has retained separate institutions of civil society, and exhibited adherence to a distinctive set of cultural symbols. But at the same time much of her population has also exhibited adherence to a set of British symbols and participated in British institutions.

Indeed, this situation has resulted in widespread terminological confusion, a confusion which has only grown with devolution. If 'nation' is not synonymous with 'state' and if people may feel a sense of belonging to more than one nation, then we have to accept that the terms 'nation' and 'national' might be referring either to Scotland, Wales and England on their own, or to the United Kingdom as a whole. The problem is that, within England at least, the terms 'British' and 'English' are often used as though they were interchangeable. English and British identities are perhaps fused rather than overlapping, raising questions about whether England can be considered a separate nation at all. Within this book at least we have striven for consistency and clarity in the use of language, though doubtless some will disagree with the decisions we have made.

Of course, for a nationalist, terminological confusion is not a problem. For such a person, national identity is an exclusive concept. Membership of one nation implies non-membership of another. Moreover, a nationalist believes that each nation has the right to independent statehood. Any other situation is a violation of his or her national sentiment (Gellner 1983). Thus, someone who is a Scottish nationalist is undoubtedly a person who wishes to dismantle the United Kingdom state.

We have here a crucial distinction. The existence of a Scottish or Welsh national identity does not itself pose a challenge to the existence of the United Kingdom. It is the way in which that national identity does or does not express itself politically which matters. In other words, Scotland and Wales may have voted for devolution, and perhaps even moved closer to independence, not as a result of their becoming nations again but because their existing sense of nationhood has been politically awakened.

Certainly, there is much evidence in this book to testify to the claim that Scotland is more clearly a nation than is Wales. People in Scotland are more likely to claim a Scottish national identity (and to disclaim a British identity) than people in Wales are to claim a Welsh identity. There are many reasons why this should be so. Wales has a long border with populous lowland England and is open to relatively high levels of immigration and penetration by people in England. It even shared the same established Church as England until after the First World War. While for some people distinctively Welsh institutions are an attraction, for others, and especially those who do not speak Welsh, British civil society has seemed more congenial. Scotland, in contrast, has a separate legal system and established Church. To this has been allied a distinctive civil society which for the most part has engaged most sections of Scottish life rather than acted as a source of division.

To some degree, then, the difference in the outcome of the referendums in Scotland and Wales in 1997 could simply be a reflection of a difference in the degree to which they are both nations. But such an account not only proves to be an insufficient explanation of the different outcomes, but is unable to explain why devolution was more popular in Scotland and in Wales than it was in 1979. For we have not uncovered any clear evidence in this book that an exclusively Scottish or Welsh national identity is more commonplace now than it was twenty years ago. Rather, what appears to have changed is the politics of national identity. Those who feel Scottish or Welsh have become more likely to want their sense of nationhood expressed through distinctive, if not necessarily independent, political institutions.

Why has this change happened? It is difficult to identify any one simple cause. However, the political climate in the UK from 1979 onwards appears to have been at least one important reason. For Scotland, at least, the experience of being ruled by a government for which it had not voted was relatively new. But probably more important in both Scotland and Wales was the apparently alien nature of that rule. In Scotland this was symbolised by the introduction of what proved to be one of the Conservative government's most unpopular policies, the poll tax, a year earlier in Scotland than in England, giving rise to the perception that Scotland was being subjected to an unwanted social experiment. In Wales, the equivalent role was performed by the increasing use of government appointed quangos to administer public policy and the exclusion of locally elected politicians. True, it would be a mistake to claim that all Conservative rule in Scotland and Wales after 1979 was politically insensitive. After all, significant new powers were devolved to the Scottish Office while Welsh-language teaching was extended in Wales. Nevertheless, the myth that rule from London meant English rule was given sufficient life to help fuel demands for home rule.

Not that we should assume that the character of Conservative rule after 1979 led inevitably to demands for devolution. Accidents played their role too. Perhaps there was no bigger accident than the 1988 Glasgow Govan by-election. There Labour made the fatal mistake of putting up a lacklustre candidate against a charismatic former Labour MP, Jim Sillars, who was standing in the by-election in the SNP's colours and whose wife had captured the very same seat for the SNP in a by-election 15 years earlier. Shocked at the apparent threat to its Scottish bastion, defeat propelled Labour into participation in the Scottish Constitutional Convention which, as noted earlier, developed the plans on which Labour's devolution plans were largely based. That body also helped to develop a consensus in favour of devolution both inside the Labour Party and more widely.

The devolution votes in 1997 are not simply or maybe even an indication that Scotland and Wales are nations again. Scotland does appear to have more of the characteristics of a nation than does Wales, but in both cases it is the way in which national identity has been politicised that mattered most. In any event, the referendum outcomes paved the way for the passage of the Government of Wales Act and the Scotland Act the following year, with even the former securing a relatively trouble-free legislative passage despite the narrow referendum victory, thanks in part to Labour's overwhelming Commons majority. On 6 May 1999 the first elections will be held to the two bodies. And a few months later, less than two years after the referendums were held, the new bodies will assume their powers.

What is this likely to mean for the future of the United Kingdom? If the demand for devolution has arisen from the politicisation of national identity, could not the creation of separate political institutions simply fuel that process further? After all, polling evidence in both Scotland and Wales suggests that voters will not necessarily regard the Scottish and Welsh elections as 'second-order' elections and vote in the same way as they would do in a Westminster election. Moreover, in both cases the nationalist party looks set to be the principal beneficiary of this process. This suggests that political parties in Scotland and Wales have been given an incentive to emphasise their Scottishness and their Welshness to the exclusion of their Britishness, and that in any dispute between London and Edinburgh or Cardiff the integrity of the United Kingdom would be bound to be the loser.

But just as we must be wary of regarding devolution as the inevitable consequence of Conservative rule after 1979, so we must be careful not to assume that devolution will inevitably lead to independence. If the new devolved institutions succeed in meeting the aspirations of their people, and if British governments accept their right to pursue different policies from those adopted at Westminster, then people in both Scotland and Wales may come to feel that the UK can accommodate their sense of nationhood. Even if Scotland and Wales are indeed nations, whether or not they will eventually want to become independent ones still remains to be seen.

Notes

1. Note that in this book we follow the lead of Butler and Ranney (1994: 1) in using the plural referendums, not referenda; they quote the editors of the Oxford English Dictionary: "Referendums is logically preferable as the plural form meaning ballots on one issue (as a Latin gerund referendum has no plural). The Latin plural gerundive referenda, meaning 'things to be referred', necessarily connotes a plurality of issues."
2. The data on voting were collected by the BBC referendum results programmes and the map was created using boundary data supplied by the UK Borders Project at the University of Edinburgh.
3. Grant number H552 255 003.
4. Grant number H552 255 004.

References

Balsom D (1996) 'The United Kingdom: Constitutional Pragmatism and the Adoption of the Referendum' in Gallagher M and Vincenzo Uleri P, *The Referendum Experience in Europe*, London: Macmillan.

BBC Political Research Unit (1998) *Conference Guide 1998*, London: BBC Research.

Bochel J, Denver D and McCartney A (eds) (1981) *The Referendum Experience: Scotland 1979*, Aberdeen: Aberdeen University Press.

Bogdanor, V. (1979) *Devolution* (Oxford, OUP)

Bogdanor V (ed) (1987) *The Blackwell Encyclopaedia of Political Institutions*, Oxford: Blackwell.

Brown A, McCrone D, Paterson L and Surridge P (1999) *The Scottish Electorate*, Edinburgh: Edinburgh University Press.

Butler D and Ranney A (1994) *Referendums Around the World: The Growing Use of Direct Democracy*, Washington, DC: American Enterprise Institute.

Constitution Unit (1996a) *An Assembly for Wales: Senedd i Gymru*, London: Constitution Unit.

Constitution Unit (1996b) *Scotland's Parliament: Fundamentals for a New Scotland Act*, London: Constitution Unit.

Constitution Unit (1996c) *Report of the Commission on the Conduct of Referendums*, London: Constitution Unit.

Curtice J (1996) 'Why the Additional Member System has won out in Scotland', *Representation*, **33**: 119-24.

Foulkes D, Barry Jones J and Wilford R. (eds) (1983) *The Welsh Veto: The Wales Act 1978 and the Referendum*, Cardiff: University of Wales Press.

Gellner E (1983) *Nations and Nationalism*, Oxford: Blackwell.

Gould P (1998) 'Why Labour Won' in Crewe I, Gosschalk B and Bartle J (eds), *Political Communications: Why Labour won the General Election of 1997*, London: Frank Cass.

Heath A and Kellas J (1998) 'Nationalisms and Constitutional Questions', *Scottish Affairs: Special Issue on Understanding Constitutional Change*, 110-27.

Neill of Bladen (Chmn.) (1998) Fifth Report of the Committee on Standards in Public Life: Standards of Public Life: The Funding of Political Parties in the United Kingdom, London: The Stationery Office, Cm. 4057.

Scottish Constitutional Convention (1990) *Towards Edinburgh's Parliament*, Edinburgh: COSLA.

Scottish Constitutional Convention (1994) *Further Steps: Towards a Scheme for Scotland's Parliament*, Edinburgh: COSLA.

Scottish Office (1997) *Scotland's Parliament*, Edinburgh: HMSO, Cm. 3658.

Welsh Office (1997) *A Voice for Wales*, London: HMSO, Cm. 3718.

1 Referendums

David Butler and Iain McLean [*]

The history of referendums

Referendums around the world

Referendums are an almost universal but occasional device of government. The United States, India, Japan, Holland, Israel are five countries that have little in common but they are distinct from every other major democracy in the world. They alone have never experienced a referendum at the nationwide level. All other countries have tried referendums - but usually only once or twice. Of the 900 referendums that have taken place at the nationwide level in the whole history of the planet just over half have occurred in Switzerland. Australia with 42 used to come next but has been overtaken by Italy with 45 (all but three since 1974).

In Switzerland, referendums are a way of life, with voters going to the polling stations four times a year to decide on issues referred to them by the parliament or by pressure groups. In every other democracy, nationwide referendums are occasional and exceptional events (although California and some other western American states have followed the Swiss path). The countries with most referendums are those where the electorate is required to endorse any changes in

---

[*] David Butler is Emeritus Fellow of Nuffield College Oxford. Iain McLean is Professor of Politics and Official Fellow of Nuffield College Oxford.

the constitution. Australia, Ireland and Denmark offer the most notable examples, but many other countries have provision for referendums as an instrument of constitutional change (France, Italy, Uruguay).

In dictatorships referendums have often been invoked, seriously or spuriously, to demonstrate popular support for the regime. Here are some prime examples:[1]

			% 'Yes' vote	% Turn-out
24 May 1934	Italy	Approval of fascist regime	99.9	99.5
28 March 1938	Germany	Approve Anschluss	99.0	99.7
15 February 1976	Cuba	Approve Constitution	99.0	98.7
16 September 1976	Egypt	Approve President Sadat	99.9	95.4
16 October 1976	Phillipines	Approve Marcos	97.9	97.2

In democracies referendums can be classed under four heads (a very selective list of examples is attached to each category): constitutional, territorial, moral, and miscellaneous.

Constitutional

It is common to seek endorsement for a new regime after a war or a revolution. It may also be a condition of constitutional amendment:

			% 'Yes' vote	% Turn-out
1 July 1937	Ireland	Approve constitution	56.5	68.3
12 March 1950	Belgium	Return of Leopold III	57.6	92.4
5 May 1946	France	Approve constitution	47.1	80.7
13 October 1946	France	Approve constitution	53.2	68.8
29 September 1958	France	Approve constitution	79.2	84.2
4 December 1974	Greece	End monarchy	69.2	75.6
5 October 1960	S Africa	Change to republic	52.3	90.7
5 October 1988	Chile	Extend president's term	43.0	n.a.
17 March 1992	S Africa	Constitutional reform	69.0	85.0

n.a. = not available

Territorial

When a country breaks up or when its relationship with other powers is at issue, political prudence, if not constitutional necessity, can lead to the calling of a referendum. The many referendums on joining the European Community or approving changes to the Treaty of Rome fall into this category:

			% 'Yes' vote	% Turn- out
13 August 1905	Norway	Separation from Sweden	99.9	84.8
29 May 1944	Iceland	Separation from Denmark	98.5	98.4
10 May 1972	Ireland	Join European Community	83.1	70.8
26 May 1987	Ireland	Single European Act	69.9	41.1
19 June 1992	Ireland	Maastricht Treaty	57.3	68.7
22 May 1998	Ireland	Abandon claim to NI	94.4	55.6
20 September 1992	France	Maastricht Treaty	51.0	69.7
10 June 1993	Denmark	Maastricht Treaty	49.0	68.7
14 October 1993	Denmark	Maastricht Treaty	56.8	86.0
28 May 1998	Denmark	Amsterdam Treaty	55.1	74.8

Moral

Issues such as conscription, prohibition, divorce and abortion often cut across party lines and governments find it expedient to refer the matter to the people:

			% 'Yes' vote	% Turn- out
29 September 1898	Canada	Alcohol Prohibition	51.3	44.0
28 October 1916	Australia	Conscription	46.2	82.7
12 May 1974	Italy	Divorce	59.1	88.1
7 September 1983	Ireland	Relax abortion ban	66.9	54.3

Miscellaneous

Other issues that divide parties may lead governments to employ the cop-out of a referendum:

			% 'Yes' vote	% Turn- out
16 October 1955	Sweden	Drive on right	18.2	53.2
13 October 1957	Sweden	New pension plan	47.7	72.4
25 June 1963	Denmark	Nature conservancy law	42.6	73.0
5 November 1978	Austria	Approve nuclear power	49.5	64.1
12 March 1986	Spain	Stay in NATO	52.6	59.4
19 September 1992	New Zealand	Change electoral system	84.7	55.2

Some referendums are binding; others are only advisory - but there are few cases where the verdict of the people has been ignored (the most conspicuous was in Sweden in 1955 when an 82% vote for continued driving on the left was accepted but, without another referendum, was overturned by government *fiat* 12 years later).

In a few cases a simple majority has not been sufficient to give legitimacy to a 'yes' vote. In some instances a 75% (Belau) or a 67% (Sierra Leone) 'yes' has been required; in others a 50% turnout (Weimar Germany); in others an affirmative from 45% or 40% of the electorate (Denmark, Scotland).

For a long time in Switzerland and, in recent years, in Italy, referendums have been the result of popular initiative. Virtually all referendums in other countries have been launched by the government of the day and a large majority have been won. Australia is the great exception: 34 of the 42 constitutional amendments put to the vote since 1901 have been defeated (although eight with majority 'yes' were invalidated because there was not a majority in at least four of the six states).

Referendums in the UK

Referendums had been discussed in Britain for more than 80 years before the first one occurred. It was, paradoxically, A V Dicey, that arch-proponent of parliamentary sovereignty, who in 1890, suggested that this check on parliamentary sovereignty should be invoked as a defence against the enactment of Irish Home Rule.

The idea was raised again in 1910 as a means of resolving disputes between the two houses of parliament, and again in 1913 as a precondition for Irish Home Rule. In other words the referendum was first brought up by the political right. Indeed, it was a Conservative, Winston Churchill, who next seriously raised the idea. In May 1945 when the issue of a long-overdue general election arose, he tried to ensure the continuance of the war-time coalition by having a referendum to authorise the postponement of a dissolution until the end of the war with Japan. It is worth quoting Clement Attlee's dismissal of the suggestion:

> I could not consent to the introduction into our national life of a device so alien to all our traditions as the referendum, which has only too often been the instrument of Nazism and Fascism. Hitler's practices in the field of referenda and plebiscites can hardly have endeared these expedients to the British heart. (Quoted by Bogdanor 1994: 36.)

It was only in 1970 that referendums became a serious possibility in the UK, when Tony Benn suggested the device to the Labour Party National Executive Committee (NEC) as a way of dealing with the Common Market issue. Benn was rebuffed; but two years later the NEC endorsed the idea (which led Roy Jenkins to resign the deputy leadership of the party). On 5 June 1975 the first and so far the only nationwide UK referendum occurred. But since 1973 seven other referendums have taken place at a lower level.

These are the eight referendums that the UK has had at the national or sub-national level:

			% 'Yes' vote	% Turn- out
8 March 1973	N Ireland	Stay in UK	98.9	58.7
5 June 1975	UK*	Stay in Common Market	67.2	64.5
1 March 1979	Scotland**	Approve devolution	51.6	63.6
1 March 1979	Wales	Approve devolution	20.9	58.8
11 September 1997	Scotland	a. Establish parliament	74.3	60.1
		b. Give it taxing powers	63.5	60.1
18 September 1997	Wales	Establish assembly	50.3	51.3
7 May 1998	London	Approve mayoral government	72.0	34.0
22 May 1998	N Ireland	Approve Good Friday deal	71.1	81.0

* Butler and Kitzinger 1976
** Bochel *et al* 1981

This is not the place for an exhaustive account of each of the referendums that have occurred in the UK. But some points may be made about each contest.

1973 Northern Ireland: In 1972 events in Northern Ireland led the Heath government to suspend the Stormont parliament and to institute direct rule from London. One element in the new package which, it was hoped, would led to a return of Belfast rule, was a referendum to determine whether the people of Northern Ireland wished to remain within the UK. The result, on a 58.7% turnout, was a 98.9% 'yes'; all the nationalist parties having urged abstention, which explains both the low turnout and the overwhelming 'yes'. The unionists were able to claim that 58% of the eligible electorate had voted for the Union.

The Northern Ireland Act of 1972 provided for a referendum every ten years, but in the circumstances of 1983 and 1993 there was no serious suggestion that further such tests of opinion should be undertaken.

1975 United Kingdom: The only UK-wide referendum produced a two to one majority in support of the government's re-negotiation of the UK's membership of the European Community, although every opinion poll in 1973 and 1974 had shown a majority in favour of leaving the Community. The key factor was the government's recommendation of a 'yes' vote, which produced a 30% switch towards support. The 'yes' campaign was also helped by the fact that all the leading figures on the 'yes' side (Harold Wilson, Edward Heath, Jeremy Thorpe, Roy Jenkins, Reginald Maudling, James Callaghan, Shirley Williams) had a decidedly positive public image, while all the leading figures on the 'no' side had a neutral or negative image (Tony Benn, Enoch Powell, Michael Foot, Peter Shore, Ian Paisley, Jack Jones, Hugh Scanlon) (Butler and Kitzinger 1976).

The 1975 referendum was devised to save the Labour Party from its own divisions. In April a special Labour conference voted by 3,724,000 to 1,981,000 to support the NEC in opposing continued British membership. Harold Wilson found it expedient to give explicit permission to ministers to break from Cabinet solidarity on this one issue outside parliament. Seven members of the Cabinet did so; one junior minister, Eric Heffer, was sacked for expressing his disagreement from the front bench while, in the post-referendum reshuffle, one dissenting minister (Judith Hart) was sacked and one (Tony Benn) was demoted.

This was only an advisory referendum but, as Harold Wilson told parliament, a majority of one for the 'noes' would be enough. However, when parliament met after the referendum and he was asked whether he would keep to his determination not to repeat the constitutional experiment of the referendum, he said "I can certainly give the Right Honourable Gentleman the assurance that he seeks." (House of Commons debate, 1975).

One significant feature of the referendum was the distribution of three leaflets to each elector, one from each of the umbrella organisations and one setting out the government's report on the re-negotiation. The 'noes' complained at the unfairness of two 'yes' leaflets being distributed at taxpayers' expense and only one 'no' leaflet. It was much the most lavish attempt at public information in any UK referendum, although in Scotland and Wales in 1997 the White Paper proposals were sent out universally; so were the terms of the Good Friday Agreement in Northern Ireland in 1998.

The Britain in Europe Campaign was embarrassingly well-financed. To avoid the charge of unfairness, the Referendum Act (May 1975) provided for public funding of £125,000 for each side, on condition that they published accounts; these later showed a 'yes' expenditure of £1,481,000, in contrast to the 'noes' £134,000. But, in fact, the resources in money and publicity skills of the 'yes' camp brought little benefit during the brief lack-lustre campaign in May and June 1975. There was no strong movement in the polls during the final phase.

1979 Scotland: This stands out as the only UK referendum with a threshold. The Cunningham amendment to the Scotland Act 1978 laid down that a 'yes' vote would be valid only if it appeared to the secretary of state that 40% of the Scottish electorate supported it. The circumstances of the 1979 referendum are discussed in more detail elsewhere in this book; see, for example, the chapters by Paula Surridge and David McCrone and by Kenneth Morgan. The 'yes' campaign won by 51.6% to 48.4%. But this was on a 63.6% turnout. So only 32.9% of the electorate were deemed to have voted 'yes'. (The result was clear but, if the margin had been larger, there could have been controversy over the known inaccuracy of the electoral register.) One interesting aspect of this referendum was the absence of party broadcasts for either side; the Labour Votes No Campaign managed to secure an injunction against party broadcasts on the grounds that the two sides would not be balanced (*Wilson v. Independent Broadcasting Authority* 1979).

The most important aspect of the campaign was the swing away from the 'yes' camp. At the beginning of the year polls indicated a 64% to 36% 'yes' intention. In the course of February the lead slipped away to a dead heat. How far this was attributable to the campaign arguments and how far to the general disillusion with the Labour government associated with 'the winter of discontent' cannot be finally determined.

It is worth noting that the outcome of the referendum alienated the Scottish National Party sufficiently for them to vote against the Labour government in the crucial confidence division of 23 March which was lost by one vote. That led to a general election and the victory of the Conservatives, the most clearly anti-devolution party.

1979 Wales: This was the most lop-sided referendum in mainland Britain. Over 80% of the voters in Labour-dominated Wales rejected an assembly proposed by a Labour government. Fear of bureaucracy and of domination by a Welsh-speaking minority appears to have been central to the Labour Votes No Campaign, as discussed in the chapters in this volume by Geoffrey Evans and Dafydd Trystan, and Kenneth Morgan. But even in Gwynedd, the most Welsh-speaking county, there was a two-to-one 'no' vote. As in Scotland, the winter of discontent had provoked an anti-government swing and the referendum gave an outlet for even Labour loyalists to express their unhappiness.

1997 Scotland: This was notable as the only double-barrelled referendum in the UK. Almost 11% more of the Scots who voted (74.3%) were willing to vote for a Scottish parliament than for giving it taxing powers (63.5%) (see the chapter by Paula Surridge and David McCrone). Three of the four main Scottish parties advocated a 'yes-yes' vote, while the Conservatives fighting a lack-lustre 'no' campaign acknowledged that they would accept the verdict and participate in any resultant arrangements. It was a pre-legislative referendum in contrast to the post-legislative referendum of 1979.

1997 Wales: This was the closest - and, perhaps, the most unsatisfactory - of UK referendums. As discussed in the chapter in this volume by Richard Wyn Jones and Dafydd Trystan, the principality voted 50.3% to 49.7% for a Welsh assembly on a 51% turnout. The last authority to report its count (Carmarthenshire) switched the overall outcome from a 'no' to a 'yes'. There were complaints that the campaign had been affected by government resources being directed to support the 'yes' campaign and by the timing of the vote - one week after the inevitable victory of those seeking endorsement for a Scottish parliament (see the chapter by David McCrone and Bethan Lewis). The (Neill) Committee on Standards in Public Life, to be discussed later, took the first of these complaints very seriously, and inserted an unexpected chapter on the regulation of referendums into its October 1998 report on the funding of political parties.

1998 London: This produced the lowest turnout, 34%, in any UK referendum, but all parties were more or less agreed on the idea of a mayor and there was no very organised opposition - although 27% did vote 'no'. The 'yes' vote was significantly higher in the central boroughs than in the more outlying suburbs.

1998 Northern Ireland: The Good Friday Agreement, painfully arrived at after months of negotiation, caused deep division among the unionists. When the referendum on it came, the issue was not whether there would be a 'yes' victory, but whether there would be a majority among the unionists. Opinion polls indicated that, despite the opposition of Ian Paisley's Democratic Unionists, as well as of a majority of the Ulster Unionist MPs, 52% of unionists did vote 'yes'. A 73% 'yes' on an 80% turnout gave authority for the election in June 1998 of an assembly and the implementation of the Good Friday proposals.

The future of referendums in the UK

Referendums in the pipeline

In 1993 the Labour Party endorsed having a referendum on a change in the electoral system. They confirmed this in their 1997 election manifesto. The home secretary repeated the assurance that the referendum would take place before the end of 1999, presumably offering the electorate a choice between the current electoral system and the form of proportional representation suggested by Lord Jenkins' Commission as the best alternative to the *status quo*. The Commission, which reported in October 1998, suggested the Alternative Vote for single member constituencies with a limited top-up from party lists which would, in some measure, redress imbalances in representation (see Jenkins 1998).

There is also the commitment of all parties to a referendum before the UK joins the European Monetary Union. The Liberal Democrats - with their long-standing commitment to referendums - have long supported this. John Major, under pressure from the Euro-sceptics in his party, in the spring of 1996 committed the Conservatives to a referendum, and Gordon Brown made a similar promise for Labour soon afterwards.

The Referendum Party, whose 547 candidates in 1997 constituted the largest new party intervention seen in a UK general election, had allegedly a single aim - to force a referendum on UK membership of the European Union. Sir James Goldsmith spent £20 million on his campaign, but was rewarded with only 3.1% of the votes and 42 saved deposits; the net impact of his efforts on the outcome for the other parties was negligible (Curtice and Steed 1997, Heath *et al* 1998). But the presence of Referendum Party candidates undoubtedly had a substantial effect on the Conservative campaign, nationally and locally.

The Nairne Commission and the Neill Committee

The British constitution has developed incrementally. Referendums, once thought incompatible with representative government and parliamentary sovereignty, have been accepted, at least as an *ad hoc* device, by each of the political parties. On the whole the eight referendums have been conducted fairly and their results have been accepted as decisive popular verdicts. There were complaints about the disparity of resources in the 1975 UK referendum on Common Market membership and in the Welsh vote of 1997. There was unhappiness about the 40% rule in the Scottish referendum of 1979. But each referendum was advisory and conditional. Each was accepted by the government of the day as a guide to future action.

   However, the country may have been lucky. The conduct of referendums can be controversial: the timing of the vote, the wording of the questions, the facilities for publicising the rival cases in officially distributed pamphlets or on the airwaves must raise problems of equity. Each of the four referendums since May 1997 was organised differently. There were no established avenues of appeal in case of controversial administrative decisions. The fact that the UK's experience of referendums has so far been relatively painless does not guarantee a happy future for the device.

   In 1996 the possibility that a Labour government might call a referendum on changing the voting system led the Electoral Reform Society, in conjunction with the Constitution Unit, to set up a commission to look at the prerequisites for fair play in referendums; the Commission was chaired by Sir Patrick Nairne who, in the Cabinet Office, had been responsible for organising the 1975 referendum. The Report's (Constitution Unit 1996) most central recommendation was for the establishment of a referendum commission to oversee the fair conduct of any future referendums (possibly as part of the wider functions of an electoral commission). The Report discussed the need for general rules of guidance as referendums multiplied. Among the themes discussed were:

- Should each referendum be subject to an individual act of parliament or should there be a general referendum act?
- Should referendums be advisory or mandatory?
- Should referendums be pre- or post-legislative (that is, should the public be asked to approve a general idea or a specific act)?
- Who should constitute the electorate, locally or nationally?
- Should there be thresholds or should a majority of one on any turnout be sufficient?

- What procedures should guide the wording of the question?
- Should multi-option referendums be allowed?
- How long should the campaign last?
- Should there be public provision of information about the issues? Should there be free distributions of literature?
- What recognition should be given to campaigning organisations?
- Should there be limits on campaign expenditure?
- Should there be public subsidy for campaigning organisations?
- Should there be any restraint on government activity during the campaign?
- Should there be any restraint on party activity during the campaign?
- What rules should established for equal access to broadcast media?
- How should the date of the referendum and the hours of polling be settled?
- Who should be responsible for the organisation of the poll?
- How should the votes be counted - by polling-district, ward, parliamentary constituency, county?

The Nairne Commission put forward tentative answers to each of these questions, but argued that they were matters for fuller debate and ultimately to be the subject matter for a statutory referendum (or electoral) commission.

As mentioned briefly above, the Neill Committee on Standards of Public Life took evidence in 1998 on whether and, if so, how referendums should be regulated. "We were disturbed", they wrote,

> in particular, by the evidence we heard in Cardiff to the effect that the referendum campaign in Wales in 1997 was very one-sided, with the last-minute 'no' organisation seriously under-funded and having to rely for financial support essentially on a single wealthy donor. The outcome of the Welsh referendum was extremely close, and a fairer campaign might well have resulted in a different outcome. (Fifth Report of the Committee on Standards in Public Life 1998)

Accordingly, they recommended that each side in future referendums be given core public funding to make its case, and that no public resources be allowed to go into the efforts by the government of the day to put its case. These rules would be policed by an election commission also proposed in the report. This would be one of its many jobs.

It is now clear that Harold Wilson's assurance that referendums would not become part of the UK's constitutional arrangements has been falsified. They have now been advocated or invoked so often (with all parties being to some degree involved) that they are unlikely to disappear from the scene. If they are to go on happening there is everything to be said for a regularisation of their procedures, rather than conducting them on a one-off basis by separate acts of parliament - and a neutral arbiter is needed to oversee them (Butler 1998).

So far, despite Nairne and Neill, there has been little principled discussion in Britain on either: the rules to mandate a referendum or to permit one, or the dangers of political manipulation of referendums. The two points are closely connected.

Rules to mandate or to permit a referendum

As we have shown, many referendums have occurred for reasons of sheer political expediency. Some issues cross-cut party lines, and are one-off questions, to which the government can live with either answer. One might have thought that driving on the left in Sweden was an excellent example, although as it turned out the government could not live with the answer. Other issues also cross-cut party lines, but in a more fundamental way - the 1975 referendum on Europe being a clear example. Others again are constitutional and/or territorial, for example all the polls in Scotland, Wales, and Northern Ireland. So what is, and what should be, the guiding principle for when to hold a referendum?

We get no help either from politicians or from constitutional experts. The records show that politicians call for referendums just when it suits them to do so. But do not suppose that constitutional lawyers are above that sort of thing. Consider that over-rated figure A V Dicey, mentioned above. Like other unionists at the turn of the last century, Dicey detested Irish Home Rule. Hence his claim that the Irish Home Rule Bills so fundamentally affected the constitution that they should not be implemented unless supported in a referendum. He well knew that Home Rule was very unpopular in England, with 80% of the UK population.

The hypocrisy of this demand was clear from 1914 onwards, when the idea of the partition of Ireland began to emerge as the only solution to the intractable problem of Protestants rejecting Home Rule and Catholics embracing it. Various Irish and Liberal politicians suggested that there should be local option - either the people directly, or their local authorities, should be allowed to vote on whether or not to come under the Home Rule parliament. Dicey and the unionists were as inflexibly opposed to allowing Fermanagh and Tyrone to vote on the Union as they were in demanding that England should vote on the Union.

Since 1979, the boot has been on the other foot. Only the Scots, the Welsh, and the Irish - or rather, electors on the register in each of these countries - have been invited to vote on their constitutional future. Those who live in England (outside London) have not. But other large questions of political manipulation surround the territorial referendums.

The dangers of political manipulation of referendums

Why were there referendums in Scotland and Wales in 1979? Why was the 40% rule imposed? Why was the 1997 referendum in Wales held a week later than that in Scotland? The short answer is one word long: politics. In 1979, a weak government, which proposed devolution only in order to salvage its vote in Scotland, could not prevent its legislation from being savaged by its own backbenchers. That process led first to the referendums, and then to George Cunningham's 40% rule. Cunningham is an expatriate Scot whose amendment was designed to wreck, not to improve, the legislation. As no government since the war has been elected with as much as 40% of the electorate voting for it, the constitutional case for the Cunningham amendment was hard to make. Or rather, if it were conceded, it would follow that governments should be elected by some radically different method than the single-member plurality system, which almost never ensures that 40% of the electorate supports the winner.

In 1997, a strong government was determined to get popular support for its devolution plans. Therefore it staged the Welsh vote, where support was known to be uncertain, a week later than the Scottish vote, where it was known to be certain. The same ploy was used by the states applying to join the EU in the most recent round - Norway, the most sceptical, had its referendum last. However, the Norwegians voted 'no'.

Possible solutions

Two possible solutions to these problems are: (1) to embed the referendum in the constitution, and (2) to permit the popular initiative.

Several countries embed the referendum in the constitution, especially by making the constitution unalterable unless the alteration is approved by referendum. Ireland is a good example. The constitution there entrenches the electoral system. The leading party (Fianna Fail), which would do better under first-past-the-post, has twice tried to change it; twice it has been rebuffed. And the 1998 referendum in the Republic of Ireland, with its overwhelming vote to abandon the Republic's constitutional claim to the north, was constitutionally mandated as well as politically expedient. That gives its result all the more authority. Of course, to get the referendum entrenched in the British constitution, we have to write it first. That will take a while, but it is better than relying on A V Dicey.

The popular initiative is sometimes thought to favour the political right. Proposition 13 in California, which launched the tax revolt movement, is often cited. But the evidence, even from California, is not all one way: there is no convincing evidence that the initiative biases outcomes in any one partisan direction. And a weakness of the present situation is that politicians may choose to put moral issues where they can live with any outcome to referendum, but not those where they cannot. Those on the British left who demanded a referendum on the EU in the 1970s could never satisfactorily explain why there should not be a referendum on capital punishment. One possible solution is that non-constitutional referendums should occur only as the result of a popular initiative.

Notes

1. The referendum results are taken from Butler and Ranney (1994) unless otherwise specified. But see also Gallagher and Uleri (1996).

References

Bochel J, Denver D and McCartney A (1981) *The Referendum Experience: Scotland 1979*, Aberdeen: Aberdeen University Press.

Bogdanor V (1994) 'Western Europe', in Butler D and Ranney A (eds) *Referendums Around the World*, Basingstoke: Macmillan.

Butler D (1998) *The Case for an Electoral Commission*, London: Hansard Society.

Butler D and Ranney A (eds) (1994) *Referendums Around the World*, Basingstoke: Macmillan.

Butler D and Kitzinger U (1976) *The 1975 Referendum*, Basingstoke: Macmillan.

Constitution Unit (1996) *Commission on the Conduct of Referendums*, London, Constitution Unit, December.

Curtice J and Steed M (1997) Appendix to Butler D and Kavanagh D, *The British General Election of 1997*, Basingstoke: Macmillan.

Fifth Report of the Committee on Standards in Public Life (1998) *The Funding of Political Parties in the United Kingdom*, Cm 4057-I, London: The Stationery Office: para 12.32.

Gallagher M and Uleri V (1996) *The Referendum Experience in Europe*, Basingstoke: Macmillan.

Heath A F, Jowell R, Taylor B and Thomson K (1998) 'Euroscepticism and the Referendum Party', in Denver D, Fisher J, Cowley P and Pattie C (eds), *British Elections and Parties Review 8: The 1997 General Election*, London: Frank Cass.

House of Commons debate, 9 June 1975: col 37.

Jenkins of Hillhead, Lord (1998) *Report of the Independent Commission on the Voting System*, London: The Stationery Office, 2 vols, Cm 4090-I and II.

Wilson v. Independent Broadcasting Authority (1979) Scottish Law Reports 279.

2 The Scottish and Welsh referendum campaigns

*David McCrone and Bethan Lewis**

The key to understanding the referendums in Scotland and Wales in 1997 lies in what happened in 1979. In that year, the Scots voted by 52% to 48% in favour of an assembly, as it was then called, while in Wales the proposal was defeated by a margin of four to one. In Scotland, this left a double-edged legacy. On the one hand, the majority had been narrow, but was enough to generate a grievance that it had been a 'yes' vote. In Wales, on the other hand, devolution had been comprehensively trounced, and was off the agenda for the foreseeable future.

By 1981, the Labour Party in Scotland had acknowledged that a majority had voted 'yes' in the 1979 referendum, and that an assembly could have defended Scotland from Thatcherism as well as extending democracy. Its 'Interim Statement on Devolution' also indicated that at some future stage, a Scottish assembly could have tax-raising powers. John Smith, who had done so much to steer the ill-fated Scotland Bill through the House of Commons, predicted that another referendum would be needed, though his early death meant that he was not to see it.

* David McCrone is Convenor of the Unit for the Study of Government in Scotland and Professor of Sociology, University of Edinburgh. Bethan Lewis is a University of Wales, Board of Celtic Studies Research Assistant based in the Institute of Welsh Politics at the Department of International Politics, University of Wales, Aberystwyth.

The devolution issue in Wales lay latent until the second half of the 1980s. The prospect of a Welsh assembly re-emerged in the discussions on the reform of local government. In this way it was eased back onto the agenda relatively painlessly. The re-election of a Conservative government in the 1987 general election despite its poor showing in Wales was a spur to the devolutionary argument, repeated even more forcefully in 1992. Meanwhile, Scotland's slipstream provided a momentum which supported the Labour Party's incremental steps towards championing Welsh devolution again.

When, in mid-1996, the announcements were made in Scotland and in Wales by the Labour leader, Tony Blair, that should his party win the general election, referendums would be dusted down and used again, there was considerable scepticism. Labour adopted an ultra-cautious approach to policy generally in the run-up to the 1997 general election, making as few promises and giving as few hostages to fortune as possible. There was suspicion in Labour's ranks, never mind in the other home rule parties, that once more a referendum was being used as device to remove Labour from political hooks. There was general agreement that postponing such a decision would remove the charge of tax-raising at least in 'middle England' where Labour had to do well to win in the general election. In Wales, Labour's devolutionists were angered by what they perceived to be a U-turn on their party's stated commitment to establish an assembly once elected to government, decided unilaterally by the British Labour Party leadership with little reference to the situation in Wales or indeed the party's Welsh hierarchy. The Liberal Democrat and Plaid Cymru leaderships had to decide their course of action. Some in these parties seriously questioned Labour's commitment to devolution in Wales, and Plaid Cymru, especially, were haunted by memories of 1979 when they believed they were left holding Labour's baby.

The two nations were being offered different forms of devolution. Scotland was to have a parliament and Wales an assembly. This reflected the fact that Scotland has its own legal system, and hence law-making powers fit more naturally into a devolved system. It was also the case that the demand for home rule - and for independence - was lower in Wales. Fear of the nationalists in both Scotland and Wales still stalked Labour. The march to home rule in Scotland since the 1979 debacle was reflected in the network of campaigning groups which drew their legitimacy from civil society rather than the political system. After the false dawn of 1992, when even the Conservatives expected to lose the general election, non-party and supra-party organisations had held the arena in Scottish social politics. There was a palpable sense that politicians could not really be trusted to deliver home rule, and that 'the people' must decide. In Wales, disillusionment with the political system was not channelled into broad-based organisations. Although the language of devolution re-entered political discourse in Wales, particularly from 1992 onwards, it seemed to be practised in a vacuum. In the absence of alternative *loci* of policy formulation, the Wales Labour Party held the floor, keeping a vice-like grip on the policy which had proved so divisive in 1979.

Home rule had an older and firmer base in Wales than in Scotland, but since the 1960s the demand had been greater in the northern kingdom, reflected in a stronger Scottish National Party, and a Labour movement which in the 1980s had undergone a more complete conversion on the road to an Edinburgh parliament. Hence, the campaigns in the two nations were separate but linked. The Welsh referendum was to come one week after the Scottish one, in part so that the Scots could provide a further boost to devolution in Wales, should it be needed. It was clear that the Welsh had the steeper mountain to climb, given that only 20% of those who voted had supported the devolution bill in 1979. The Scots on the other hand simply had to hold and develop their majority of 1979. The campaigns looked crucial.

The Scottish Referendum Campaign

The referendum announcement and its context

That there was to be a referendum in Scotland on home rule came as a considerable shock to most Scots. In May 1996 the political editor of *The Scotsman* newspaper had written that the Labour Party was about to revise its revenue-raising plans for a Scottish parliament, and was roundly attacked for his pains. "Total nonsense", said the then shadow secretary of state for Scotland, George Robertson, who dismissed it as "wearisome speculation". So it did not prove, for on 26 June, Blair and Robertson announced in Edinburgh that there would be a referendum on the tax-raising element. *The Scotsman* felt vindicated, and expressed its alarm along with the shadow minister nominally in charge of devolution, John McAllion, who knew nothing about it and resigned in disgust. It became clear that Labour saw the referendum as the way to shoot Conservative secretary of state Michael Forsyth's 'tartan tax' fox, but opponents argued that it seemed simply to sell the pass. Much politicking took place in smoke-filled rooms, and the Scottish Labour executive acquiesced by 20 votes to 4 after it was promised consultation on wording.

The row continued, however, and in September the Scottish Labour executive met again, this time announcing a solution: not one, but two referendums. The press poured scorn on the plans: "Oh no, it's two referendums", said *Scotland on Sunday*; "the road to ridicule", said *The Scotsman*. At one stage, it looked as if there might have to be five hurdles to a Scottish parliament with tax-raising powers: voting 'yes' to Labour in a general election; 'yes' in a referendum on a Scottish parliament; 'yes' to it having tax-raising powers; 'yes' in an election to a Scottish parliament; and 'yes' in a further referendum to activate this power. A week later, the byzantine formula was dropped: "Robertson reverts to plan A", said *The Scotsman* in mockery. This left Labour looking foolish; its Liberal Democrat allies in the Scottish Constitutional Convention (see below) embarrassed; Forsyth cock-a-hoop that his tartan tax jibe was hitting home; and the SNP thinking that the home rule apple was about to drop into its lap, once it had sorted out what it would recommend to its supporters if a two-question referendum came to pass. A couple of defections by Labour Party members occurred but far fewer than the SNP hoped or Labour feared.

The long campaign

Although the campaign for a 'yes' vote in a referendum began formally in mid-1996, it was much older than that. The scars from the previous campaign in 1979 persisted. Then, 52% of Scots who voted declared their wish for a parliament, but insufficient to meet the hastily gerrymandered 40% rule (the Cunningham amendment) whereby that percentage of the **electorate** was required to vote yes to endorse the parliament, not 40% of the **turnout** (see also the chapter by David Butler and Iain McLean in this volume). For supporters of constitutional change the results of the 1992 general election and the return of the Conservative government had been a significant setback, especially to the Scottish Constitutional Convention which had been established with cross-party support in 1989. Scotland had had a number of Conventions on home rule during the 1920s and 1940s, but none as broad as this one. It was underpinned and partly funded by the Convention of Scottish Local Authorities, and its membership included Labour, the Liberal Democrats, the Greens and the Democratic Left, as well as the Scottish Trades Union Congress (STUC), and the churches. The Conservatives and the SNP excluded themselves from participation. James Mitchell (1992) argued that the 1992 general election result had the same impact as the referendum of 1979: though a numeric majority of the electorate had voted for constitutional change by voting for pro-devolution parties, the failure to realise expectations was a psychological blow to the opposition parties. Initial efforts after 1992 to bring all the opposition parties, including the SNP, together were made by Campbell Christie, the general secretary of the STUC and key player in the Scottish Constitutional Convention, but they failed.

The period immediately after 1992 witnessed the setting up of several organisations which had the aim of keeping the constitutional question high on the political agenda. Democracy for Scotland, Scotland United and Common Cause were three such bodies, and the Women's Co-ordination Group was also established to continue pressing the case for equal representation of men and women in a Scottish parliament. Although the different groups continued to exist, an umbrella organisation, the Coalition for Scottish Democracy, was established in 1995 and was instrumental in setting up a Scottish Civic Assembly. The assembly had representatives from a wide range of non-party organisations in Scotland and played a role in articulating an alternative to the government's approach to policy issues in Scotland. These organisations were designed to add an extra-parliamentary edge to the demand for home rule, while the Scottish Constitutional Convention concerned itself mainly with designing and promoting the parliament itself.

The launching of the Scottish Constitutional Convention's final document, *Scotland's Parliament, Scotland's Right*, on St Andrew's Day in November 1995 was significant because it represented a consensus of view between two of Scotland's main political parties and among a wide range of organisations in Scottish civil society on a scheme for a Scottish parliament.

Before the announcement in mid-1996 that there was to be a referendum on Scottish home rule if Labour won the forthcoming general election, the line of argument advanced by the Scottish Labour Party and by its leader, George Robertson, was that the mandate for constitutional change had already been given by the fact that around 75% of voters in Scotland consistently voted for parties which supported reform. The party argued that it was a sufficient mandate that Labour should win a general election on a platform that included plans to set up a Scottish parliament. In these circumstances, the reaction from Scottish political activists to the British party leadership's decision to hold a referendum on the issue was somewhat predictable. Labour was accused of once again betraying the hopes and aspirations of Scots for home rule and Scottish Labour was criticised for being under the control of the British leader, Tony Blair. It was interesting to compare the response of the media and commentators north and south of the border to the change of policy. For those in England, the decision seemed politically sensible and a way of endorsing and strengthening the plans for a Scottish parliament. In Scotland, on the other hand, the initial reaction was to interpret the decision as potential political suicide, leaving Labour open to losing electoral ground to the SNP, and one that could seriously endanger the setting up of a parliament. To understand the mood in Scotland that followed the decision to hold a referendum, it has to be placed in the context of memories of the referendum experience in the 1970s. Among those who had been part of the 'yes' campaign in 1979, it was interpreted as another obstacle in the long road to home rule, and, anxieties were raised that history would repeat itself especially if the referendum was subject to a 40% rule or other condition (Jones 1997).

The debate became more heated when it was announced that there were going to be two questions, the first asking people in Scotland if they wanted a Scottish parliament and the second directed at the tax-varying powers. The split over the decision to hold a referendum was rehearsed at executive meetings of the Scottish Labour Party where attempts were made to limit the damage by restricting it to a straightforward question on whether or not to establish a parliament. At one stage, following a particularly difficult executive meeting, a so-called compromise of three questions was proposed, a decision that only added fuel to the debate. In the event, a final decision was made for a two-question referendum - one on the parliament and one on the tax question - and Tony Blair arrived in Scotland to explain why the decision had been taken, at one stage saying that it had originated from a proposal from his shadow secretary of state for Scotland, George Robertson. When he became prime minister, Tony Blair replaced Robertson with Donald Dewar who had been shadow secretary of state previously, and who was untainted by the series of U-turns on the referendum issue. The argument was made that, without a referendum, the plans for a parliament were open to attack from supporters of the *status quo*; this would be a particular danger, it was claimed, for the decision over tax-varying powers that had already been the subject of attack from Michael Forsyth and others. The latter point was, of course, related very directly to the Labour Party's policy on taxation and its determination to rid itself of the image of a tax-raising party. The argument was also put by the Labour leadership that a 'yes' vote in the referendum would ease the passage of a Scotland Bill through the House of Commons and help entrench the Scottish parliament, making it less vulnerable in the future, should the Conservatives return to power at Westminster.

The SNP, not surprisingly, jumped at the opportunity handed to it to make political capital from the decision, accusing George Robertson of being a puppet of Tony Blair and stating that once again policy in Scotland was being driven from south of the border. Tony Blair was even compared by some to Margaret Thatcher in that he was accused of being insensitive to the political situation in Scotland. The storm mounted as the SNP got hold of a research report based on evidence from focus groups, carried out on behalf of the Scottish Labour Party, which showed that Blair was identified with moving Labour to the right and that Labour was seen to be back-tracking on the commitment to home rule (Jones 1997). The Scottish Liberal Democrats reiterated their strong opposition to the holding of a referendum on the grounds that the mandate for such constitutional change had already been demonstrated by the Scottish electorate. They were particularly opposed to the second question on taxation, fearing that a parliament without the ability to raise revenue would not have the type of powers envisaged in the plans of the Scottish Constitutional Convention.

Those within the Scottish Labour Party who opposed the referendum decision found their positions under threat as the party moved closer to the general election and demonstrated its willingness to impose party discipline. Suspicions within the party mounted and were fuelled by the news that a group of senior Labour activists in Scotland broadly sympathetic to Tony Blair and the policies of New Labour had formed a group called The Network (*The Scotsman* 29 January 1997). At the elections for the Scottish executive which followed in March 1997, a number of well-known members on the left lost their positions, reflecting the change in the balance of power in the party in Scotland.

These developments meant that many Labour activists in Scotland entered the official election campaign with mixed feelings. They desperately wanted a change of government, but the shift away from the type of policies they supported and the referendum issue severely damaged morale. However, with an election imminent, the majority view was that there was little option but to accept the decisions and move into the campaign. While some of the party's supporters were disillusioned, if the object was to get a change of government, then the Labour Party was the only means to achieve it.

Having won the election so handsomely, the new prime minister lost no time in appointing Donald Dewar as secretary of state for Scotland. Dewar's aim was to get the programme for setting up a Scottish parliament established as quickly as possible. There were to be two questions in the referendum, asking for 'yes'/'no' answers to each: "I agree/do not agree that there should be a Scottish parliament"; and "I agree/do not agree that a Scottish parliament should have tax-varying powers". A mere fortnight after the election victory, the referendum bill was published, with a view to getting it royal assent by mid-July. By the end of that month, the White Paper was published.

The short campaign

Campaigning for a 'yes, yes' vote immediately got underway, and learning from the 1979 fiasco, an all-party umbrella group was set up as Scotland FORward. The group's chairman was Nigel Smith, a businessman who had been involved in the home rule movement without being associated with any single political party. The group was funded from trade union and business sources, notably the STUC. Its aim was to provide a single, unifying force for the campaign so that the logo 'FOR' (from 'FORward') could be reproduced in the colours of Labour, SNP and Liberal Democrats. In late June 1997, some five weeks after the Scotland FORward campaign was launched, Think Twice was launched to campaign for a double 'no' vote. It was severely hobbled by the fact that the Conservative Party was its only backer. The lack of Conservative political leadership north of the border led to Michael Ancram running the campaign. Ancram was MP for the English seat of Devizes, and was not helped by the fact that in 1987 the Edinburgh South electorate had voted him out as their MP. The 'no' campaign split into a series of almost-theological nuances. As well as those arguing for a double 'no' vote to both questions in the referendum, there were also proponents of 'no, yes'. They argued that there should not be a Scottish parliament, but if there had to be one, it should have full tax-varying powers to encourage fiscal responsibility. There was also those who supported a 'yes, no' position - largely associated with business persons in Scotland - who did not wish to deny their patriotic credentials, but did not want higher taxes. Faced with an almost united 'yes, yes' campaign in which all three main parties played a part, the opposition faced an uphill task.

Public opinion

As shown in table 2.1 early polls showed substantial leads on both question: three to one on the principle of a Scottish parliament, and two to one in favour of it having tax-varying powers.

The Conservatives found it impossible to focus their fire. Some wanted the bill ambushed in the House of Lords; others wanted an indepen-dence option on the ballot (hoping to split the 'yes' vote); some wanted outright opposition to the principle of devolution; others wanted the party to acquiesce in what was proving to be, in John

Smith's words, "the settled will of the Scottish people".

Table 2.1

Opinion polls of Scottish referendum vote intention

Question 1: I agree/do not agree that there should be a Scottish parliament.
Question 2: I agree/do not agree that a Scottish parliament should have tax-
varying powers.

		Question 1				Question 2		
		Yes	No	Don't know		Yes	No	Don't know
(a) System Three polls for								
The Herald								
May 1997	%	64	21	15	%	53	28	19
June 1997	%	68	21	11	%	56	26	18
July 1997	%	65	19	16	%	54	27	19
August 1997	%	61	23	16	%	47	32	11
September 1997	%	61	20	19	%	45	31	14
(b) ICM polls for *The Scotsman*								
January 1997	%	69	27	4	%	59	33	8
March 1997	%	71	26	3	%	58	34	8
April 1997	%	64	28	8	%	52	34	12
June 1997	%	72	22	6	%	61	32	7
July 1997	%	68	22	10	%	55	36	9
August 1997	%	66	23	11	%	55	38	9
September 1997	%	63	25	12	%	48	40	12

The SNP had its opponents of a devolved parliament too. After all, the fundamentalists claimed, the party stood for independence, not devolution. The party leader Alex Salmond replied that he would support a "positive" White Paper. When this was duly published in late July, the party's national council voted in early August to support the 'yes, yes' campaign with very few dissidents, notably the party's erstwhile leader, Gordon Wilson, who called it a "devolution swamp". Labour and the Liberal Democrats who had worked together in the Constitutional Convention welcomed this conversion to the principle of home rule. A few Labour activists with long memories of 1979 refused to associate themselves with what they saw as an SNP attempt to use the devolved parliament as a stepping stone to full independence. A few other excursions and alarms from business opponents such as the governor of the Bank of Scotland were rapidly stamped upon by Scotland FORward campaigners before they got out of hand. High profile personalities like Sean Connery, and even dissident businessmen like the boss of the transport company Stagecoach, helped to give the 'yes' campaign gloss.

At the very end of August, Diana, Princess of Wales, was killed. 'No' campaigners wanted the whole thing put on ice, ostensibly 'as a mark of respect', while Donald Dewar decreed a week's moratorium on the campaign. The campaign was foreshortened. Some thought that her death and funeral would generate an out-pouring of Britishness, and feared the referendum would be lost. The weekend before the referendum had one poll showing a shortening of the 'yes'/'no' gap on the second - tax - question to a mere eight points. The Scottish CBI and the Scottish Chambers of Commerce produced poll evidence from their members that most thought the business climate would worsen. Two days before the referendum, Lady Thatcher entered the fray when she came to Glasgow on her lecture trail. She warned against "resentful English nationalism" and the threat to the union. The 'yes' campaign took comfort from this familiar recruiting sergeant for home rule, and even the Think Twice campaign declined her help through gritted teeth. In television debates, the party leaders, Donald Dewar, Alex Salmond and Jim Wallace, complemented each other's skills and demolished the opposition 'no' campaigners who included recycled Conservatives and the redoubtable but isolated Tam Dalyell, whose famous West Lothian question seemed to have lost its capacity to mobilise if not to bamboozle.

The result of the referendum confirmed their worst fears. On a turnout of 60% (respectable in the circumstances of a very out-of-date electoral register), 74% voted 'yes' on the first question, and 63% on the second. Only Orkney, and Dumfries and Galloway, voted 'no' on the second question (53% and 51% respectively). The "unfinished business" of which the late Labour leader John Smith had spoken of in the context of home rule, as well as the longest electoral campaign in Scottish history - since mid-1996 - was over.

As we have seen, both ICM polls for *The Scotsman* and System Three polls for *The Herald* showed consistent support of around three to one for a parliament in principle (the first question), and on tax-varying powers (the second question), around two to one. ICM's final poll (discounting 'don't knows') gave a 'yes' vote on the first question of 72%, and on the second question of 59%, compared with actual results of 74% and 63.5% respectively. System Three's final poll put the predicted result at 75% and 59%. Both polling organisations slightly under-estimated the 'yes' vote on the second question, possibly the result of differential turnout. The make-up of the Scottish vote is discussed in more detail in the chapter in this volume by Paula Surridge and David McCrone.

At the end of the day, it appears that Scottish voters had made up their minds how to vote some time before. Certainly, the polls suggest little attrition to the 'no' campaign. To suggest that it was all over bar the voting on 11 September would be to discount the success of the 'yes' campaign in holding its line. The parties supporting the campaign focused on what united rather than divided them. To the accusation that they were strange enough bedfellows, with the SNP seeking independence and the others home rule, the reply that the Scottish people would decide in due course what constitutional outcome they wanted seemed to do the trick. Using the same 'yes, yes' message on party posters but in the different party colours gave a sense of cohesion. Private polling for Scotland FORward had suggested that the 'yes' vote was vulnerable on the tax question, and yet it managed to keep a firm hold of the agenda. The British deputy Labour leader John Prescott told the governor of the Bank of Scotland, who raised issue of the impact of higher taxation on investment, rather brusquely to go away and play with his money. The strategy to prevent even the smallest forest fire breaking out into inferno had worked.

The Welsh referendum campaign

The referendum announcement and its context

With Tony Blair's announcement on 27 June 1996 that there would be referendums on Labour's devolution proposals, the Welsh political scene was thrown into flux. The media focused on the turn-around in Labour policy and the manner in which the decision had been made. It appeared that Ron Davies, the shadow Welsh secretary of state, was totally excluded from discussions leading to the decision and had been publicly denying that a referendum was to be held or was necessary up to 48 hours before the announcement was made (*The Western Mail* 27 June 1996). Another member of the shadow Welsh Office team, it was reported, became aware of the policy change only through an article in a newspaper.

Although answering the charge that devolution would be imposed on the Welsh public by a Labour government and welcomed by some MPs and elements of the media, announcement of the referendum unleashed a series of alternative and certainly more testing challenges for the Labour Party to address in Wales. The announcement meant that those Welsh Labour MPs who had barely concealed their hostility to devolution were prompted by the furore to vocalise their opposition publicly. Fuel to their fire was the decision that the assembly would be elected by a degree of proportional representation (PR) - an appendage to the referendum announcement. It seemed Ron Davies had secured Blair's backing for an element of PR in the assembly elections, arguing that it would assist in obtaining support of other parties for a 'yes' vote in the referendum. At a heated meeting at Wales Labour Party headquarters in early September 1996, Tony Blair explained his position to the Welsh Labour Executive and attained their compliance to look again at the electoral system for the assembly. Meanwhile pro-devolutionists within and outside the party questioned the Labour leadership's commitment to devolution.

Analysis of Tony Blair's motives followed. He was accused of bowing to Tory claims that devolution would be imposed on the Scots and the Welsh, preoccupied by the approaching general election. This contentious constitutional issue would be shelved until after the election had been won. Some referred to the utility of the referendum mandate in clearing the devolution proposals' passage through parliament. In June 1996, above all, the decision was perceived as displaying little reference to Welsh circumstances and being largely dictated by Scottish concerns. Nonetheless, the Labour Party in Wales accepted that they were faced with a *fait accompli*, and recognised that they had a difficult task ahead of them to win the referendum.

A campaign was required and had to be constructed. There was little to build upon in Wales, unlike Scotland. Wales had had no Constitutional Convention and the Welsh public were largely ignorant of the issue of devolution and displayed little enthusiasm for it. It had not been widely discussed in the public domain. Indeed, the Wales Labour Party had ensured that the development of devolution policy from the late 1980s onwards was confined within the party's ranks. Foremost among the various reasons for this approach was the shadow of 1979, and the highest priority placed upon avoiding party division - a concern which shaped the Welsh party's devolution proposals. Having rejected an initiative in 1992 for a Welsh Con-stitutional Convention, the Wales Labour Party decided instead to establish a Policy Commission which engaged in a consultation process during 1993 and 1994. Public meetings were held in six venues throughout Wales where oral and written evidence were accepted. However, in contrast with the profile of the Scottish Constitutional Convention, this exercise barely registered with the Welsh public.

While the Scottish Constitutional Convention's activities and recommendations were disseminated through a flourishing Scottish media, there is no Welsh national media to compare with that which exists in Scotland. This compounded the implications of the absence of a wide-ranging discussion of devolution involving the institutions of Welsh civil society and the range of political parties. The main 'Welsh' daily newspapers, *The Western Mail* and *The Daily Post*, have readerships concentrated in south Wales and north Wales respectively. Indeed, *The Daily Post* is Liverpool-based with a north Wales edition. Compared with the most widely read papers in Wales, *The Daily Mirror* and *The Sun*, their readership is small. Only 13% of the Welsh population are readers of either *The Western Mail* or *The Daily Post* according to one estimate (*UK Press Gazette* 27 March 1998).

The penetration of Wales-based terrestrial television to homes in Wales is incomplete too. Up to 10% of Welsh households, mainly in north-east Wales cannot receive Welsh television signals.[1] In addition, approximately 35% of the Welsh population live in 'overlap areas' covered by English transmitters, compared to only 2.5% in Scotland (Institute of Welsh Affairs 1996). Thus a significant proportion of people in Wales do not access the Welsh-based media and consequently received very little information regarding Welsh devolution and the referendum campaign. The coverage by the London-based media of events in Wales was scant to say the least. This situation certainly had an impact on the referendum campaign; it also highlighted the broader problem facing the nascent Welsh polity.

The 'yes' camp

The 'yes' campaign in Wales seemed to consist of three main strands: the Labour government after 1 May 1997; the cross-party Yes for Wales campaign; and the Wales Labour Party. While Labour's role in these three vehicles is relatively clear, categorising the key input of the other pro-devolution parties is certainly more difficult. Focusing initially on this three-fold classification, there was generally a high degree of co-ordination between the campaigns and at times they could not be distinguished. However, relationships between them were also fraught with tensions.

Yes for Wales filled the need, perceived by senior Welsh Labour MPs, to have a cross-party and non-party campaign which in particular was not closely allied with the Labour Party. Peter Hain MP, in collaboration with Leighton Andrews, the Welsh-born chair of a London political consultancy, set about drawing together a number of leading figures from different aspects of Welsh society to form a steering group. Hain, along with Ron Davies, was present at the first meeting on 20 December 1996. Other participants included academics, trade unionists and media figures. At this gathering, officials were chosen and broad strategies decided upon and after the initial meeting Hain and Davies retreated from the picture. The campaign could thus more confidently claim that it:

> is deliberately non-Party, and is representative of the civic life of Wales: North and South, East and West, rural and industrial, denominational and non-denominational, voluntary, private and public organisations, cultural, sporting, business, trade unions, youth and students. (Yes for Wales papers 1997)

While in Scotland the Constitutional Convention had been fulfilling this role since 1989, Yes for Wales was set up only nine months prior to the referendum. It was not officially launched until 10 February 1997, and did not build up steam until after the Labour general election victory.

Meanwhile, the Wales Labour Party appointed Andrew Davies, a former party official, as a special projects officer with responsibility for the devolution campaign. His remit to educate and inform the Welsh public and particularly Labour Party activists had been rendered largely redundant by the delay in his appointment until 1 April 1997. The 1 May general election meant that there was further delay before the referendum reached the top of Labour's list of priorities. Discussion of devolution was minimal during the election campaign, which was tightly controlled by party headquarters in London and was largely homogeneous across Britain.

Labour's landslide victory left the coast clear for the effort to secure the implementation of their devolution plans. From their position in government, a degree of strategic direction for the referendum campaigns was injected by a Welsh Office committee chaired by the secretary of state. Its members included Peter Hain, then a new Welsh Office minister, who took a prominent role in the campaign, drawing on his extensive campaigning experience. The committee included also the Welsh Office special advisers, Nick Ainger MP (Ron Davies's parliamentary private secretary), members of the Wales Labour Party executive and officers of the party, as well as the leader of the Welsh Local Government Association. The final element in the committee's make-up was the central (British) party link, Allan Barnard.

Described by one participant as the most tense campaign he had ever been involved in, it was the London/Cardiff conflicts which were perhaps the most emotive in view of the subject of the campaign. The sources of tension, from the Welsh perspective, were the perceived ignorance in Millbank (Labour's British headquarters in London) of

Welsh circumstances and what was believed to be apathy, even hostility, at the highest levels to Welsh devolution. One very senior figure within the central (that is, British) Labour Party administration was said to be under the impression up to a very late stage that the referendum was to be held in September of the following year! The production of scratch cards to promote a 'yes' vote, despite the objections of Welsh Labour officials, epitomised to some the heavy-handedness of central input and its lack of awareness of the Welsh context. Indeed, Millbank's man in Wales soon became known as the 'governor-general' by senior figures in the Wales Labour Party.

Yet London had the resources and the campaigning expertise desperately lacking in Wales and involvement of Labour's central administration was therefore indispensable. Their spin doctors, and tried and tested formulae, were transported over Offa's Dyke. Focus groups were conducted at two locations: Maesteg in the south Wales valleys, and Wrexham in the north-east. Views as to their utility were contradictory. The groups confirmed that Tony Blair was Labour's ace card and consequently great emphasis was placed on his support for devolution in Labour's campaigning material. One sceptic has since claimed, in an interview with one of the authors, that the exercise was a London device, totally unsuited to Welsh circumstances, particularly in those areas targeted - simple questions on social background designed to break the ice entailed descent into a group therapy session.

Yes for Wales' strategy was characterised by launches of numerous local branches and groups such as Students Say Yes, Actors Say Yes and Women Say Yes. Coupled with periodic announcements regarding the latest personalities from the world of sport and entertainment to call for a 'yes' vote, the profile in the media was impressive. Less impressive was the national Yes for Wales campaign's grasp of the practical aspects of campaigning. Delays in producing leaflets at crucial stages necessitated emergency action by some local groups to produce their own leaflets. Yes for Wales cannot be assessed in general terms, however. Its role and composition varied between areas and over time.

One assertion which can be made generally, is that canvassing during the campaign was extremely limited. Otherwise, strategies varied as did the level of activity. Of particular relevance in this regard was the position of the Labour Party in different areas and the role of its activists. In those areas where the Labour Party's electoral dominance was most complete, its campaigning machine was weakest, as it was unaccustomed to the task (see McAllister 1980, Hain 1998). Lack of energy and enthusiasm after the general election was another factor which minimised Labour grass roots participation in the campaign in certain areas. Reports of Plaid Cymru members delivering Labour leaflets in Cardiff and in north-east Wales in the final weeks of the campaign graphically illustrate this phenomenon.

The 'no' camp

A formal 'no' campaign was not launched until 22 July 1997. Just Say No's leadership consisted of an unlikely grouping of disillusioned Labour activists and Welsh Conservatives. It was a merger of two separate initiatives. The Conservatives had been seeking to establish a 'no' campaign in the period following the general election and had identified businessman Robert Hodge as an appropriate figurehead. Meanwhile veteran Rhondda Labour Party members Carys Pugh and Betty Bowen had established their own campaign. The contact between the two groups was made by Viscount Tonypandy, former (Labour) speaker of the House of Commons and a long-standing opponent of devolution.

Just Say No's campaigning activities differed significantly from those of Yes for Wales. Their activities were concentrated around leafleting in public places and there was little local organisation (Woods 1998). They had their own supportive personalities: for example, footballer Gary Speed, to counter Ryan Giggs' declared support for a 'yes' vote. However, financially and in terms of media savvy they could not compete with the 'yes' campaign - or so it seemed. Yet the final result suggests that the 'no' campaign may have been relatively successful in conveying its message. It was simple and appealed to the major fears of the voters - cost, bureaucracy and the break-up of the Union. Many people may also have been repulsed by the slick 'yes' campaign. As the media and sporting elite declared their support for a 'yes' vote and urged their compatriots to do the same, many ordinary Welsh people may well have questioned the relevance of this message to their own lives.

Dissenting Welsh Labour MPs provided an alternative source of opposition to the assembly plans. Llew Smith, MP for Blaenau Gwent, was the most prominent of the 'rebels', asserting soon after the announcement of the referendum his intention to campaign for a 'no' vote. Allan Rogers (Rhondda) and Ray Powell (Ogmore) also publicly broke ranks while a number of others[2] displayed varying degrees of apprehension regarding their party's proposals (McAllister 1998). These MPs refrained from formally joining the Just Say No campaign, but co-ordination of activities between the campaign and Llew Smith, at least, was acknowledged after the referendum. Above all, the dissenting figures within the Labour Party provided the media with stories which were difficult to squeeze out of the largely uninspiring 'no' campaign. Claims by Llew Smith of bullying by Ron Davies, then secretary of state for Wales, due to his non-adherence to the party line, were particularly fruitful. *The Western Mail* gleefully reported that "Ron-gate rumbles on" (1 July 1997). As for the effect on the eventual result, majority 'yes' votes were recorded in the constituencies of all the major protagonists, yet it is impossible to measure whether the magnitude of these endorsements was diminished by the stance of the local MP. Similarly the effect on their constituencies of those MPs who were conspicuous by their absence during the campaign can only be speculated upon.

A new form of politics?

"Working together has been a rewarding experience . . . This campaign has been a good example of how more can be gained by co-operation". These were the words of the secretary of a constituency Labour Party to the chair of the local Yes for Wales group - an Independent Green town councillor - shortly after the referendum. This represented the ideal of cross-party co-ordination to secure a 'yes' vote and the aspiration of what could happen with the creation of the assembly.

  Part of the rationale for establishing Yes for Wales was to secure the involvement of the Liberal Democrats and Plaid Cymru in the 'yes' effort. Plaid Cymru's participation was viewed by the Welsh Labour hierarchy as crucial. Of key importance, it was also a highly complex role. In the immediate aftermath of the referendum announcement Plaid campaigned for a four-question referendum.[3] Following the general election in May 1997, the party had to decide whether it would publicly declare support for a 'yes' vote and, if so, whether it would also campaign under the umbrella of the Yes for Wales campaign. Some voices within the party claimed that the proposal to create such an emaciated institution, so much weaker than that on offer in Scotland, was an insult to Wales and could not be supported. The ghost of 1979 loomed large over these deliberations. There were doubts regarding Labour's commitment to devolution and fears that Plaid Cymru would again find themselves doing the lion's share of the work while some Labour MPs were campaigning against. Most compelling, however, was the instinctive support of Plaid Cymru members and supporters for this devolutionary measure and the feeling that if they did not play a positive role they may not have the opportunity again to influence the course of Welsh politics so fundamentally. Thus it soon became clear that Plaid would recommend a 'yes' vote, but further consideration of their campaigning strategy was required.

Senior figures within the party were anxious that taking too prominent a role in the campaign would confirm fears among a section of the electorate that devolution was part of the nationalist agenda, giving credence to the 'slippery slope' argument. In a meeting of the National Council of the party in July 1997, it was decided that Plaid Cymru would campaign publicly for a 'yes' vote. This position was arrived at following numerous meetings between senior Plaid Cymru figures and Welsh Office ministers, Yes for Wales officials and Wales Labour Party campaigners. Assurances were secured that the government's commitment to a 'yes' vote was total and that it would pull out all the stops to ensure that the referendum was won.

Plaid Cymru set in motion its well-honed campaigning machine but its **public** role in the campaign was low key owing to the concerns outlined. It campaigned under the banner of Yes for Wales while providing a significant proportion of workers in some areas. In their Westminster constituencies Plaid campaigners conducted widespread telephone canvassing, and similarly in other areas such as the Rhondda and Cardiff. It was a sophisticated effort which earned the respect of those Welsh Office figures with whom they liaised closely.

The meetings between Plaid Cymru, the Liberal Democrats, and senior figures within various strands of the campaign, established the theme of co-operation and co-ordination which seemed to be epitomised by the scenes at the main counting centre in Cardiff in the early hours of 19 September 1997. After victory for the 'yes' campaign had been secured, Ron Davies and Welsh Office ministers as well as Dafydd Wigley and Richard Livsey, the Plaid Cymru and Welsh Liberal Democrat leaders respectively, stood on the stage, hands joined aloft in celebration.

To what extent this level of co-operation was replicated at grass roots level is difficult to gauge. Again it varied between localities and over time. Taking the composition of the Yes for Wales groups as an indication of the variability, in some areas the Labour and Yes for Wales campaigns were virtually co-terminous, while in others such as Llanelli the Labour Party did not feature. Here the membership was largely composed of Plaid Cymru and minority socialist parties, while the Labour Party and the Liberal Democrats were absent (Woods 1998). Alternatively, in Neath and parts of Cardiff a wide range of parties and organisations were involved.

Public opinion

Campaigners were acutely aware of the crucial role of the media in the formation and representation of public opinion in the run-up to the referendum. According to one key 'yes' campaigner, "there was a big charm offensive by government ministers to win over editors", and it seemed to succeed as newspaper editorial positions were generally sympathetic to the devolution proposals.

The press and television media employed a notion of balance which proved to be particularly contentious. 'Yes' campaigners complained that by giving 50:50 coverage to the Yes and No camps the media were over-representing the level of support for the 'no' campaign. The media's definition of balance was said to ignore the fact that three of the four main parties had declared their support for a 'yes' vote. Indeed, the television media in particular were accused of sustaining, even creating, the 'no' campaign by striving to represent equality between the two camps.

The absence of a national 'Welsh' media certainly had repercussions in terms of informing the electorate of the issues at hand and it was probably one explanation for the high proportions who stated in opinion polls that they were undecided how they would vote (see table 2.2). This figure was consistently between 26% and 36% throughout the campaign. In Scotland, the proportion of 'don't knows' was significantly lower, indicating that Scots had over the years become engaged by the issue of devolution. The Welsh polls did however for the most part predict a 'yes' vote and a *Western Mail*/Beaufort poll at the end of August saw a lead of 20 points for the 'yes' camp. In the event, the most accurate representation of the final result came from a *Guardian*/ICM poll published on 11 September - ironically considered an anomaly by many at the time. The huge discrepancy between this poll and previous figures at the end of August was interesting in view of the suspension of the campaign during early September following the death of Diana, Princess of Wales. There is no conclusive evidence that the incident prompted a reversion to the *status quo*, but there was a firm feeling within the 'yes' camp that the campaign's suspension severely dented their positive momentum.

Support for the idea that a 'yes' vote was the "settled will of the Scottish people" is reflected in the finding from the Referendum Studies that 29% of Scots said they had made up their mind to vote in the September referendum before the general election in May, compared to 19% of people in Wales.

Table 2.2
Opinion polls of Welsh referendum vote intention[4]

Date		Yes	No	Don't know
October 1996	%	39	32	28
March 1997	%	41	33	27
April 1997	%	34	37	30
July 1997	%	39	27	34
July 1997	%	43	29	28
August 1997	%	42	22	36
September 1997	%	37	36	26
September 1997	%	37	29	34

The polls counted for nothing on 18 September, and in the early hours of the 19th with the final result from Carmarthenshire, the Welsh people provided the mandate to establish a Welsh assembly, by the margin of 6,721 votes on a turnout of 50%. The make-up of the Welsh vote is discussed in more detail in the chapters by Richard Wyn Jones and Dafydd Trystan and by Geoffrey Evans and Dafydd Trystan in this volume. The campaign had been incidental to the lives of many. There were significant obstacles to effective campaigning in Wales, and particular problems which belonged to the 1997 referendum campaign. Yet a 'yes' vote was secured, overturning the huge negative majority registered in 1979. Even if the campaign did not capture the imagination of a significant proportion of the Welsh people, in view of the marginal result it was crucial to delivering the necessary affirmation. It also set a challenge for the Welsh assembly to touch people's lives in a way the campaign had not.

Conclusion

The results of the referendums in Scotland and Wales confirmed that constitutional change is well established on the political agenda. Despite the narrowness of the Welsh result, few in either country thought afterwards that the outcome was not settled. The 'no' campaigns quietly folded their tents and 'normal' politics returned. Except that little would be the same again. The Conservative journalist Michael Fry who had helped to found the 'no, yes' campaign in Scotland declared that "The Union is over bar the shouting. Its end is a matter of time, whether a few years or a couple of decades" (*The Herald*, 24 September 1997). By this he meant that the authority of the

Westminster crown-in-parliament as the basis of sovereignty in the UK could no longer be sustained in the face of the new parliament and assembly.

In both countries, Labour soon found itself embroiled in a controversy over the siting of the new institutions. In Scotland, the old Royal High School building on Calton Hill had been the preferred site since Labour had refurbished it in the 1970s for the assembly, and the city council had bought it in the 1980s with this aim in mind. It was later judged to be too small for the purpose of a modern parliament, and some close to the centre of power in Labour's Scotland even considered it a 'nationalist shibboleth', which was odd given its 20-year association with home rule rather than independence. Ultimately a central city site was found at Holyrood for a new custom-built building without the practical or political problems of Calton Hill.

In Wales, the almost universally favoured location for the assembly, Cardiff City Hall in the capital's impressive civic centre, was the topic of extended and often hostile discussions between the Welsh Office and Cardiff County Council. Financially, and increasingly politically, it was ruled out by Ron Davies, then secretary of state. Other options, outside Cardiff, were then considered and the next episode in the saga was the Cardiff or Swansea question. With an announcement on 13 March 1998, the Swansea campaigners' hopes were dashed. Yet a final decision had still not been made and further consideration was deemed necessary of two sites in Cardiff Bay. A waterfront site centred on the Pier Head building was eventually settled upon. It was an affair which proved as emotive as, if not more so than, the referendum itself.

The government put itself on the defensive on this and other issues. In the first opinion polls after the referendum, the Scottish electorate began to discriminate between voting for Westminster and voting for Edinburgh. While Labour had a commanding lead over the SNP, their main rivals, for Westminster elections, the lead has narrowed considerably when it comes to Scottish elections. By the early months of 1998, the SNP had drawn level with Labour for Scottish elections and then overtook them by the middle of the year. While SNP support fell back under sustained Labour attack throughout the rest of the year, there was still a considerable differential between voting preferences for Westminster where Labour had a 15-20 percentage point advantage over the SNP, and those for Holyrood where Labour had a lead of only a couple of points over their main rival. A simple 'how would you vote?' question is plainly not enough, for under the Additional Members System of voting, Scots will have two votes, one for an MSP elected from the 73 constituencies, and the other for an 'additional member' selected from party lists for each of the current

European constituencies (seven 'additional members' from each of eight constituencies, making 56 'additional members' in total). While votes for constituency MSPs will be counted by first-past-the-post system, the 'additional member' seats will be allocated correctively to reflect the percentage of votes received by the political parties. While Labour is doing better than the SNP on the first vote, the positions are reversed on the second, largely because Labour voters are more likely than SNP voters to switch. Independence for Scotland is not apparently the shibboleth of former years. As analysis of the Scottish electorate elsewhere in this book shows (see the chapter by Paula Surridge and David McCrone), most Scots thought just after the referendum that their country would be independent within 20 years, and viewed such an outcome with equanimity. No such claims could be made in Wales partly because the dearth of polls has meant that the voting intentions and political preferences of the Welsh public are gauged very infrequently. Polls have however displayed a swell in support for Plaid Cymru when respondents are asked how they would vote in assembly elections, indicating the likelihood of their being the second party in the assembly, still a significant distance behind Labour (*Western Mail* 27 July 1998 and 1 October 1998). Plaid Cymru is also likely to benefit from the element of proportionality in the voting system, with 20 'additional members' elected from five regional lists plus each of the 40 constituencies returning one member each, elected by the first-past-the-post system. More worrying for Labour in Wales are the repercussions of Ron Davies's 'lapse of judgement' one Monday evening in October 1998. His resignation as secretary of state for Wales and the prospective Labour leader in the assembly has robbed the party and the new institution of a popular figure who had succeeded in building a broad consensus behind devolution. As a result, the Labour Party in Wales was in disarray and faced a potentially damaging contest to replace Davies as its candidate for First Secretary. Whether these events will affect Labour's electoral fortunes in Wales will be seen in the May 1999 assembly elections.

The Government of Wales Bill was published on 27 November 1997, and the Scotland Bill three weeks later. The Bills made their way through Westminster without much trouble to become law on 31 July and 19 November 1998 respectively. The referendums confirmed the Scottish and Welsh mandates, and have given the parliament and assembly legitimacy beyond Westminster. How Scotland and Wales had got to this position is possible to describe, but no one can say where the road will take them.

Notes

1. BBC Wales figures, 1998.
2. The other MPs were: Denzil Davies (Llanelli), Ted Rowlands (Merthyr Tydfil and Rhymney), Alan Williams (Carmarthen East and Dinefwr), and Alan Williams (Swansea West).
3. The options which Plaid Cymru wanted put in the referendum were: the *status quo*, Labour's executive assembly, a law-making parliament, and full self-government in Europe.
4. The polls listed derive from various sources from the period October 1996 to September 1997, based on varying sample sizes and designs, and slightly differing questions; all were reported in the *Western Mail* newspaper. In the absence of regular polls in Wales from a consistent source, these figures are the only publicly available indication of public opinion over the period.

References

Hain P (1998) 'Welsh Warning', *Tribune*, 19 June 1998.

Institute of Welsh Affairs (1996) *The Road to the Referendum: requirements for an informed and fair debate*, Cardiff: IWA.

Jones P (1997) 'Labour's Referendum Plan: Sell-Out or Act of Faith?', *Scottish Affairs* **18**, winter.

McAllister I (1980) 'The Labour Party in Wales: The Dynamics of One-Partyism', *Llafur* **3**: 79-89.

McAllister L (1998) 'The Welsh Devolution Referendum: Definitely, Maybe?', *Parliamentary Affairs* **51**: 149-65.

Mitchell J (1992) 'The 1992 Election in Scotland in Context', *Parliamentary Affairs* **45**: 612-26.

Woods M (1998) 'Local Campaigning in the Welsh Devolution Referendum, 1997', paper presented to the Elections Parties and Opinion Polls 1998 Annual Conference, University of Manchester, September.

Yes for Wales papers (1997) National Library of Wales.

3 The 1997 Scottish referendum vote

Paula Surridge and David McCrone [*]

When people in Scotland voted in September 1997 by three to one to set up a Scottish parliament, and by two to one for it to have tax-varying powers, it was easy to forget that having a referendum at all had been a highly contentious exercise to begin with. As the chapter by Bethan Lewis and David McCrone on the referendum campaigns makes clear, the device of a referendum was adopted by the Labour Party for a variety of reasons. There was little doubt that Labour was serious about devolving power to Scotland and Wales, but it was nervous that it would be difficult to steer government legislation through the thickets of the Westminster parliament. After all, many in the party saw the debacle over devolution in the 1970s as one of the hammer blows to a dying Labour government, and while Labour was much more sympathetic to devolving power than it had been in the pre-Thatcher era, memories of the 1979 referendum remained vivid. The Scottish National Party (SNP) also had a place in Labour demonology as it had helped to deliver the *coup-de-grâce* to the Labour government in the 1979 vote of confidence, even though, in James Callaghan's memorable phrase about SNP MPs, "it proved that turkeys could vote for Christmas after all". So it came to pass, the SNP

[*] Paula Surridge is Lecturer in Sociology, University of Salford. David McCrone is Convenor of the Unit for the Study of Government in Scotland and Professor of Sociology, University of Edinburgh.

lost 9 of their 11 Westminster seats in the 1979 general election, and went through its own period of upheaval. One effect was that scepticism about fighting for devolution rather than independence entered the SNP's soul. It voted in 1989 to withdraw from the Scottish Constitutional Convention, a body set up after the 1987 general election to draft proposals for a Scottish parliament, with the support of Labour and the Liberal Democrats. Faced with an implacable Conservative government, Labour was able to re-educate itself as a home rule party, with few but the predictable opponents in its ranks.

Labour had no way of knowing in advance just what a sweeping victory it would gain in the general election of May 1997. In particular, it had been rattled by the 'tartan tax' campaign run by Michael Forsyth, the Conservative secretary of state for Scotland, and it believed, like most politicians in the western world, that electorates do not vote for higher taxes. Hence introducing a second vote on tax-varying powers had the benefit for Labour of neutralising this vexed question. While Labour Party members went along with the party's decision to hold a referendum, activists in the home rule movement generally were more suspicious of the Labour leadership's motives, particularly about the tax question.

The outcome of the referendum removed these fears. The votes cast in favour of both the principle of a devolved parliament and its tax-varying powers were so convincing, that, in the late John Smith's phrase, the "settled will of the Scottish people" underwrote the legitimacy of the parliament.

From 1979 to 1997

It is important to see the 1997 Scottish referendum vote in a wider political context, and not only that of the May 1997 general election result. The sense of there being 'unfinished business' derived from the debacle of the 1979 referendum when a majority of those Scots who voted supported an assembly, but in insufficient numbers to meet the 40% of the electorate in favour which had been set as a hurdle by opponents of devolution. The results in 1997 were considerably more emphatic than that of 1979, with 74% of the votes cast being in favour of the setting up of the parliament and 63% in favour of the parliament having tax-varying powers. Even if a 40% rule had existed in 1997, with a turnout of just over 60% the votes cast on 11 September would have exceeded it.

Table 3.1
Scottish referendum vote and social characteristics, 1979 and 1997

	1979				1997			
	Yes	No	Did not vote	N	Yes	No	Did not vote	N
Age								
18-34	% 38	34	28	196	% 49	15	35	164
35-54	% 39	34	27	235	% 57	14	27	257
55-64	% 24	49	27	90	% 65	17	16	94
65+	% 41	41	18	124	% 52	26	21	161
Housing tenure								
Owner	% 29	51	20	263	% 52	21	25	423
Non-owner	% 43	29	29	385	% 61	9	30	253
Religion								
Catholic	% 37	28	36	87	% 71	5	23	105
Non-Catholic	% 37	39	24	561	% 52	19	27	570
Sex								
Male	% 40	34	26	319	% 58	14	27	291
Female	% 34	41	25	329	% 53	19	26	385
Party identity								
Conservative	% 17	63	21	199	% 15	59	26	123
Labour	% 44	27	29	243	% 66	7	27	336
Liberal etc.	% 34	39	27	62	% 45	32	23	51
SNP	% 77	3	21	68	% 76	1	22	122
National identity*								
Scottish	% 46	33	21	359	% 57	16	26	621
British	% 24	45	31	246	% 46	26	27	373
English	% 27	64	9	11	% 38	29	33	28
Class identity								
Working class	% 41	32	27	446	% 64	8	27	479
Non-working class	% 29	50	21	202	% 52	20	26	197
Occupation								
Manual	% 45	28	27	242	% 62	7	30	302
Non-manual	% 33	43	24	406	% 50	24	24	374

* The categories used were not mutually exclusive in 1997 (i.e. a respondent could claim more than one national identity). The 1979 question limited respondents to a single national identity.

It would appear, then, that between 1979 and 1997 changes occurred in Scotland to make the 'will of the people' considerably more settled. Using data from the 1979 Scottish Election Survey and the 1997 Scottish Referendum Study (for details of the 1979 and 1997 Scottish Election Studies and the 1997 Scottish and Welsh Referendum Studies, see the Introduction and the Technical Appendix of this book), we can compare the behaviour of different social groups at each referendum. Table 3.1 shows how various groups within Scottish society voted in 1979 and on the first question of the 1997 referendum.[1]

Table 3.1 clearly demonstrates one of the key differences between the 1979 and 1997 referendums. In 1979, there were divisions between social groups in their support for a Scottish parliament. Those who were broadly middle class (non-manual occupation, home owners, non-working class identifiers) voted 'no' in 1979. By 1997 these divisions had lessened such that the only social group to have a majority of 'no' voters were those who identified with the Conservative Party. Although support for the parliament varied among different groups in 1997, a majority voted 'yes' even among middle-class groups. In this sense the Scottish parliament was indeed the 'settled will of the Scottish people' as no group could claim a majority dissension. It is also interesting to note that abstentions did not vary substantially between social groups at either referendum.

In this chapter we use data from the 1997 Scottish Referendum Study to try to understand the basis of this support for a Scottish parliament. As referendums are rare events there are no general theories of voting behaviour at referendum to draw upon. Thus, using the literature of support for political parties in Scotland and the widespread imagery used in the Scottish media, we hypothesise three main sets of reasons for a 'yes' vote in the 1997 referendum. (See Brand *et al* 1993, 1994 and Brown *et al* 1998, 1999 for more detailed discussion of voting behaviour at general elections in Scotland.) First, voting for a parliament might be seen as a way of expressing national identity, as an emotive affirmation of one's Scottishness. Second, there may be rationalistic reasons for a 'yes' vote. That is to say that people in Scotland may have voted for a Scottish parliament because they believed that the establishment of a Scottish parliament would lead to either their personal circumstances improving (egocentric voting) or to circumstances in Scottish society improving (sociotropic voting) (Kinder and Kiewit 1981). In contrast, those who support the emotive explanation argue against a rational explanation on the grounds that constitutional questions come well down the list of reasons people give for voting preferences at general elections (Finlay 1997; Edwards

1989). A third possible view is that what matters to people is good government and democratic efficiency, and that support for a Scottish parliament drew on considerable discontent over how Scotland was governed. We shall consider each of these arguments.

Rational voting and the referendum result

If the people of Scotland cast their votes at the referendum along rational principles we should expect to find a strong relationship between the expectations people had of the parliament and their voting behaviour. As we are dealing with a snap-shot picture of the electorate we cannot be sure about the direction of causality in these analyses. For example is it the case that people supported a parliament because they expected it to have positive outcomes or did they say they expected positive outcomes because they supported a parliament? In order to the test the propositions set out above we have assumed throughout that support for the parliament is the dependent variable.

The Referendum Study asked respondents a series of questions about what they expected of the parliament. The first of these was

> *Now supposing that a Scottish parliament within the UK were set up. As a result of this Scottish parliament, would unemployment in Scotland become higher, lower or would it make no difference?*

Similar questions were asked about taxation the economy, education, the NHS and social welfare. The results, displayed in table 3.2, show that people were able to make distinctions between the different policy areas.

The table shows that most of the people of Scotland expected taxes to go up as a result of the Scottish parliament (76%). This suggests that if people were voting rationally it was not along the 'pocket book' model which has often been used at general elections (Heath *et al* 1991). While the question is not specific to the respondent's personal position and so cannot be interpreted purely in terms of the pocket book model, it is unlikely that a 'rational' voter, in the egocentric sense, who expected higher taxes would vote for the parliament.

Table 3.2
Expectations of Scottish parliament in policy areas

	Taxa-tion	Econ-omy	Unemploy-ment	Educa-tion	NHS	Welfare
	%	%	%	%	%	%
A lot better/lower*	0	18	5	28	23	13
A little better/ lower	3	46	38	42	42	46
No change	20	24	38	25	28	35
A little worse/ higher	65	10	15	3	5	4
A lot worse/ higher	11	2	3	0	1	1
N	657	657	657	657	657	657

* Lower/higher refers to taxation and unemployment

However, if we further partition the sample into, on the one hand, those who expected taxes to be higher, and on the other, those who expected taxes to be unchanged or to be lower, we find that 61% of the 'pessimists' voted 'yes' on both referendum questions, whereas 83% of the 'optimists' did the same. Thus, although there is some difference between the two groups, there is little evidence that referendum vote was driven by the pocket book.

Rather, the evidence suggests that people voted according to the expectations they had of a Scottish parliament in terms of policy outcomes. If we assume that taxation is the cost that has to be paid in order to receive policy benefits we can further our understanding of the voting process by setting the expected costs against the expected benefits. Thus, we constructed a scale based on the number of benefits (excluding taxation) that respondents expected from the Scottish parliament. This ranges from 0, a respondent who expected everything to either stay the same or get worse, to 5, a respondent who expected improvement in all of the policy areas. The distribution on this scale is shown in table 3.3.

It can be deduced from table 3.3 that people in Scotland were able to differentiate between policy areas; it was not the case that most people were either totally optimistic or totally pessimistic about the effects of a parliament.

Table 3.3
Number of expected benefits of Scottish parliament (excluding taxation)

	Number of benefits expected
	%
0	19
1	9
2	8
3	9
4	25
5	31
N	*657*

As table 3.1 showed, there is little evidence that factors such as social class, gender or national identity are the key to these results; we could find little variation in support for a parliament in terms of any of these background social characteristics. As we have reported elsewhere (Brown *et al* 1999), further modelling of the data confirms this: expectations of the parliament remain a significant predictor of referendum vote even after other social characteristics were taken into account. Our conclusion is that people supported a Scottish parliament because they believed that it would improve the quality of public welfare in Scotland. In addition, we believe that this is consistent with a rationalistic model of vote choice along sociotropic lines. In other words, voters voted according to 'welfare rationality' for which they were prepared to accept higher taxation as a reasonable cost.

Democratic effectiveness

The second hypothesis we test is that people wanted a Scottish parliament because it would improve how Scotland is governed. The Referendum Study asked people three related questions:

Would a Scottish parliament give ordinary Scottish people more say in how Scotland is governed, less say, or would it make no difference?

Would a Scottish parliament give Scotland a stronger voice in the United Kingdom, a weaker voice in the United Kingdom, or would it make no difference?

Would a Scottish parliament give Scotland a stronger voice in Europe, a weaker voice in Europe, or would it make no difference?

Table 3.4 shows the distribution of responses to these questions.

Table 3.4
Expected democratic effectiveness of Scottish parliament

	Say in government of Scotland	Scotland's voice in UK	Scotland's voice in Europe
	%	%	%
More/stronger	79	70	60
No difference	16	17	22
Less/weaker	2	10	11
Don't Know	2	4	6
N	676	676	676

Nearly four out of five respondents expect the parliament to be more responsive to people in Scotland, 70% think that it would give Scotland a stronger voice in the UK, and 60% that it would do the same for Scotland in Europe. These responses tend to cluster together, so that 78% of those who expect the parliament to give Scots more say in government also expect it to give Scotland a stronger voice in the UK, and 68% expect this also to hold for Europe. Optimism was strongest among those who voted 'yes, yes', so that 92% of 'yes, yes' voters expected the parliament to give people in Scotland more say, compared with only 43% of those who voted 'no, no'. A similar differential operated with regard to Scotland's voice in the UK, and in Europe, with 85% of 'yes, yes' voters taking an optimistic view of the former, and 80% for the latter, compared with 24% and 13% of those who voted 'no, no'.

Again we are faced with the possibility that our assumed direction of causality is incorrect. However, we believe that these results show that people in Scotland expected the parliament to improve democratic effectiveness, as well as to lead to positive policy outcomes. In order to address the possibility that attitudes to democratic effectiveness are an artefact of people's social location further modelling was conducted. But again we find factors such as age, gender, social class, housing tenure and educational level are unrelated to expectations of democratic effectiveness (see Brown *et al* 1999 for further details of the statistical modelling). We can conclude that optimism about democratic renewal was spread across all social categories.

A further issue is how these expectations of democratic effectiveness relate to policy expectations. Using logistic regression models of the expectations of democratic effectiveness we find that there is an association between expectations of people having more say in government and expectations of improvements in unemployment, taxes, the economy and social welfare, but none with health and education, with those who feel most positive about policy expectations also feeling most positive about democratic expectations. As regards Scotland's voice in the UK, there is an association with expectations about the economy and social welfare; for Scotland's voice in Europe, the only association is with the economy. What is striking about these results is that the associations between expectations in different policy areas do not correspond with the division of powers between Edinburgh and Westminster. Thus, Westminster retains control of the economy and large measures of social welfare (social security) but Scots do not appear to measure democratic effectiveness in terms of two of the key powers where the Scottish parliament actually does have control - health and education. In other words, as we shall see later, there is likely to be an inner dynamic in terms of the Scottish parliament seeking to meet expectations about democratic effectiveness in areas which are not part of its remit - the economy and social welfare.

National identity

If relationships between expectations of democratic effectiveness and expectations of policy outcomes are present but complex, what can be said about links between these and national identity? Let us take a step back to explore whether national identity is a key factor in explaining the demand for a Scottish parliament. The view that a parliament is primarily an expression of national identity - that it is an end in itself - has some currency among political commentators. It lies behind an argument, less common now than in the past, that a parliament is an irrelevance to the 'real needs' of the Scottish people for better services - health, education, jobs and so on. Put simply, did people vote for a Scottish parliament primarily as an expression of their Scottishness? In other words, is its affective quality more important than its effective quality?

To measure national identity we use a question, known as the Moreno scale, which asks respondents to rank their Scottish and/or British identity so we can begin to explore how national identity is related to referendum vote (Moreno 1988):

> *Which, if any, of the following best describes how you see yourself?*
> *Scottish, not British*
> *More Scottish than British*
> *Equally Scottish and British*
> *More British than Scottish*
> *British not Scottish*
> *Other*

Unfortunately, the sample size for respondents who identify themselves as more British than Scottish is very small (this reflects the distribution of identities within the population of Scotland. Less than 6% describe themselves as 'More British than Scottish' or 'British not Scottish'.). Thus, it is sensible to comment on only the first three categories. Here we do find some association with national identity. As seen in table 3.5, those who ranked their Scottish and British identities equally were split almost equally between 'yes' and 'no' voting on the second question of the referendum. However, even this group had a small majority in favour of the principle of a parliament (the first referendum question).

Table 3.5
National identity and Scottish referendum vote

	Scottish not British	More Scottish than British	Equally Scottish and British	More British than Scottish	British not Scottish
	%	%	%	%	%
Yes, yes	80	78	46	27	29
Yes, no	12	8	10	27	7
No, no	7	14	42	47	64
No, yes	-	-	1	-	-
N	157	148	139	16	17

Further modelling of this relationship shows that, once expectations of the parliament in terms of democratic effectiveness and policy outcomes are taken into account, national identity is no longer a significant predictor of referendum vote (see Brown *et al* 1999 for further details). As table 3.6 shows, the relationship between national identity and expectations of the parliament is itself complex. The table shows the proportion within each national identity category who expected improvements in the democratic effectiveness shown.

Table 3.6

Expected democratic effectiveness of Scottish parliament and national identity

	Scottish not British	More Scottish than British	Equally Scottish and British	More British than Scottish	British not Scottish
% saying that a Scottish parliament would give ...					
More say in Scottish government	86	84	70	68	57
Scotland stronger voice in UK	77	82	54	50	48
Scotland stronger voice in Europe	65	70	50	50	25
N	*213*	*216*	*190*	*23*	*21*

Whereas 85% of those who felt more Scottish than British or Scottish not British believed that the parliament would give Scots more say in government, the proportion was 63% among the small group (7% overall) who felt more or wholly British. In other words, across the spectrum of national identity, a clear majority of people were optimistic in their expectation of the parliament's democratic effectiveness. But when this measure of national identity is added to the earlier model of democratic effectiveness, it is less strongly associated with democratic expectations than are policy expectations. In sum, there is no reason to think that the Scottish parliament is primarily about articulating a sense of Scottishness in isolation from expectations about improvements in social welfare and democratic effectiveness. (For a fuller discussion of these issues see Brown *et al* 1999, chapters 6 and 7.) Indeed, the importance of expectations about the parliament turns out to be one of the main differences between

Scotland and Wales, as shown in the chapter by John Curtice in this volume.

Our analysis points to people in Scotland wanting a parliament because most have expectations that it will make a difference to their lives in terms of the services they want it to provide. Those are the grounds on which its effectiveness is likely to be judged, rather than as an affective expression of nationhood. This is not to say that being Scottish does not matter to people, merely that it does not discriminate as to whether or not they are in favour of a parliament. Further evidence to support this claim is found by looking at the priorities people in Scotland think the parliament should have. Choosing from a list of areas including increasing national pride, giving people more say in government and improving the standard of living, the most common response was to give people more say (28%), followed closely by increasing the standard of living (27%) and improving education (23%). Promoting a sense of national pride with just 4% came below all other categories except leaving the UK.

Debating the future

Much of the debate about devolution over the past 20 years or so has been less about its actual merits and de-merits, than what, if anything, it might lead to. Both Conservatives and Nationalists have tended to believe that home rule will ultimately lead to independence, with the Conservatives warning against the 'slippery slope' effect of a domestic parliament, and the SNP seeing it as a stepping stone along the way. What do people think is likely to happen in the future? The Scottish Referendum Survey asked:

> *At any time in the next twenty years, do you think it is likely or unlikely that Scotland will become completely independent from the United Kingdom?*

Table 3.7
Expectations of Scottish independence

	%
	%
Very likely	19
Quite likely	41
Quite unlikely	25
Very unlikely	16
N	*638*

A clear majority (60%) think independence likely, considerably more than the 39% who favour it themselves (37%). How are expectations about independence and people's preferences related? Of those sympathetic to independence (it was their first or second choice of constitutional arrangement), 69% think it likely to come about in the next 20 years. Of those who did not prefer independence as their first or second choice, 49% expect it to happen. Put another way, of those who expect independence to come about, two-thirds are not opposed to it. This suggests that for a majority of Scots there is no cognitive or value barrier to independence, something borne out by opinion polls in the months following the referendum. For example, in ICM polls for *The Scotsman* in June, July, September and November 1998, the proportions claiming that they would vote for independence in a referendum were 56% (35% against), 49% (44% against), 51% (38% against) and 49% (43% against) respectively. What these data perhaps suggest perhaps is less how people might vote if there actually was a referendum on independence and more that there is no majority resistance to independence.

What, if anything, is likely to drive any move towards independence? Using a statistical model of whether people thought independence was very or quite likely, on the one hand, or not likely on the other, we find that social class, gender, age and education do not explain whether people expect independence. (There is a weak association with housing tenure, but it is of little consequence as it explains little of the variation.)

How are policy expectations associated with expectations about independence? As we can see from table 3.8, the more optimistic people are about improvements in education, health and social welfare, the more likely they are to expect independence. This suggests perhaps that when it comes to those powers in the hands of the Edinburgh parliament - education, health and, to some extent, welfare - majorities may also expect independence to come about as an outcome of success in these areas. Turning to expectations about the state of the economy, unemployment and taxation, both those who are optimistic and those who are pessimistic are equally likely to expect independence to come about.

These results suggest that there may be different routes to independence. On the one hand, it could come about because people who are optimistic about policy outcomes over which the devolved parliament has control (education, health and social welfare) believe that independence will follow as these are extended. Alternatively it may come about because people are pessimistic about what the parliament can do in areas which are controlled by Westminster (the economy, unemployment and taxation). To put it another way, if the parliament makes a success in those areas it does control, then extending its powers might seem the natural thing to do. If people believe the parliament is unsuccessful because it does not control unemployment, taxation and the economy, then an obvious line of attack is to argue for independence.

Table 3.8
Proportion expecting Scottish independence
by expected effects of Scottish parliament

	Taxa-tion		Econ-omy		Unemploy-ment		Educa-tion		NHS		Welfare	
		N		*N*		*N*		*N*		*N*		*N*
% expecting ...												
Better/lower*	66	25	66	406	62	277	65	456	64	421	63	370
Neither	57	144	42	171	51	257	44	176	50	196	53	249
Worse/higher	59	485	53	78	66	117	44	21	38	37	50	34

* Lower/higher refers to taxation and unemployment

This analysis shows how closely policy issues are associated with support for the parliament. We predict that much of the debate about further constitutional change will be framed by these policy issues. In that respect, those who have argued that people are much more interested in 'real' politics - the delivery of services - than in purely constitutional politics are correct. On the other hand, they are wrong insofar as the distinction between these two realms is artificial, because they are linked together in the minds of the electorate.

Issues of identity are associated with views on independence as we might expect. Thus, three-quarters of people who feel they are Scottish not British expect independence to come about, compared with fewer than half (46%) of those who feel equally Scottish and British. Identity in these terms does seem to operate over and above the effect of policy expectations when it comes to expectations about independence, even though we found that identity was not a strong predictor of vote in the referendum.

We should take care not to argue that expectations about policy outcomes, expectations about democratic effectiveness, and national identity are entirely separate dimensions. Our task has been to show that there is in fact no hard-and-fast distinction between the politics of constitutional change and the politics of policy outcomes, at least in the case of Scottish voters.

Political parties

Plainly politics is not simply or mainly about debates of policy expectations, but about competition between political parties. How Scottish politics unfolds will primarily be about changing party fortunes. We are able to get some inkling of how these might develop in terms of people's first or second party preferences. Using the 1997 Scottish Election Survey, we find that 60% of the sample were close to Labour (gave the party as either their first or second preference), 43% the SNP, 31% the Liberal Democrats, and 17% close to the Conservatives. This highlights the relative unpopularity of the Conservatives in Scotland. Analysis we have conducted elsewhere (Brown *et al* 1999, chapter 5) suggests further that the Conservatives are isolated in terms of policy preferences. This is evident in table 3.9, which shows the proportion of each 'pool' of supporters agreeing with various policy statements. The gap between their supporters and supporters of other parties is greater than 10 percentage points on the following issues: private medicine, education, redistribution of wealth, tax and spend, stricter trade union laws, the EU Social Chapter, nationalisation and defence cuts. On the other hand, Labour and the SNP sympathisers are close on each issue, to the extent that on no measure are they more than a few percentage points apart. Evidently the two biggest parties in Scotland, Labour and the SNP, are competing on a similar policy agenda; and the Conservatives are far adrift from the electorate's prevailing policy preferences. These findings confirm earlier work on the 1992 and 1997 Scottish Election Studies which demonstrated the similarities between Labour and SNP voters (Brand *et al* 1994, 1995; Brown *et al* 1999).

Table 3.9
Policy preferences by pools of party support*, Scotland

% saying ...	Conser-vative	Labour	Lib. Dem.	SNP
Government should put more money into the NHS [a]	88	98	97	97
Government should encourage the growth of private medicine [a]	39	24	27	24
Government should spend more money on education [a]	91	97	94	96
Government should get rid of private education in Britain [a]	12	34	25	33
The cleverest children should be selected for education in separate schools [b]	46	22	32	24
It is a good thing for schools to be made to compete against each other for pupils [b]	50	19	27	20
People who break the law should be given stiffer sentences [b]	75	85	76	87
Life sentences should mean life [b]	82	88	85	90
Prisons should try harder to reform prisoners rather than just punishing them [b]	61	81	82	77
People should be allowed to use their cars as much as they like, even if it causes damage to the environment [b]	33	23	25	27
For the sake of the environment, car users should pay higher taxes [b]	20	27	30	22
Income and wealth should be redistributed towards ordinary working people [b]	39	78	63	79
Government should spend more money to get rid of poverty [a]	84	98	94	97
It would be better if everyone paid less tax and had to pay more towards their own health care, schools and the like [b]	21	14	15	12
Taxes should be as low as possible, and people should have to provide more for themselves even if it means that some people suffer [b]	13	6	5	6
Everyone's taxes should go up to provide better old age pensions for all [b]	45	58	60	62
Government should increase taxes and spend more on health, education and social benefits [c]	48	77	79	77

Table 3.9 (Contd)

% saying ...	Conser-vative	Labour	Lib. Dem.	SNP
Government should introduce stricter laws to regulate the activities of trade unions [a]	42	30	30	30
Government should give workers more say in running the places where they work [a]	61	79	67	83
The British government should sign up to the Social Chapter so that British workers have the same rights at work as everyone else in Europe [d]	15	50	45	49
The law should set a minimum wage so that no employer can pay their workers too little [e]	48	83	76	82
There should be more nationalisation of companies by government [f]	7	42	33	39
Government should spend less on defence [a]	38	69	62	69
Government should give more aid to poor countries in Africa and Asia [b]	31	39	46	30
N	*146*	*494*	*253*	*359*

* The pool of support for each party consists of those people who reported voting for the party in the 1997 general election and also people who gave that party as their second preference

Notes on coding of response categories:

a. % choosing 'definitely should' or 'probably should' (other categories being 'doesn't matter either way', 'probably should not' and 'definitely should not')

b. % choosing 'agree strongly' or 'agree' (other categories being 'neither agree nor disagree', 'disagree' and 'disagree strongly')

c. the options offered against this were 'Government should reduce taxes and spend less on health, education and social benefits' and 'Government should keep taxes and spending at the same level as now'

d. the option offered against this was 'The British government should not sign up to the Social Chapter because it would cost too many British workers their jobs'

e. the option offered against this was 'There should be no minimum wage because a minimum wage set by law would cost too many low paid workers their jobs'

f. the options offered against this were 'There should be more privatisation of companies by government' and 'Things should be left as they are now'

Our final piece of evidence is how respondents to the Referendum Study said (in September 1997) they would vote in the elections to the Scottish parliament: 54% said Labour, 24% the SNP, 13% Conservative, and 8% Liberal Democrat. These levels of support are likely to change as the debate in Scotland continues in the run-up to the parliament's first elections in May 1999. This is even more likely than is usual in political behaviour as the debate is not only about party competition but also about the electoral system itself. The parliament will be elected under a system of PR which will allow voters to cast two votes, one for a local constituency MP and one for an MP from a party list. It is unclear at the time of writing the extent to which the Scottish electorate will be informed about the electoral system and will engage in sophisticated forms of political behaviour in response. In table 3.10 we look at where support for parties in the Scottish parliament is likely to come from.

Table 3.10
Intended vote in elections to Scottish parliament
by vote in 1997 general election

	Intended vote in Scottish parliamentary elections			
	Conservative	Labour	Liberal Democrat	SNP
Vote at 1997 general election	%	%	%	%
Conservative	98	2	12	0
Labour	1	94	14	15
Liberal Democrat	0	1	73	4
SNP	0	3	1	81
Other	1	0	0	0
Base	*88*	*314*	*47*	*131*

We can see only 81% of likely SNP votes will come from people who voted nationalist in the general election of 1997. Both Labour and the Conservatives are very reliant on those who voted for their party in 1997. The Liberal Democrats are more similar to the SNP with 73% coming from Liberal Democrat general election votes. Most of Labour's 'defectors' benefit the SNP (15% of the SNP vote), but there is little reciprocity, with only 3% of Labour's Scottish parliamentary vote likely to come from 1997 SNP voters.

This analysis further confirms that Labour and the SNP are largely competing for the same pool of voters, and helps to explain the fierce rivalry between the parties. It may also provide a small measure of comfort for the Conservatives who are likely to gain some representation in the Scottish parliament through the proportional representation mechanism of its electoral system.

The Scottish parliamentary elections

What then is likely to determine how people will vote in the first elections to a Scottish parliament in May 1999? We can identify four types of explanation: people's policy expectations; whether or not they think the parliament will be democratically effective; the expectations they have about Scottish independence; and how far people trust each of the parties to stand up for Scotland's interests. We can examine how these influence likely vote by means of logistic regression models, which are summarised in table 3.11.

First it is clear that trust in the party to stand up for Scotland's interests is important for all parties, in fact it would appear that this is the prime factor in explaining party choice for the parliament election. We can see from table 3.12 below, that only one in ten people in Scotland trust the Conservatives to work in Scotland's interests. It is also clear that Labour and the SNP are most trusted with Scotland's interests, with the latter having the highest 'just about always' rating. Whilst this is in part a reflection of the distribution of party support in Scotland it is not a simple reflection of party preference. Even among Conservative identifiers only 50% said that they trusted the party to work in Scotland's interests just about always or most of the time.

Table 3.11
**Logistic regression model of intended vote
at elections to Scottish parliament**

	Conser-vative		Labour		Lib. Dem.		SNP	
	B	SE	B	SE	B	SE	B	SE
Constant	-3.67	(0.78)	-0.17	(0.48)	-2.99	(0.87)	-5.57	(0.75)
Expectations of improvements in								
Economy	-0.65	(0.47)	0.39	(0.28)	-1.00*	(0.48)	1.04**	(0.38)
Unemploy-ment rate	-0.11	(0.37)	-0.26	(0.26)	0.15	(0.45)	-0.07	(0.32)
Taxation	0.90	(0.51)	-0.48*	(0.22)	0.59	(0.49)	-0.21	(0.26)
NHS	-0.61	(0.55)	-0.24	(0.36)	1.46*	(0.63)	-0.30	(0.46)
Education	-0.82	(0.51)	-0.02	(0.37)	-0.24	(0.61)	0.31	(0.50)
Social welfare	-0.43	(0.41)	0.10	(0.24)	-0.27	(0.42)	0.13	(0.29)
Democratic effectiveness								
Stronger voice in UK	0.44*	(0.19)	-0.08	(0.13)	0.11	(0.24)	-0.08	(0.16)
Stronger voice in EU	-0.05	(0.21)	-0.02	(0.12)	-0.39	(0.23)	0.28	(0.15)
Say in govern-ment	0.25	(0.17)	-0.40*	(0.14)	0.23	(0.22)	0.26	(0.18)
Trust (party) to work in Scotland's interest	2.53**	(0.35)	2.09**	(0.21)	1.21**	(0.35)	2.51**	(0.41)
Expect inde-pendence in 20 years	0.27	(0.33)	-0.13	(0.20)	-0.31	(0.35)	-0.02	(0.26)
Preference for independence	-0.40	(0.45)	-0.58**	(0.21)	-1.02*	(0.46)	1.80**	(0.26)

* significant at 5%; ** significant at 1%

Table 3.12
Trust in each party to work in Scotland's interests

	Conservative	Labour	Liberal Democrat	SNP
	%	%	%	%
Just about always	2	11	2	28
Most of the time	8	49	26	34
Only sometimes	31	33	42	20
Almost never	56	4	11	11
Don't know	2	3	19	7
N	*674*	*674*	*674*	*674*

Attitudes to independence separate Labour and Liberal Democrat voters from the SNP supporters, with those most in favour of independence intending to vote SNP, confirming that attitudes to independence will become a key issue in Scottish politics. However, people's expectations of independence do not play a part in influencing voting behaviour for the parliament. Expectations that people held of the parliament were also surprisingly weak in determining voting intentions. Those who expected higher taxes were less likely to be intending to vote Labour and those who expected improvements in the economy were more likely to be SNP supporters, while those expecting improvements in the NHS were more likely to support the Liberal Democrats. Overall, however, there is little significant influence of expectations of the parliament on people's voting intentions. Similarly, the measures of democratic effectiveness had little impact, with the exception of those who expected the parliament to give Scotland a stronger voice in the UK being more likely to support the Conservatives and those who thought it would give people a greater say in government less likely to support Labour. While these results may seem unusual it is possible that this is a reaction to there being a Labour government in the UK. The models presented in table 3.11 seem to suggest that the key influence on voting behaviour for the Edinburgh parliament will be the extent to which the parties convince the voters that they have Scotland's best interests at heart.

Conclusion

We have shown that most voters have strong expectations of the Scottish parliament, both with regard to desired policy outcomes and democratic effectiveness. These expectations hold regardless of social location, and we can conclude that they reflect majority Scottish opinion regardless of class, age and gender. Above all, we find that desire for a parliament is related to people's expectations that it will improve the quality of their lives in terms of policy outcomes and not simply as a means of improving democracy in Scotland. Hence, to juxtapose affective desire for a parliament with what some have called 'real' politics of education, health, jobs and housing, misses the point that the institution is seen by many in the electorate as the means to improving these, rather than as an end in itself.

What is likely to happen next? Since the referendum, there has been considerable turbulence in the opinion polls in Scotland. While Labour maintains a lead in polls asking about Westminster elections (averaging a 14-point lead in the second half of 1998 in the System Three/*Herald* monthly polls), the gap is much narrower when people are asked about the Edinburgh election. Indeed, the same polling company found the SNP narrowly ahead for Edinburgh elections for much of 1998. Only in September 1998 did Labour reverse this lead so that by the end of the year it had a one-point lead over the SNP. Predictions as to how these party preferences translate into seats is particularly problematic in a two-vote contest, but polls in 1998 suggest that Labour would have around a 6 to 11 seat advantage over the SNP, and would need to rely on Liberal Democrat support to have an effective majority. Of course, as we suggested earlier, such estimates may change in the run-up to the election.

Why should there be such a difference between Westminster and Edinburgh elections? We should not be surprised at this, as it is frequently a feature of political systems with devolved systems of power (as discussed in the chapter in this volume by Anthony Heath and Bridget Taylor). In Catalunya, for example, support for the nationalist coalition, *Convergença i Unió*, is much stronger in autonomous elections (around 40%) than it is for all-Spanish *Cortes* elections (around 25%), so that CiU and the Socialist Party vie for supremacy in much the same way as is likely to happen in Scotland.

The Scottish political agenda over the last decade or so has been dominated by Labour and the SNP. This has helped to shape political values and opinion, while also being a reflection of these values. Survey data consistently show that there is little by way of political values and attitudes to distinguish the typical Labour voter from the typical SNP voter. That is why both parties are locked into an intense political battle: they are each competing for the same broad and sizeable swathe of Scottish public opinion, and in turn this helps to shape the political discourse of Scotland at the present time. With the two parties neck-and-neck in the opinion polls in the race to be the largest party in a Scottish parliament (though not, of course, for Westminster where Labour have a 15-20 percentage point lead in the opinion polls), this nationalist-leftist discourse is reinforced.

Will the Scottish parliament matter? Our analysis shows very clearly that what people want from a parliament relates to policy preferences. It is not simply a vehicle for expressing Scottishness *per se*. Nonetheless, the parliament is likely to reinforce national identity partly because the weight of people's expectations of policy outcomes is likely to lead the parliament to find its share of powers unduly restrictive. If the parliament fails to make an impact on matters such as the state of the economy or managing social security, which are reserved for Westminster, then it is in a position to claim that it requires further powers to respond effectively to the desires of the Scottish electorate. In other words, standing up for Scotland's interests may well require seeking further powers for the Scottish parliament, and if this evolves incrementally towards independence, our evidence is that a majority of people in Scotland will not object. Matters of policy, identity and constitutional politics are entering a new and uncharted era.

Notes

1. For the purposes of this comparison the first question in the 1997 referendum is treated as equivalent to the single question asked in the 1979 referendum.

References

Brand J, Mitchell J and Surridge P (1993) 'Identity and the Vote: Class and Nationality in Scotland', in *British Parties and Elections Yearbook 1993*, London: Frank Cass.

Brand J, Mitchell J and Surridge P (1994) 'Social Constituency and Ideological Profile: Scottish Nationalism in the 1990s', *Political Studies* **42**.

Brand J, Mitchell J and Surridge P (1995) 'Will Scotland Come to the Aid of the Party?', in Heath A, Jowell R and Curtice J (eds) *Labour's Last Chance?: The 1992 Election and Beyond*, Aldershot: Dartmouth.

Brown A, McCrone D and Paterson L (1998) *Politics and Society in Scotland*, London: Macmillan, 2nd edition.

Brown A, McCrone D, Paterson L and Surridge P (1999) *The Scottish Electorate*, Macmillan: Basingstoke.

Edwards O D (ed) (1989) *A Claim of Right for Scotland*, Edinburgh: Polygon.

Finlay R J (1997) *A Partnership for Good? Scottish Politics and the Union Since 1880*, Edinburgh: John Donald.

Heath A, Jowell R, Curtice J, Evans G, Field J and Witherspoon S (1991) *Understanding Political Change*, London: Pergamon.

Kinder D and Kiewit D (1981) 'Sociotropic Politics: The American Case', *British Journal of Political Science* **11**.

Moreno L (1988) 'Scotland and Catalonia: the Path to Home Rule' in McCrone D and Brown A, *The Scottish Government Yearbook 1988*, Edinburgh: Unit for the Study of Government in Scotland.

4 The 1997 Welsh referendum vote

Richard Wyn Jones and Dafydd Trystan[*]

Just 6,721 votes separated the 'yes' and 'no' camps when the result of the referendum on the government's proposals for a Welsh assembly was finally announced in the makeshift counting centre at the Welsh College of Music and Drama in Cardiff during the early hours of the 19 September 1997. These votes represented a mere 0.6% of those cast during the previous day's poll; or a tiny 0.3% of the total eligible electorate. (The full referendum results are given in the Introduction to this volume.) Nonetheless, they were enough to secure the most grudging of mandates for the creation of a National Assembly for Wales - a body whose establishment will surely represent the most profound transformation in the structures of governance in Wales since the Acts of Union of 1536-1543.

The result of the referendum has generated many questions about the nature of contemporary Welsh society and politics, some of which are addressed in this book. This chapter focuses on two in particular, using the 1997 Welsh Referendum Study (for further details about the Welsh Referendum Study, see the Introduction and Technical Appendix of this book). First, why was it that a proposal actively supported by political parties that had gained over 75% of the vote in

---

[*] Richard Wyn Jones is Lecturer in the Department of International Politics at the University of Wales Aberystwyth. Dafydd Trystan is Tutor in the Department of International Politics, University of Wales Aberystwyth.

the 1997 general election, and in particular by the three parties which had subsequently represented all of the Westminster seats in Wales, fail to attract more than 50.3% of the vote in the referendum (and on a lower turnout)? Second, why was it that an issue that both sides of the argument had presented as a 'make or break' issue for the future of Wales, and indeed the UK as a whole, failed to attract more than a modest turnout when it was put to the voters?[1] Of course, these questions are of more than academic interest; they relate directly to the future prospects of the National Assembly itself. We will seek to answer them by analysing the effects of party cues and national identity cues on referendum vote.

The chapter is organised into four sections: the first focuses on the inter-relationship between party cues and referendum vote; the second on the inter-relationship between national identity and referendum vote. The third section then addresses the mutual implication of national identity and party identification in the Welsh context, while the fourth section concludes the chapter by summarising our findings.

Partisan alignment and referendum vote

Party cue theory would lead us to expect a significant relationship between patterns of partisan alignment and referendum vote.[2] That is, voters would tend to follow the recommendation of the party with which they identify when deciding how to vote in the referendum.

Table 4.1
Party identification and Welsh referendum vote

		Yes	No	Did not vote	N^3
Labour	%	34	24	42	366
Conservative	%	7	62	30	138
Plaid Cymru	%	71	6	24	72
Liberal Democrat[4]	%	18	45	37	49
None	%	27	13	60	30
All	%	31	31	38	681

Table 4.1 seems to indicate that there were clear distinctions along party lines. These ranged across a spectrum: Plaid Cymru identifiers voting 'yes' by a margin of around 12 to 1, and also the most likely to vote; Labour identifiers (53% of the sample) supporting their party's devolution proposals by a margin of 3 to 2, but the least likely of all party identifiers to vote; Liberal Democrats opposing devolution by just over 2 to 1; and Conservative identifiers voting 'no' by a decisive nine to one margin. This suggests at least a *prima facie* case that partisan alignment was an important factor in the referendum vote and that voters may have been making their decisions along party lines.

Parties and referendum vote

However, to establish if partisan alignment was important, we need to explore the clarity of party cues in the referendum. That is, what did the voters perceive each party to be recommending, and how unified did they perceive each party to be in terms of these recommendations? For if party recommendations were unclear or if parties were perceived to be badly divided on the issue of devolution, then we might conclude that party cues were weak, thus casting doubt on the relative significance of party cues in influencing referendum vote. Furthermore, we need to consider the relationship between the strength of party identification and referendum vote. For example, if Labour 'yes' voters were disproportionately likely to be strong Labour identifiers, one might conclude that party identification was a significant factor in the referendum vote. Conversely, if there is no relationship between the degree of attachment to the party and voting patterns in the referendum, this may also lead us to question whether party cues were important in this instance.

We shall therefore consider the strength of party identification and referendum vote, perceived party recommendations and perceived party divisions. This will form the basis for the consideration of each of the four parties in turn.

Table 4.2
Strength of party identification and Welsh referendum vote

		Yes	No	Did not vote	N
Labour					
Very strong	%	47	27	27	*90*
Fairly strong	%	40	24	36	*168*
Not very strong	%	15	22	63	*106*
Conservative					
Very strong	%	0	90	10	*20*
Fairly strong	%	3	67	30	*69*
Not very strong	%	17	44	40	*48*
Plaid Cymru					
Very strong	%	88	0	13	*24*
Fairly strong	%	63	13	25	*32*
Not very strong	%	68	0	33	*15*
Liberal Democrat					
Very/fairly strong	%	21	41	39	*29*
Not very strong	%	16	47	37	*15*

Base: respondents without a party identification excluded.

Note: Liberal Democrat categories (very and fairly strong) combined due to very small numbers.

Table 4.3
Perceived party recommendations in the Welsh referendum

		Yes	No	Did not recommend	Don't know	N
Labour Party						
All voters	%	80	2	5	13	*686*
Labour identifiers	%	82	1	5	12	*368*
Conservative Party						
All voters	%	2	72	5	20	*686*
Conservative identifiers	%	2	79	7	13	*140*
Plaid Cymru						
All voters	%	72	1	3	25	*686*
Plaid Cymru identifiers	%	92	0	2	6	*71*
Liberal Democrats						
All voters	%	39	4	9	48	*686*
Liberal Democrat identifiers	%	46	3	26	24	*49*

Table 4.4
Perceived party divisions in the Welsh referendum

		United	Divided	Neither or both	Don't know	N
Labour Party						
All voters	%	44	35	2	19	*686*
Labour identifiers	%	46	34	0	19	*368*
Conservative Party						
All voters	%	39	33	2	26	*686*
Conservative identifiers	%	48	31	4	18	*140*
Plaid Cymru						
All voters	%	68	4	1	28	*686*
Plaid Cymru identifers	%	93	2	0	6	*71*
Liberal Democrats						
All voters	%	32	15	3	50	*686*
Liberal Democrat identifiers	%	50	16	0	24	*49*

The Labour Party and referendum vote

In the context of the relationship between referendum vote and partisan alignment, those respondents who describe themselves as Labour Party identifiers are clearly vitally important. Not only was the assembly a Labour Party proposal, but the party's identifiers account for over half of the Welsh electorate. Furthermore, when consideration is given to the transformations that have occurred between the 1979 and 1997 referendums, it becomes clear that the key shift has been in the voting patterns of Labour identifiers, as discussed in the chapter by Geoffrey Evans and Dafydd Trystan in this book.

Table 4.2 suggests that strength of partisan alignment may well be an important element in understanding the referendum vote among Labour identifiers. Those respondents who identified very or fairly strongly with Labour supported devolution by almost 2 to 1, while those whose degree of Labour identification was weakest ('not very strong') were opposed by a margin of 4 to 3. Furthermore, and crucially given the final result of the referendum, those with the strongest identification were most likely to turn out to vote.

Moreover, the evidence suggests that the Labour Party managed to communicate its position on devolution relatively effectively both to its own supporters and to the wider electorate. Table 4.3 shows that 82% of Labour identifiers correctly identified the Labour Party's position as recommending a 'yes' vote. This was despite the potential confusion created by the divisions within Labour ranks exposed during the referendum campaign as three of its MPs opposed devolution, and another three publicly expressed varying degrees of scepticism - divisions that, as table 4.4 indicates, were noted by a significant proportion of Labour identifiers, and indeed, of the electorate as a whole.

The Conservative Party and referendum vote

In contrast to the situation in Scotland where there has been a significant tradition of support for devolution within the Conservative Party, the party in Wales has been consistently hostile towards any proposal to establish a Welsh parliament or assembly. During the referendum campaign the party was initially hesitant about taking an official position on devolution, but, as shown in the chapter in this volume by David McCrone and Bethan Lewis, the Conservatives were to provide the organisational backbone for the Just Say No campaign. Thus the positive relationship between strength of attachment to the

Conservative Party and opposition to an assembly demonstrated by table 4.2 again confirms that there was indeed a relationship between degree of partisan alignment and referendum vote. Furthermore Conservative scepticism on devolution was widely recognised: 79% of Conservative identifiers recognised that their party was recommending a 'no' vote (table 4.3).

The findings on divisions in Conservative ranks is more difficult to interpret. As table 4.4 demonstrates, 33% of all respondents and 31% of Conservative identifiers perceived the party to be divided on devolution. But while there were a few dissident Conservative voices who argued in favour of an assembly, most notably Viscount St Davids and Phil Pedley, these were not high profile figures. So, given the relatively low level of knowledge of the devolution proposals themselves demonstrated by the Welsh Referendum Survey (see below), it is hard to credit that such large proportions were aware of the nuances of Conservative internal politics. A more plausible explanation may be the existence of a more generalised perception of the Conservative Party as riven with division in the run-up to the 1997 general election.

Plaid Cymru and referendum vote

The strongest supporters of devolution in the 1997 referendum were Plaid Cymru identifiers (table 4.1). But while the party's whole *raison d'être* is the recognition of Welsh nationhood through the establishment of a Welsh layer of democratic governance, Plaid Cymru approached the referendum warily. Having been traumatised by its experiences in 1979, when it felt that it had been betrayed by the Labour Party's lack of support for its own devolution proposals, Plaid Cymru was determined not to endorse the government's proposals until the Wales Labour Party had demonstrated its commitment to them (Wyn Jones and Lewis 1999). Thus it was only in mid-July 1997 that Plaid Cymru finally extended its full support to the cross-party Wales campaign - a decision which seems subsequently to have been supported by all sections of Plaid Cymru.

Tables 4.3 and 4.4 indicate that the party's position was widely understood both among party identifiers and the electorate in general (with 92% of the former and 72% of the latter correctly identifying Plaid Cymru's position), and that the party was widely perceived to be united on the matter (with 93% of the party's identifiers and 68% of the whole sample describing the party as united on devolution). This suggests that the party cue was strong, and that party cue theory provides an explanation of Plaid Cymru identifiers' referendum vote.

Liberal Democrats and referendum vote

Liberal Democrat identifiers provide an interesting exception to the association between partisan alignment and referendum vote observed thus far. As table 4.2 indicates, even those classifying themselves as 'fairly strong' Liberal Democrat identifiers were hostile to devolution by a margin of more than two to one. This was despite the Liberals' long-standing commitment to a parliament for Wales stretching back over a century and more, and the Liberal Democrat leadership's endorsement of a 'yes' vote at the referendum.

Given the small number of Liberal Democrats in our sample (reflecting the rather low level of Liberal Democrat voting in Wales - 12.4% in the 1997 general election), there is obviously a danger in reading too much into the findings. That said, given that Liberal Democrat supporters were the only party identifiers to go against their party's recommendation in the referendum vote, they are clearly an interesting case to consider when exploring the validity of party cue theory in explaining the referendum vote.

One possible explanation of the apparent Liberal Democrat anomaly is that the party cue was not strong. The findings presented in table 4.3 provide some partial support for this, in that 50% of Liberal Democrat identifiers either did not know which course of action their party was recommending or believed that their party had made no recommendation. Table 4.4 indicates that 16% of the party's identifiers perceived the Liberal Democrats to be divided, even though there was certainly no public dissension from the leadership's pro-assembly stance. Furthermore, findings from successive British Election Surveys indicate a more general lack of awareness of Liberal Democrat policies (Heath *et al* 1985: 87-106; Heath *et al* 1994: 199-200). On this basis, we might explain the Liberal Democrat anomaly on the grounds that the party cue was not strong.

However as we proceed to the next sections on the inter-relationship between national identity and referendum vote, and the mutual implication of partisan alignment and national identity, another explanation for the behaviour of Liberal Democrat supporters at the referendum suggests itself: namely that the effects of party cue on Liberal Democrat identifiers is mediated by the effects of their national identity profile.

National identity and referendum vote

Any attempt to understand or to measure national identity is a task fraught with difficulties. Not only can a number of different factors impact upon any given individual's sense of national identity, including ancestry, place of birth, place of residence, language and so on. But the relative importance of these various elements of national identity is often both context-dependent and subject to change over time; and all of these in ways of which the individual concerned is often unaware at a conscious level. In Wales, national identity is an especially complex phenomenon. As a 'stateless nation', to use David McCrone's felicitous phrase (McCrone 1992), Wales has not had a state apparatus to underpin a distinct identity. Rather its identity has been created and recreated in the context of a complex and often contradictory relationship with the dominant English/British neighbour to the east. Furthermore, Welsh identity in the modern age has been transformed by very significant movements of population both into and out of Wales in response to changes in the economic underpinnings of society in Wales. The result of this legacy is a pattern of overlapping and conflicting identities so complex that Raymond Williams was once moved to write that the Welsh have "some of the most radical identity confusions of any modern people" (Williams 1990: 66).[5]

The Welsh Referendum Survey explored the nature of national identity in Wales using two distinctly different approaches. One was to ask respondents to choose a single, exclusive category which best corresponds to their perceptions of their own national identity, for example: Welsh, British, English:

> *Please say which, if any, of the words on this card describes the way you think of yourself. Please choose as many or as few as apply.*

> *British*
> *English*
> *European*
> *Irish*
> *Northern Irish*
> *Scottish*
> *Welsh*
> *Other (please say what)*
> *None of these*

Subsequently if respondents chose more than one description they were then asked:

And if you had to choose, which one best describes the way you think of yourself?

The second used the Moreno scale (Moreno 1988), already described in the chapter by Paula Surridge and David McCrone on Scotland, to probe feelings of national identity in terms specifically of Welshness and/or Britishness, by asking respondents to place themselves on a spectrum:

> *Welsh, not British*
> *More Welsh than British*
> *Equally Welsh and British*
> *More British than Welsh*
> *British, not Welsh*
> *Other*

Using exclusive identity categorisations we find that the majority of the sample describe themselves as Welsh (63%), though a significant minority (26%) describe themselves as British. However an approach which focuses on possible overlapping senses of identity shows that when offered the choice of identifying themselves in non-exclusive terms, 68% claim some form of dual Welsh and British identity compared to 17% who view themselves as exclusively Welsh and 12% as exclusively British.[6]

Tables 4.5a and 4.5b demonstrate, on both measures a clear relationship between national identity and referendum vote. In the case of the singular or exclusive measure of national identity (table 4.5a), Welsh identifiers were more likely to vote in favour of the establishment of an assembly than those who identified themselves as British or English; they were also more likely to turn out. Similarly when responses to the Moreno scale are plotted against referendum vote (table 4.5b) it is apparent that those towards the Welsh end of the spectrum (that is, those describing themselves as Welsh not British or more Welsh than British) were significantly more likely to support devolution than those who felt equally Welsh and British or subscribed to a more or exclusively British identity. Respondents towards the Welsh end of the spectrum were also more likely to turn out.

Table 4.5
National identity and Welsh referendum vote

(a) Singular categories

		Yes	No	Did not vote	N
Welsh	%	39	26	35	427
British	%	15	44	41	175
English	%	17	31	52	42
Other	%	28	25	47	36

(b) Moreno scale[7]

		Yes	No	Did not vote	N
Welsh not British	%	43	23	34	113
More Welsh than British	%	43	25	31	166
Equally Welsh and British	%	25	34	41	225
More British than Welsh	%	16	37	46	67
British not Welsh	%	13	45	42	82

This in turn raises the issue of what are roots of national identity in the Welsh context? We shall focus on three factors in particular - place of birth, age and language - and seek to explore their relationship with self-ascribed identity and with referendum vote.

Place of birth, national identity and referendum vote

Wales has seen a relatively large influx of population in recent decades, many of whom are 'lifestyle migrants' who move to Wales after retirement or to live and work in a more pleasant environment. While two-thirds of our sample were born in Wales, 21% said they were born in England. To what extent have these individuals been assimilated into some form of Welsh identity? Table 4.6 plots place of birth against responses to the Moreno scale. Obviously not all those born in England have moved into Wales as 'lifestyle migrants', indeed in some parts of Wales, babies are routinely born in English hospitals! Nonetheless we find that those born in England are significantly more clustered towards the British side of the Welsh-British spectrum than those born in Wales.

Table 4.6
Place of birth and national identity, Wales

		Welsh not British	More Welsh than British	Equally Welsh and British	More British than Welsh	British not Welsh	Other	N
Wales	%	23	32	38	4	2	1	457
England	%	1	5	21	25	39	9	145
Somewhere else	%	6	20	26	19	17	12	29

When the association between place of birth and referendum vote is examined directly (table 4.7) we find that while those born in Wales favoured devolution by the narrow margin of 55% to 45%, those born in England were opposed by a margin of 2 to 1. Furthermore we observe a divergence in patterns of participation, with those born in England significantly less likely to vote than other respondents.

Table 4.7
Place of birth and Welsh referendum vote

		Yes	No	Did not vote	N
Wales	%	35	29	36	454
England	%	18	36	46	141
Somewhere else	%	29	35	37	30

Age, national identity and referendum vote

Work in Scotland has demonstrated that the younger age groups are becoming increasingly less British and more Scottish than their elders in terms of their self-ascribed identity (Brown *et al* 1999). As this phenomenon is often explained in terms of the dilution in the popular memory of second world war British patriotism/nationalism and the decline of the post-war welfare state settlement (Brown *et al* 1999), there is reason to suppose that such a generational shift may also be occurring in Wales. Table 4.8 provides some suggestion that this might be the case. Certainly we find a relationship between age and national identity with younger members of the electorate feeling more Welsh than older electors who feel more British.[8]

Table 4.8
Age and national identity, Wales

		Welsh not British	More Welsh than British	Equally Welsh and British	More British than Welsh	British not Welsh	Other	N
18-24	%	25	23	35	10	7	0	60
25-34	%	24	26	26	13	8	3	120
35-44	%	19	22	36	5	12	5	136
45-54	%	17	23	31	11	14	5	133
55-64	%	11	28	37	8	8	8	85
65+	%	8	26	35	12	18	2	152

Table 4.9 demonstrates somewhat contradictory patterns of association between age and referendum vote. Those under the age of 45 who turned out to vote were more likely to support the establishment of an assembly than were older people. However, the former group were significantly less likely to vote. This suggests that any electoral impact arising from differences in national identity between age groups in Wales is not enough to offset the more generalised alienation from the institutions of political representation apparently felt by younger people. (For evidence relating to the 1997 general election see Denver and Hands 1997.)

Table 4.9
Age and Welsh referendum vote

Age		Yes	No	Did not vote	N
18-24	%	19	15	66	62
25-34	%	31	21	48	119
35-44	%	33	23	44	135
45-54	%	31	43	27	131
55-64	%	36	37	27	84
65+	%	32	40	29	147

Language, national identity and referendum vote

Previous work on national identity in Wales has argued that 'cultural attachment' was an important and politically significant element of Welsh identity, and that knowledge of the Welsh language - or a positive attitude towards the language - was a key element in determining the strength or otherwise of this attachment (Balsom *et al* 1984). Table 4.10 provides strong evidence of a relationship between linguistic competence and national identity. The Welsh Referendum Survey asked each respondent to classify him/herself into one of three linguistic groups: speak Welsh fluently; speak Welsh but not fluently; and cannot speak Welsh. Overall 17% of respondents claimed to speak Welsh fluently, 12% said they speak some Welsh but not fluently, while 71% of the sample were non-Welsh speakers. On the Moreno scale of national identity, fluent Welsh speakers tend to place themselves firmly to the Welsh end of the spectrum while non-Welsh speakers tend more towards the British end.

Table 4.10
Welsh linguistic competence and national identity

		More Welsh than British	Equally Welsh and British	More British than Welsh	British not Welsh	Other	N
	Welsh not British						
Fluent Welsh speaking	% 32	41	26	2	0	0	*113*
Non-fluent Welsh speaking	% 17	28	35	10	8	2	*83*
Non-Welsh speaking	% 13	21	34	12	15	5	*491*

When the relationship between linguistic competence and referendum vote is examined, strong patterns again emerge (table 4.11). Fluent Welsh speakers supported the establishment of a Welsh assembly by almost 4 to 1, while those who do not speak Welsh were opposed by a margin of around 3 to 2. As with the findings in relation to country of birth, there is also clear differentiation in turnout along linguistic lines, with 79% of fluent Welsh speakers in the sample claiming to have voted in the referendum, compared to 57% of those who do not speak the language.[9] All of which suggests that not only is the ability to speak Welsh an important element underpinning Welsh identity, but that it also had a significant bearing on referendum vote.[10]

Table 4.11
Welsh linguistic competence and referendum vote

		Yes	No	Did not vote	N
Fluent Welsh-speaking	%	61	18	21	*111*
Non-fluent Welsh-speaking	%	31	34	35	*83*
Non-Welsh speaking	%	24	33	43	*485*

Analysis using the singular categories of national identity provides broad confirmation of the relationships identified so far in this section between place of birth, linguistic competence, age and national identity. When we model Welsh identity (*versus* not Welsh identity) we find (table 4.12) that birth and linguistic competence have significant effects, while age in this instance is not significant. Thus both a birthplace outside Wales and non-Welsh speaking have a significant positive association with non-Welsh identity.

Table 4.12
Logistic regression model of exclusive Welsh identity

	B		SE
Place of birth			
(Wales)			
England	-3.26	**	(0.28)
Somewhere else	-2.91	**	(0.51)
Welsh speaking			
(Fluent)			
Non-fluent	-1.37	*	(0.55)
Non-Welsh speaking	-2.04	**	(0.47)
Age			
(18-34)			
35-54	0.08		(0.28)
55+	-0.31		(0.28)
Constant	3.29	**	(0.48)
N		*638*	

* significant at 5%; ** significant at 1%[11]

Knowledge, expectations and national identity

Before drawing firm conclusions on the relationship between patterns of national identity and referendum vote it is also necessary to probe people's levels of information about the government's devolution proposals. It may be, for example, that Welsh identifiers were more positive about devolution and more likely to turn out to vote because they had greater knowledge of the proposals, perhaps because of greater exposure to Wales-based print and television media. If they did have more knowledge of the proposals, this might call into question the significance of national identity in influencing referendum vote. On the other hand, if it appears that levels of information regarding the proposals were **not** closely linked to national identity, while expectations of the Welsh assembly were, this would reinforce the argument that national identity was important in determining referendum vote.

In order to probe these issues further we first consider the results of the devolution knowledge quiz in relation to positions on the Moreno scale of national identity. The devolution quiz, which is also discussed in the chapter in this volume by Lindsay Paterson and Richard Wyn Jones, consists of seven questions in the Referendum Survey designed to probe respondents' knowledge of the government's devolution proposals. These ranged from whether the establishment of a Welsh assembly would mean that people would need passports to travel between England and Wales, to whether the assembly would be elected by a system of proportional representation; respondents were asked to answer "true" or "false" to each (see the survey questionnaires in Appendix II to this volume). As these examples demonstrate, the questions were not difficult; rather the reverse. The aim was certainly not to catch people out. Nonetheless the results reveal a lack of information about key elements of the proposals. Just 16% of the sample succeeded in answering all seven questions correctly, while almost a third (31%) managed to answer only four or fewer questions correctly. However, as table 4.13 (where we have calculated the mean score of correct answers - with a potential range 0 to 7 - for each Moreno national identity category) demonstrates there is no clear association between national identity and having correct information about the devolution proposals. The mean score of those at the exclusively British end of the spectrum was only slightly lower than those with an exclusively Welsh identity, while all those whose sense of national identity included both Welsh and British elements had a mean score similar to that of the exclusively Welsh.

Table 4.13
National identity and Welsh devolution knowledge quiz

National identity	Mean quiz score
Welsh not British	5.1
More Welsh than British	5.1
Equally Welsh and British	5.0
More British than Welsh	5.1
British not Welsh	4.6
Other	5.6
N	*670*

Strikingly, however, despite this apparent lack of association between national identity and levels of information about the devolution proposals, an association does emerge between national identity and expectations of the assembly. Another battery of questions in the survey probed respondents' expectations of the proposed assembly. As tables 4.14a and 4.14b demonstrate, almost 50% thought that the establishment of an assembly would lead to improvement in the standard of the NHS and improvement in the Welsh economy. As shown in the chapters by Paula Surridge and David McCrone and by John Curtice in this volume, these questions turn out to have had a critical impact in Scotland.

In Wales, however, within these overall figures, there are marked contrasts in expectations between those who see their identity as exclusively or primarily Welsh and those who see their identity as equally Welsh and British, or as predominantly British. The predominantly Welsh identifiers (42% of the sample) account for 67% and 70% respectively of those who believe the establishment of an assembly will bring about improvements in the Welsh economy and the standard of the NHS in Wales. Given that, as we have seen, there was no significant difference in terms of information levels along national identity lines, it seems likely that these clear distinctions in terms of expectations are themselves a reflection of the role of national identity in influencing how the devolution proposals are perceived. All of this tends to support the argument that national identity may have been an important influence on the referendum vote.

Table 4.14
Expectations in Wales and national identity about the:

(a) Health service

	Welsh not British	More Welsh than British	Equally Welsh and British	More British than Welsh	British not Welsh	Other
	%	%	%	%	%	%
A lot better	21	13	9	2	0	9
A little better	32	44	35	42	26	27
No difference	35	37	42	42	68	55
A little worse	6	4	9	9	4	9
A lot worse	1	0	4	5	0	0
N	*108*	*158*	*205*	*59*	*78*	*22*

(b) Economy

	Welsh not British	More Welsh than British	Equally Welsh and British	More British than Welsh	British not Welsh	Other
	%	%	%	%	%	%
A lot better	18	10	4	3	3	9
A little better	35	45	31	31	18	18
No difference	35	34	43	43	51	50
A little worse	6	9	14	16	24	23
A lot worse	2	0	6	7	1	0
N	*108*	*157*	*206*	*58*	*80*	*22*

The mutual implication of partisan alignment and national identity

In theoretical terms, we have demonstrated from the survey data that two explanations of the referendum vote – one based on party cues and the other on national identity – appear to play some role in the attempt to understand the outcome of the referendum. However it is important to note that these are not separate or mutually exclusive explanations. Rather, in the Welsh context at least, patterns of partisan alignment and patterns of national identity are related or mutually implicated.

 Prior to the 1997 Welsh Referendum Survey, the last major study of voters' attitudes in Wales was the 1979 Welsh Election Survey conducted by Denis Balsom and his colleagues (Balsom *et al* 1983; Balsom *et al* 1984; Balsom 1985 - see the Introduction to this volume for further details about this study). Their work posited a significant relationship between partisan alignment and the different senses of national identity that exist in Wales. Specifically, and to attempt to summarise this work, it was argued that:

- Those voters in Wales with a British national identity were more likely to be Conservative supporters than those who saw their national identity as Welsh, who tended to support Labour or Plaid Cymru.
- Among Welsh identifiers the minority exhibiting strong Welsh 'cultural attachment', defined as knowledge of - or positive attitudes towards - the Welsh language, regular exposure to Welsh-based media, and nonconformist religious affiliation, were more likely to be Plaid Cymru supporters than the majority among whom identification with the Labour Party predominated.

The position of Liberal (as the party then was) supporters did not feature in this work. Nonetheless an analysis of recent Welsh electoral trends suggests that Liberal Democrat support is becoming increasingly concentrated in what Balsom termed 'British Wales' (Balsom 1985; Trystan 1999).

Evidence from the 1997 Referendum Survey confirms that these relationships largely hold. Table 4.15 shows that supporters of the four main political parties in Wales have rather distinct profiles in terms of their national identities, as expressed on the Moreno scale. We see that Plaid Cymru support is very much clustered towards the Welsh end of the spectrum; Liberal Democrat and Labour support is fairly evenly spread across identities, with some bias among Labour identifiers towards the Welsh end; and Conservative support is very much concentrated at the British end of the spectrum.

Table 4.15
Party identification and national identity, Wales

		Welsh not British	More Welsh than British	Equally Welsh and British	More British than Welsh	British not Welsh	Other	N
Labour	%	18	24	35	10	10	3	367
Conservative	%	6	19	35	12	22	5	140
Plaid Cymru	%	41	37	21	1	0	0	71
Liberal Democrat	%	8	31	33	13	12	2	48

Note: Respondents without a party identification excluded.

Next we further consider partisan alignment by contrasting Labour identification with Conservative, Plaid Cymru and Liberal Democrat identification. Here we use logistic regression modelling to test the effect on party identification both of national identity and of those factors identified earlier as associated with individuals' sense of national identity: age, language and place of birth.[12]

The models shown in table 4.16 suggest that there are significant differences between Labour and Conservative identifiers and between Labour and Plaid Cymru identifiers, while there are no significant identity-related differences between Labour and Liberal Democrat identifiers.

Table 4.16
Logistic regression model of partisan identification

	Labour Conservative[13]		Labour Plaid Cymru[14]		Labour Liberal Democrat[15]	
	B	**SE**	**B**	**SE**	**B**	**SE**
Place of birth						
(Wales)						
England	-0.59	(0.33)	-0.40	(0.73)	-0.33	(0.55)
Somewhere else	-0.28	(0.60)	5.03	(17.04)	0.89	(1.36)
Welsh speaking						
(Fluent)						
Non-fluent	0.75	(0.47)	2.94 *	(0.59)	-0.11	(0.60)
Non-Welsh						
speaking	0.95 **	(0.38)	3.67 *	(0.41)	0.98	-(0.54)
Age						
(18-34)						
35-54	-0.51	(0.30)	-0.17	(0.43)	-0.46	(0.42)
55+	-0.68 *	(0.30)	0.72	(0.47)	-0.09	(0.45)
National identity[16]						
(Primarily Welsh)						
Equally Welsh and						
British	-0.46	(0.27)	0.44	(0.41)	-0.14	(0.39)
Primarily British	-0.82 *	(0.38)	1.55	(1.14)	-0.35	(0.60)
Constant	1.17 **	(0.41)	-	(0.38)	1.74 *	(0.57)
N	446		387		368	

* significant at 5%; ** significant at 1%

Focusing upon Labour-Conservative identification Labour score highly among non-Welsh speakers, however this may be linked to the widespread collapse of the Labour vote in Welsh-speaking Wales between 1966 and 1997. In 1966 Labour held all the seats in Welsh-speaking Wales; by 1997 all but one, Carmarthen East and Dinefwy, were represented by Plaid Cymru. Thus Welsh speakers who would have traditionally supported the Labour Party have now moved decisively to Plaid Cymru, while the Conservatives have retained a minority level of support among this group.

Those over 55 are more likely to favour the Conservatives, as are respondents describing themselves as primarily British. While there are clearly several patterns of distinction between Labour and Conservative identifiers, the same cannot be said when one compares Labour and Plaid Cymru identifiers.

Here we find that there are no significant differences between Labour and Plaid Cymru supporters in terms of place of birth, age or national identity, but that Welsh speakers are far more likely to support Plaid Cymru,[17] while non-Welsh and non-fluent Welsh are strongly associated with Labour identification. The results are highly significant, despite the relatively small number of Plaid Cymru identifiers in the sample. Thus it is the Welsh language that differentiates strongly between Plaid and Labour supporters, net of national identity.

Clearly the most important finding from these analyses is the highly significant role of language in distinguishing between Plaid Cymru and Labour supporters, who are otherwise indistinguishable (in terms of the characteristics considered). And of course Labour *versus* Plaid support is the crucial issue in post-devolutionary Welsh electoral politics. Between them the parties account for almost two-thirds of voters in Wales, and Plaid is the major threat to Labour. Clearly, as we have seen in the context of the Welsh referendum, there are associations not only between both national identity and referendum vote, and party identification and referendum vote, but also between national identity and party identification. Next, therefore, we try to look more closely at these associations by unpacking the key variables.

Table 4.17[18] confirms that patterns of national identity influenced voting patterns among party identifiers, as well as strength of party attachment (table 4.2). Among identifiers with each of the parties, those with primarily Welsh national identity were more likely to vote 'yes' in the referendum, and in the case of Labour and Plaid Cymru were more likely to turn out, than were those tending towards the British end of the spectrum.

Table 4.17
Party identification, national identity and Welsh referendum vote

		Yes	No	Did not vote	N
Primarily Welsh Labour	%	41	21	38	154
Equally Welsh and British Labour	%	30	25	45	129
Primarily British Labour	%	24	26	50	72
Primarily Welsh Conservatives	%	12	56	32	34
Equally Welsh and British Conservatives	%	11	64	26	47
Primarily British Conservatives	%	2	71	27	48
Primarily Welsh Liberal Democrat	%	26	47	26	19
Equally Welsh and British Liberal Democrats	%	27	53	20	15
Primarily British Liberal Democrafts	%	0	31	69	13
Primarily Welsh Plaid Cymru	%	80	6	15	55
Equally Welsh and British Plaid Cymru	%	47	7	47	15

Conclusion

In order to think further about these relationships we suggest considering the Welsh referendum vote in terms of both direct and indirect effects. Our thesis is that party cues had a direct and significant impact on the vote. Furthermore we would suggest that national identity had both direct effects and indirect effects via partisan cues on referendum vote. Thus our understanding of patterns of referendum choice may be summarised schematically:

Figure 4.1
Understanding the Welsh referendum vote

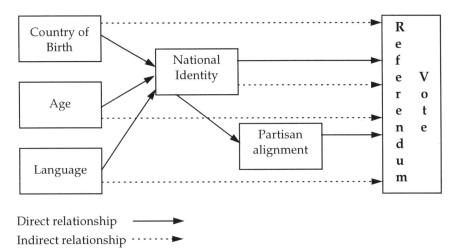

Direct relationship   ⟶
Indirect relationship ┈┈┈▶

Having demonstrated the inter-relationship between aspects of national identity and partisan alignment, we now consider how all of these factors impacted upon referendum vote (see table 4.18). This model clearly demonstrates the direct effects of both partisan alignment and national identity on referendum vote, with party identification having the biggest effects. We have already seen that national identity also plays a role in patterns of party identification, and that in turn national identity is linked to an individual's place of birth and linguistic competence. It should be noted that place of birth, age and language (barely) do not have a significant independent direct effects on vote once national identity is taken into account.

Table 4.18
Logistic regression model of Welsh referendum vote

	Yes/No[19]		Voted/Not voted[20]	
	B	**SE**	**B**	**SE**
Place of birth				
(Wales)				
England	0.61	(0.51)	-0.24	(0.30)
Somewhere ekse	-0.97	(1.66)	-0.91	(0.57)
Welsh speaking				
(Fluent)				
Non-fluent	0.86 *	(0.44)	-0.42	(0.41)
Non-Welsh speaking	0.33	(0.49)	-0.67	(0.34)
Age				
(18-34)				
35-54	-0.10	(0.38)	0.85 **	(0.23)
55+	-0.14	(0.38)	1.27 **	(0.25)
National identity				
(Primarily Welsh)				
Equally Welsh and British	-0.21	(0.30)	-0.42	(0.22)
Primarily British	-1.54 **	(0.57)	-0.48	(0.33)
Partisan alignment				
(Labour)				
Conservative	-2.37 **	(0.40)	0.38	(0.40)
Liberal Democrat	-1.57 **	(0.48)	-0.25	(0.36)
Plaid Cymru	1.24 *	(0.60)	0.17	(0.49)
Constant	0.57	(0.38)	0.68	(0.46)
N	*339*		*545*	

* significant at 5%; ** significant at 1%

However patterns of 'yes'/'no' choice is only one aspect of the referendum vote. We must also consider turnout, and in this case the regression analysis provides a very different picture.

We see that the most significant factor in terms of turnout is age rather than partisan alignment or national identity, with younger people less likely to turn out. Nonetheless there is some evidence to support the notion that national identity and language may each play some role too in differential patterns of turnout.[21]

Given the narrowness of the referendum majority in favour of the establishment of an assembly and the relatively low turnout in the poll, no one involved in the devolution project in Wales can be under any illusions concerning the magnitude of the challenges facing the newly established National Assembly as it attempts to establish broad public legitimacy. However the analysis of the referendum vote allows us to delineate the contours of these challenges more precisely. Specifically attitudes towards devolution appear to reflect patterns of partisan alignment and national identity. As identified by Ron Davies in the Preface to this volume, the challenge will be to generate a sense of legitimacy for the National Assembly which is non-partisan and extends to all of those who live in Wales.

The success or failure of this task seems to largely depend on the ability of those involved in the devolution process to turn the rhetoric of inclusivity that has characterised Welsh politics since the 1997 general election into reality. Our analysis suggests that the whole notion of inclusivity needs to be more broadly cast. The discussion of inclusivity has so far concentrated on voting procedures for the National Assembly elections, and the structures and standing orders within which assembly members should operate. But while all this is undoubtedly important and may well ameliorate some of the partisan-based suspicions about the assembly, it may not be enough to overcome the fact that attitudes towards devolution seem also to be coloured by national identity. Thus the challenge for the National Assembly for Wales will be to both embody and imbue a sense of national identity which can incorporate all those living in Wales. Given the heterogeneous nature of the Welsh population, this must inevitably be a civic identity based on identification with institutions and place, and the values that they represent, rather than ethnic markers such as place of birth and ancestry, as also argued in the chapter in this volume by Lindsay Paterson and Richard Wyn Jones. It may well be that it is the success, or otherwise, of the assembly in fostering such a sense of national identity that will ultimately decide the true significance of those dramatic events in Cardiff in the early hours of 19 September 1997.

Notes

1. Under the headline "What Happens if we Vote NO", a Yes for Wales campaign newsletter predicted that "Wales will get left behind. Decisions will be taken behind closed doors in Whitehall, not by the people we elect in Wales. Scotland will sail ahead in the race for jobs and inward investment. We need an Assembly to stand up for Wales and make a strong case for Wales.". A leaflet published by the Just Say No campaign declared that "September the 18th is Make or Break Day for Wales. A Welsh Assembly will **destroy Britain** and the unity of its people The Assembly represents a grave danger to Wales. **A danger to services, jobs, enterprise and our strong position within the UK**." (Emphasis in the original.)

2. It has been shown that voters take their cue from parties on some issues (see Flickinger 1994, Heath *et al* 1990).

3. The base *N*s in the tables are weighted unless otherwise stated in this chapter.

4. It should be noted that, though the number of Liberal Democrats in our sample is rather small, the differentiation from the null hypothesis for Liberal Democrat 'yes' and 'no' votes is significant at the 0.05 level.

5. Given "the long Welsh experience of a precarious and threatened identity" (Williams 1990: 59), it is perhaps not surprising that identity has been the central preoccupation of much of the writing on Wales. Among the most interesting discussions are Humphreys 1983, Williams 1990, Williams 1991, Smith 1993, and Jones 1998.

6. The chapter by John Curtice in this volume deals in more detail with the correspondence between analyses using each of the two measures of national identity.

7. The 26 respondents who gave other responses to the Moreno question are not included in this and subsequent tables unless otherwise stated.

8. We cannot be sure, however, whether this is a cohort effect or a life-cycle effect. The pattern could also owe something to retirees who have moved in from England and may feel less Welsh.

9. This pattern of differential turnout is confirmed by analysis of the referendum result on a county basis, which shows that those areas with the highest proportions of Welsh speakers, such as Gwynedd, Ceredigion, Carmarthen and Ynys Mon, had significantly higher turnouts than the other county boroughs of Wales.

10. The causal direction may not always be one way - people who feel Welsh may learn to speak Welsh.

11. Model chi-squared 289.45; degrees of freedom 6; -2 log likelihood 538.13.

12. We recognise that these are not the only factors associated with national identity and intend to explore the inter-relationships between class, religion, region and national identity in further work.

13. Model chi-squared 29.144; degrees of freedom 8; -2 log likelihood 491.060.

14. Model chi-squared 154.077; degrees of freedom 8; -2 log likelihood 213.129.

15. Model chi-squared 10.825; degrees of freedom 8; -2 log likelihood 252.826.

16. In the series of logistic regression models that follows we have constructed a summary version of the Moreno question using three categories - primarily Welsh (Welsh not British, and more Welsh than British); equally Welsh and British; and primarily British (more British than Welsh, and British not Welsh).

17. It should be noted that opinion polls conducted since the referendum which ask about voting in the National Assembly elections have shown a significant increase in support for Plaid Cymru among those who do not speak Welsh.

18. For table 4.17 we use three categories of national identity again: primarily Welsh (Welsh, and more Welsh than British); equally Welsh and British; and primarily British (British, and more British than Welsh).

19. Chi-squared 128,945; degrees of freedom 11; -2 log likelihood 349,502.

20. Chi-squared 59,865; degrees of freedom 11; -2 log likelihood 671,814.

21. The cross-tabulation suggests associations between turnout and both language and national identity. In the logistic regression model each of these factors marginally fails to meet the formal statistical significance test, each being significant at 0.06 not at 0.05 on a rather small sample. We would suggest therefore that both national identity and language may each have a role in differentiation in turnout.

References

Balsom D (1985) 'The Three Wales Model', in Osmond J (ed) *The National Question Again*, Llandysul: Gomer.

Balsom D, Madgwick P J and Van Mechelen D (1983) 'The Red and the Green: Patterns of Partisan Choice in Wales', *British Journal of Political Science* **13**: 299-325.

Balsom D, Madgwick P J and Van Mechelen D (1984) 'The Political Consequences of Welsh Identity', *Ethnic and Racial Studies* **7**: 160-81.

Brown A, McCrone D, Paterson L, Surridge P (1999) *The Scottish Electorate: The 1997 General Election and Beyond*, London: Macmillan.

Denver D and Hands G (1997) 'Turnout', *Parliamentary Affairs* **50**: 720-32.

Flickinger R S (1994) 'British Political Parties and Public Attitudes towards the European Community: Leading, Following or Getting Out of the Way?', in Broughton D, Farrell D M, Denver D and Rallings C (eds), *British Elections and Parties Yearbook 1994*, London: Frank Cass: 197-214.

Heath A, Jowell R and Curtice J (1985) *How Britain Votes*, Oxford: Pergamon.

Heath A F, Jowell R, Curtice J and Evans G (1990) 'The Rise of a New Political Agenda?', *European Sociological Review* **6**: 31-49.

Heath A, Jowell R and Curtice J (1994) *Labour's Last Chance? The 1992 Election and Beyond*, Aldershot: Dartmouth.

Humphreys E (1983) *The Taliesin Tradition: A Quest for the Welsh Identity*, London: Black Raven Press.

Jones R M (1998) *Ysbryd y Cwlwm: Delwedd y Genedl yn ein Llenyddiaeth* Caerdydd: Gwasg Prifsygol Cymru.

McCrone D (1992) *Understanding Scotland: The Sociology of a Stateless Nation*, London: Routledge.

Moreno L (1988) 'Scotland and Catalonia: The Path to Home Rule' in McCrone D and Brown A, *The Scottish Government Yearbook 1988*, Edinburgh: Unit for the Study of Government in Scotland.

Smith D (1993) *Aneurin Bevan and the World of South Wales*, Cardiff: University of Wales Press.

Trystan, D (1999) *Wales at the Polls 1900-1999*, Cardiff: Welsh Academic Press.

Williams G A (1991) *When Was Wales?*, London: Penguin.

Williams R (1990) *What I Came to Say*, London: Hutchinson Radius.

Wyn Jones R and Lewis B (1999) 'The Welsh Devolution Referendum', *Politics* **19**: 1, 37-46.

5 Why was 1997 different?

*A comparative analysis of voting behaviour
in the 1979 and 1997 Welsh referendums*

Geoffrey Evans and Dafydd Trystan*

In 1979 as the embers of the Callaghan administration finally dimmed, the Welsh electorate rejected devolution by an overwhelming majority of four to one. In 1997 they said 'yes', albeit by the smallest of margins. In the intervening 18 years the pattern of support for devolution in Wales had been transformed. The aim of this chapter is to understand this transformation and to try to explain why 1997 was so different. We begin by considering the broader political and social context. We then examine and test explanations of changes in patterns of voting behaviour between 1979 and 1997 using the 1979 Welsh Election Survey and the 1997 Welsh Referendum Survey (for information about these see the Introduction and (for the 1997 study) the Technical Appendix).

The lack of continuity between many of the questions asked in the two surveys restricts the inferences that can be made from their comparison. Even the comparisons of the more evidently equivalent measures require acceptance of certain methodological assumptions. Nonetheless, these difficulties are not likely to prove fundamentally problematic - especially when we examine the relationships between different concepts, such as national identity, or orientations towards devolution and independence, rather than just look at the changes in

---

* Geoffrey Evans is Faculty Fellow, Nuffield College Oxford. Dafydd Trystan is Tutor in the Department of International Politics, University of Wales Aberystwyth.

the distribution of answers to questions on such issues. And as we shall see, it is the changing patterns of relationships between referendum vote and the potential influences on it - partisanship, identity, region and class - rather than changing distributions of these characteristics that are of most significance for understanding electoral change in Wales. Yet even these quite far-reaching changes do not themselves quite explain why 'no' turned to 'yes'. The final piece of the puzzle is perhaps the most intriguing. It is also the one that provides most cause for concern with regard to the claims to democratic legitimacy of the new Welsh assembly: our analysis indicates that in 1997 the changing campaign context and its impact on differential turnout between members of the electorate who did and did not want devolution for Wales changed, at the eleventh hour, 'no' to 'yes'.

The changing political context

That the political context changed dramatically between the two referendums is undeniable. The process which led to the 1979 referendum began with the nationalist surges in Scotland and Wales during the mid 1960s (see Trystan 1999), and the subsequent establishment by the then Labour government of the Crowther/Kilbrandon Commission in 1968 to examine sub-state governance in the UK.[1] The Labour manifestos for the general elections of 1974 contained a commitment to legislate for devolution largely in line with the recommendations of the Kilbrandon Commission. But following the election of October 1974 discontent with Labour's position grew, particularly among Welsh Labour backbenchers. By 1975 the strategy of the anti-devolutionists was to call openly for a referendum, arguing that the proposals had "failed to carry the movement" (cited in Jones 1983: 26). After initial opposition, the government capitulated and conceded a referendum - a capitulation which was shortly to be followed by the defeat of the Scotland and Wales Bill on the guillotine on 22 February 1977, by 29 votes (Jones 1983). Following this defeat, separate Bills for Wales and Scotland were introduced in the following parliamentary session, which were then subjected to highly damaging parliamentary scrutiny for almost the whole of the parliamentary session. The opponents of devolution, most prominently Welsh Labour MPs Leo Abse and Neil Kinnock, lost no opportunity in raising doubts and fears regarding the proposed assembly, so by the beginning of the referendum campaign itself the pro-devolutionists were already facing an uphill struggle of immense magnitude.[2]

While the pro-devolutionists were poorly organised and demoralised from the very beginning, following the tortuous passage of the Wales and Scotland Acts through parliament, the 'no' campaigners were organised and effective. There was a specific Labour Party 'no' campaign, ably led by Neil Kinnock and Leo Abse among others, the Labour No Assembly Campaign. This was complemented by the umbrella No Assembly Campaign which raised further doubts about the devolution project in the minds of the electorate (Jones and Wilford 1983). Those Labour MPs and members campaigning against were not disciplined by the Labour Party, and indeed in some instances the government contrived to create even greater problems for the 'yes' campaign.[3] Thus while it must be noted that the government provided official endorsement of the devolution proposals, this endorsement was neither united nor emphatic. It was no surprise therefore when on 1 March 1979 the people of Wales rejected devolution. The scale of the defeat surprised many, but the defeat itself was widely expected.

Compare that to 1997. At the time of both the 1997 devolution referendums the Labour government was still very much enjoying its honeymoon period. Labour supporters (who account for over 50% of the Welsh voters) had waited for 18 years for a Labour government and the sense of excitement regarding the prospects for the new government was palpable. Moreover, the method of holding the referendum avoided many of the dangers of 1979. There was no parliamentary scrutiny of the devolution proposals prior to the referendum and those pro-devolutionists who had reservations regarding the scheme for devolution largely held their fire until after 18 September.[4]

Furthermore, the institutional context of Welsh politics had been transformed between 1979 and 1997, with significant growth in the functions of the Welsh Office, and the widespread development of Welsh quangos (Osmond 1995).[5]

The situation in 1997 also differed in terms of the degree of Labour division. While there continued to be much disquiet among a significant minority of Labour Party activists, the overall endorsement provided was strong (see the chapters by David McCrone and Bethan Lewis, and by Richard Wyn Jones and Dafydd Trystan in this volume). There was no Labour No Assembly Campaign in 1997, and those Labour MPs who declared that they would vote 'no' were marginalised and played no active part in the campaign.[6] The possibly profound importance of this aspect of the campaign will become clear later.

Social change

We might consider also the idea that the social context in Wales changed in ways that influenced the 1997 referendum outcome. The thesis that political changes reflect social development has widespread endorsement and Wales undoubtedly did change in the 18 years between the two devolution referendums. In particular, it is likely that Wales became more middle class and more educated between 1979 and 1997, and independence movements often have their leadership and strongest support among the educated middle classes. If this assumption holds and changes have been marked enough, we might have at least part of an answer to our conundrum. A range of evidence of the changing social context of Welsh politics is given in table 5.1.

Table 5.1
The changing social character of Wales 1979 and 1997[7]

	1979	N	1997	N	1979-97 % change
Objective class					
% middle class	46.9	402	53.6	353	+6.7
% working class	52.7	452	46.4	305	-6.3
Subjective class					
% middle class	24.1	207	19.4	136	-4.7
% working class	67.7	581	65.9	448	-1.8
% no educational qualifications	54.7	469	35.1	241	-19.6
% women in full-time work	35.7	155	48.9	192	+13.2
% women looking after home	46.8	203	20.9	82	-25.9
% regular church attendance	16.8	144	14.6	100	-2.2

Interestingly, the main point to be taken from this table is that in many respects there has not been a great deal of change. Certainly, changes in patterns of self-ascribed social class are not large: of those defining themselves as belonging to one class or another, the vast majorities, near to 75% in both 1979 and 1997, claim to be working class, with a small increase in 1997 in the proportion of respondents ascribing themselves to no class. However we should note that the proportion of respondents with no qualifications fell from 54% of the sample in 1979 to 35% in 1997 - although 35% remains an unusually high proportion without qualifications compared with the rest of the UK. Finally, despite the much-discussed decline of religiosity in Wales, the proportion of regular church attendees remained largely unchanged between 1979 and 1997.

In one respect, however, there has been marked change: the evidence on gender and employment reflects a profound transformation in the Welsh economic structure. From an industrial base largely built upon the male-dominated coal and steel industries, the Welsh economy endured a significant degree of restructuring during the 1980s. The feminisation of the labour force is clear, with a significant growth in the number of women in work and a fall of over 50% in the proportion of women looking after the home. This is related to the growth of light manufacturing industries in Wales, where up to 60% of the labour force is female (*Digest of Welsh Statistics* 1997).

The question is: are these compositional changes in the Welsh electorate in themselves likely to account for the difference in outcomes between the two referendums? The simple answer is no, given that the most relevant changes are of small magnitude.[8] Moreover, as we shall see below, it is clear that the middle class, the educated, and working women are **not** more pro-devolution than are other groups. There appears to be little in the changing social structure of Wales to account for the political change evident in 1997.

An emerging national identity?

But social change is not just about social structure. When examining questions of sovereignty and regional autonomy, notions of regional and ethnic identity loom large. Despite the efforts of many theorists the resurgence of nationalism and claims for autonomy bear no obvious relationship to economic and social development (Gellner 1983). And in Wales if the years between 1979 and 1997 saw an increase in Welsh national identity and this provides a basis for 'yes' voting, then it could help explain why 1997 was different. Over time comparability on the national identity question is not exact unfortunately, as the options offered to respondents were a little different in the two surveys. However, we do have several different ways of addressing the issue of national/regional identity which are directly comparable and which can serve to bolster any conclusions.

(For the wording of the questions asked in Wales, see the chapter by Richard Wyn Jones and Dafydd Trystan.)

Table 5.2
Changing patterns of identity in Wales 1979 and 1997

	1979	N	1997	N	1979-97 % change
% fluent in Welsh	19.7	169	16.5	113	-3.2
% born in Wales	78.8	675	72.4	457	-6.4
National identity	%		%		
Welsh	58.6	479	62.7	429	+4.1
British	33.5	274	25.7	178	-7.8
English	7.9	65	6.0	42	-1.9

Table 5.2 shows an increase in the proportion of the sample affirming a Welsh identity by 1997, though a decrease in the proportion speaking Welsh fluently or born in Wales. But these movements are all rather small in magnitude. Moreover, the changes in the proportions born in Wales and speaking Welsh are in a contrary direction to that which would be expected to account for an increase in pro-devolution voting. These aspects of social change cannot in themselves take us very far in understanding electoral developments in Wales.

The politics of national identity

Alternatively, however, the nature of the devolution question may have changed – the debate over devolution may have been more about national identity in 1997 than it was in 1979. If this was the case, then even if the proportion of the electorate in Wales professing a Welsh identity had not changed greatly, its political impact - in terms of the propensity to cast a 'yes' vote, and to turn out to do so - may well have had somewhat greater effect on the referendum result (see also John Curtice's chapter for a comparison of national identity in Wales and Scotland in 1997).

In table 5.3 we do see some interesting changes. Place of birth was not significant to referendum vote in 1979, when those born in Wales and those born in England were equally hostile to devolution; but it was significant in 1997, with little change among those from England, but significant change among those who were born in Wales, becoming more pro-devolution. This change in the pattern of association with vote did not occur for Welsh speakers and non-Welsh speakers; however, there was change in patterns of turnout. In 1997 Welsh speakers were even more likely to vote than in 1979 - a reflection of the issue's importance and perhaps the perceived chance of victory, while the converse is true for those who do not speak Welsh.

Table 5.3a
National identity and Welsh referendum vote 1979 and 1997

	1979				1997				1979-97
	Yes	No	Did not vote	N	Yes	No	Did not vote	N	Yes/no shift[9]
Welsh	% 21.7	42.0	36.3	479	% 39.3	25.5	35.1	429	+26.6
English	% 10.8	33.8	55.4	274	% 14.6	31.7	53.7	178	+7.3
British	% 9.5	62.8	27.7	65	% 14.9	44.0	41.1	42	+12.2

Table 5.3b
Place of birth and Welsh referendum vote 1979 and 1997

	1979				1997				1979-97
	Yes	No	Did not vote	N	Yes	No	Did not vote	N	Yes/no shift
Wales	% 17.3	47.9	34.8	675	% 35.8	27.2	37.1	457	+30.3
England	% 13.0	51.4	35.6	146	% 18.1	36.8	45.1	145	+12.8

Table 5.3c
Welsh linguistic competence and referendum vote 1979 and 1997

	1979				1997				1979-97
	Yes	No	Did not vote	N	Yes	No	Did not vote	N	Yes/no shift
Fluent Welsh speaker	% 36.1	34.9	29.0	169	% 60.6	16.3	23.1	113	+28.0
Non-Welsh speaker	% 11.2	51.6	37.1	614	% 24.2	33.3	42.5	490	+24.3

Overall, we find only small pro-devolution movements among British and English identifiers between 1979 and 1997, but a significant shift among Welsh identifiers. Furthermore, fewer people define themselves as British in 1997 than was the case in 1979. The same patterns can be observed for place of birth, while Welsh language speakers were relatively more likely to turn out (and in the main vote 'yes') in 1997 than 1979. So both the growing propensity of a Welsh identity and its increased relevance to the devolution issue appear to be of some - if not overwhelming, as the differences observed are not large - importance for explaining the different outcomes in the two referendums.

The Welsh referendums as second-order elections

An alternative view is that electoral change reflects changes effected 'from above', that is by political parties: it is the parties' actions, rather than any social, 'bottom-up', changes, that best explain why electorates change their preferences. One such theory, discussed in the chapter in this volume by Anthony Heath and Bridget Taylor, proposes that voters in 'second-order elections' vote on the basis of the government's general popularity rather than on the specific issues ostensibly under consideration.[10] If voters' reactions to referendums reflect their feelings towards the government of the day, then we would expect the 1997 referendum result to have been strongly influenced by Labour's endorsement of devolution, in conjunction with the party's remarkable popularity at that time.

For this account to hold we need to show in the first instance that: (i) government popularity ratings in 1997 were far higher than in 1979; and (ii) the government provided a clearer endorsement of devolution than in 1979.

That the government's general popularity relative to the opposition was higher in autumn 1997 than at the time of the 1979 referendum is not in dispute; there is a wealth of public opinion poll data on such matters. But most such data refers to Britain as a whole, or at least to England and Wales together, and we should not assume that the Welsh follow the same path as the English. Recent examples of polls of views in Wales on the current Labour government, for example, show a surprisingly low level of satisfaction with the government's record. Given that Labour has achieved over 60% support (for UK general elections) in these polls, an average satisfaction rating of 38% may cause some alarm.[11]

Views in Wales on the popularity of the main parties are illustrated by answers to the following questions.[12]

Table 5.4

Attitudes in Wales towards the parties 1979 and 1997

1979: let us say that you gave each of the parties a mark out of ten, a mark according to how much or how little you like it

1997: choose an expression from this card to say how you feel about the . . . party

Party score	1979 score	1997 rating	1979-97 change
Labour	3.4	3.7	+0.3
Conservative	2.7	2.4	-0.3
Liberal (Democrats)	2.4	3.0	+0.6
Plaid Cymru	1.7	2.9	+1.2
N	*829*	*681*	

Note: the base is the whole sample for each survey.

The party popularity scores asked in 1979 using an 11-point response scale indicate a clear bias towards the Labour Party among the Welsh electorate and against the Conservatives, as would be expected given the relative levels of voting for the two parties. While there are no directly comparable questions in 1997, respondents were asked to rate their feelings towards each party on a 5-point scale (from strongly in favour to strongly against). The answers on these scales indicate there was a significant growth in popularity between 1979 and 1997 for the Labour Party and a contrasting decline in Conservative fortunes. Whereas the Labour advantage in terms of positive ratings in 1979 was quite modest, at just under 15 points, by 1997 it is over 47 points. Table 5.4 also suggests an electorate-wide increase in positive attitudes towards Plaid Cymru.

These data are consistent with a growth in the popularity of Labour between 1979 and 1997. However, we should note also that the proportion of the Welsh sample with a Labour identity, or voting Labour or intending to vote Labour should there be an election tomorrow (asked in 1997), was not very different between the two surveys (54% Labour in 1997, 52% in 1979). Table 5.5 also shows some growth in support for Plaid Cymru.

Table 5.5
General election vote in Wales 1979 and 1997

Vote	1979		1997		1979-97 % change
	%	N	%	N	
Did not vote/not eligible	11.2	96	10.4	71	-0.8
Conservative	27.7	238	17.6	120	-10.1
Labour	45.3	389	51.4	353	+6.1
Liberal (Democrat)	6.6	57	8.5	59	+1.9
Plaid Cymru	5.8	50	9.7	67	+3.9
Other responses	3.2	28	2.3	16	-0.9

Note: Table adapted from Balsom 1983, based on BBC Wales-Abacus Poll 21/22 February 1979.

As we noted above, however, the government's views on Welsh devolution in 1997 were more positive and better prepared than they were in 1979. This difference in the government's endorsement and presentation of the devolution option we would expect to be reflected in the public's perceptions of the parties' positions on, and commitment to, this issue. In table 5.6 below we provide some evidence of how people saw the main parties' positions on devolution at the time of each referendum.

Table 5.6a
Perceptions of parties' support for devolution in Wales in 1979

Party/grouping		Mainly for	Evenly split	Mainly against	Don't know
The government	%	53.6	17.2	14.0	15.1
Labour MPs	%	39.0	34.0	10.0	17.1
Conservative Party	%	6.3	12.1	58.6	23.0
Plaid Cymru	%	79.2	3.7	2.6	14.5
Liberal Party	%	21.0	20.5	16.5	42.1

Note: Table adapted from Balsom 1983, based on BBC Wales-Abacus Poll 21/22 February 1979.

Table 5.6b
Perceived party recommendations on Welsh devolution in 1997

Party/recommendation		Yes	No	Did not recommend	Don't know	N
Labour						
All respondents	%	80.4	2.0	4.6	13.0	*686*
Labour identifiers	%	81.6	0.8	5.2	12.4	*368*
Conservative						
All respondents	%	2.3	71.9	5.3	20.4	*686*
Conservative identifiers	%	2.1	78.7	6.7	12.5	*140*
Plaid Cymru						
All respondents	%	71.6	1.2	2.5	24.7	*686*
Plaid Cymru identifiers	%	92.2	0	1.6	6.2	*71*
Liberal Democrats						
All respondents	%	39.3	4.3	8.7	47.7	*686*
Liberal Democrat identifiers	%	46.2	3.4	26.3	24.1	*49*

The evidence again is not identically comparable, but it is clear enough. In 1997 respondents had a very clear view of where the government stood, while in 1979 there was considerable diversity of opinion on the positions of both the Labour government and Labour MPs on devolution. In 1997 the public perception was overwhelming in its judgement that the Labour Party was recommending a 'yes' vote. In 1979, in contrast, fewer than two in five respondents saw Labour MPs as mainly for the proposals, and even more surprisingly, given that devolution was a government proposal, barely half of respondents thought that the government was mainly in favour.

Party cues and electoral change

The difference in popularity of the government at the time of the two referendums cannot by itself account for the difference in the referendum results. However, the more clear-cut endorsement of devolution in 1997 by the Blair government, *vis-à-vis* the Conservatives in particular, could translate into differences in voting behaviour if voters' preferences are shaped by party cues as argued in the chapter by Richard Wyn Jones and Dafydd Trystan. That voters have at times taken their cue from parties on at least some issues is an established finding in research on the rise of 'new' issues.[13] The undoubted difference in the endorsement of a 'yes' vote by Labour in 1997 compared with 1979 might thus have translated into more 'yes' voting by Labour partisans in 1997 - but not by Conservative partisans. Levels of turnout by Labour supporters might also have increased as the party, with morale running high, mobilised its support more effectively than in 1979.

For this account to hold we would expect to find a far bigger gap between Labour and Conservative supporters in 'yes'/'no' voting in 1997 than in 1979. In particular, Labour supporters should show the biggest increases in 'yes' voting compared to 1979 while Conservatives might even be unchanged. Table 5.7 shows that this is exactly what happened.

Table 5.7
Party identification and Welsh referendum vote 1979 and 1997

	1979				1997				1979-97
	Yes	No	Did not vote	N	Yes	No	Did not vote	N	Yes/no shift
Labour %	16.7	44.0	39.3	448	% 34.4	23.8	41.8	366	+31.6
Conservative %	7.8	66.2	26.0	219	% 7.2	62.3	30.4	138	-0.2
Plaid Cymru %	75.5	6.1	18.4	49	% 70.8	5.6	23.6	72	+0.2
Liberal Democrats %	12.3	61.5	26.2	65	% 18.4	44.9	36.7	49	+12.4

We might also predict changes in patterns of turnout - with Labour's core voters being relatively more inclined to vote in 1997 than in 1979.[14] As we can see in table 5.7, however, this is not the case.

If changes in the effects of partisanship can help explain the difference between 1979 and 1997, we would further expect a change in the social basis of support. We would expect regional propensities to have changed as the Labour voting valleys in the south became disproportionately more supportive in 1997 than in 1979. The same follows for changes in the class basis of 'yes' voting, with a disproportionate growth among the working class.

Table 5.8
Subjective class identification and Welsh referendum vote 1979 and 1997

		1979				1997				1979-97
		Yes	No	Did not vote	*N*	Yes	No	Did not vote	*N*	Yes/no shift
Middle class	%	21.7	53.1	25.1	*207*	% 30.1	42.9	27.1	*133*	*+12.2*
Working class	%	15.7	46.6	37.7	*581*	% 31.6	29.1	39.2	*446*	*+26.8*

As seen from table 5.8 this is evidently the case: the working class clearly became more pro-devolution in its vote between 1979 and 1997. As we can see from table 5.9, so did the relatively working-class, Labour-supporting areas in the south. A strong shift can also be seen in the Plaid stronghold of Gwynedd in the north.

Table 5.9
Region and Welsh referendum vote 1979 and 1997[15]

County		1979*			1997			1979-97
		Yes	No		Yes	No	*N*	Yes/no shift
Clwyd	%	21.6	78.4	%	33.3	66.6	*60*	*+11.7*
Dyfed	%	28.1	71.9	%	57.5	42.5	*40*	*+29.4*
Gwent	%	12.1	87.9	%	32.8	67.2	*61*	*+20.7*
Gwynedd	%	34.4	65.6	%	84.3	15.7	*51*	*+49.9*
Mid Glamorgan	%	20.2	79.8	%	62.7	37.3	*67*	*+42.5*
Powys	%	18.5	81.5	%	35.3	64.7	*17*	*+16.8*
S. Glamorgan	%	13.1	86.9	%	47.5	52.5	*59*	*+36.4*
West Glamorgan	%	18.7	81.3	%	45.3	54.7	*64*	*+26.6*

* 1979 official referendum results.

To sum up, compared with 1979, in 1997 there was a small increase in levels of support for the Labour Party; a considerably greater pro-'yes' increment from being a Labour supporter (but not lower rates of abstention); and changes in patterns of class and regional support which are consistent with a party cue effect. In contrast, Conservative supporters were as opposed to saying 'yes' in 1997 as they were in 1979.[16]

Further considerations: timing and turnout

Explanations that focus on the role of partisan cues and the growing political salience of national identity do appear to go some way to accounting for the changes we have observed. There are, however, further differences in the character of voting in the two referendums which are both intriguing and consequential.

In both years far more 'yes' voters made their minds up how to vote in the last week than did 'no' voters. In 1979 this made little impact on the results, but the 1997 outcome was effectively decided by pro-devolution voters making their minds up in the last week.

Table 5.10a
Welsh referendum vote by time of decision 1979

	Yes	No
	%	%
Only shortly before	30.1	12.3
One to two months before	11.6	12.8
Long time before	54.1	74.4
Other responses	4.1	0.5
N	146	414

Table 5.10b
Welsh referendum vote by time of decision 1997

	Yes	No
	%	%
In week before	38.7	27.8
In month before	13.2	18.5
Between general election and referendum	16.0	22.4
Before general election	32.1	29.8
Other responses	-	1.5
N	210	210

In both years also, far more people who did not vote would have voted 'no' than 'yes' – see table 5.11 - but whereas in 1979 this pattern reflected quite closely the pattern of opinion in the electorate as a whole, in 1997 it did not. Opponents of change were more likely not to vote in 1997 than in 1979. In other words, as can clearly be seen from the right-hand columns of table 5.11, the 1979 result reflected the electorate's views on devolution, but our survey indicates that the 1997 result did not.

Table 5.11
Preferences for Welsh devolution of different groups 1979 and 1997

	All non-voters	Non-voters with prefer-ences	All voters	All who expressed a preference	All voters plus non-voters who "cared a good deal" about the result
	%	%	%	%	
1979					
Yes	17.6	23.3	26.1	26.1	n a
No	58.1	76.7	73.9	74.7	n a
Don't know/ would not say	24.3				
	%	%	%	%	%
1997					
Yes	32.4	36.3	50.2	46.2	49.5
No	41.1	63.7	49.8	53.8	50.5
Don't know/ would not say	35.2				

Moreover, table 5.12 shows that this was not due to a lack of interest in the result of the referendum among non-voting opponents of devolution. So, for example, more non-voters who nonetheless cared a great deal about the result would have voted 'no' rather than 'yes'.[17] Had just these concerned (and informed) opponents of devolution voted at the same rate as those who were pro-devolution, the result would have been reversed: a rare occasion when the strategy of 'free riding' - that is of not voting and letting other people do it for you - was perhaps a big mistake.

Table 5.12
Levels of involvement by Welsh devolution preference in 1997

	Cared a good deal	Interested in politics[18]	Score on scale of knowledge about referendum issues	N
Yes	64.3%	3.05	5.13	272
No	52.4%	3.06	5.23	317

Note: excludes respondents who did not express a preference.

Why was there differential turnout between pro- and anti-devolution voters in 1997?

Table 5.12 shows that similar levels of general political interest and knowledge about the devolution plans, and only small differences in caring about the result, were to be found among pro- and anti-devolution respondents. To measure knowledge about the referendum issues, we use the knowledge 'quiz' discussed by Richard Wyn Jones and Dafydd Trystan in the previous chapter. Table 5.13 presents multivariate statistical models that attempt to account for differences in turnout between these groups by controlling for these and a range of other factors - media consumption, national identity, party identity - that might have affected turnout. The dependent variable is whether respondents voted or not. The technique used is logistic regression, which is the most suitable technique for modelling the prediction of dichotomous choices - that is, voted or did not vote - of this sort. To interpret the models in table 5.13, it need only be remembered that the coefficients are the log-odds of voting rather than not voting and that a positive coefficient indicates an increased likelihood of voting.

  The first model includes only whether respondents had a 'yes' or 'no' preference. It simply tells us what we know already: that electors who favoured devolution were more inclined to turn out and vote. The second model includes political interest, knowledge, and whether respondents cared about the result. The coefficient for a 'yes'/'no' vote drops a little - from 0.59 to 0.47 - so these characteristics do account for a proportion of the differential turnout. The third model shows, however, that this remaining difference in turnout between pro- and anti-devolution respondents does not change even when we take into account a further extensive set of variables. This analysis - and many others not shown - indicates that the coefficient for differential turnout between pro- and anti-devolution respondents cannot be removed by controlling statistically for relevant differences between pro- and anti-devolution respondents. In other words, we cannot explain away differential turnout as a result of political interest, concern, knowledge or a range of other factors that informed commentators or general political science theory might propose to explain it.

Table 5.13
Logistic regressions of turnout in the Welsh referendum in 1997

	Model 1		Model 2		Model 3	
	B	**SE**	**B**	**SE**	**B**	**SE**
Devolution preference						
No	-	-	-	-	-	-
Yes	.59**	(.19)	.47 *	(.21)	.48 *	(.24)
Knowledge of issues			.14	(.07)	.13	(.07)
Cared who won			1.52**	(.23)	1.46**	(.22)
Interest in politics			.21	(.11)	.21	(.11)
Media consumption[19]						
BBC1 Wales					.08	(.31)
BBC1 other					-.21	(.33)
HTV Wales					-.22	(.30)
ITV other					.01	(.34)
National identity						
English					-.51	(.31)
British					.25	(.23)
Welsh					.06	(.26)
Party identification						
Labour					-	-
Conservative					.33	(.29)
Liberal Democrat					.27	(.43)
Plaid Cymru					.60	(.43)
None					.46	(.47)
Constant	.68	.12	-1.33	.39	-1.40	(.51)
Chi-square	9.0	1 df	104.1	4 df	113.7	15 df

* significant at 5%; ** significant at 1%

There is also a further intriguing aspect of the different levels of turnout between 'yes' and 'no' voters which is shown in table 5.14.

Table 5.14
Logistic regression of the decision to turn out among pro- and anti-devolution groups, Wales, 1997

	Pro-devolution		Anti-devolution	
	B	**SE**	**B**	**SE**
Knowledge of issues	.25 *	(.10)	0.37**	(.10)
Care about result	1.32**	(.34)	1.68**	(.29)
Interest in politics	.20	(.18)	.21	(.14)
Constant	-1.30	(.54)	-.89	(.51)
N	272		317	
Chi-square	41.94	3 df**	56.05	3 df**

* significant at 5%; ** significant at 1%

Here we can see that the pro-devolutionists' tendency to turn out is influenced by their knowledge of the devolution issues - the informed tend to vote more than the uninformed. But this does not apply to anti-devolutionists. Among anti-devolutionists, those who did not vote were not significantly less informed than those who did. Non-voting anti-devolutionists were also significantly more informed (average score 4.78) about the issues than pro-devolutionists who did not vote (average score 4.38). The failure of these informed anti-devolution electors to get to the polls to the same extent as the informed pro-devolutionists is hard to understand except in terms of the institutional context of the campaign. As we have already seen that it was not differences in levels of knowledge or interest or concern about the result that explained differential turnout, we are forced back to an account which emphasises the failure to mount a coherent 'no' campaign and to canvass and put forward the 'no' case. The asymmetry in terms of resources and impact between the two campaigns - 'yes' and 'no' - is undeniable, and in our statistical analyses of electors' decisions to turn out and cast their vote we can find no empirical support for an alternative explanation.

Conclusion

The timing of the Welsh referendum of 1997 could not have been better in terms of securing a 'yes' vote. The new Labour government was still enjoying its honeymoon period, little opportunity had existed for left-wing discontent to grow, and the Scots had already a week earlier voted resoundingly for the establishment of a parliament in Edinburgh. Furthermore the speedy pre-legislative referendum ensured that there was little time for the deficiencies of the government's devolution proposals to be examined. The 'no' campaign in Wales was a damp squib. In contrast, the political context of the referendum of 1979 was hostile indeed for the then Labour government. It had lost its majority during 1976 and was reliant on the Liberals and other smaller parties to ensure success for its legislative programme. The referendum took place shortly after the 'winter of discontent' and amidst the resurgence of the Conservative Party under the leadership of Margaret Thatcher. Crucially in the context of devolution the government was also reliant on its own recalcitrant backbenchers. These different political contexts in 1979 and 1997 can be seen to have influenced electors' behaviour; to have changed the pattern of support and opposition to devolution; and in the final instance, to have undermined the turnout among 'no' voters sufficiently for a 'yes' result to have crept in under the wire - despite 'yes' being the minority choice for Wales.

This is not to deny that, although the increase in the proportion of the population of Wales affirming a Welsh identity between 1979 and 1997 was small, Welsh national identity increased in political salience. As we have seen two notable developments have occurred. People with a Welsh national identity have become more pro-devolution. And Plaid Cymru, the nationalist party, has become markedly more acceptable to the mass of the population in Wales. This also can be understood in political terms. As there was no marked social change that might account for why a Welsh identity became more politically salient, this too is likely to be a political creation. Perhaps the Labour government should thank Plaid Cymru for its work in this area, for without the politicisation of Welsh identity, the swing from 1979 to 1997 would not have been enough.

But is it enough? Our evidence suggests that even with the significant changes between 1979 and 1997 the Welsh assembly could be argued to lack legitimacy. Referendums in theory invoke the spirit of direct democracy and seek to ascertain the opinions of the electorate on important political issues. On this basis the Welsh referendum result may be called into question - not only is a 50% turnout a poor basis upon which to make a claim of representativeness, but also because by a small majority, the Welsh electorate actually preferred the pre-devolution constitutional *status quo*. That they failed to make their voice heard representatively in terms of the referendum vote appears to be as much to do with the strength of the pro-'yes' political forces and the failure of the 'no' campaign to play its part in mobilising anti-devolution opinion.

However the question remains as to what extent the Welsh referendum was a genuine call to the people. As others have noted in this volume (see chapters by David McCrone and Bethan Lewis, and Lindsay Paterson and Richard Wyn Jones), the practicalities of the 1997 Welsh referendum had more to do with political expediency and internal Labour Party politics than the invocation of the spirit of direct democracy. That the result failed accurately to reflect public preferences suggests that the recent recommendations of the Neill Commission are indeed addressed to a genuine problem in the conduct of referendums. For Wales, however, the die is already cast. Having said this one cannot and should not underestimate the large scale transformation that has occurred in Welsh views on devolution between 1979 and 1997. Given that this transformation delivered only the most grudging of mandates for the assembly, significant challenges lie ahead in developing the legitimacy of the National Assembly for Wales across all sections of the population.

Notes

1. The Royal Commission on the Constitution was established under the Chairmanship of Lord Crowther in 1968. It sat from 1969 to 1973, reporting in October 1973. Upon Lord Crowther's death in 1972, Lord Kilbrandon was appointed to chair the Commission (Kilbrandon 1973).
2. This was confirmed by a BBC Wales poll a month before the referendum which put support for an assembly at 33%, with 46% intending to vote 'no', and 21% undecided (Balsom 1983: 204).
3. In particular the amendment introducing the threshold of 40% of the registered electorate endorsing the proposal as a condition for enacting the Wales Act was moved technically in parliament by the late John Smith for the government to bring Wales into line with Scotland, an earlier attempt to introduce the amendment having been stymied by a parliamentary filibuster by pro-devolutionists Welsh MPs (James and Lindley 1983).
4. Notably in this instance, the Institute of Welsh Affairs produced a report critical of some aspects of the devolution proposals soon after the vote on 18 September (Institute of Welsh Affairs 1997).

5. Though the process of administrative devolution is clearly an important element of the development of Welsh politics in the late twentieth century, an analysis of this process and its development is beyond the scope of this chapter.

6. There is some debate as to the precise role of Blaenau Gwent Labour MP Llew Smith in the 'no' campaign. He undoubtedly played some role in assisting Carys Pugh and Betty Bowen (two Labour activitists prominent in the Just Say No campaign), though he did not have a high profile during the campaign.

7. All figures for 1979 in this chapter are taken from the 1979 Welsh Election Study, unless otherwise stated. Objective class is as coded from occupation. Subjective is the answer to a series of questions about respondent's own class.

8. We could do a shift-share analysis here, but it is apparent that it would not show any important effects as these changes are rather small compared with the change in the referendum result.

9. In order to calculate 'yes/no' shift 1979-97 non-voters have been excluded, and the percentage of 'yes' and 'no' voters recalculated accordingly. The differences between 1979 and 1997 are reported under 'yes/no' shift in this table and all subsequent tables unless otherwise stated.

10. This explanation has often been used to account for the outcome of European and local government elections (McLean *et al* 1996).

11. Data taken from Beaufort/BBC Opinion Polls conducted in July and November 1998.

12. In the 1979 Welsh Election Survey respondents were asked "let us say that you gave each of the parties a mark out of ten points, a mark according to how much or how little you like it". A score for each party was then calculated, and divided by two in order to facilitate comparability between the 1979 data and the 1997 data. In 1997 respondents were asked to "choose a phrase from this card to say how you feel about the . . . party". The five options ranged from strongly in favour to strongly against. A score for each party was then calculated by using a scale from 1 (strongly against) to 5 (strongly in favour). Though the scales are clearly not exactly comparable, the relative changes in attitudes towards the various parties do offer scope for investigation.

13. Thus attitudes towards Britain's relations with the European Union have been shown to be influenced in this way (Flickinger 1994) as well as those on 'green' and related 'new politics' issues (Heath *et al* 1990).

14. It is difficult to assess whether the Labour Party was more active in mobilising supporters in 1997 than in 1979. Certainly, the proportion of our sample who report being canvassed by a party or other political representative is vanishingly small. Labour was reported as the most

common canvasser in 1997, but only 2.2% of respondents reported a visit from them.

15. The results reported for 1979 in this table are actual county-wide results. For 1997 due to local government reorganisation comparable figures are not available and therefore the figures reported are from the Welsh Referendum Survey 1997. Though one cannot read too much into the 1997 samples based on small numbers in each county, the broad pattern of growth is consistent and therefore general inferences may be drawn.

16. There is an alternative account to the party cue model. This *'rational choice'* model proposes that people switch parties because of party position on devolution. It may be that Welsh voters switched to Labour by 1997 because the party was pro-devolution. To test this we need to examine whether those who switched to Labour between 1992 and 1997 are more pro-devolution than those who remained Conservative. Likewise for 1979, did those who left Labour between 1974 and 1979 have more anti-devolution attitudes? Unfortunately, the data required to test these ideas are simply not available. An examination of switchers in 1997 showed that of those who switched from the Conservatives following the general election, none joined the 'yes' camp, the others being divided two to one between those who did not vote at all and those who voted 'no' - thus suggesting that parties' stances on devolution had little impact on the partisan choice of these respondents. Of those who switched from Labour, almost half did not take part in the referendum vote, and of those who did vote, two-thirds chose to vote 'no'; only one of the nine switchers who placed themselves in the 'no' camp, said at the time of the referendum that they would vote for the Conservatives. The amount of party switching between the general election of 1997 and the time of the referendum is far too small to allow inferences to be drawn with confidence, but it provides no evidence to support the view that switching was prompted by party positions on devolution.

17. Respondents were asked: "Would you say you cared a good deal about the results of the recent referendum in Wales, or that you didn't care very much?".

18. Respondents were asked: "How much do you generally have in what is going on in politics ... a great deal, quite a lot, some, not very much, none at all?"

19. Respondents were asked: "Which if any of these television stations do you watch regularly?"

References

Balsom D (1983) 'Public Opinion and Welsh Devolution' in Foulkes D, Jones J B and Wilford R A (eds) *The Welsh Veto: The Wales Act 1978 and the Referendum*, Cardiff: University of Wales Press: 197-215.

Digest of Welsh Statistics 1997 (1997) Cardiff: The Welsh Office.

Flickinger R S (1994) 'British Political Parties and Public Attitudes towards the European Community: Leading, Following or Getting Out of the Way?', Broughton D, Farrell D M, Denver D and Rallings C (eds*) British Elections and Parties Yearbook 1994*, London: Frank Cass: 197-214.

Foulkes D, Jones J B and Wilford R A (eds) (1983) *The Welsh Veto: The Wales Act 1978 and the Referendum*, Cardiff: University of Wales Press.

Gellner E (1983) *Nations and Nationalism*, Oxford: Blackwell.

Heath A F, Jowell R, Curtice J and Evans G (1990) 'The Rise of a New Political Agenda?', *European Sociological Review* **6:** 31-49.

Institute of Welsh Affairs (1997) *Making the Assembly Work*, Report of the IWA Constitution Working Group, Cardiff: IWA.

James M and Lindley P (1983) 'The Parliamentary Passage of the Wales Act, 1978', in Foulkes D, Jones J B and Wilford R A (eds), *The Welsh Veto: The Wales Act 1978 and the Referendum*, Cardiff: University of Wales Press: 34-61.

Jones J B (1983) 'The Development of the Devolution Debate', in Foulkes D, Jones J B and Wilford R A (eds), *The Welsh Veto: The Wales Act 1978 and the Referendum*, Cardiff: University of Wales Press: 19-33.

Jones J B and Wilford R A (1983) 'The Referendum Campaign: 8 February/March 1979' in Foulkes D, Jones J B and Wilford R A (eds), *The Welsh Veto: The Wales Act 1978 and the Referendum*, Cardiff: University of Wales Press: 118-51.

Lord Kilbrandon (1973) *Royal Commission on the Constitution 1969-73*, London: HMSO.

McLean I, Heath A and Taylor B (1996) 'Were the 1994 Euro- and Local Election in Britain Really Second-Order? Evidence from the British Election Panel Study', in Farrell D, Broughton D, Denver D and Fisher J (eds), *British Elections and Parties Yearbook 1996*, London: Frank Cass.

Osmond J (1995) *Welsh Europeans*, Bridgend: Seren.

Trystan D (1999) *Wales at the Polls 1900-1999*, Cardiff: Welsh Academic Press.

6 Is Scotland a nation and Wales not?

Why the two referendum results were so different

John Curtice[*]

The outcomes of the two devolution referendums held in September 1997 were very different. In Scotland, despite a suspension of campaigning following the death of Diana, Princess of Wales, less than a fortnight before polling day, as many as 60% turned out to vote, just 11 points lower than in the 1997 general election, while nearly three out of four voters voted 'yes'. In Wales in contrast, only half the electorate turned out to vote, and of those only just over half voted 'yes'. Indeed, 'no' votes outnumbered 'yes' votes throughout the count until the very last result from Carmarthenshire was declared. In short, while Scotland voted for her proposed new parliament with enthusiasm, Wales came close to inflicting upon Tony Blair his first serious electoral reverse since becoming Labour's leader.

The chapters by Paula Surridge and David McCrone and by Richard Wyn Jones and Dafydd Trystan have already examined the Scottish and Welsh patterns of voting, while the chapter by Geoffrey Evans and Dafydd Trystan has looked at why the Welsh result was different in 1997 from 1979. In contrast, the aim of this chapter is to examine why the two 1997 results in Scotland and Wales were so different from each other. Why did Wales nearly vote 'no' when Scotland voted overwhelmingly 'yes'? And why did so many more electors stay at home in Wales than in Scotland. In particular, we explore the degree to

---

[*] John Curtice is Professor of Politics at the University of Strathclyde and Deputy Director of CREST.

which we can account for these differences by examining the pattern of national identity in the two countries. Did Scotland vote 'yes' and Wales almost 'no' because Scotland's population has a shared sense of a distinctive national identity which is lacking in Wales? And can such a difference account for the reluctance of people in Wales to vote all?

Our starting point therefore is to ask whether voting for or against devolution in the two countries was primarily an expression of national identity. After all, when it comes to elections it is commonly argued that the way in which people vote is influenced by their membership of social groups (Lipset and Rokkan 1967). Elections are regarded as an occasion for the mobilisation of social cleavages. What we are doing here is to ask how far we can use such an approach to account for referendum outcomes as well.

An alternative view would argue that although social cleavages may provide a long-term anchor to voting behaviour, on examination they cannot account very effectively for overall election outcomes as these can reflect short-term as much as long-term influences. Thus, for example, it has been argued that only about one-third of the decline in support that Labour suffered between 1964 and 1987 can be accounted for by changes in the social composition of the electorate (Heath *et al* 1991). To explain the remainder we have to look at political changes, including the appeals made by the parties, changes in the number of Liberal candidates, and changes in the franchise. In short, in order to understand the outcome of elections we have to look at the political context within which voters cast their vote.

The Scottish and Welsh referendums provide us with an unusually good opportunity to examine the validity of these two perspectives. For in many respects the two referendums provide us with a natural experiment. While the details of the two devolution schemes were different (see the Introduction to this volume), the two countries were being asked to vote for much the same principle. And they were invited to do so within a week of each other. As a result some of the factors that are sometimes thought to influence the outcome of referendums, such as the popularity of the incumbent government, (Franklin *et al* 1994, 1995; Gallagher 1996) or the state of the economy, were identical for the two referendums. Indeed, in general, any UK-wide influences on voting behaviour were the same for the two referendums, so whatever explains the difference between the two outcomes must be something that distinguishes Scotland from Wales.

Meanwhile, as is evident from the chapters by Paula Surridge and David McCrone, and by Lindsay Paterson and Richard Wyn Jones, there were differences in the politics of devolution in the two countries. In Scotland, the government's proposals were the result of extensive deliberation over nearly a ten-year period in the Scottish Constitutional Convention, a body which contained not only representatives from a wide range of organisations in Scotland but also members of both the Labour Party and the Liberal Democrats. It thus reflected a process of widespread consultation, at least among some of the elites of Scottish society. In Wales in contrast the government's proposals had been both originated largely within the confines of the Labour Party and formulated more recently, with significant amendments made as little as twelve months before Labour came to power. Maybe the reason why Wales was less enthusiastic about devolution was because it had been less extensively discussed and argued for in the Welsh context.

The 1997 Scottish and Welsh Referendum Studies are well placed to exploit the opportunity afforded to us (for details of the Referendum Studies see the Introduction and Technical Appendix). For the most part, respondents in the two countries were asked either the same question or functionally equivalent ones. We can thus undertake a systematic comparison of the attitudes and identities that electors in the two countries brought to the voting decision and thereby aim to identify why they behaved so differently. On occasion, we can also compare our answers with those given by respondents in England to the 1997 British Election Study, just months before the referendums, enabling us to examine whether Scotland and Wales vary in the extent to which they are different from England. (For details of the 1997 British Election Study, see the Introduction to this volume.)

The surveys also have a second important quality; they mirror the difference in the actual outcome in the two countries. In Wales, 50.2% of those who said they voted said that they voted 'yes', virtually identical to the 50.3% who actually did so. In Scotland, the proportion saying they voted 'yes' was at 77%, just three points higher than the actual result. True, a much higher proportion of survey respondents claimed to have voted than the proportion of the electorate that was officially recorded as having voted. But this is a common finding in survey research that reflects inadequacies in the official figures as much as it does the limitations of surveys (Swaddle and Heath 1989). Encouragingly for our purposes, the difference in the claimed level of turnout in the two surveys, 11 points, almost exactly matches the difference of 10 points between Scotland and Wales in the official statistics.

Explaining the difference

In Scotland, people were asked to vote on two questions. The first was whether they wanted a Scottish parliament at all, the second whether they wanted that body to have 'tax-varying' powers, that is the ability to raise or lower the standard rate of income tax by up to three pence in the pound. In Wales, where it was not proposed that the assembly should have such tax-varying powers, voters were simply asked whether they wanted the assembly to be established. (The precise wording of the referendum questions is given in the Introduction to this volume.) Throughout this chapter we compare voting behaviour on the first question in the Scottish referendum, that is for the principle of a parliament, with voting behaviour in respect of the one and only question asked in Wales.

If we start from the presumption that voters' attitudes towards the principle of devolution reflected their sense of national identity, we can identify three classes of possible reason as to why support was much more lukewarm in Wales than it was in Scotland. The first and simplest is that people living in Wales are less likely to share a common sense of national identity which, among other things, also makes them feel different from people living in the rest of the United Kingdom. There is, after all, good reason why we might think this should be so. Wales, in contrast to Scotland, is a country divided both by language and by national origin. According to the 1991 Census, nearly one in five people in Wales speak Welsh, providing much of the foundation of electoral support for Plaid Cymru, as shown in the chapter by Richard Wyn Jones and Dafydd Trystan in this volume. In contrast in Scotland, Gaelic is spoken by only just over 1% of the population. Meanwhile nearly a quarter of people living in Wales were born outside the principality, whereas this is true of only just over one in ten people living in Scotland (ONS 1996; GRO(S) 1996). And the more we find ourselves able to rely upon differences in the distribution of national identity in the two countries in order to account for the difference in the referendum outcomes, the more we can claim that it was underlying cleavages rather than politics that mattered.

Our other two possible explanations in contrast admit of the possibility that the political context in which voters cast their vote was important to the outcomes. The first of these is that the two countries might have differed in the degree to which national identity was associated with voting 'yes' or 'no'. Perhaps, for example, people in Wales are just as likely to feel Welsh as people in Scotland are to feel Scottish, but that in Wales, feeling Welsh or otherwise was less likely to be translated into support for or opposition to devolution. If so, this would suggest that there was a difference in the degree to which the campaigns for and against devolution in the two countries tapped into or politicised feelings of national identity.

Our second possibility is that perhaps national identity was associated with referendum vote just as much in Wales as it was in Scotland, but that for any given identity voters in Wales were simply less likely to vote 'yes'. Thus for example, feeling Welsh rather than British might have made just as much difference to the probability that any individual voter in Wales voted 'yes' as feeling Scottish rather than British made a difference to the behaviour of voters in Scotland. But at the same time, those in Wales who felt Welsh might have been less likely to vote 'yes' than were those in Scotland who felt Scottish, while at the same time those in Wales who felt British were also less likely to vote 'yes' than were their counterparts in Scotland. Such a pattern would suggest that factors other than national identity itself also played an important role in the two outcomes. Perhaps, for example, voters in the two countries differed in their views about the merits or de-merits of existing constitutional arrangements independently of their national identity, and voted accordingly. Or they may have differed in their perceptions of the consequences of devolution. To find either pattern would suggest that the politics of devolution in the two countries mattered to the outcomes.

Although in many respects the surveys are ideal for our purpose, we should also recognise their limitations. It is difficult with any survey which interviews its respondents just once to distinguish between the motivations that voters bring to the ballot box and the impact of the strategies pursued by politicians to woo them. Many of the indicators available in a survey will reflect the combination and interaction of both influences. Thus, for example, voters who say that the Welsh assembly would give them more say in how they are governed may well have been reflecting the arguments used by 'yes' campaigners that this indeed would be one of the consequences of devolution. But it could also be the case that any respondent who feels Welsh rather than British would be inclined towards a belief that any Welsh rather than UK-wide body would be more likely to give them more say, irrespective of what 'yes' campaigners may have said. And at the same time we have to be aware that in agreeing that the assembly would give them more say, 'yes' voters may well simply be rationalising a decision that they arrived at for completely different reasons.

Even so, we can still make considerable progress. For the more that we can account for the difference in the referendum outcome in the two countries simply with reference to measures of national identity, the more clearly we shall be able to argue that a cleavage based account is a sufficient explanation. The more that we have to refer to arguments about devolution or the Union, the less plausible this position will be. To begin our examination we need to investigate our key variable, national identity.

National identity in Scotland and Wales

The United Kingdom is a multi-national state. As a result it is a polity of overlapping identities (Heath and Kellas 1998). On the one hand there is a sense of British identity which all can share, and associated with which is a set of affective symbols which are to be found in all corners of the kingdom, such as the union flag or the national anthem. At the same time there is a sense of being English, Scottish, Welsh, Ulster or Irish, each an identity with its own set of symbols and culture. The unity of the UK has long appeared to rest on whether people feel British as well as English, Scottish, Welsh, Ulster or Irish. When, as in nineteenth-century Ireland, those who profess adherence to the 'local' identity, in this case Irish, do so to the exclusion of any sense of Britishness (or indeed feel antipathy towards Britishness) then the UK appears under threat (Gellner 1983).

The importance of 'dual' identities in the United Kingdom has been recognised in survey research through the use of the so-called Moreno question, as previously discussed in the chapters by Paula Surridge and David McCrone and by Richard Wyn Jones and Dafydd Trystan (Moreno 1988). Table 6.1 shows the distribution of national identity measured in this way in the Referendum Surveys in Scotland and Wales, together with the results obtained in England in the 1997 British Election Survey.

Two points clearly stand out. The first is that while over four in ten people in Wales feel Welsh more than British (if indeed they feel British at all) only a quarter of those living in England regard themselves as English more than British. Welshness is more likely to be regarded as something that is distinct from Britishness than is the case with Englishness. Note indeed that almost half of those living in England regard themselves as equally English and British, for many of whom doubtless the two terms are synonymous.

But while some people in Wales appear to have a sense of Welshness that they feel is distinct from Britishness, a far larger proportion of people in Scotland consider their British identity, if any, to be secondary to their Scottish identity. No less than two-thirds of people living in Scotland said that they are wholly or predominantly Scottish

(66% compared with 43% Welsh in Wales). In short, our expectation that people living in Scotland would be more likely to have a distinct sense of identity than people in Wales is confirmed. Have we then stumbled across a simple explanation for the difference in the outcomes in the two countries?

Table 6.1
Scottish, Welsh and English national identity

	Scotland	Wales	England
	%	%	%
Scottish/Welsh/English, not British	33	17	8
More Scottish/Welsh/English than British	33	26	18
Equally Scottish/Welsh/English and British	29	34	49
More British than Scottish/Welsh/English	3	10	15
British, not Scottish/Welsh/English	3	12	10
N	*653*	*659*	*2383*

Source: For England, the 1997 British Election Study.

Not quite. Consider what outcome we might have expected in the two countries if referendum votes had simply been an expression of national identity. In that event, we might anticipate that all those who felt wholly or predominantly Scottish or Welsh would have voted in favour of devolution while those who felt wholly or predominantly British would vote against. Meanwhile we might anticipate that those who felt equally Scottish/Welsh and British would divide evenly between 'yes' and 'no'. On these assumptions we would expect 79% of those living in Scotland to vote yes, only two points more than actually claimed in our survey to have done so. But even though the expected 'yes' vote in Wales is much lower, 61%, it is still 11 points above what actually happened.

On this evidence, then, it would seem that we can conclude that differences in the distribution of national identity in the two countries are not sufficient to explain the difference in the referendum result in the two countries (even if everyone had voted in line with their national identity). The gap in referendum outcomes appears to be almost twice what we might have expected. But of course it might be questioned whether our measure of national identity is adequate. Perhaps if we were to use an alternative indicator we would be better able to capture the difference in national identity in the two countries.

As well as the Moreno question, respondents were asked to choose from a list (British, English, European, Irish, Northern Irish, Scottish or Welsh) which best describes the way they think of themselves. Respondents who chose more than one were then asked which **best** describes how they think of themselves (see the chapter by Richard Wyn Jones and Dafydd Trystan for the precise wording of the questions). This provides another indicator of national identity.

Table 6.2
Alternative measure of Scottish, Welsh and English national identity

	Scotland	Wales	England
	%	%	%
Scottish/Welsh/English only	45	27	18
Sccotish/Welsh/English more than British	40	36	16
British more than Scottish/Welsh/English	14	32	20
British only	1	3	40
Neither British nor Scottish/Welsh/English	1	3	6
N	670	684	2549

Note: In Scotland and Wales, British also includes a small number of persons who described themselves as English.
Source: For England, the 1997 British Election Study.

A summary of the results obtained in response to these questions is given in table 6.2. We identify five different groups. First are those who in Scotland said that they were Scottish, or in Wales said they were Welsh, and who did not say that they were either British or English. Next are two groups who described themselves both as Scottish/Welsh and also as British/English. We distinguish them according to which they said **best** describes themselves. Meanwhile our final two groups are those who describe themselves as British or English, but not as Scottish/Welsh, and those who did not consider any of these labels were appropriate for themselves. The table contains equivalent information for people living in England, from the 1997 British Election Study.

This measure confirms that people living in Scotland are more likely to feel Scottish than people living in Wales are likely to feel Welsh. No less than 45% of people in Scotland feel exclusively Scottish compared with 27% Welsh in Wales. But once again, the difference in the distribution of national identity does not clearly translate into the difference in referendum outcomes. If we assume that all those who were exclusively Scottish/Welsh voted 'yes', together with a half of those in the two groups who felt both British and Scottish/Welsh, we would acquire a 72% 'yes' vote in Scotland, and a 61% vote in Wales. Although in the remainder of this chapter we use the Moreno question, we have checked all of the results reported using this alternative measure. Not only did it prove to be highly correlated with the Moreno measure, but also unless otherwise noted our substantive findings were clearly confirmed.

The surveys also contain a series of questions which tap how much pride people have in various cultural symbols commonly associated with Scottishness or Welshness respectively. National pride is, of course, not the same thing as national identity, but we might anticipate that those who regard themselves as Scottish or Welsh would be more likely to have a positive affective orientation towards the symbols of their culture. In Scotland we asked about six such symbols, and in Wales seven. In each case factor analysis suggested that, with the exception of pride in the landscape, all of these symbols form part of a single underlying dimension, and that this dimension is closely correlated with a further item that simply asked people whether they felt proud of being Scottish or Welsh.

Table 6.3
Sources of national pride in Scotland and Wales

% very proud of:	Scotland	Wales
The Scottish/Welsh landscape	84	72
William Wallace/the Welsh rugby team	40	49
Scottish music/Male voice choirs	40	46
Scottish/Welsh community spirit	40	45
Tartan/the Eisteddfod	39	35
The Gaelic/Welsh language	11	32
The Welsh chapels	n a	22
Mean pride scale score	3.9	3.9
Minimum N	675	684

Note: Where more than one item is included in a row, the first mentioned item is that administered in Scotland, the second the one in Wales.
Mean pride scale score: the average level of pride across all items except the landscape, where a 5 = very proud and 1 = not at all proud; n a = not asked.

What we find is that pride in the affective and cultural symbols often associated with Welshness is just as widespread among those living in

Wales as is pride in the equivalent symbols among those living in Scotland. The Welsh are much more likely to be proud of the Welsh language than Scots are of Gaelic, and are also somewhat more proud of Welsh male voice choirs or the Welsh rugby team than Scots are of Scottish music or William Wallace. Indeed, only when it comes to their national landscape do Scots clearly have a higher level of pride than those living in Wales do. In short, looking at measures of national pride rather than national identity only makes it even more remarkable that the two countries should have voted so differently.

Of course, what the Moreno scale taps, in contrast to our indicators of national pride, are respondents' attitudes towards Britishness. And a further measure suggests that this is indeed something which does distinguish the two countries. In Scotland, just 37% said they feel very proud of being British, whereas no less than 63% said the same in Wales. Moreover, factor analysis suggests that feeling pride in being British is not particularly correlated with feeling pride in being Scots or Welsh or with pride in the symbols of Scottishness or Welshness. An adequate measure of national identity in Scotland and Wales needs, as the Moreno question does, to tap into feelings of Britishness as well as those of Scottishness/Welshness.

National identity and referendum voting

Having examined the distribution of national identity in the two countries, we still need to consider how far voting behaviour in the referendums was associated with national identity. Are we correct to anticipate that those who felt Scottish/Welsh and not British were most likely to vote in favour of devolution while those who felt British and not Scottish or Welsh were least likely to do so? And does any association hold equally well in both countries? In table 6.4 we show for each country how referendum voting behaviour varied according to national identity. For each response to the Moreno question it shows the proportion reporting having voted 'yes', 'no', or not having voted at all.

Our basic premise is indeed fulfilled. In each country, those who felt exclusively or primarily Scottish/Welsh were more likely to vote in favour of devolution and less likely to vote against than those who felt exclusively or primarily British. Feelings of national identity evidently did make a considerable difference to the way in which people voted.[1]

But there also appear to be two important differences between the countries. First, those who feel primarily or exclusively Welsh were less likely to support devolution than were those who felt primarily or exclusively Scottish. Equally, those who feel exclusively or primarily British were less likely to support the creation of an assembly in Wales than they were a parliament in Scotland. In other words, for any given combination of feeling Welsh and British, support for devolution in Wales was lower than among those with the equivalent combination of feeling Scottish and British in Scotland.

Table 6.4
Scottish and Welsh national identity and referendum vote

(a) Scotland

		Yes	No	Did not vote	N
Scottish/not British	%	67	6	27	211
More Scottish than British	%	60	11	29	211
Equally Scottish and British	%	44	33	23	188
More British than Scottish	%	41	34	26	23
British/not Scottish	%	25	49	27	21

(b) Wales

		Yes	No	Did not vote	N
Welsh/not British	%	43	23	34	106
More Welsh than British	%	44	25	32	166
Equally Welsh and British	%	26	34	41	227
More British than Welsh	%	16	37	47	70
British/not Welsh	%	13	45	42	84

Second, the two countries differ also in the pattern of association between turnout and national identity. In Scotland there is no sign of an association, with close to a quarter not voting in each and every category of national identity. In contrast, in Wales there is a clear association, with those feeling exclusively or primarily British being less likely to turn out than those who feel exclusively or primarily Welsh, as also discussed in the chapter by Geoffrey Evans and Dafydd Trystan. In other words national identity appears to have made a difference to the turnout in Wales, whereas it did not do so in Scotland.

Both patterns mean but one thing for our analysis. They confirm the suspicion we had already formed that the difference in the outcome in the two countries, whether it be in the proportion voting in favour or in the proportion deciding to vote at all, cannot simply be accounted for by the differences between them in the distribution of national identities. Rather, the pattern of association between national identity and voting behaviour differed in important respects in the two cases. We need to try and tease out why this was so.

One other pattern might also be thought to be present. It would appear that national identity seems to have been more strongly associated with the decision to vote in favour or against devolution in Scotland than in it was in Wales. For example, there is a 43-point difference between the exclusively Scottish and the exclusively British in the proportion voting 'no' in Scotland, whereas the equivalent gap in Wales is only 22 points. Indeed, more complex statistical analysis confirms the existence of a statistically significant interaction effect in this table. However, this is one occasion when a finding using the Moreno question is not confirmed by the alternative measure of national identity, and thus we cannot rule out the possibility that it may simply be an artefact of measurement.[2]

Non-voting

Of the two main patterns in table 6.4, we begin by exploring why the association between turnout and national identity was different in the two countries. The fact that in Wales those who felt British were less likely to turn out than were those who felt Welsh clearly raises some important questions. Were the opponents of devolution less likely to vote in the Welsh referendum than its advocates? And given the narrowness of the outcome, does that mean that the majority of people in Wales did not in fact support the government's proposals for devolution, as argued in the chapter by Geoffrey Evans and Dafydd Trystan?

There seems indeed to be little doubt that in both cases the answer is in the affirmative. This conclusion is supported by evidence from both the surveys and the election results themselves. In the surveys those who said they did not vote were asked how they were likely to have voted if they had gone to the polling station. Some were adamant they would have cast a blank ballot while others said they were not sure. But three-quarters of non-voters in Scotland and two-thirds in Wales felt able to give an answer. And, as table 6.5 shows, the answers they gave were very different in the two countries.

In Scotland non-voters indicated that they favoured devolution by a ratio of just over three to one, very similar to the distribution of opinion among those who did vote. There seems to be little doubt that the outcome of the Scottish referendum was a faithful reflection of the 'settled will' of the Scottish people. But in Wales the picture is very different. Far from reflecting the even division of opinion among those who went to the polling station, a clear majority of those who did not turn out but who expressed a view on devolution indicated their opposition to the government's proposals.

Table 6.5
The referendum preferences of non-voters in Scotland and Wales

	Scotland	Wales
	%	%
Yes	64	24
No	20	41
Don't know	10	20
Would not vote	6	15
N	*172*	*263*

Such a finding should not be surprising given the election results themselves. The result of the referendum was declared separately for each of the 22 local authority districts in Wales. Of these districts, 11 had a majority of 'no' voters. In these districts turnout was no less than 27 points lower than it was in the general election less than five months earlier. In contrast in the other districts of Wales where 'yes' voters were in a majority, turnout was only 20 points lower than in the general election. In short, those parts of Wales with a higher 'no' vote also saw more electors stay at home.

Far from signifying the 'settled will' of the electorate in Wales, the outcome of the devolution referendum depended on the reluctance of those opposed to devolution to turn out. If we combine the reported vote of those respondents who said they voted with the reported preference of those who said they did not vote then (leaving aside those non-voters who did not reveal any preference), we find that in Scotland 77% were in favour of devolution, exactly the same figure that we obtain from looking only at those who voted. But in Wales this calculation produces a figure of just 46%. In other words, if turnout had been higher in Wales it is likely that the government's proposals would have been defeated quite comfortably.

So it seems then that one reason at least why turnout was lower in Wales than in Scotland is that the referendum failed to engage that part of the electorate in Wales who felt strong ties to Britain, perhaps because they felt it was largely irrelevant to their concerns. In Scotland in contrast all parts of the electorate appear to have been equally engaged.

The referendum certainly appeared less important to the people of Wales than it did to those of Scotland, as demonstrated by the analysis of 'second-order' elections in the chapter by Anthony Heath and Bridget Taylor. Thus, for example, in Scotland, no less than 65% felt that the result of the referendum would make a great deal or quite a lot of difference to their country, whereas in Wales only 35% took that view. Similarly 72% of respondents in Scotland said that they cared a good deal about the outcome of the referendum, compared with 51% in Wales.[3] Moreover, such feelings were clearly related to propensity to vote. For example, in Scotland just 15% of those who said that the outcome would make a great deal of difference reported not voting compared with 37% of those who felt it would make not very much difference or none at all. In Wales the equivalent figures were 9% and 48%.

Moreover, those in Wales who felt primarily or exclusively British were particularly likely to think that the outcome of the referendum would not make much difference. We see this in table 6.6, which shows the relationship between national identity and how much difference respondents thought the referendum result would make. In constructing this table we have treated the latter as an interval-level measure in which those who thought the referendum would make a great deal of difference are given a score of 5, those who thought quite a lot of difference a score of 4, and so on, with those thinking it would make no difference at all being scored 1 and those who did not know, 0.[4] We label this measure the 'mean impact score'.

There are clear differences in the table between Scotland and Wales. In Wales the more British someone felt, the less likely it was that they thought that the outcome of the referendum would make much of a difference. In Scotland there is no such pattern. Here we have a clear indication that the referendum campaign failed to engage the more British half of Wales' population in particular. But we should also note that even those who feel primarily or exclusively Welsh were less likely than their counterparts in Scotland to feel that the outcome of the referendum would make a difference. So, the Welsh electorate in general were less engaged in their referendum, and not only those who feel a tie to Britain.

Both findings have one clear implication. The difference in the level of turnout in the two countries was not just a consequence of differences in their distribution of national identity. As noted by Ron Davies in the Preface to this volume, the referendum failed to spark the interest of the people of Wales in the same way that it did in

Scotland. Evidently, the politics of the way in which the proposals were presented and debated in the two countries made a difference.

Table 6.6
Scottish and Welsh national identity and
perceived impact of the referendum

	Mean impact score			
	Scotland		Wales	
		N		N
Scottish/Welsh, not British	3.6	213	2.9	106
More Scottish/Welsh than British	3.6	216	2.7	169
Equally Scottish/Welsh and British	3.6	190	2.5	228
More British than Scottish/Welsh or British, not Scottish/Welsh	3.6	44	2.4	156

Voting Yes or No?

Now we turn to the other pattern that we found in table 6.4, that irrespective of their national identity people in Wales were less likely to vote in favour of devolution than were people in Scotland. It will be helpful here if we develop a simple statistical model of referendum voting behaviour in Scotland and Wales combined. The dependent variable in this model is whether or not the respondent voted 'yes' rather than 'no' in the referendum. As this is a dichotomous dependent variable we use logistic regression. We then include two simple independent variables. The first is the respondent's national identity as measured by the Moreno question, but where thanks to their paucity in Scotland, we combine (as in table 6.6) those who feel primarily British with those who feel exclusively British. In each case the model tells us the impact on the probability of a person voting 'yes' rather than 'no' of being in each of the other three Moreno categories compared with this combined category.[5] The second variable is whether or not the respondent lives in Wales; respondents who live in Wales have a value of 1 on this variable while those living in Scotland have a value of 0. This variable therefore measures the degree to which the proportion of the vote cast in favour of devolution in Wales was lower than it was in Scotland for any given position on the Moreno national identity question.[6]

Table 6.7
Logistic model of Scottish and Welsh national identity and referendum vote

	Voted Yes *versus* voted No	
	B	SE
National identity		
Scottish/Welsh, not British	2.27	(.29)*
More Scottish/Welsh than British	1.80	(.27)*
Equally Scottish/Welsh and British	.71	(.26)*
Wales	-.98	(.16)*
Constant	.50	(.09)
N	*886*	

* significant at 5%

Note: The parameter coefficients for national identity are simple contrast coefficients that measure the impact on vote of being in that category rather than feeling primarily or exclusively British.

This model is simply a more formal way of examining some of the evidence presented in table 6.4, and confirms the conclusions reached there. Thus we find that the more someone felt Scottish or Welsh rather than British, the more likely it was that they voted in favour of rather than against devolution. At the same time we see that those living in Wales rather than Scotland were less likely to support devolution even after taking into account their national identity. National identity is not then a sufficient explanation of the difference in the outcome in the two countries.

What might be the explanation? We proceed by examining a variety of possible explanations in turn in order to see whether they help to reduce the size of the 'Wales' coefficient in the model. If they do, we can claim to have identified what it is that produced such a different result in Wales from Scotland. We start by looking at explanations based on features (apart from national identity) of the sociology and social psychology of the two countries, that is explanations that might still be compatible with a social cleavage approach to explaining the difference in devolution outcomes. The most obvious such feature must be the language division in Wales.

Table 6.8 enables us to examine the possible impact of the language divide in Wales on support for devolution. It shows the proportion of those who turned out in Wales who supported devolution, broken down not only by national identity but also by language. As we noted earlier, Gaelic-speaking is not widespread in Scotland and indeed was not asked about in the survey, so for Scotland we simply show the proportion voting 'yes' by national identity alone.

Table 6.8
Scottish and Welsh national identity, Welsh speaking and referendum vote

% of voters voting 'Yes'	Scotland		Wales			
			Welsh-speaking		Non-Welsh speaking	
		N		N		N
Scottish/Welsh, not British	92	160	73	35	55	30
More Scottish/Welsh than British	84	151	76	52	53	64
Equally Scottish/Welsh and British	57	151	56	33	38	101
More British than Scottish/Welsh or British, not Scottish/Welsh	45	33	25	9	26	77

Note: Those classified as 'Welsh-speaking' are all those who said they could speak Welsh, irrespective of fluency. Non-voters are excluded from the base.

As shown in the chapter by Richard Wyn Jones and Dafydd Trystan, whether or not someone is a Welsh speaker clearly did make a difference to the probability that they voted 'yes', at least among the majority of Welsh speakers who do not feel predominantly or exclusively British. Thus, for example, among those Welsh-speaking voters who feel exclusively Welsh, nearly three-quarters voted in favour of devolution, compared with just over half of those who feel Welsh but do not speak Welsh. Even so, it is also clear that this is not a sufficient explanation of the difference in the level of support for devolution in the two countries. For even among Welsh speakers, support for devolution was lower for any given position on the Moreno scale than it was among the equivalent category of voters in Scotland. Thus unsurprisingly we find that if we were to add a 'Welsh-speakers' term to the model we would simply increase the size of the Wales coefficient rather than reduce it.

Another feature that we might wish to consider is party identification (Butler and Stokes 1974). One possible explanation of the way that people vote in referendums is that they simply follow the advice of the party with which they feel an emotional affinity (Svensson 1984; Tonsgaard 1992), especially if that party is thought to be united in support of a particular position. All of the parties made their positions clear on the devolution proposals in the two countries, with in each case the nationalists, Labour and the Liberal Democrats calling for a vote in favour while the Conservatives were against.[7] So perhaps more people voted 'no' in Wales simply because more people there identify with the Conservatives?

In fact there is little difference in the level of Conservative identification in the two countries. In both around one-fifth say that generally speaking they consider themselves to be Conservatives: 21% in Scotland and 17% in Wales. More noticeable is a difference in the distribution of Labour and nationalist identification. Just 11% identify with Plaid Cymru whereas 20% consider themselves to be a Scottish Nationalist. And while 55% are Labour identifiers in Wales, the equivalent figure in Scotland is 50%. But of course this latter difference should matter only if the nationalist parties were significantly more likely to persuade people to vote 'yes' than were Labour.

Table 6.9
Scottish and Welsh party identification and referendum vote

% of voters voting 'Yes'	Scotland		Wales	
		N		*N*
Conservative	20	*90*	10	*99*
Labour	91	*246*	59	*213*
Liberal Democrat	58	*40*	30	*31*
SNP/Plaid Cymru	99	*96*	92	*47*

In practice, as table 6.9 shows, we find that identifiers with all three pro-devolution parties were less likely to vote 'yes' in Wales than they were in Scotland. At the same time, Conservative identifiers were more united in their opposition in Wales than in Scotland. The contrast between the two countries is greatest for the two non-nationalist devolution parties, that is Labour and the Liberal Democrats.[8] According to the surveys, fewer than two in three Welsh Labour identifiers who voted supported the government's plans while fewer than one in three Liberal Democrats did so. As a result, the difference between Labour and Plaid Cymru supporters in their level of support for devolution was far greater than the difference between Labour and SNP supporters.[9]

Interesting though these patterns may be, adding party identification to the model would do little to explain why the outcome in Wales was different from that in Scotland. For while doing so confirms that party identification did indeed appear to influence devolution voting independently of national identity (albeit apparently in the wrong direction so far as Liberal Democrats are concerned), the fact that the distribution of party identification is so similar in the two countries means that the addition does nothing to reduce the size of the Wales term in our model. In fact it is increased.

Grievances and expectations

So, looking more widely at the sociology and social psychology of Scotland and Wales has failed to contribute to our ability to explain the difference in the two referendum outcomes. Evidently we do indeed need to look at voters' views as to the merits or otherwise of the constitutional provisions put before them. If they do help us to account for the difference, then it would appear that we will have to conclude that the politics of devolution in the two countries mattered We have already seen in the chapter by Paula Surridge and David McCrone how important expectations of the parliament apparently were to voting in the Scottish referendum.

One impetus towards the introduction of devolution was undoubtedly the fact that in none of the elections won by the Conservatives between 1979 and 1992 did either Scotland or Wales give a plurality of their votes to the Conservatives. As a result these two parts of the UK enjoyed regimes for which they had not voted and policies which they did not support. Thatcherism might have appealed to the voters of England, but not to voters in Scotland or Wales (Brown *et al* 1999; Curtice 1996). What devolution would enable these two parts of the UK to do is to implement a more left-wing policy agenda than appeared to be acceptable to voters in England (Brown *et al* 1998; Osmond 1998; Paterson 1994).

If this argument is correct, we should be able to demonstrate that those who adopt a more left-wing position were more likely to vote for devolution. But if it is to account for the difference in the referendum outcome in Scotland and Wales, we will have to amend the argument somewhat. We would have to demonstrate that people in Scotland adopted a more left-wing position, independent of national identity, than was the case in Wales.

In the referendum surveys we included a set of items which between them have been shown to form a scale that measures the degree to which respondents adopt a left-wing or right-wing view on major economic issues[10] (Evans and Heath 1995; Evans *et al* 1996). The scale ranges from 1 which is the most left-wing position to 5 which is the most right-wing. However as table 6.10 shows, looking at ideology is not of much help to us in our task, for in practice there is relatively little difference between Scotland and Wales in the overall level of support for left-wing rather than right-wing propositions.

Table 6.10
Scottish and Welsh national identity and ideological differences

Mean left/right scale score	Scotland		Wales	
		N		*N*
Scottish/Welsh, not British	2.4	*208*	2.6	*101*
More Scottish/Welsh than British	2.6	*211*	2.6	*156*
Equally Scottish/Welsh and British	2.7	*182*	2.7	*207*
More British than Scottish/Welsh or British, not Scottish/Welsh	2.8	*43*	2.7	*140*
All respondents	2.6	*644*	2.6	*604*

There is though one feature of table 6.10 that we should note. In Wales a respondent's position on the national identity scale makes no difference to their chances of being left-wing rather than right-wing on economic issues. In Scotland, however, those who feel exclusively or primarily Scottish are more likely to adopt a left-wing position than those who feel primarily or exclusively British. This confirms the suggestion made by Brown *et al* (1999) that one of the consequences of the debate about devolution in Scotland is that arguments about economics and equality have become intertwined with arguments about nationalism, and that it is this that makes Scotland most distinctive in her attitudes towards the role of government. Here then we see a clear sign of a difference in the character of the debate in Scotland and Wales, albeit not one that enables us to explain the difference in the two referendum outcomes.[11]

Of course, the debate about the merits or otherwise of devolution has not simply been about its possible implications for the ideological direction of public policy. That debate has also seen the articulation of alleged grievances. One is simply that who ran Scotland and Wales in the 1980s appeared to be determined by votes cast in England. Another comprises claims about the degree to which Scotland and Wales are or are not advantaged economically by their membership of the UK. It might be that such arguments have had greater force in Scotland than in Wales, and that it is the resulting greater sense of 'grievance' about existing arrangements in the UK that accounts for the higher level of support for devolution in Scotland.[12]

Such an explanation has partial force. Asked whether they had ever felt angry about the fact that it is English voters who mainly decide who runs their country, only 29% of people in Wales said they had felt very angry compared with no less than 41% on Scotland. Even more strikingly, just 16% of people in Wales think England's economy benefits more from having Wales in the UK, whereas no less than 48% of Scots take this view of their own country's membership. Moreover, answers to these questions are strongly correlated with referendum vote. For example, in Scotland no less than 94% of voters who felt very angry that it was English voters who decide who runs their country supported the 'yes' camp compared with just 41% of those who were not angry. However, these items are also correlated with national identity. As a result if we add them to the model we find that only the one item about the supposed power of English voters is significantly associated with referendum vote independently of national identity.

The debate about devolution was not of course just about grievances. It was also about the alleged benefits of devolution for the governance of Scotland and Wales. Here, of course, also the differences in what was being proposed for Scotland and Wales might also have had an impact as considered in the chapters by Paula Surridge and David McCrone and by Anthony Heath and Bridget Taylor. We asked our respondents about a range of possible consequences that might flow from devolution. The responses to six such items are shown in table 6.11. The items in the table fall into three pairs. The first pair consider the implications of devolution for the affective and constitutional status of Scotland and Wales as a nation, the second pair look at the instrumental consequences of devolution, while the last might be considered to address the degree to which the public felt that devolution would improve their sense of engagement with the political process. In each case, expectations were clearly different in the two countries.

Scots clearly had higher expectations of devolution than did the Welsh. Thus for example, a half of people living in Scotland thought devolution would increase the standard of living in their country compared with just a quarter of people living in Wales. Meanwhile just over three-quarters of people in Scotland felt that devolution would give ordinary people more say in the way their country is governed, compared with only just half in Wales. The two countries also differed in their evaluation of what devolution would mean for their future as nations. Scots were more likely than the Welsh to believe both that it would give them more pride in their country and that it would eventually lead to independence.

Table 6.11

Expectations of devolution in Scotland and Wales

% say more likely as result of devolution	Scotland	Wales
Scottish/Welsh will eventually leave the UK	42	21
Give Scots/Welsh more pride in their country	77	54
Increase standard of living in Scotland/Wales	50	29
Improve standard of education in Scotland/Wales	71	50
Give ordinary Scots/Welsh people more say in how Scotland/Wales is governed	79	54
Give Scottish/Welsh stronger voice in the UK	70	50
Minimum N	*674*	*684*

Moreover, voters' expectations were strongly associated with the way that they voted. In Scotland those who thought devolution would increase the standard of living in their country were no less than 42 points more likely to vote 'yes' than were those who did not think the standard of living would increase. In Wales the equivalent figure was as much as 66 points. If we undertake the same calculation for those who thought that devolution would give ordinary people more say in the running of their country, we find differences of 51 points in Scotland and 58 in Wales.

There is however one item for which this is not true. This is voters' expectations of what devolution would mean for the future of the UK. In Scotland those who thought that devolution would make independence more likely were only 13 points less likely to vote 'yes' than those who thought was not the case. The equivalent figure in Wales is just 14 points. Almost undoubtedly, this reflects the fact that the possibility that devolution would lead to independence was for some an attraction and for others a disincentive. In any event, of all the arguments that were put up against devolution by its opponents, the claim that it would result in the break-up of the UK was evidently one less likely to affect the aggregate outcome (but see also the chapter by Anthony Heath and Bridget Taylor, particularly with reference to Wales).

But so far as the other items in table 6.11 are concerned, it seems as though we might have the means to account for the differences in the two referendum outcomes. For we have identified items which discriminate sharply between 'yes' and 'no' votes in Scotland and Wales and on which the distribution of responses in the two countries differed. In table 6.12 we show what happens if we add the four items that cover the perceived instrumental and 'engagement' consequences of devolution to the logistic model, together with the item discussed earlier about power of English votes in deciding who runs Scotland and Wales.

Table 6.12
Expanded model of referendum vote in Scotland and Wales[13]

	Voted Yes *versus* voted No	
	B	**SE**
National identity		
Scottish/Welsh, not British	1.46	(.41)*
More Scottish/Welsh than British	.95	(.37)*
Equally Scottish/Welsh and British	.67	(.36)
Wales	-.54	(.23)*
Expectations		
More say	1.14	(.25)*
Stronger voice in UK	1.68	(.25)*
Increase standard of living	1.31	(.27)*
Improve education	1.01	(.25)*
Angry England decides	.74	(.15)*
Constant	2.12	(.38)*
N	*879*	

* significant at 5%

All five items are strongly correlated with voting 'yes' in the referendum. Moreover, they also serve to reduce the size of the Wales coefficient, which although still statistically significant, is now -.54 rather than -.98. So differences in the expectations that people in Scotland and in Wales had of devolution play an important role in explaining why the referendum outcome in the two countries was so different, even though they do not furnish us with a complete explanation.[14] It appears that, as with turnout, differences in the politics of devolution in the two counties mattered.

We should, of course, be careful in the implications that we draw here. As we warned at the beginning of this chapter, when we ask people to say what they think the consequences of devolution would be, we are in many ways inviting them to provide a rationalisation for a decision that they may well have made for completely different reasons. Equally, we must be aware that national identity will doubtless have helped shape people's expectations of devolution. However, as we cannot account for the difference in the outcome in the two countries without including variables which tap voters' reported attitudes towards devolution, it does appear that the difference in the outcome in the two countries was not simply the result of the distribution of national identity in the two countries. People in Scotland and Wales had different expectations of devolution, and did so we would suggest at least in part because of differences in the way that the devolution debate was conducted in the two countries. In short politics mattered, not just social cleavages.

Conclusion

The Welsh referendum nearly proved to be a disaster for the then still new Labour government. Its devolution proposals for the principality, one of the key elements of its extensive programme of constitutional reform, came close to defeat. Indeed, as we have demonstrated victory was secured only because many electors who were not enamoured of the proposals did not feel sufficiently motivated to register a 'no' vote. Such a narrow victory meant that the referendum largely failed in its original objective of demonstrating such widespread support for devolution that parliament would feel duty bound both to implement it without significant amendment and not to tamper with it in future without the backing of another popular vote. Although Labour's large Commons majority meant that the Government of Wales Act still had a largely untroubled passage, the new Welsh assembly will start its life without a clear bedrock of legitimacy. One of its key tasks will be to develop such foundations for itself. In contrast, the new Scottish parliament will begin its life as the embodiment of the 'settled will' of the Scottish people, with apparently more prospect that its powers will grow rather than any concern that they might diminish.

In part, the contrast in the outcome of the two referendums does reflect differences in the pattern of national identity in the two countries. Scots are indeed more likely than the Welsh to think of themselves as a nation that is distinct from the rest of the United Kingdom. But this is far from a sufficient explanation. What also seems to have mattered was the character of the debate about devolution in Wales. In contrast to Scotland, that debate was less inclusive and less intense. As a result fewer people in Wales were convinced of either the instrumental or the affective benefits of devolution. Of course, we would acknowledge that one of the reasons why the debate took the character that it did, and indeed why a more limited form or devolution was proposed for Wales compared with Scotland, might well have been the weaker sense of a distinct national identity in Wales. The behaviour of elites may well be a reflection of the social divisions in their country. Even so, as discussed further by Ron Davies in the Preface and in the chapter by Lindsay Paterson and Richard Wyn Jones, our analysis suggests that how elites respond to the circumstances in which they find themselves makes a difference to political outcomes.

If our analysis is correct, it also has important implications for the way in which the government might handle future referendums. The outcome in Wales shows not only that referendum outcomes are not determined simply by social cleavages, but also that they are not just a reflection of the popularity of the incumbent government. Even newly elected popular governments are in danger of losing a referendum if the proposition is one for which public opinion has not already been well prepared.

It is widely anticipated that the current Labour government hopes to hold a referendum on Britain's possible entry into the single European currency in the wake of a second election victory in 2001 or 2002, hoping that it can profit from the honeymoon created by such a victory. Given the unpopularity of a single currency to date (Curtice and Jowell 1998; Evans 1998) our analysis of what happened in the Scottish and Welsh referendums suggests such a strategy may well not be enough. The government may well need to declare its hand and implement a programme of persuasion long before referendum day if it wants to be sure that we will eventually support the Euro.

Notes

1. We certainly take the view that national identity mattered more to the outcome in Scotland than suggested by Surridge *et al* (1998). They use the alternative measure of national identity to examine the relationship between voting intention in the referendum at the time of the 1997 general election and national identity. They note that 63% of those who described themselves as British were in favour of the creation of a Scottish parliament, not much lower than the 72% recorded among those who are Scottish. However, they fail to distinguish between those who ascribed to only one of these labels and those who ascribed to both. As a result there is a substantial overlap in the composition of their two groups with the inevitable consequence that the levels of support for the Scottish parliament in them were similar. See also note 2.

2. The pattern of association between our alternative measure of national identity and referendum voting behaviour is shown in the following table. Note that in Scotland there is a 29-point gap between the first and third rows of the table in the proportion voting 'yes', very similar to the equivalent gap of 27 points in Wales.

Table 6.13
Alternative measure of Scottish and Welsh national identity and referendum vote

(a) Scotland

		Yes	No	Did not vote	N
Scottish only	%	68	6	26	283
Scottish more than British	%	50	22	29	269
British only/British more than Scottish	%	39	39	21	103

(b) Wales

		Yes	No	Did not vote	N
Welsh only	%	43	20	37	173
Welsh more than British	%	37	30	33	249
British only/British more than Welsh	%	16	42	43	238

3. In contrast, levels of interest in politics in general differed little between the two countries: 36% of people in Scotland and 32% in Wales said that they were interested in politics a great deal or quite a lot. The differences reported in this paragraph can thus be interpreted as evidence of differences in the degree to which the two referendums engaged their populations and are not a reflection of differences in the propensity of the two populations to be interested in political issues.

4. Examination of this latter group revealed that they were least likely to turn out at all, and thus their answer can reasonably be regarded as an indication of disengagement from the referendum.

5. We have also modelled Moreno national identity as an interval-level variable. Doing so has no material impact on the results reported here.

6. As we might anticipate from our earlier discussion, we also find that there is a small but statistically significant interaction between referendum vote, national identity as measured by the Moreno question, and whether or not the respondent lives in Wales, indicating that the association between national identity and vote is weaker in Wales than in Scotland. However,

as noted earlier this finding is not replicated if we use the alternative measure of national identity. Moreover including the interaction term increases both the size of the Wales coefficient and its standard error. Thus it does not help us to understand why the 'yes' vote was lower in Wales than in Scotland while its inclusion makes the model less stable. In contrast with the interaction term excluded, the results reported here for the Moreno question are replicated almost exactly if we use instead the alternative measure of national identity.

7. Note however that voters in Scotland consistently had a clearer idea of the position of the parties than was the case in Wales. In Scotland 82% of people said that they thought the Conservatives recommended a 'no' vote, compared with only 72% in Wales. Meanwhile 90% of people in Scotland thought that Labour were in favour, compared with 80% in Wales. The equivalent figures for the nationalist parties are 86% and 70%, and for the Liberal Democrats, 57% and 39%. Respondents' views of the parties' positions in Wales are also examined in the chapter by Richard Wyn Jones and Dafydd Trystan.

8. These figures indeed reflect perceptions of how united the parties were on devolution. In Scotland 15% thought that Labour was divided on the issue, compared with as many as 35% in Wales. Equally, while 33% thought the Conservatives were divided in Wales, 46% took this view in Scotland.

9. Note however that if we add interaction terms for party identification and Wales to the model only the term for Labour approaches statistical significance.

10. The items are as follows:

    Ordinary working people get their fair share of the nation's wealth
    There is one law for the rich and one for the poor
    There is no need for strong trade unions to protect employees' working conditions and wages
    Private enterprise is the best way to solve the country's economic problems
    Major public services and industries ought to be in state ownership
    It is the government's responsibility to provide a job for everyone who wants one

    Note that three of the items are worded in a right-wing direction and three in a left. In constructing the scale, the scoring is made consistent across items.

11. As one might anticipate the left-right scale proves to be significantly associated with referendum vote independently of national identity, also reducing the Wales coefficient slightly. However it proves to be insignificant after the variables tapping hopes and grievances, discussed below, are added.

12. After all Wales had not given a plurality of its votes to the Conservatives since 1859, so the experience of not having voted for the government in

power was not a new one. Scotland, in contrast, had backed the Conservatives at each of their three election victories of the 1950s.

13. The parameter coefficients for national identity are simply contrast coefficients that measure the impact on vote of being in that category rather than feeling primarily or exclusively British. The parameter coefficients for the 'expectations' variables are also simple contrast coefficients. They show the impact on vote of saying devolution would have the stated consequence versus saying it would have either the opposite effect or none at all. 'Angry England decides' is treated as an interval level variable. Those who said they were 'very angry' are scored 3, those 'somewhat angry', 2, and those 'not angry', 1.

14. The item on whether or not devolution would give the Scots and the Welsh more pride in their country proved not to be significantly correlated with referendum vote independently of all the other variables in the model. The survey also contained a range of other items which tapped perceptions of the benefits or otherwise of devolution. But no others proved to be both independently significantly associated with vote and capable of reducing the size of the Wales coefficient. Two criticisms of devolution which were significantly associated with referendum vote were that it would cost too much to set up and run and that it would pay too much attention to the central belt of Scotland/south Wales, but the inclusion of these items in the model served only to increase the size of the Wales coefficient.

References

Brown A, McCrone D and Paterson L (1998) *Politics and Society in Scotland*, 2nd edition, London: Macmillan.

Brown A, McCrone D, Paterson L and Surridge P (1999) *The Scottish Electorate*, London: Macmillan.

Butler D and Stokes D (1974) *Political Change in Britain*, London: Macmillan.

Curtice J (1996) 'One Nation Again?', in Jowell R, Curtice J, Park A, Brook L and Thomson K (eds), *British Social Attitudes: the 13th Report*, Aldershot: Dartmouth.

Curtice J and Jowell R (1998) 'Is there Really a Demand for Constitutional Change?', *Scottish Affairs*, Special Issue on 'Understanding Constitutional Change'.

Evans G (1998) 'How Britain Views the EU', in Jowell R, Curtice J, Park A, Brook L, Thomson K and Bryson C (eds), *British - and European - Social Attitudes: How Britain Differs*, Aldershot: Ashgate.

Evans G and Heath A (1995) 'The Measurement of Left-Right and Libertarian-Authoritarian Values: A Comparison of Balanced and Unbalanced Scales', *Quality and Quantity* **29**: 191-206.

Evans G, Heath A and Lalljee M (1996) 'Measuring Left-Right and Libertarian-Authoritarian Values in the British Electorate', *British Journal of Sociology* **47**: 93-112.

Franklin M, Marsh M and Wlezien C (1994) 'Attitudes towards Europe and Referendum Votes - A Response', *Electoral Studies* **13**: 117-21.

Franklin M, van der Eijk C, and Marsh M (1995) 'Referendum Outcomes and Trust in Government: Public Support for Europe in the Wake of Maastricht', *West European Politics* **18**: 101-17.

Gallagher M (1996) 'Conclusion', in Gallagher M and Uleri P V (eds), *The Referendum Experience in Europe*, London: Macmillan.

Gellner E (1983) *Nations and Nationalism*, Oxford: Blackwell.

General Register Office (Scotland) (1996) *1991 Census: Monitor for New Parliamentary Constituencies in Scotland*, Edinburgh: GRO(S).

Heath A, Jowell R, Curtice J, Evans G, Field J and Witherspoon S (1991) *Understanding Political Change: The British Voter 1964-87*, Oxford: Pergamon.

Heath A and Kellas J (1998) 'Nationalisms and Constitutional Questions', *Scottish Affairs*, Special Issue on 'Understanding Constitutional Change'.

Lipset S and Rokkan S (eds) (1967) *Party Systems and Voter Alignments: Cross-National Perspectives*, New York: Free Press.

Moreno L (1988) 'Scotland and Catalonia: The Path to Home Rule', in McCrone D and Brown A, *The Scottish Government Yearbook 1988*, Edinburgh: Unit for the Study of Government in Scotland.

Office for National Statistics (1996) *New Parliamentary Constituency Monitor: 1991 Census: Wales*, London: ONS.

Osmond J (1998) *New Politics in Wales*, London: Charter '88.

Paterson L (1994) *The Autonomy of Modern Scotland*, Edinburgh: Edinburgh University Press.

Surridge P, Paterson L, Brown A and McCrone D (1998) 'The Scottish Electorate and the Scottish Parliament', *Scottish Affairs*, Special Issue on 'Understanding Constitutional Change'.

Svensson P (1984) 'Class, Party and Ideology: A Danish Case Study of Electoral Behaviour in Referendums', *Scandanavian Political Studies* (new series) **7**: 175-96.

Swaddle K and Heath A (1989) 'Official and Reported Turnout in the British General Election of 1987', *British Journal of Political Science* **19**: 537-70.

Tonsgaard O (1992) 'A Theoretical Model of Referendum Behaviour', in Gundelac, P and Siune K (eds), *From Voters to Participants: Essays in Honour of Ole Borre*, Aarhus: Politica.

7 Were the Scottish and Welsh referendums second-order elections?

Anthony Heath and Bridget Taylor[*]

There has been a great deal of work in Britain over the years on voting in general elections and the influences that shape people's decisions about which party to support. There is also a growing literature on the way in which people vote in European or local elections, and the differences between these and general elections. Voting in referendums, however, has inevitably been little studied because there have been so few in Britain. Our aim in this paper is to make a start and to explore some of the general characteristics of voting, and of non-voting, in referendums. We take the Scottish and Welsh referendums of 1997 as our exemplars, but our primary research objective is to develop a more general understanding of the nature of voting in referendums. In particular we focus on the theory of second-order elections, which has been applied very successfully to understanding the differences between general, European and local elections. How far can this theory be applied to referendums?

Of course referendums differ from elections in some important ways. Referendums do not elect representatives to a governing body, whether a parliament or council. Many referendums, including the 1997 devolution referendums, are not binding upon the government to act in accordance with the majority preference, but merely advisory. Finally, in a referendum the ballot is cast not for a party but in response, affirmative or negative, to a question formally on a single issue (or two

[*] Anthony Heath is Professor of Sociology at Nuffield College Oxford. Bridget Taylor is Research Officer in CREST at Nuffield College Oxford.

connected issues in the case of the 1997 Scottish referendum). This is not to deny, of course, either that parties may play a major role in cueing their supporters' preferences, or that the policy issue which is the subject of the referendum may be embedded in an integrated policy manifesto.

The concept of second-order elections

Reif and Schmitt introduced the notion of second-order national elections as a conceptual framework for the analysis of European election results:

> [T]he 'first-order' elections in parliamentary systems are the national parliamentary elections . . . There is a plethora of 'second-order elections': by-elections, municipal elections, various sets of regional elections, those to a second chamber and the like . . . Many voters cast their votes in these elections not only as a result of conditions obtaining [in] . . . the second-order arena, but also on the basis of factors in the main political arena of the nation. (1980: 8-9)

They predicted that second-order elections would have a lower level of participation than first-order ones; that they would offer brighter prospects for small and new political parties; and that governing parties would do badly. Perhaps most crucially, Reif claimed that voting in second-order elections was based on "the political situation of the first-order arena at the moment when the second-order election is being held" (Reif 1984: 8). Voting in these second-order elections can be thought of as a way in which voters communicate to the national government (and to the other political parties) their views on its current performance and electoral prospects (compare with van der Eijk *et al* 1996).

The theoretical rationale behind these claims is that "there is less at stake as compared to first-order elections" (Reif 1984: 8). Since less is at stake, there is less incentive to turn out and vote; there is less need to worry about whether one's vote is wasted or not, since in a sense all votes are wasted anyway, and so one is more free to vote for minor parties that have no realistic chance of forming the government; and there is less point in collecting or using information about the specific political arena when making one's decision.

There are several reasons to think that the theory of second-order elections might apply to referendums in Britain. First, turnout has tended to be relatively low in referendums. As David Butler and Iain McLean have shown in their chapter in this volume, British referendums have generally had lower turnouts than have general elections over this period. The Common Market referendum in June 1975, for example, had a turnout of 64.5% compared with the turnouts of 79% and 73% in the two general elections of 1974. The Scottish referendum of 1979 had a turnout of 63.6% compared with a turnout of 76.8% among Scots in the general election of that year. The Welsh referendum had a turnout of 58.8% compared with 79.4% among the Welsh in the general election. And in 1997, the Scottish referendum turnout of 60.1% was again substantially down on the 71.3% of Scots who voted in the general election earlier in the year, while in Wales the referendum turnout was only 51.3% compared with 73.4% in the general election.[1]

These turnouts are not as low as those in European elections, for which the concept of second-order election was devised (between 32% and 36% in Britain), but they are low enough to suggest that some of the characteristics of second-order elections may have been present in the 1997 referendums, and in the Welsh referendum in particular.

Second, it has also been suggested by various writers that the contrast between the outcomes of the 1979 and 1997 devolution referendums may have something to do with the popularity of the sponsoring governments, as discussed in the chapter by Geoffrey Evans and Dafydd Trystan in this volume. Thus in the early months of 1979, Callaghan's Labour government was suffering from declining popularity as the 'winter of discontent' finally destroyed Labour's tenuous hold on office. In contrast, in the autumn of 1997 Tony Blair's New Labour government was still in its honeymoon period and was riding high in public esteem. The theory, then, that the outcome of a referendum depends at least in part on "the political situation of the first-order arena at the moment when the second-order election is being held" seems to have some merit.

Third, it could well be argued that 'less was at stake' in the Welsh devolution referendum than in the Scottish referendum. Whether less was at stake in the Scottish referendum than in a general election is arguable, and cannot perhaps be objectively decided. In a sense, of course, the Scottish referendum was indeed second-order in that, had Labour failed to win the general election, there would surely have been no referendum at all on Scottish devolution. Certainly, the Conservative Party had no intention of introducing one. Whatever the merits of this argument, it is not unreasonable to suppose that less was at stake in the Welsh than in the Scottish referendum, since the Welsh assembly was due to be given many fewer powers than the Scottish. (A fuller discussion of this is given in the Introduction to this volume.) In this sense the theory of second-order elections looks highly plausible as an account of the differences between the two referendums.

On the other hand, the theory of second-order elections was not designed to be applied to referendums. Future elections to the Scottish parliament and the Welsh assembly may well fit the theory, but it is unlikely that Reif and Schmitt would have wished to apply their predictions to constitutional referendums. Most obviously, something was indeed at stake in both Wales and Scotland, namely whether to introduce new constitutional arrangements. And the question(s) on which voters were being asked to decide were unambiguously ones that related to the second-order arena.

In this paper we begin by focusing on the issue of turnout. How far can the low turnout, and in particular the lower turnout in Wales, be explained by how much was at stake? In the second part of the paper we then turn to look at our respondents who reported that they had turned out to vote. What were the primary influences on the way they voted? Were they guided by factors specific to the first-order or to the second-order arena? And was there a difference between Wales and Scotland of the sort predicted by the theory of second-order elections?

Turnout and how much was at stake

As we noted above, turnout is expected to be lower in second-order elections because less is at stake. In Wales, given the limited powers granted to the proposed assembly, it indeed appears that less might be at stake than in Scotland.

We begin, then, with this key explanatory concept and ask what our respondents' perceptions were of how much was at stake. To ascertain respondents' perceptions, we asked:

> *Some people say that it makes no difference which side wins elections, things go on much the same. How about the last general election when the Labour Party won? How much difference do you think that result will make?*

> *And what about the recent referendum? How much difference do you think the result of that will make?*

Table 7.1 shows the distributions of the answers given to these two questions by our respondents in Wales and Scotland respectively. In Scotland, we see that the distribution of answers was very similar for the referendum and for the general election, although there were somewhat more don't knows about the referendum. If we combine the three categories of great deal, quite a lot and some we find that altogether 82% of Scottish respondents felt that the referendum would make a difference, almost exactly the same figure as for the general election (83%). This suggests that electors in Scotland may in fact have seen the referendum as first-order in nature, as important as a general election.

Table 7.1
How much difference the general election/referendum
will make, Scotland and Wales

	Scotland		Wales	
	General election	Referendum	General election	Referendum
	%	%	%	%
How much difference:				
a great deal	29.9	30.0	25.1	12.3
quite a lot	34.9	35.4	31.6	22.9
some	18.3	16.9	24.7	19.5
not very much	11.4	8.0	13.2	21.8
none at all	2.3	1.3	1.6	6.4
don't know	3.2	8.5	3.8	17.1
N	676	676	686	686

In Wales however, there was a marked difference between the two sets of answers; 55% for the referendum compared with 80% for the general election. Clearly, the Welsh did not feel that as much was at stake in their referendum, and this is hardly surprising given the differences in the powers of the proposed new institutions.

As we might expect from the theory of second-order elections, these differences in perception were quite closely linked to differences in turnout. In table 7.2 we cross-tabulate these perceptions by the respondents' reports of their turnout in the referendums.

In general, we see much the same pattern in both countries of declining turnout as we move down the columns from people who thought the referendum would make a great deal of difference to those who did not know whether or not it would make any difference. Thus, of Scottish respondents who thought that the referendum would make a great deal of difference, 85% reported that they had voted. In Wales the corresponding figure was 90%. Of Scottish respondents who felt they did not know what difference it would make, 45% said they had voted while among the Welsh the corresponding figure was 37%. The range in turnout rates is thus slightly larger in Wales than in Scotland, but the overall pattern is broadly the same.

Table 7.2
Turnout by difference the referendum will make, Scotland and Wales

	Scotland		Wales	
% turnout		*N*		*N*
How much difference:				
a great deal	85.2	*203*	90.6	*85*
quite a lot	73.2	*239*	72.2	*158*
some	73.7	*114*	67.7	*133*
not very much	66.0	*53*	55.1	*147*
none at all	-	*9*	43.2	*44*
don't know	44.8	*58*	37.1	*116*
All	73.7	*676*	62.1	*683*

Table 7.2, then, suggests that the different distributions in the two
countries of how much was thought to be at stake can largely account
for the overall difference in turnout. In other words, turnout was lower
in Wales than in Scotland simply because less was thought to be at stake.
This seems a very plausible interpretation, since there is no good reason
to suppose that the Welsh are in general more apathetic, less interested
or less willing to engage in politics. Certainly their participation in
general elections is, if anything, higher than the Scots, while the
percentage who reported that they took a lot of interest in politics was
much the same in the two countries (36% in Scotland and 32% in Wales).
Interestingly the proportions who said they had read the official
summary documents about the devolution proposals were almost
identical in the two countries (at 42%).

We can test our interpretation rigorously with a series of logistic
regression models (table 7.3). We begin in model A by establishing the
base-line difference between the two countries and we simply regress
turnout on country of residence. The parameter estimate for 'country' in
this model is a measure of how big the difference in turnout is between
the two countries. (The parameter estimate is measured on the logit scale
and is in fact identical to the log odds ratio of reported turnout in the
two countries.) As we can see, the parameter estimate is highly
significant - five times its standard error.

Our next step is to see if we can account for the difference between the
countries in turnout by introducing measures of how much was thought
to be at stake. If how much was at stake can account for the difference,
then its inclusion in the model should reduce the 'country' parameter to
a level where it is no longer significant. Model B therefore adds our

respondents' perceptions of how much difference the referendums would make. We take the don't knows as the reference category and the parameter estimates therefore compare the propensity to turnout of the other categories with that of the don't knows. As we can see, there is no significant difference in turnout (controlling for country) between the respondents who said don't know and those who answered none, but all the other groups have significantly higher propensities to turn out and vote.

However, the main feature of interest in Model B is the change in the estimated size of the 'country' parameter. As we can see, this shrinks from a highly significant 0.60 in Model A to a non-significant 0.23 in Model B. We have therefore largely succeeded in explaining the difference in turnout between Scotland and Wales.[2]

Table 7.3
Logistic regressions of turnout in Scottish and Welsh referendums

	Model A[3]		Model B[4]		Model C[5]	
	B	**SE**	**B**	**SE**	**B**	**SE**
Constant	1.67	(.19)	.08	(.27)	0.37	(.52)
Country	.60 ***	(.12)	.23	(.13)	-0.32 *	(.14)
Difference referendum makes						
great deal			2.15 ***	(.24)	1.45 ***	(.26)
quite a lot			1.26 ***	(.20)	0.75 ***	(.21)
some			1.05 ***	(.21)	0.69 **	(.23)
not much			0.76 *	(.30)	0.53 *	(.23)
none at all			0.01	(.13)	-0.06	(.34)
don't know			0		0	
Party identification						
strong					0.91 **	(.35)
fairly strong					0.68 *	(.32)
not very strong					0.34	(.33)
none					0	
Political interest					0.35 ***	(.07)
Knowledge about referendum					0.17 **	(.05)
N	1357		1357		1291	

* significant at 5%; ** significant at 1%; *** significant at 0.1%

In Model C we add some further control variables. Previous research on turnout has suggested that political interest, sense of political efficacy, and strength of attachment to one's party are related to turnout (see for example, Schmitt and Mannheimer 1991). One other variables is also of interest. As described in the chapter by Richard Wyn Jones and Dafydd Trystan in this volume, the Referendum Surveys also included measures of respondents' knowledge about the devolution proposals; we might expect more knowledgeable electors to be more likely to turn out, and if the Welsh were less knowledgeable about the referendum, this could in principle help to explain the difference in the Welsh and Scottish turnout.

The results of Model C suggest that some of the new measures, notably strength of party attachment, political interest and political knowledge, do help to explain individual differences in turnout. (Note that Lindsay Paterson and Richard Wyn Jones in the next chapter in this volume find that overall levels of knowledge about devolution were not lower in Wales than in Scotland.) They all have highly significant parameter estimates and, crucially, the overall fit of the model is improved. It is also notable that the inclusion of these additional measures substantially reduces the estimates associated with how much was at stake. (This is because the additional variables are themselves associated with perceptions of how much difference the referendum would make.)

So far the results are closely in line with the theory of second-order elections. In Scotland, the election was apparently seen as a first-order election, but in Wales it was clearly second-order. And this difference largely explains the difference in turnout.

Now this may be, as we suggested earlier, simply because of the objective differences in the powers of the two elected bodies. However, it may also be that different national identities led people to take different views of the importance of the referendums. The theory of second-order elections describes first-order elections as the national parliamentary elections, but this rather begs the question of what is to count as the nation. As we have seen in previous chapters in this volume, many Scottish electors, and a smaller proportion of Welsh electors, see themselves as Scottish (or Welsh) rather than British. Accordingly, they may well come to see any future elections to a Scottish parliament as the first-order national elections.

In the meantime we can check whether national identity was related to people's perceptions of the referendums. Table 7.4 cross-tabulates perceptions of how much difference the referendum and general election were expected to make by the Moreno measure of national identity. (For a more detailed account of this measure see Paula Surridge and David McCrone's chapter in this volume, and John Curtice's on comparison with an alternative measure of national identity.)

Table 7.4
Scottish and Welsh national identity and perceived
perceptions of how much was at stake

% saying the referendum/
general election would make a difference

	Scotland			Wales		
	Refer- endum	General election difference	N	Refer- endum	General election difference	N
Scottish/Welsh, not British	68.8	-8.0	215	43.0	+21.6	114
More Scottish/Welsh than British	67.7	+1.4	. 217	33.8	+23.5	169
Equally Scottish/Welsh and British	61.5	0.0	192	34.1	+21.2	226
More British than Scottish/Welsh	60.0	+10.0	20	42.9	+24.7	70
British, not Scottish/ Welsh	57.9	+15.8	19	23.2	+20.7	82

The first column in each panel shows the percentage who felt that the referendum would make a difference (the proportions saying a great deal plus quite a lot plus some difference). As we can see in both Wales and Scotland, there is a clear gradient (of roughly similar magnitude in both countries) with people who see themselves as Scottish or Welsh rather than British being much the most likely to say that the referendum would make a difference. Thus in Scotland 69% of respondents who felt Scottish not British thought the referendum would make a difference, compared with only 58% of people who felt themselves to be British not Scottish. In Wales all the figures were much lower, but the gradient is fairly similar running from 43% among the Welsh not British down to 23% among the British not Welsh.

The second column compares these perceptions of the referendum with perceptions of the general election. Thus, among the Scottish not British only 60% said that the general election would make a difference, 8.0 percentage points lower than the figure for the referendum. The second column gives these gaps between the referendum and general election figures. As we can see, people who felt equally Scottish and British felt that the referendum and the election were about equally important, while the 'British not Scottish' respondents gave substantially greater importance to the general election (+16 points). A similar pattern is not, however, really evident in Wales, where of course all the differences are positive.

People with exclusively Scottish national identities thus seem to have seen the referendums as more significant than did the people who identified themselves as British not Scottish. Indeed, for people who saw themselves as Scots rather than British the first-order context does indeed seem to be the Scottish one, rather than the British elections to the Westminster parliament. Conversely, people who did not see themselves as Scottish, probably English who happened to be resident in Scotland at the time, were rather clear that for them the first-order context was the Westminster elections. Possibly this may reflect lack of interest in what was going on in Scotland, and perhaps these respondents felt that questions of devolution were more ones for Scots to decide and ones in which they should not interfere themselves. We do not however have the data to explain their apparent lack of concern with Scottish devolution.

The first-order context

A crucial aspect of the theory of second-order elections is that voting in such elections is based on "the political situation of the first-order arena at the moment when the second-order election is being held" (Reif 1984: 8). The respondents' current party preferences can be used as a reasonable proxy for measuring their assessment of the political situation in the first-order arena. While there will be many factors that will impinge on the Westminster parliamentary arena - the economic performance of the economy, the internal divisions of the parties over Europe, the government's success or otherwise in implementing its manifesto commitments - all these things are likely to affect the current standing of the parties. Current standing thus gives us a summary measure of the state of play in the first-order arena.

So one simple question to start with is whether people simply voted along the lines of their current party preferences. Moreover, given the evidence which we have seen so far suggesting that the Welsh referendum had more of the characteristics of a second-order election, the natural expectation is that voting along party lines would have been more prevalent in Wales than in Scotland. The question is complicated by the fact that in Wales the Labour Party was more divided over devolution than it was in Scotland, but in a sense that is an issue specific to the second-order context. What we need to know is whether the popularity of the parties in the Westminster context had a stronger influence in Wales than in Scotland.

In table 7.5 we therefore cross-tabulate our respondents' current (Westminster) party preference by their vote in the two referendums. In Wales there was of course only one question in the referendum, whereas in Scotland there were two (for the precise wording of the referendum questions see the Introduction to this volume).

In table 7.5 we focus simply on the first of the two Scottish questions.

Table 7.5
Yes vote and current party preference, Scotland and Wales

% 'Yes' vote	Scotland	N	Wales	N
Conservative	19.7	66	6.3	80
Labour	88.9	252	59.5	220
Liberal Democrat	62.9	35	24.2	33
SNP/Plaid Cymru	96.9	96	98.1	52
Don't know	51.7	29	44.8	29

Note: The base is those who reported voting in the referendum.

Table 7.5 runs directly counter to the expectation that the Welsh referendum would have more of a second-order character. We see that, in Wales, Labour and Liberal Democrat supporters were much more likely to cross party lines than they were in Scotland. In both countries, as we have seen in earlier chapters, the Labour and Liberal Democrat parties had fairly unequivocally endorsed 'yes' votes in the two referendums, but whereas in Scotland 89% of voters who currently preferred Labour voted 'yes', in Wales this figure was down to 63%.

Some of the difference might have been a result of confusion about the parties' recommendations (on Wales, see Richard Wyn Jones and Dafydd Trystan's chapter in this volume). But if we restrict ourselves to respondents who correctly identified their party's recommendation, we still find a very substantial failure to follow the party line in Wales.

The results of tables 7.5 and 7.6 should not surprise us. Given the closeness of the vote in Wales, and the very high support for Labour there, it follows logically that many Labour supporters must have gone against their party's recommendation. In a sense, we are merely redescribing the outcomes of the referendums. We therefore need to be particularly careful not to draw causal conclusions from these cross-tabulations. The large proportion in Scotland who voted in accordance with Labour's recommendations does not mean that Scots were voting the way they did out of obedience to the party line. It may rather have been the case that the Labour Party's recommendation was more in line with public opinion in Scotland than it was in Wales. In other words, the causal direction may run the other way: it was public opinion that determined what questions the Labour government put to the Welsh and Scottish electorates.

Table 7.6

Yes vote among respondents who correctly perceived their current party's recommendation, Scotland and Wales

% 'Yes' vote	Scotland	N	Wales	N
Conservative	16.7	60	5.8	69
Labour	88.7	239	59.0	195
Liberal Democrat	62.1	29	35.0	20
SNP/Plaid Cymru	95.8	95	96.1	51

Note: The base is those who reported voting in referendum and correctly perceived their current party's recommendation.

The second-order context

An alternative way of looking at the problem is to ask whether the role of factors specific to the second-order arena were more or less important in Wales than in Scotland. Of course in one sense the questions asked in the referendums were by definition factors specific to the second-order arena. However, we can go behind the simple question on the referendum paper (or the not quite so simple dual question in Scotland) in order to ask what were the more specific considerations that led people to vote the way they did. We can also ask whether these considerations had the same character that can usually be found in general elections, such as the economy and so on, or whether they were *sui generis*.

To tap this, we asked people:

> *Which of the following comes closest to your views about a Welsh assembly: A Welsh assembly would make it more likely that Wales eventually leave the United Kingdom, make it more likely that Wales stay in the United Kingdom, or would it make no difference?*

And would a Welsh assembly give Wales a stronger voice in the United Kingdom, a weaker voice in the United Kingdom, or would it make no difference?

Would a Welsh assembly give Wales a stronger voice in Europe, a weaker voice in Europe, or would it make no difference?

And would a Welsh assembly give the Welsh more pride in their country, less pride in their country, or would it make no difference?

Would a Welsh assembly give ordinary Welsh people more say in how Wales is governed, less say, or would it make no difference?

Would a Welsh assembly increase the standard of living in Wales, reduce the standard of living, or would it make no difference?

Would a Welsh assembly improve the standard of education in Wales, reduce the standard of education, or would it make no difference?

Which of these, if any, do you think should be the most important for a Welsh Assembly to bring about?
And which, if any, should be the second most important?
And which, if any, should a Welsh assembly not try to bring about?

> *Improving education in Wales*
> *Giving Wales a stronger voice in the United Kingdom*
> *Giving the Welsh more pride in their country*
> *Giving Wales a stronger voice in Europe*
> *Increasing the standard of living in Wales*
> *Giving ordinary Welsh people more say in how Wales is governed*
> *Making it more likely that Wales eventually leaves the United Kingdom*

Equivalent questions were asked in Scotland. Some of these considerations, notably the standard of living and the standard of education, are the kinds of issue that dominate party politics at Westminster. They are the bread and butter (almost literally) of first-order British politics where there are generally large differences between the Labour and Conservative Parties. The other considerations are ones that are more specific to Wales and Scotland and essentially concern how the nations of Wales and Scotland are to be governed. They are concerned with the process of government itself.

We should also note that our questions distinguish the likely empirical effects of a Welsh assembly or Scottish parliament from the normative matter of the voters' own value priorities. On standard decision-making theory, both aspects should be important: thus if one thinks that the assembly will make no difference to the achievement of a particular outcome, then the value one attaches to that outcome becomes irrelevant

to how one should vote. Conversely, if one thinks that establishing an
assembly will, for example, make it more likely that Wales will become
independent, whether this makes one more or less likely to vote 'yes'
will depend on the value one attaches to independence.

To simplify matters, however, we begin by considering our
respondents' value priorities. These are reported in table 7.7. (We
exclude the second most important priorities since there were no
significant differences at all between respondents in Scotland and Wales
in the distribution of their second priorities.) As with table 7.5, we
restrict our analysis to respondents who reported that they had voted in
the referendum.

Table 7.7
Value priorities in Scotland and Wales

	Most important		Important not done		
	Scotland	Wales	Scotland	Wales	
	%	%	%	%	
More likely eventually to leave UK	2	0	58	78	***
Give stronger voice in the UK	11	15	2	1	
Give stronger voice in Europe	5	9 *	1	1	
Give the Scots/Welsh more pride in their country	3	4	1	1	
Give ordinary people more say in how Scotland/Wales is governed	28	20 **	1	1	
Increase standard of living	26	23	1	0	
None/Don't know	2	2	36	18	***
N	493	417	482	415	

Note: The base is those who reported voting in the referendum.
* significant at 5%; ** significant at 1%; *** significant at 0.1%

As we can see, there was substantial consensus between the two
countries over the most important priority for a parliament/assembly.
Both Scottish and Welsh voters were likely to give priority to improving
education, increasing the standard of living, and a greater say in
government. On most of these objectives, very similar proportions of
Scottish and Welsh voters gave them top priority. The main difference
was in the priority given to more say in government, 20% of the Welsh
but 28% of Scottish voters giving it first priority.

However, there was a much bigger difference when we look at things that a parliament/assembly should **not** do. 78% of Welsh but only 58% of Scottish voters said that it was very important that Wales/Scotland should **not** become more likely to leave the UK. The proportions in both countries who were committed to remaining within the UK is impressive, but in Wales it was an overwhelming majority.

How, then, did these value priorities relate to the way in which people voted? Although economic and welfare considerations were more or less equally valued in the two countries, these sorts of considerations could still have played a different role in people's decision-making in Wales and Scotland. Scots, for example, might have been more influenced by political considerations, such as having more say in government, whereas the Welsh may have been more guided by economic and welfare concerns. In other words, were the specifically second-order constitutional issues more important in Scotland and the bread-and-butter issues of Westminster politics the more important in Wales?

We therefore carry out separate logistic regressions in the two countries to explore the way that the respondents' value priorities were related to a 'yes' vote. In the case of the first value priority, we include all seven considerations listed above, namely leaving the UK, gaining a greater voice in the UK, and so on. We take the standard of living as our reference category. The parameter estimates thus compare the influence of the other categories with that of the standard of living. We found that the second-ranked value priorities were not associated with the way one voted, and so we excluded these from the analysis. But we did include respondents' judgements of what it was important should **not** be done. Given the very skewed distribution of responses, we grouped all the small categories (such as the standard of living, education and so on) into a single category thus giving three categories in total.

Table 7.8 yields two striking conclusions. First, exactly the same value priorities in the two countries account for a 'yes' vote. Thus in both countries giving ordinary people more say in how they are governed is significantly associated with a 'yes' vote. And a desire not to leave the UK is also significantly associated with a 'no' vote in both countries alike.

Second, and perhaps even more surprisingly, the magnitudes of these associations with vote are effectively indistinguishable in the two countries. While the parameter estimate for more say in how Scotland/Wales is governed appears rather larger in Scotland (1.15) than it does in Wales (0.70), the standard errors are quite large and we cannot reject the null hypothesis that the association is the same (at around 0.95). Similarly, although the estimate for not leaving the UK appears slightly larger in Scotland (at 2.73) than in Wales (2.13), the difference could easily be explained by sampling error.[6]

Table 7.8

Logistic regression of Yes vote and value priorities, Scotland and Wales

	Scotland		Wales	
	B	**SE**	**B**	**SE**
Most important to bring about				
Leave UK	4.82	(14.5)	3.6	(13.5)
Voice in UK	.27	(.39)	.61	(.35)
Voice in Europe	.82	(.62)	.86	(.42)
More pride	-.02	(.69)	.07	(.60)
More say	1.15 **	(.33)	.70 *	(.32)
Standard of living	0		0	
Quality of education	.38	(.32)	.00	(.30)
None	8.83	(12.69)	-2.3	(1.17)
Most important not to bring about				
Leave UK	-2.73 ***	(.44)	-2.13 ***	(.37)
Something else	-1.67 *	(.65)	-1.51 *	(.62)
None	0		0	
Constant	2.81	(.37)	1.54	(.40)
Model improvement	110.1	(9 df)	69.7	(9 df)
N	482		415	

* significant at 5%; ** significant at 1%; *** significant at 0.1%

Two other parameter estimates need to be discussed: in both Scotland and Wales there are large estimates associated with a positive desire to leave the UK (4.8 and 3.6 respectively) and with the category none (8.8 and 2.3 respectively). However, table 7.7 showed that there were tiny numbers of respondents who gave leaving the UK as their most important positive priority, while very few people indeed said that none of the seven considerations was important. This means that the estimates in table 7.8 are also based on tiny numbers and hence they have huge sampling errors. We cannot therefore attach any real meaning to these parameter estimates, although of course the pattern of association makes good *a priori* sense. However, we would need a much larger sample in order to pursue this further.

So far, then, it appears that, while the absolute numbers opposed to leaving the UK are very different in the two countries, the way in which it influenced a 'yes' vote is very similar. In other words, the same sort of influence worked in the same sort of way in the two countries.

As a final step we can add current party preference to the model to explore whether this too worked in the same way in the two countries. This is done in table 7.9. However, we make one minor change to the model: since we had a large number of categories in table 7.8 that had no significant association with vote, we combine these and thus simplify the model.

Table 7.9

Logistic regression of Yes vote, issues and current party, Scotland and Wales

	Scotland		Wales	
	B	SE	B	SE
Most important to bring about				
More say	0.79 *	(.35)	1.07 *	(.34)
Something else	0		0	
Most important not to bring about				
Leave UK	-2.04 ***	(.43)	-2.02 ***	(.42)
Something else	-0.80	(.78)	-1.32	(.74)
None	0		0	
Current preference				
None	0		0	
Conservative	-1.63 **	(.52)	-1.51 **	(.59)
Labour	1.73 ***	(.45)	1.51 **	(.48)
Liberal Democrat	0.36	(.55)	.07	(.62)
SNP/Plaid Cymru	2.21 **	(.66)	4.41 ***	(1.11)
Constant	1.71	(.56)	0.57	(.54)
Model improvement	199.9	(7df)	176.7	(7df)
N	472		407	

* significant at 5%; ** significant at 1%; *** significant at 0.1%

Since they include both current preferences and value priorities, the models reported in table 7.9 tell us about the effects of each variable, controlling for the others. In this respect of course it differs from the simpler analysis of party preference shown in table 7.5. The crucial point is that the new models reported in table 7.9 take account of the distributions of respondents' value priorities and the way in which these are associated with a 'yes' vote. As we saw from table 7.7, there are some large and important differences between Scotland and Wales in the distributions, particularly with respect to leaving the UK.

What table 7.9 indicates is that, once we have taken account of these differences in the distributions, the impact of current party preference is much the same in the two countries. Thus in Scotland the parameter estimate associated with a Labour preference is 1.73 while in Wales it is 1.51. Given the size of the standard errors, it is clear that we cannot reject the null hypothesis that the impact of a Labour preference is the same in both countries.[7] Both countries are also alike in that the estimate associated with a Liberal Democrat preference is not significantly different from zero.

This gives a very different interpretation of our previous finding that Labour and Liberal Democrat supporters were much more likely to cross party lines in Wales than they were in Scotland. As a simple description of the behaviour of voters in the two countries, the original statement based on table 7.5 is of course still correct. However, in understanding **why** voting across party lines was more prevalent in Wales, it is clear that we now need to take account of respondents' value priorities. It now appears that a current preference for the Liberal Democrats had little or no direct impact on the vote in either country: the fact that Scottish Liberals tended to vote along the lines of their party's recommendation simply reflects the fact that the party's recommendation happened to be more in tune with their supporters' value priorities. Liberal Democrats in Scotland tended to vote 'yes' because of their value priorities not because they were following the party's recommendation.[8]

In the case of Labour supporters, however, the party's recommendation does seem to have had some impact on voting 'yes', albeit one of much the same magnitude in both countries. The absolute difference in the extent to which Labour supporters voted along party lines in the two countries, however, largely follows from the fact that Labour supporters in Wales were more apprehensive about the risk of leaving the UK. In a sense Labour had a tougher job to do in Wales, since their supporters' value priorities differed substantially from those of their supporters in Scotland. (One could argue that this was in part self-inflicted, as Ron Davies does in his Preface, since the Labour Party in Wales did not seem to include or engage the electorate in the development of proposals for devolution, in contrast to Scotland: see also the chapter on the campaigns by David McCrone and Bethan Lewis, and on civil society by Lindsay Paterson and Richard Wyn Jones.) Of course, Labour politicians recognised the different constraints placed upon them by public opinion in the two countries, and hence proposed different constitutional arrangements in Wales and Scotland. While in one sense the Labour leadership got it right, in another sense it now appears that the proposed arrangements in Wales were not sufficient to allay fears that devolution might eventually lead Wales to leave the UK. In this respect, then, it may be that Labour got it wrong.

Conclusion

The results of our analysis are in one sense clear-cut although in another they are rather puzzling. The straightforward result is that most of the differences between Wales and Scotland in the turnout and in the 'yes' vote can be simply explained by the different distributions of public perceptions and value priorities in the two countries. In Wales, electors were less likely to feel that the new constitutional arrangements would make a difference than they were in Scotland. In Wales, electors were more apprehensive about the risks of leaving the UK that might follow from the new constitutional arrangements. These are perhaps the two key findings for understanding the level of turnout and the size of the 'yes' vote.

However, the implications for the theory of second-order elections are more puzzling. The theory correctly suggested that, since less was believed to be at stake in Wales, electors would be less likely to turn out and vote. However, the theory was wrong in suggesting that voters would be influenced by different factors in casting their ballots when less was at stake. Instead, voters in the two countries seemed to be influenced by exactly the same kinds of factor and by much the same magnitudes.

As we suggested at the beginning of this chapter, the theory of second-order elections was not developed to account for constitutional referendums.

It may well be that, when elections to the Welsh assembly and Scottish parliament are held in 1999 that the predictions of the theory will hold up much better. We may well find that, in Scotland, there is a greater discrepancy than in Wales between how people vote in the Westminster elections and how they vote in their own national elections (to the Scottish parliament or Welsh assembly). In Wales, it may be that the assembly elections will look more like second-order elections with voters casting their ballots on the basis of their judgements about the performance of the parties at Westminster. In Scotland, in contrast, the elections to the parliament may look more like first-order elections with Scottish considerations dominating the vote rather than Westminster considerations.

Notes

1. The ageing of the electoral register in the months between the general election and the referendums accounts for a small proportion of the observed decline in turnout, but most of the difference is likely to be real.
2. We also checked whether the impact of how much was at stake differed in the two countries. However, we were unable to reject the null hypothesis that the parameters were the same in both countries.
3. Model improvement: 26.2; degrees of freedom: 1.
4. Model improvement: 137.1; degrees of freedom: 6.
5. Model improvement: 195.6; degrees of freedom: 11.
6. We can test the hypothesis more rigorously by combining the two samples and testing the model that postulates the same effects in both countries. The chi-squared degrees of freedom for this model is 8.65 for 7 df, p = .279. This is a rather good fit and indicates that the discrepancies between this model and the observed patterns could easily be accounted for by sampling error.
7. Again we test this formally by pooling the datasets and using a loglinear model. The model that postulates that all the associations with a 'yes' vote have the same strength in the two countries yields an excellent fit to the data - chi-squared = 51.8 for 43 degrees of freedom, p = .168.
8. Strictly speaking we should remember that a parameter of zero indicates that there is no difference between respondents who currently prefer the Liberal Democrats and those who currently have no party preference in their propensity to vote 'yes', controlling for the other variables in the model. However, the claim that a Liberal Democrat preference had no net impact on vote seems quite a reasonable interpretation of the strict finding.

References

Reif K and Schmitt H (1980) 'Nine Second-Order National Elections', *European Journal of Political Research* **8**: 3-45 and 145-62.

Reif K (1984) 'National Electoral Cycles and European Elections 1979 and 1984', *Electoral Studies* **3**: 244-55.

Schmitt H and Mannheimer R (1991) 'About Voting and Non-Voting in the European Elections of June 1989', *European Journal of Political Research* **19**: 31-54.

Van der Eijk C, Franklin M and Marsh M (1996) 'What Can Voters Teach Us about Europe-Wide Elections; What Can Europe-Wide Elections Teach Us about Voters?', *Electoral Studies* **15**: 149-66.

8 Does civil society drive constitutional change?

The case of Wales and Scotland

Lindsay Paterson and Richard Wyn Jones [*]

What is civil society?

In recent times the concept of 'civil society', along with its apparent extension 'civic society', has played a prominent part in political discourse not only in Scotland and Wales, but more generally - most prominently of all perhaps during the overthrow of the communist states in Eastern Europe. Yet, despite its ubiquity, the meaning of civil society remains deeply ambiguous and indeed, superficially at least, contradictory. This is as true at the theoretical level as it is on the perhaps less reflexive level of political practice. Thus, for some commentators, civil society appears as an inherently conservative set of institutions which act as a bulwark against progressive social change (Kumar 1993; Nairn 1997), while others view civil society as the potential locus for a revitalised radical democratic project (Keane 1988; Marquand 1996; Hirst 1994). Indeed, the noted German social theorist Axel Honneth has argued that "in the course of over two hundred years of political theory, [civil society] has acquired so many strands and strata of meaning that today it appears to lack any definite contours" (1993: 19). But this confusion and lack of clarity can be overstated. In fact, much effort has now been expended in delineating

---

[*] Lindsay Paterson is Professor of Educational Policy at the University of Edinburgh. Richard Wyn Jones is Lecturer in the Department of International Politics at the University of Wales, Aberystwyth.

and clarifying the contours of the concept. The resulting literature offers a rich account of the different, and often competing, understandings of civil society which exist at both the everyday and more self-consciously theoretical levels (see Hall 1995; Keane 1988; by far the most comprehensive discussion is in Cohen and Arato 1992).

This section seeks to draw from this literature in order to highlight some of the accounts of civil society that seem to be particularly relevant for understanding the politics of home rule in Wales and Scotland. The chapter then discusses recent developments in Wales and Scotland in the light of these theories. The second section deals with the very different histories of civil society in the two countries. Then, in the third section, we deal with the reactions of civil society to the governments of Thatcher and Major and to the proposals for home rule which were tabled by the Labour government in 1997. The fourth section uses survey data to investigate the meaning which people in Wales and Scotland attach to national identity: have the different political, cultural and civic histories of the two countries produced different understandings of identity? Then the fifth section uses survey data to examine the 1997 referendums; the question is, again, whether the different histories yielded different levels of knowledge and different relationships between identity and politics.

The concept of civil society was given its first influential formulation in Hegel's *Philosophy of Right* (1942), although drawing on eighteenth-century ideas from, among others, Adam Ferguson. He posited the *bürgerliche Gesellschaft* (bourgeois or civil society) as a characteristic feature of modernity. This was a sphere distinct from the state but including what might be termed economic society, that is the various institutions and practices of production and exchange, as well as the institutions and practices of cultural production and reproduction. Among its key institutional elements were professional associations. Hegel argued that the role of the state was to bring order to this realm of competing private interests - to bring a unity and harmony to civil society that it was not capable of either attaining or maintaining of its own volition. According to this conceptualisation, therefore, although civil society was certainly influenced by the political realm - that is, on this understanding, the state - and indeed depended on it for its continued functioning, it was not itself political.

A more recent, and equally influential, interpretation of civil society has developed from the work of the Sardinian Marxist Antonio Gramsci (1971). This posits civil society as including all those institutions in the cultural sphere in which public opinion is formed and through which ideas and values become sedimented, including, *inter alia*, the education system, the media, voluntary bodies and social movements of all kinds. According to this conceptualisation, civil society is distinct from both the state **and** the market. However, this is not to say that civil society is somehow non-political: far from it. According to this view, it is in civil society that the ideational basis that allows for the functioning of both political and economic society is created and recreated. Ultimately, it is in and through the institutions of civil society that a particular order is legitimated or becomes de-legitimated: it is in civil society that the struggle for hegemony takes place.

The latter Gramscian reading of civil society incorporates the former Hegelian version within itself. From the Gramscian perspective, the suggestion that civil society is inherently stolid, staid and non-political depends on a series of separations between public and private and between politics and economics that are themselves **intensely** political. Indeed those assumptions about the political passivity of civil society and its dependency on the state have served to legitimate a particular political order. In contrast, far from viewing civil society as inevitably conservative, proponents of the Gramscian understanding of civil society have argued that it can (potentially) form the locus for the generation of new, more inclusive and participative structures of democratic governance. For although the relative autonomy of civil society has been increasingly undermined by the incursions of both market relations and the state, it nonetheless remains the sphere in which more normative concerns are articulated (in comparison to the more instrumental considerations that predominate in political and economic society). Moreover its real, if indirect, political influence means that the normative concerns of civil society can transform the institutions of society as a whole.

Civil society in Wales and Scotland

Wales

"For Wales, see England" - so read the now notorious entry in the 1888 edition of *Encyclopaedia Britannica*[1] which has acted as goad to subsequent generations of nationalists in Wales. But the fact remains that even if reducing Wales to England is grotesquely misleading, little in Welsh history can be understood without reference to the relationship with the English neighbour. For it is this relationship - often complex and uneasy, always unequal - which has provided the context in which the institutions of Welsh society have developed.

English domination over Wales was a fact long before the final conquest by Edward I's forces in 1282. In the ninth century native rulers paid homage at the English court (Jenkins 1970). Equally significant perhaps, despite long and embittered resistance, by the middle of the twelfth century the Welsh church had been induced to submit to the jurisdiction of the primate of England at Canterbury (Williams 1997). The subjugation of Wales was no doubt aided by the fact that, despite a common language, common customs, and a common legal system, the country was "politically fragmented and dynastically divided" (Davies 1984: 55). Attempts by thirteenth-century native rulers Llywelyn ap Iorweth and Llywelyn ap Gruffudd to build a unitary feudal Wales, independent from English rule, all floundered in the face of a combination of the centrifugal forces in Welsh society and the increasingly centralised power of the English monarchy.

With the 1284 Statute of Rhuddlan, Edward I formalised English control over Wales through what one authority has described as "the first colonial constitution" (Cam 1962). The hybrid system of governance established by the statute was to last until the Acts of Union of 1536 and 1543. It was based on a division of political and indeed legal authority between the Principality, namely those areas in the north and west forfeited to the crown following the slaying of Llywelyn ap Gruffudd, and the Marches in the south and east where power and authority was divided between feuding lordships. This already complex pattern was overlaid by a distinction between conqueror and conquered, native and settler, which also remained basic to the governance of the country (Davies 1989). So while Welsh customs and practices, including the Welsh legal system, persisted, they did so in a weakened, discriminated-against form. It was the general discrimination against the native population that eventually fuelled the great rebellion of Owain Glyndŵr from 1400 to 1409, the aims of which included not only the establishment of an independent state, but also the re-establishment of the autonomy of the Welsh church and the foundation of independent university institutions in Wales (Davies 1995).

The failure of Glyndŵr's revolt had the effect of hastening a process that had already been underway for some time whereby the social elite in Welsh society became increasingly integrated into the English state. This process was given further impetus following the ascension of the Tudors (a family with its origins in Wales) to the English throne after a campaign in which the Welsh had played a prominent part. Indeed, in Wales the rise of the Tudors was widely seen as representing the moment in which the Welsh regained mastery of *Prydain* (Britain) -

their historic birthright. However, as the historian Glanmor Williams points out:

> Fidelity to the Tudors sprang not only out of sentiment but also as a result of the gains accruing from a growing participation in a whole complex of institutions that, beside the sovereign and the dynasty, included common law and Parliament, the courts of justice great and small, and the whole apparatus of local government and administration (1997: 399).

Thus when Henry VIII implemented the Acts of Union, their main significance was not perceived as lying in the fact that they attempted to annex and assimilate Wales to England, even though that was indubitably the case. Rather they were largely welcomed on the basis that, as they swept away the remnants of Welsh laws and customs, they also extended the same formal status to the King's Welsh subjects as that granted to the English, thus allowing the more powerful among the former to involve themselves in the affairs of state and society on equal terms.

As we saw in the introduction to this chapter, civil society is a feature of modernity: it is only with modernity that social institutions can (potentially at least) develop the complexity and relative autonomy that we associate with civil society. Establishing a universally accepted chronology for the emergence of modernity in Wales has proven to be an elusive goal. Nonetheless, if we trace the emergence of the modern state in these islands to the Tudor period - a not unreasonable assumption - then it is clear that, even before this time, Wales had long been extensively integrated into the English (and then the British) state. In the Tudor period itself, integration was completed and formalised through the Acts of Union. As a result, and, as we shall see, in contrast to the situation in Scotland, civil society in Wales developed within a British context with no significant administative structures or institutions surviving from a pre-conquest or pre-'union' era. Therefore, as civil society developed in Wales, its 'Welshness' - the extent to which the prefix Welsh could be meaningfully attached to the institutions and practices of civil society - has remained a matter of doubt.

In the initial post-union period, structures of governance and authority, including those of the church, were dominated by a small elite which clearly favoured the greatest possible degree of assimilation with England. However they presided over a deeply divided society with a central cleavage over-determined not only by differences in political and economic power, but also in language and culture, and subsequently (especially after 1811) in religion.[2] This was essentially to remain the case well into the nineteenth century, for Wales's overwhelmingly rural and relatively backward economy did not allow the development of a relatively autonomous, urbanised middle strata - the foundation of Hegel's *bürgerliche Gesellschaft* - which could successfully challenge the power of the gentry (Jenkins 1993).

During the nineteenth century, however, rapid and far-reaching economic developments and accompanying social transformations, coupled to the slow extension of the franchise, brought about fundamental shifts in the balance of power in Welsh society. In particular the election of Henry Richard as MP for Merthyr in 1868 announced the growing political power of the radical and nonconformist middle class - or at least the male portion of it. The concerns of the newly empowered middle class became important political issues, including in particular the disestablishment of the Church in Wales, finally agreed in 1914. Moreover, civil society institutions and organisations began to proliferate with the creation of myriad bodies including the long-cherished University of Wales in 1893. Attempts were even made by the short-lived Cymru Fydd movement to place home rule on the political agenda (Morgan 1981; Morgan 1998).

In retrospect, the activism of the Welsh nationalists in the last decades of the nineteenth century (for this is how many of the leading Welsh Liberal politicians of the day styled themselves) seems to have established a pattern which has been followed by successive generations of nationalists whatever their party affiliations. Setting aside the many important differences between them in terms of emphasis or, indeed, in terms of their desired end-goal, we can say that Welsh nationalists have pursued an essentially two-pronged strategy aimed at:

- securing political recognition and expression of Welsh difference and distinctiveness, for example through the structures of the Westminster parliament or through some measure of home rule;

- ensuring recognition and expression of Welsh difference and distinctiveness among the institutions of civil society – whether through the establishment of new bodies such as the University or the National Library (established in 1907), the reform of actually existing institutions such as the Trades Union Congress (which established the Wales TUC in 1974), or, on occasion, the establishment of parallel Welsh civil society organisations such as the Farmers Union of Wales (in 1955) or the women's movement Merched y Wawr (in 1966).

However nationalists - with nationalism understood in these broad terms - have always faced powerful countervailing assimilationist trends; indeed forces so powerful that at various times they have seemed to many to be unstoppable (for example Williams 1991: 296-305). In the twentieth century these have included, *inter alia*: rapid anglicisation and secularisation, with both processes seeming to undermine apparently central elements of Welsh identity; very significant flows of population both into and out of Wales in response to the rise and fall of the Welsh economy and to wider changes in UK society; the growing role of the state in almost every facet of social life; and a very powerful unionist ideology centred on the Labour movement. Nonetheless, a recognisable Welsh civil society has gradually emerged. At least part of the explanation for this seems to lie in the fact that institutionalisation has developed a momentum of its own, with the establishment of the Welsh Office (1964) being crucial. For as the administration of government in Wales has become increasingly devolved in areas such as health, education, planning and economic development, those bodies and social organisations affected by the activities of government have had increasingly to operate in a Welsh context.

Even after the 1979 referendum and the advent of Thatcherism, the trend towards administrative devolution continued with so-called quangos, such as the Welsh Development Agency, the Cardiff Bay Development Corporation and the Countryside Council for Wales playing an increasingly prominent role in the governance of Wales. It was the Conservatives' determination to ensure that this system of devolved administration remained firmly under their control that eventually led to renewed demands for political devolution in the 1990s. The Conservatives' practice of using non-elected place-men (sic) to run the quangos proved highly controversial in traditionally anti-Conservative Wales (Osmond 1995). Indeed, one of the arguments most favoured by supporters of devolution in the run-up to the 1997 referendum was that an assembly would ensure that the much-reviled quangos would be made democratically accountable. Ironically therefore, through their own actions, Conservatives appear to have eroded the legitimacy of the very constitutional *status quo* to which they were so attached.

The establishment of the assembly will surely serve as a catalyst for the further development of Welsh civil society. This however will be no simple task. Compared to Scotland at least, administrative devolution has been relatively limited: there is no separate Welsh legal system for example. As a result Wales has lacked many of the strong professional organisations central to Hegel's conception of civil society. Moreover, other important elements of Welsh civil society are weak. For example, only 13% of the daily newspapers read in Wales are Wales-based, while up to a third of television viewers receive their signal from English transmitters and therefore cannot watch Wales-focused news and current affairs programmes (Wyn Jones and Lewis 1999). Welsh civil society remains a fragile plant.

Scotland

The starting point for understanding the role of civil society in Scotland is the Union of 1707 between the Scottish and English parliaments (Fry 1987; Harvie 1994; Lenman 1981; Lynch 1991; McCrone 1992; Paterson 1994; Scott 1979; Whatley 1994). Before that, Scotland - unlike Wales - had been a fully independent state since the early fourteenth century[3] and had been in voluntary dynastic union with England since 1603. During the period of its independence, Scotland had had a weak central state and fairly strong regional political systems (Grant 1984; Wormald 1981). This strength of localities against the centre was reinforced by the effects of the sixteenth-century reformation, which took a much more extreme form in Scotland than in England (Marshall 1992; Wormald 1981). Thereafter, the local presbytery was the fount of moral, political and cultural authority, laying the basis for the emergence of a truly modern civil society in the eighteenth and nineteenth centuries.

   In the context of this strong local society and relatively weak central state, the key point about the 1707 Union was that it was partial. It did not interfere with any of the civic pillars of Scottish independence. It secured the continuing separateness of Scots law and the Scottish legal system, it guaranteed the autonomy of the education system and of local government, and - above all - it safeguarded the dominant Presbyterian church. These institutions mattered more to Scots than the parliament which was lost: unlike in England, the parliament had never been central to national life, and, in particular, the general assembly of the church was a much more significant source of legislation than the parliament. That was ultimately because parliament was believed to be mainly about foreign affairs, not about domestic social policy.

   The general principles of this odd constitutional arrangement then remained remarkably unscathed for about two centuries. For most of the eighteenth century, social life locally was overseen by the church, by local government (elected on a very limited franchise) and by the sheriff, the local judge who also co-ordinated networks of *ad hoc* committees overseeing social life. Although this system was reformed in the nineteenth century, the changes merely reinforced tendencies that were already present (Fry 1987; Checkland and Checkland 1984; Harvie 1994; Hutchison 1986; Paterson 1994). Local government was renovated in 1832, significantly widening the franchise and extending its responsibilities. Other local agencies emerged alongside it, usually - as in the previous century - led by the sheriff. By the end of the century, there were boards to oversee such matters as the poor law, education, public health, prisons, agriculture and the development of the Highlands and Islands. That they were needed was largely because of the decline in influence of the church, especially after it split disastrously in 1843.[4] An ethic of public service could grow up in this soil while remaining distrustful of the state: Scottish politics largely consisted of voluntary activity sponsored by local institutions (Checkland 1980). This was Hegel's professional society at its most autonomous and triumphant.

Aspects of that had changed profoundly by the middle of the twentieth century, but developments in the 1930s were no more straightforward than those a century earlier. The main point is that there developed a separate Scottish agency of the central state, the Scottish Office, which, from humble beginnings in 1885, grew to be responsible for implementing most social policy by the 1970s. It had or acquired ultimate charge of education, health, social work, housing, economic development, the environment, agriculture, fishing, law, sport, and the arts. The main omission from its responsibilities was the large area of social security. Around that hub there developed a network of consultation, agencies, local government and pressure groups. These were not just the meek instruments of directives from London; in significant respects, they helped to make policy (Paterson 1998a).

Even in this era of growing state power, moreover, there remained scope for local autonomy. Elected local government itself still had significant powers over education, social work, the environment, housing, local transport, and local planning. The Scottish Office - like government departments in many states - could not manage everything itself, and so ceded real powers to various committees overseeing, for example, the health service or economic development. Although appointed by government, these committees were regarded by government as enjoying real autonomy so far as operational matters were concerned. Around these committees - and frequently providing members of them and staff for them - were pressure groups, professional associations, and trade unions, each pulling the official committees into civil society and away from the state. It is because of these roots in Scottish civic life that quangos have not generated nearly so much hostility in Scotland as in Wales.

Unifying the whole structure, moreover, was the system of Scots law, still independent so far as its institutional structures were concerned (Thomson 1995). Until the 1960s, moral coherence came also from the still strong culture of Presbyterian Protestantism (a culture which grew in strength despite institutional schisms) (Brown 1987). These institutions and the government agencies' leadership of Scottish opinion was helped by the continuing distinctiveness of the Scottish media: newspapers read in Scotland are overwhelmingly Scottish, and the Scottish parts of the new broadcast media - catering for almost the whole country - gradually acquired greater Scottish distinctiveness and greater cultural self-confidence (MacInnes 1992, 1993).

Civil society mobilisation in Scotland and Wales

Scotland

The first signs of popular unease about the Scottish governing system came in the 1960s, as the Scottish National Party started to attract a significant share of the vote (Brown *et al* 1998; Fry 1987; Harvie 1994; Paterson 1994). The SNP favoured outright independence, but the other three main parties - Labour, Conservative, and Liberal - responded by proposing various schemes for an elected assembly with limited powers. The weak Labour government of 1974-79 eventually managed to get one such proposal onto the statute book, but it was endorsed only narrowly in a referendum held in 1979, and was never implemented. Although numerous factors were responsible for the reluctance of the electorate to support the assembly more enthusiastically - including the limited nature of its powers, the unpopularity of the government which proposed it, and the still minority appeal of the SNP's proposals for independence - the underlying explanation is probably that most people hoped that the old system of partial and local autonomy could still work.

The problem for that majority, and for the constitution, was that the old ways turned out not to be available after all. Margaret Thatcher's government came to power in 1979 with a hostility to civil society that was unprecedented in modern British Conservatism. Following several tenets of New Right thinking, she regarded it as a conspiracy by professionals against lay people, as restricting the market freedoms without which no other freedom could be secure, and as a repository of the corporatism which had prevented both Labour and Conservative governments from modernising the British economy. So, throughout Britain, she abolished many of the most overtly corporatist of the public bodies (for example, those which grouped trade unionists, employers and government), she appointed increasing numbers of her own ideological supporters to the many committees which remained, and she eroded the autonomy of local government, the universities, and other previously partly independent public institutions.

None of this was deliberately anti-Scottish. It only appeared so in Scotland because Scotland - especially the Scottish middle class - remained quite attached to corporatism, civil society, and institutional impediments to state power. It had these predilections because of the nearly three centuries in which Scottish autonomy had depended on such institutional arrangements.

Scottish civil society in the early 1990s had thus come to inherit a putative national tradition of Scottish government. It embodied those currents of British social democracy which had been dominant in the twentieth century, but which could be traced also in the presbyterian philanthropy of the nineteenth century. It inherited the autonomy of the social networks of the welfare state, the autonomy of the boards and the local government which ruled Scotland domestically at the height of nineteenth-century industrialism, and the autonomy of the local parish which was the Union's immediate legacy. The expectations of local autonomy - however tenuously based on any constitutional theory - had come to be regarded as rights, and, in popular views, the Scottish civic institutions were held to constitute national identity (Cohen 1996; Hearn 1998; McCrone 1992), a sense of popular sovereignty which was believed to be older and more legitimate than the sovereignty of the parliament at Westminster (Mitchell 1996; Paterson 1998b).

The reaction of Scottish civil society to Thatcherism took disparate forms (Brown *et al* 1998). They lobbied against particular policies, they sought to resurrect corporatist ideas, they used the Scottish Office itself as a way of putting discreet pressure on the government internally, and, in a few notable instances such as the poll tax, they opposed government policy outright. In due course, the unsatisfactory compromises forced by this fragmented opposition brought together most parts of civil society to devise a scheme for an elected Scottish parliament that might prove to be more acceptable than the one which failed to be clearly endorsed in 1979. The vehicle between 1989 and 1996 was the Scottish Constitutional Convention, grouping the Labour Party and the Liberal Democrats, and representatives of numerous bodies in civil society such as local government, trade unions, churches, women's organisations, and organisations representing minority ethnic groups.

The Convention was a curious combination of rhetoric about a renewal of democracy with a continuation of the semi-secretive world of the committees and boards that had run the Scottish welfare state. There was some reality to the claims that the Convention represented a broad spectrum of Scottish society. It did, after all, contain 59 of the 72 MPs, and did embrace a much wider range of civil society groups than the Conservative government could claim to speak for. But it was also socially narrow and very traditional in its composition and style, reflecting the male-dominated and middle-class nature of Scottish civic society in general.

This dual character of the Convention - radical as well as conservative - was hardly surprising, because it was drawing on the various strands that had led to the questioning of Scotland's current constitutional position - a leftist critique of the Scottish Office bureaucracy, a popular frustration with a decade of radical Conservative rule in the face of overwhelming Scottish opposition, and the frustration among Scotland's political elite that the Conservative government had excluded it from power for so long. A civic society was bound to be more ideologically confused than a merely civil society in Hegel's sense, but also more truly representative of the nation. Gramsci would have recognised the ideological tensions which the confusion caused.

The proposals which it produced reflected this ambivalence. They were radical on matters such as the use of proportional representation in the electoral system, the need to increase the participation of women in elected politics, the importance of an open and scrutinising committee system, and the desirability of entrenching the powers of local government.

The critics of the Convention process argued that these radical strands were outweighed by the caution of entrenched interests. The Convention did not propose to reduce the number of Scottish MPs at Westminster (although the 1997 Labour government eventually did - see the Introduction to this volume). It did not propose to abolish the post of the secretary of state for Scotland. Most controversially of all, it did not propose to change fundamentally the way in which Scottish public expenditure is financed. The controversy arises because Scotland receives more than its population share of identifiable public expenditure in the UK.

Nonetheless, the key point is that this coalition won overwhelmingly. It persuaded the Labour government to adopt its proposals almost unamended in July 1997, and then persuaded a clear majority of the electorate to endorse them in the referendum. The slow process of manoeuvre and adjustment which the Convention encouraged had the effect of gradually aligning popular views with the views of civil society (Paterson 1998c). From being an impediment to constitutional change as it had been until the 1970s, civic Scotland had become its midwife. Civil society continues to influence the shape of the parliament through the Consultative Steering Group that is setting out its standing orders and operating practices.

Wales

Although civil society in Wales has become increasingly Welsh in terms of its outlook and frame of reference, its direct political role has hitherto been very limited. Indeed, Welsh civil society seems to have been deliberately excluded from almost all of the important discussions in the late 1980s and 1990s on the form that political devolution might take (Wyn Jones and Lewis 1998). It was only in the immediate run-up to the 1997 referendum that any attempt was made to establish broad-based legitimacy for Labour's devolution proposals; and it is only since the referendum that any serious attempts have been made to involve civil society organisations in discussions concerning the operation of the National Assembly.

Part of the explanation for this lack of civil society mobilisation before 1997 lies in the relative weakness of Welsh civil society. Moreover, as appears to be the case in England, but unlike the situation in Scotland and Northern Ireland, no significant actors in Welsh politics seem to have been aware of the (potential) importance of civil society in promoting and legitimising social and political transformation.[5] That said, the narrowness of the devolution debate in Wales - indeed, the almost total lack of any public discussion of the issue until the summer of 1997 - was also a reflection of the Labour Party's hegemonic domination of the Welsh political landscape, and the proven ability of devolution to create deep divisions within the party's ranks in Wales.

Labour has enjoyed a dominant position in Wales since the 1920s. In the intervening period this dominance has remained unassailed; indeed, apart from a period in the immediate aftermath of the Camarthen by-election in 1966 when it briefly appeared that Plaid Cymru might finally be on the verge of its much vaunted 'break-through', Labour's position in its Valleys heartland has remained essentially unchallenged. Even in the dark days of the early 1930s and early 1980s, Wales remained doggedly loyal to Labour. The durability of this hegemony has been built on the party's ability to construct and hold together a coalition of different interests in Wales. In relation to the 'national question', this coalition has extended from those who view themselves in self-conscious terms as the inheritors of the nineteenth-century Welsh radical tradition, to self-styled 'internationalists' who often seem to have regarded the survival of any element of Welsh distinctiveness beyond the very banal as a hindrance to the establishment of the (British) socialist commonwealth. It was these latent tensions within the Wales Labour Party between the 'Red Dragon and the Red Flag' (Morgan 1995) which erupted into prolonged, embittered and very public conflict when the Callaghan government tried to force devolution onto the statute books in the late 1970s (Foulkes *et al* 1983).

This domination coupled with the deep scars left by the 1979 experience - of major internal dissent, and, of course, overwhelming voter hostility - shaped the way in which the Labour Party, and indeed other organisations and political parties, handled devolution on its return onto the political agenda in the late 1980s (Wyn Jones and Lewis 1998, 1999). For *all* concerned, Labour's internal politics were the main focus of attention: affecting them was the main aim. Thus when proposals for a Welsh Constitutional Convention were briefly floated in 1992 by the Wales TUC following prompting by the Campaign for a Welsh Assembly, their only real purpose was to bring pressure to bear on the Labour Party. As a result, when the proposition had the desired effect of forcing the party to take devolution more seriously by establishing its own consultation exercise to head off pressure for a broader forum, the idea of a convention was allowed to die an unremarked death (Wyn Jones and Lewis 1998). Although the rhetoric of civil society was deployed in Wales, this was done in an essentially instrumental manner simply as a way of influencing Labour. Few if any seem to have been aware at that time that civil society-focused initiatives might also be important in their own right.

Given Labour's domination of Welsh politics, and given also that it was the only party that might realistically be expected to deliver devolution, the focus on its internal debates was entirely rational. If devolution was part of that party's platform, then a Labour general election victory would do the rest - or so ran the logic. Broader civil society mobilisation was not only unnecessary but risky given the proven divisiveness of devolution and the likelihood that broader public discussion would highlight the splits within Labour and push the party onto the defensive. However, Tony Blair's unexpected decision to announce that a Labour government would hold a pre-legislative referendum on its devolution proposals radically altered the context of devolutionary politics in Wales. From then on, mobilising opinion beyond the very small numbers involved in Labour's policy-making process would become essential rather an optional extra.

After Labour's general election victory on 1 May 1997, the devolution debate in Wales broadened out considerably (in Wales as elsewhere, Blair's aim of keeping devolution off the political agenda in the run-up to the election by announcing a post-election referendum was largely successful). Under the watchword of 'inclusivity' the then Welsh secretary Ron Davies led serious and sustained efforts to consult and co-operate with other interested parties (see also Ron Davies's Preface to this volume). In the run-up to the referendum this involved the establishment of a close if informal alliance with other pro-devolution political parties, and in particular with Plaid Cymru. Since 18 September 1998, civil society organisations have been involved in the debate over the shape of the National Assembly through the work of the National Assembly Advisory Group (1998).

However, what is important to note is that the undoubtedly genuine attempt to involve civil society organisations as partners in the devolution process is happening only at the instigation of the government and is of very recent origin. There are as yet very few signs of autonomous initiatives from civil society itself. In this sense, devolution in Wales may be best understood as part of a process of creating and animating Welsh civil society (Osmond 1998). So while Welsh civil society was not the precursor of devolution, it may yet be among its progeny.

The meaning of national identity in Wales and Scotland

Wales

Given the comparative paucity of survey data relating to Wales, it is difficult to make cross-time generalisations concerning the (changing?) nature of Welsh identity. It is unclear, for example, what effect the growing institutionalisation of Welsh identity since the late nineteenth century, already alluded to in this chapter, has had on the ways in which people in Wales conceive (consciously or unconsciously) of their national identity. We can however posit that such a process will eventually lead to a form of identity that places more stress on civic characteristics in addition to - or in place of - ethnic markers (see also the chapter by Paula Surridge and David McCrone in this volume and

McCrone 1998). That is, places and institutions (and the values they embody) will increasingly become the foci of national sentiment rather than simply ancestry and place of birth.

Despite the limitations of the data, evidence from the Welsh Referendum Study suggests that Welsh identity does contain civic as well as ethnic characteristics. (Details of the Scottish and Welsh Referendum Studies are given in the Introduction and Technical Appendix to this volume.) Civic ideas would be most closely associated with defining identity in terms of residence, ethnic with defining it in terms of descent. As table 8.1 illustrates, living in Wales and being born of Welsh ancestors are perceived as being similarly important elements of Welsh identity, even if place of birth is still regarded as the most important marker. It would be unwise in this context to read too much into the fact that only 43% of respondents regard the ability to speak Welsh as being very important or fairly important to Welsh identity given that the language can be interpreted as both an ethnic and civic marker - the latter in the sense that the revival of Welsh in recent years has been a paradigmatic example of civic activism whereby non-Welsh speakers have consciously embraced the language for themselves or their children.

Table 8.1
Attitudes to definitions of Welsh identity

	Whole sample	Born in Wales	Born in England	Born elsewhere
% saying very or fairly important to being truly Welsh				
to have Welsh parents or grandparents	66	68	58	60
to have been born in Wales	80	85	66	76
to be living in Wales	68	71	60	63
to speak Welsh	43	45	42	35
N	*686*	*457*	*145*	*29*

The survey also provides some evidence that those who support devolution have a more civic sense of Welsh identity than those who were opposed, with 74% of 'yes' voters citing living in Wales as very important or fairly important to Welsh identity compared to 59% of those who voted 'no'. This is perhaps not surprising given that the establishment of an assembly is a further expression of civic nationhood.

Without doubt, the crucial complicating factor in terms of understanding the dynamics of national identity in Wales is that a significant proportion of the population are incomers who have migrated to Wales, many from England (according to the 1991 census 23% of the population were born outside Wales, 19% in England (*Census Report for Wales* 1993)). How this group's members understand Welsh identity may well have implications for their propensity to adopt (or reject) that identity. In particular, if they have an exclusively ethnic understanding of Welshness then they will be precluded (by definition as it were) from sharing in it. Table 8.1 suggests that while those born in England also combine ethnic and civic elements in their understanding of Welsh identity, there is no evidence to suggest that they give the civic element (living in Wales) greater weight than do those respondents born in Wales.

More generally, it is important to note that overlapping senses of national identity are prevalent in Wales. For example, the Welsh Referendum Study asked people to place themselves on a scale ranging from Welsh not British to British not Welsh and found that while 17% identified themselves as having an exclusively Welsh identity and 12% exclusively British, fully 68% adopted a form of identity categorisation containing elements of both. That said, national identity did have a significant effect on attitudes towards devolution, with those towards the more exclusively Welsh end of the spectrum being more favourably disposed to the government's proposals (see the chapters by Richard Wyn Jones and Dafydd Trystan, and by John Curtice, in this volume). Given this fact as well as the relatively large proportion of incomers in the Welsh population, the interaction between the political devolution and the evolution of Welsh identity is of particular interest. Will the assembly, and a stronger Welsh civil society, foster a sense of national identity which will be embraced by all those living in Wales whatever their origins? That is clearly what its champions hope will occur. But nor is it beyond the bounds of possibility that the increasing divergence between Wales and England that is sure to follow from devolution may generate a sense of alienation between incomers and the National Assembly for Wales.

Scotland

The debate leading up to the referendum on a Scottish parliament in September 1997 inevitably raised many issues about the definition of national identity, and people opposed to or sceptical about the Labour government's scheme claimed that any element of democratic self-government could exacerbate ethnic particularism (for example, Lang 1994; Lloyd 1997). This debate was accompanied by a strengthening sense of Scottishness. For example, both the Scottish Election Survey (fieldwork mainly in May and June 1997) and the Scottish Referendum Study (fieldwork in September and October) asked people how they rated their Scottishness compared to their Britishness, on a scale from Scottish not British to British not Scottish. In the earlier survey, 23% said they were Scottish not British; in the later one, the proportion had risen to 32%. This raised the sense of exclusive Scottishness to levels it had not reached since Thatcher was in power: in July 1986, for example, the proportion was 39% (Brown *et al* 1998: 209).

On the other hand, as shown in the chapter by Paula Surridge and David McCrone in this volume, there was much evidence that ethnic or exclusive definitions of identity did not play an important part in the referendum vote in Scotland. More specifically, table 8.2 shows attitudes to the definition or source of identity. As in Wales, respondents were asked how important to Scottish identity was having Scottish parents or grandparents, being born in Scotland, and living in Scotland. Table 8.2 shows the percentages saying that these features were very or fairly important. There are two points to note. The first is that - again as in Wales - there is clearly majority agreement that all these features are important: respondents do not draw a rigid distinction between civic and ethnic ideas. The second point is the rise in the proportion endorsing a civic definition, from 67% to 78%. This general rise was in fact the same among people who expressed an exclusively Scottish identity (72% to 83%), and was greater among those who intended to vote in favour of a parliament (from 71% to 84% among those intending to vote 'yes' on the first referendum question, and from 73% to 85% among those intending to vote 'yes' on the second). Moreover, the civic definition was most popular among Labour and SNP supporters (respectively 82% and 84% in the Referendum Study), quite important among Liberal Democrats (73%), and somewhat weaker although still strong among Conservatives (63%). That Conservative proportion had risen from a much lower 48% in the earlier Scottish Election Study. (Details of the Scottish Election Study are given in the Introduction to this volume.)

This evidence from the survey data suggests that a civic identity was intensified during the referendum campaign, and that it was more popular among people intending to vote 'yes' or supporting the home rule parties than among opponents or Conservatives. Respondents found no difficulty in combining a civic view of identity with voting in favour of a Scottish parliament, or with holding an exclusive sense of

Scottish identity, or with also believing that birth and descent matter to identity too.

Table 8.2
Attitudes to definitions of Scottish identity

% saying very or fairly important to being truly Scottish	1997 Scottish Election Study	1997 Scottish Referendum Study
... to have Scottish parents or ... grandparents	76	73
... to have been born in Scotland	84	85
... to be living in Scotland	67	78
N	*851*	*676*

The only qualification to this conclusion from the Referendum Study concerns the views of the small group of residents in Scotland who were born in England (a much smaller proportion than in Wales, at about 7%). They did not share the apparent majority view that supporting a Scottish parliament was quite consistent with a civic notion of identity. Only 43% of them voted 'yes' on the first referendum question, and 30% on the second (out of 30 such respondents who voted). So, if there was a perception that the referendum vote was mainly about ethnicity, this lay with English incomers more than with any other group.[6]

So the main conclusion from this analysis is how similar are attitudes to national identity in Wales and Scotland. Despite the differences in history, people in both countries were open to a broadly civic view of identity, and tended to combine that mainly with a dual identity that, on the whole, gave greater prominence to the Scottish or Welsh component than to the British one.

The referendum votes

Scotland

The consequence of the Constitutional Convention process was to confirm home rule as the 'common sense' of Scotland, the 'settled will of the Scottish people' (a phrase of the late Labour leader John Smith which became the common parlance as soon as the referendum result was declared). Compared to the 1970s, Labour in Scotland was almost unanimously in favour (or at least not actively opposed, the only notable exception being Tam Dalyell MP), local government expressed no opposition in public, and other key conservative institutions had either grown to be enthusiastically in favour (for example the main churches) or diplomatically kept quiet (for example, the university leaderships (Paterson 1998d) and - most significantly - most private business (Brown *et al* 1998)).

The electorate's access to information was aided by the media, which had, if anything, become more distinctively Scottish in the 1990s than earlier. (For example, *The Sun* in Scotland became aggressively Scottish from 1991, in a circulation battle with the most popular daily, *The Daily Record*.) Even right-wing papers supported 'yes' votes editorially in the 1997 referendum (for example, *The Daily Express* and *The Scotsman*). Indeed, the only paper with significant Scottish circulation which advocated 'no' votes was *The Daily Mail*. This almost complete agreement was in stark contrast to the position in the 1979 referendum (Bochel *et al* 1981).

Table 8.3
Referendum vote by broad preference for the government of Scotland

% 'Yes' vote	Scottish parliament	Tax powers	N
Independence outwith EU	96	84	*43*
Independence in EU	97	86	*137*
Home rule with tax powers	92	87	*172*
Home rule without tax powers	75	19	*39*
No elected body	4	2	*97*

Note: excludes those who did not vote in the referendum

The stability of opinion on home rule which this civic leadership reflected and nurtured was evident in the consistent levels of support for a parliament in surveys and polls conducted regularly throughout the 1980s and 1990s (Brown *et al* 1998: 160). The success of the 'yes' campaigners in the referendum can be interpreted in one sense as their capacity to mobilise almost all of that general and long-standing support, despite claims by opponents that the polls were not reflecting any considered opinions. For example, in the Referendum Study, as well as specific questions about the referendum, respondents were also asked a question about preferences for Scottish government which has become standard in Scottish polls and surveys. Table 8.3 shows that the referendum votes map quite consistently onto the responses to the standard question. In the light of this, it is not suprising that nearly half of voters said they were unaffected by the campaign in August and September 1997 (45% saying that they had made up their minds before this), and that only 17% said they made up their minds in the final week before the vote on 11 September.

Table 8.4
Knowledge of proposals for Welsh assembly/Scottish parliament

	% correct answer	
	Wales	**Scotland**
The assembly/parliament will be elected by a system of proportional representation	56	67
The assembly/parliament will *not* be able to change the basic rate of income tax in Wales/Scotland	65	66
People will need passports to travel between Wales/Scotland and England	93	94
The current plan is eventually to reduce the number of MPs from Wales/Scotland at the parliament in London	40	58
The assembly/parliament will have the power to introduce the death penalty in Wales/Scotland	81	23
The assembly/parliament will control the way in which the Scottish/Welsh Office's budget is spent	82	85
The UK government, not the assembly/parliament, will make all decisions about defence	72	76
N	*686*	*676*

Note: The preamble to these questions read out by the interviewer was: Now a quick quiz about the government's proposals for a Scottish parliament/Welsh assembly. For each thing I say, please tell me if you think it is true or false. If you don't know, just say so and we'll skip to the next one. Remember - true, false or don't know.

There were quite high levels of knowledge about the proposals for the Welsh assembly and Scottish parliament (tables 8.4 and 8.5). In Scotland, only on the issue of the death penalty was there widespread ignorance (an assumption perhaps that, because the parliament would not have the power to legislate on abortion, it could not have the power to introduce capital punishment). There was almost no difference in the levels of knowledge between 'yes' voters and 'no' voters. People who abstained were not so knowledgeable, but even they were quite well-informed. For example, the proportions getting five or more of the items in table 8.4 correct were 64% among people who voted 'yes' on the first referendum question, 65% among those who voted 'no', and 50% among those who did not vote.

Table 8.5
Knowledge of proposals for Welsh assembly/Scottish parliament - summary

	% getting at least this number correct	
Number correct	Wales	Scotland
0	100	100
1	97	100
2	94	98
3	90	93
4	80	82
5	67	61
6	46	31
7	16	6
N	*686*	*676*

Further analysis of the Referendum and Election Surveys has shown, moreover, that people had well-developed expectations of the parliament, and that these were the strongest influences on their vote (Brown *et al* 1999, chapter 6). That, too, suggests that people had quite a lot of faith in the capacity of the civic élites to use the new institutions wisely. It is probably in part because of these high expectations that 72% of respondents said that they cared a lot about the outcome, not far short of the proportion who had cared about the result of the general election (83% among Referendum Study respondents) (see also the chapter by Anthony Heath and Bridget Taylor in this volume). The proportion was similar among 'yes' and 'no' voters, but much lower among those who abstained (46%).

Wales

In contrast to the position in 1979 when one view of the desirable constitutional order was clearly dominant, namely that Wales was best served by the *status quo*, by 1997 the situation had changed dramatically. The previously overwhelming consensus in favour of direct rule from Westminster - with perhaps an admixture of administrative devolution - had broken down. However it had not been replaced by any consensus as to what other governmental structure might be preferable. Rather the referendum result revealed a divided population: half of the electorate either apathetic, or confused, or both, and not registering any preference; the other half almost equally divided between opponents and supporters of the government's devolution proposals (see also the chapter by Richard Wyn Jones and Dafydd Trystan in this volume). This state of affairs can be explained in terms of Gramsci's account of the role of civil society. It will be recalled that Gramsci argued that hegemony is produced and reproduced through civil society. What seems to have occurred in Wales is that while - as in Scotland - the excesses of Thatcherism and the 'quango state' undermined the legitimacy of the *status quo*, the lack of any broad debate on alternatives meant that no other view could permeate through society and become hegemonic: hence the inconclusive or at least unconvincing nature of the 1997 referendum result.

Table 8.6
Referendum vote by broad preference for the government of Wales

	% 'Yes' vote	N
Independence outwith EU	93	15
Independence in EU	98	47
Home rule with tax powers	80	84
Assembly without tax powers	74	105
No elected body	2	163

Note: Excludes those who did not vote in the referendum.

The lack of public debate may well have had implications for voter mobilisation during the referendum itself, and not only in terms of turnout. Table 8.6 shows that a quarter of those who cast their vote in the referendum and who favoured an assembly without tax powers (that is what was on offer) actually voted 'no'. This surprising and certainly counter-intuitive finding may well be a further indication of the difficulty which both sides had in mobilising their vote in a context shaped by a general lack of public engagement and interest (see also the chapter by Geoffrey Evans and Dafydd Trystan in this volume). The amount of ground they had to make up is further underlined by the fact that only 19% of respondents reported that they had decided how to vote in a referendum on devolution prior to the general election in May: beyond a narrow group, devolution simply had not been an issue.

That said, it is important to note in this respect that there appears to be no simple relationship between knowledge and mobilisation. In fact, Welsh voters were not particularly badly informed about the devolution proposals put before them, as table 8.4 indicates. Table 8.5 shows that, in both Wales and Scotland, over two-thirds of respondents managed to give the correct answers to five of the seven survey questions concerning the assembly or parliament. This lack of difference is consistent with the point made above, that levels of knowledge in Scotland were similar among 'yes' voters and 'no' voters. In Wales the proportion of 'yes' voters answering at least five of the questions correctly was 80%, compared to 78% of 'no' voters and 49% of those who did not vote (for further discussion of the relationship between knowledge and referendum vote in Wales see the chapter by Richard Wyn Jones and Dafydd Trystan, and the chapter by John Curtice, in this volume).

Of course, the fact that the establishment of an assembly did not enjoy 'common sense' status in Wales in September 1997 does not mean that this will not change. One of the striking features of the opinion polls conducted since the referendum is that they indicate a further erosion in the support for the pre-devolution constitutional order (BBC Wales, July 1998, November 1998). However, as yet, this has not been replaced by consensus in support of the assembly: a Scottish-style parliament and even independence have garnered equal levels of support. Indeed, given the problematic nature of the new constitutional settlement in Wales with its complex and convoluted division of responsibilities and powers, it may be that when a consensus does finally emerge from a Welsh civil society now more engaged in the politics of devolution, it might be for a governmental structure with substantially more power than the one currently being established. Although the road to the establishment of a layer of devolved democratic government for Wales has been tortuous, the creation of the National Assembly in 1999 is unlikely to denote the end of that journey.

As with the analysis of national identity, these survey data concerning the referendums show a great deal of similarity between Scotland and Wales. Despite the wholly different levels of civil society mobilisation, the levels of knowledge among the electorate were broadly similar. Knowledge at the individual level therefore does not explain the different outcomes of the referendums. That is probably because mere knowledge is not the same as political mobilisation. In other words, the absence of much difference between Scotland and

Wales in the survey evidence forces us back to the vast differences in the roles of civil society as the best explanation of the different referendum outcomes.

Conclusion

The civil societies in Wales and Scotland have produced different kinds of debate about home rule, different sets of proposals, and different results in the 1997 referendums, reflecting their differing degree of autonomy and capacity to mobilise popular support. As we argued in the early sections of this chapter, civil society in Scotland has a long record of leading popular opinion. It commands popular respect as the institutional embodiment of civic identity, and so when it came to support a Scottish parliament in the 1980s and 1990s, it lent its credibility to the entire project of home rule. That could not be true in Wales. Civil society there has been weaker anyway, but also has not been able to play the same role of national leadership. It was simply not involved in the 1997 referendum to any significant extent, and so mobilisation of popular opinion was much more difficult to achieve.

For the future, the implications are that the civic culture into which the new assembly and parliament will be inserted will be crucial. In Scotland, the record of national leadership which civic institutions have shown will be a potential brake on the parliament's freedom of action. In Wales, by contrast, the relative weakness of civil society might offer the assembly a great deal of scope. The irony, then, is that the very success of the civic campaigning for a parliament in Scotland may be the biggest democratic obstacle which that parliament faces, while the much more tentative origins of the Welsh assembly could present it with the best legacy it could have.

Thus the cases of Wales and Scotland do not provide straightforward support for the argument that civil society drives constitutional change. Scottish civil society was probably crucial in leading the 1997 campaign for home rule, and in that sense placed itself at the head of a radical renewal. But, in 1979, it had been the main obstacle to change, and its conservatism and civic power may well constrain the new parliament after 1999. The absence of a coherent Welsh civil society has probably hindered constitutional renewal; but it may allow the new assembly to be more radical than it could have been had there been rival national institutions to contend with. Civil society, then, has no simple relationship to democratic renewal. It neither facilitates constitutional change nor is straightforwardly an impediment to it. As always, political outcomes are not structurally determined: they have to, and can, be fought for.

Notes

1. In the entry for England no mention is actually made of Wales.
2. In 1811, the Calvinistic Methodists split from the established Anglican Church decisively shifting the religious balance in Wales towards nonconformism. The bulk of the Welsh population became staunchly nonconformist in outlook while the anglicised elite strata remained loyal to Anglicanism (Davies 1993).
3. Before the fourteenth century, Scotland had enjoyed broken periods of semi-independence, punctuated by invasion from England and much internal conflict.
4. The Church of Scotland split over the issue of lay patronage of ministerial posts. This appeared to contradict the guarantee in the Treaty of Union that the church would be free of secular interference. The majority of the church resented lay patronage, and around one half of its ministers and congregationas left to form their own Free Church.
5. This is especially curious given that Gramsci's work has influenced a whole generation of Welsh historians and was also frequently cited as an influence by leading figures in Plaid Cymru – including then party president Dafydd Elis Thomas – when that party shifted to the left in the early 1980s (Wyn Jones 1996). Part of the explanation may be that political thought in Wales has been much exercised by the concept of 'community' (Williams 1990; Wyn Jones 1995). But while it is clear that this concept has been used in ways which attempt to articulate some of the normative ideas associated with civil society, it seems to have encouraged a tendency to succumb all too often to a naïve localism devoid of any coherent account of the inter-relationship between state, individuals and social institutions. In this sense, whatever the inherent vagueness of civil society as a concept, it does seem to be more analytically and politically useful than that of community.
6. Incomers from other places in the survey sample voted clearly in favour of a parliament, but were too few in number (only nine of them) to allow us to draw any conclusions.

References

Bochel J, Denver D and Macartney A (1981) *The Referendum Experience*, Aberdeen: Aberdeen University Press.

Brown A, McCrone D and Paterson L (1998) *Politics and Society in Scotland*, London: Macmillan, 2nd edition.

Brown A, McCrone D, Paterson L and Surridge P (1999) *The Scottish Electorate: the 1997 General Election and Beyond*, London: Macmillan.

Brown C G (1987) *The Social History of Religion in Scotland 1780-1914*, London: Methuen.

Cam H M (1962) *Law-Finders and Law-Makers in Medieval England*, London: Merlin Press.

Census Report for Wales 1991 (Part 1) (1993) London: HMSO.

Checkland O (1980) *Philanthropy in Victorian Scotland: Social Welfare and the Voluntary Principle*, Edinburgh: John Donald.

Checkland S and Checkland O (1984) *Industry and Ethos: Scotland 1832-1914*, London: Edward Arnold.

Cohen A P (1996) 'Personal Nationalism: A Scottish View of Some Rites, Rights, and Wrongs', *American Ethnologist* **23**: 802-815.

Cohen J L and Arato A (1992) *Civil Society and Political Theory*, Cambridge, Mass.: MIT Press.

Davies J (1993) *A History of Wales*, London: Penguin.

Davies R R (1984) 'Law and National Identity in Thirteenth-Century Wales', in Davies R R, Griffiths R A, Jones I G and Morgan K O (eds), *Welsh Society and Nationhood: Historical Essays Presented to Glanmor Williams*, Cardiff: University of Wales Press.

Davies R R (1989) 'Frontier Arrangements in Fragmented Societies: Ireland and Wales', in Bartlett R and MacKay A (eds), *Medieval Frontier Societies*, Oxford: Clarendon Press.

Davies R R (1995) *The Revolt of Owain Glyndŵr*, Oxford: Oxford University Press.

Foulkes D, Barry Jones J and Wilford R A (eds) (1983) *The Welsh Veto: The Wales Act and the Referendum*, Cardiff: University of Wales.

Fry M (1987) *Patronage and Principle: a Political History of Modern Scotland*, Aberdeen: Aberdeen University Press.

Gramsci A (1971) *Selections for the Prison Notebooks*, edited and translated by Hoare Q and Nowell Smith G, London: Lawrence and Wishart.

Grant A (1984) *Independence and Nationhood: Scotland 1306-1469*, London: Edward Arnold.

Hall J A (ed) (1995) *Civil Society*, Cambridge: Polity.

Harvie C (1994) *Scotland and Nationalism: Scottish Society and Politics 1707-1994*, London: Allen Unwin, 2nd edition.

Hearn J (1998) 'The Social Contract: Re-framing Scottish Nationalism', *Scottish Affairs* **23**: 14-26.

Hegel G W F (1942) *Philosophy of Right*, (translated with notes by Know T M, London: Oxford University Press.

Hirst P (1994) *Associative Democracy*, Cambridge: Polity.

Honneth A (1993) 'Conceptions of Civil Society', *Radical Philosophy* **64**: 19-22.

Hutchison I G C (1986) *A Political History of Modern Scotland, 1832-1924*, Edinburgh: John Donald.

Jenkins D (1970) 'Law and Government in Wales before the Act of Union', in Andrews J A (ed), *Welsh Studies in Public Law*, Cardiff: University of Wales Press.

Jenkins G H (1993) *The Foundations of Modern Wales 1642-1780*, Cardiff: University of Wales Press.

Keane J (ed) (1988) *Civil Society and the State*, London: Verso.

Kumar K (1993) 'Civil Society: An Inquiry into the Usefulness of an Historical Term', *British Journal of Sociology* **44**: 375-401.

Lang I (1994) 'Taking Stock of *Taking Stock*', speech to Conservative Party conference, reprinted in Paterson L (1998b) *A Diverse Assembly: the Debate on a Scottish Parliament*, Edinburgh: Edinburgh University Press: 232-37.

Lenman B (1981) *Integration, Enlightenment and Industrialisation: Scotland 1746-1832*, London: Edward Arnold.

Lloyd J (1997) 'What's the Story?', *New Statesman* **8** (August): 37-38.

Lynch M (1991) *Scotland: A New History*, London: Century.

McCrone D (1992) *Understanding Scotland: The Sociology of a Stateless Nation*, London: Routledge.

McCrone D (1998) *The Sociology of Nationalism*, London: Routledge.

MacInnes J (1992) 'The Press in Scotland', *Scottish Affairs* **1**: 137-49.

MacInnes J (1993) 'The Broadcast Media in Scotland', *Scottish Affairs* **2**: 84-98.

Marquand D (1996) 'Community and the Left', in Radice G (ed), *What Needs to Change*, London: HarperCollins.

Marshall G (1992) *Presbyteries and Profits*, Edinburgh: Edinburgh University Press.

Mitchell J (1996) *Strategies for Self-Government*, Edinburgh: Polygon.

Morgan K (1995) 'Red Dragon and the Red Flag: The Cases of James Griffiths and Aneurin Bevan', *Modern Wales: Politics, Places and People*, Cardiff: University of Wales Press.

Morgan K O (1981) *Rebirth of a Nation: Wales 1880-1980*, Oxford: Clarendon Press/University of Wales Press.

Morgan P (1998) 'Y Deinosor a'r Sarff - Sut maeCenedligrwydd yn Newid', Lecture to a conference on 'Wales and Scotland: a crisis of identity?' Cardiff, October 1998.

Nairn T (1997) *Faces of Nationalism*, London: Verso.

National Assembly Advisory Group (1998) Report to the Secretary of State for Wales (http://www.assembly.wales.gov.uk/NAAG/as-00.html)

Osmond J (1995) *Living in Quangoland*, Planet: The Welsh Internationalist **110** (April/May): 27-36.

Osmond J (1998) *The New Politics in Wales*, London: Charter 88.

Paterson L (1994) *The Autonomy of Modern Scotland*, Edinburgh: Edinburgh University Press.

Paterson L (1998a) 'Scottish Home Rule: Radical Break or Pragmatic Adjustment?', *Regional and Federal Studies* **8**: 53-67.

Paterson L (1998b) *A Diverse Assembly: The Debate on a Scottish Parliament*, Edinburgh: Edinburgh University Press.

Paterson L (1998c) 'Does Civil Society Speak for the People?' Evidence from a survey of Scottish teachers, paper submitted for publication.

Paterson L (1998d) 'Scottish Higher Education and the Scottish Parliament: The Consequences of Mistaken National Identity', *European Review* **6**: 459-74.

Scott P H (1979) *1707: the Union of Scotland and England*, Edinburgh: Chambers.

Thomson J M (1995) 'Scots Law, National Identity and the European Union', *Scottish Affairs* **10**: 25-34.

Whatley C A (1994) *'Bought and Sold for English Gold'? Explaining the Union of 1707*, Glasgow: Economic and Social History Society of Scotland.

Williams G (1991) *When Was Wales?*, Harmondsworth: Penguin.

Williams G (1997) *Wales and the Reformation*, Cardiff: University of Wales Press.

Williams R (1990) *What I Came to Say*, London: Hutchinson Radius.

Wormald J (1981) *Court, Kirk and Community: Scotland 1470-1625*, London: Edward Arnold.

Wyn Jones R (1995) 'Care of the Community: Contemporary Welsh Political Thought', *Planet: The Welsh Internationalist* **109**: 16-25.

Wyn Jones R (1996) 'From Community Socialism to Quango Wales: The Amazing Odyssey of Dafydd Elis Thomas', translated from an article by Richard Wyn Jones in the Welsh language journal *Tu Chwith* by Meg Elis and Richard Wyn Jones, *Planet: The Welsh Internationalist* **119**: 59-70.

Wyn Jones R and Lewis B (1998) 'The Wales Labour Party and Welsh Civil Society: Aspects of the Constitutional Debate in Wales', paper presented to the Annual Conference of the Political Studies Association Annual Conference, University of Keele.

Wyn Jones R and Lewis B (1999) 'The 1997 Welsh devolution referendum', *Politics* **19**: 1, 37-46.

9 Welsh devolution: the past and the future

The British Academy lecture: 18 September 1998

Kenneth O Morgan [*]

This historic day, 18 September 1998, recalls for me not one anniversary but two. Of course, it marked the very narrow endorsement of Welsh devolution in the referendum on which I was a television commentator, immured, oddly enough, in Cardiff castle. But a few hours later came the publication of my official biography of Lord Callaghan. One launch of it took place in Cardiff City Hall, hailed that day by the leader of the council as the building that would house the new Welsh assembly. The coincidence of these two events was striking, not only for me perhaps. In March 1979 the Callaghan government had been brought down, the first to be defeated on a vote of no confidence in the House of Commons since that of Ramsay MacDonald 55 years earlier. And it was devolution, not the industrial troubles of the 'winter of discontent', that finally laid it low. While the three Plaid Cymru MPs, in an interesting comment on the ethos of Welsh politics, voted for the Labour government in March 1979, the 11 Scottish National Party (SNP) members voted against, and the government fell by just one vote. One commentator was subsequently to see Callaghan as the last Labour prime minister, whose life was appropriately being written by the University of Wales's last vice-chancellor - both forecasts proving to be quite untrue. But the whole affair re-emphasised the political distinctiveness of Scotland and

[*] Kenneth O Morgan FBA is an Honorary Fellow of The Queen's College, Oxford, Research Professor of the University of Wales, Aberystwyth and Honorary Professor of the University of Wales, Swansea.

Wales, with the former's much stronger sense of national and territorial identity. The Scots had at least voted in favour of devolution, if narrowly, on 1 March 1979, while the Welsh, even in Gwynedd, rejected it almost contemptuously by an overall majority of almost four to one.

Eighteen years later the world had moved on. Again it was Scotland that was to trigger political change. Wales, as we know, now endorsed devolution on a low turnout of only 50% but in a major shift of electoral opinion which commentators have tended to under-estimate. The referendum this time brought not catastrophe but Catatonia - 50.3% of the voters woke up that wet morning (assuming they had been to bed at all) and thanked the Lord they were Welsh. But again it was the Scots who would lead the way, not a candle in the wind but a beacon of hope. Their elected body, endorsed by three-quarters of the voters, would be a genuine parliament with legislative and taxation powers. It would open up fundamental issues for the British polity and constitution, and their relationship with Europe and a wider world. In the run-up to the Scottish elections in May 1999, the opinion polls showed a strong surge of support for the SNP. All this is likely to have its impact on Wales too - not in the Welsh assembly being dominated by Plaid Cymru (which seems unlikely in any future one can foresee), but in pressure in Wales that its own body should have stronger powers and a more credible role. We historians are erratic prophets. But it seems to me highly probable that, as so often in the past, Wales will emulate changes north of the border. This will happen much more rapidly this time than the 79 years it took to follow Scotland in having a secretary of state. In the past, one of the more famous insults to which the Welsh took offence was that contained in the *Encyclopaedia Britannica*, an entry which encapsulated all the patronising indifference shown by the Victorians towards the Welsh identity - "for Wales - see England". A hundred years on, in a very different social and cultural context, in which English nationalism seeks a role and a rebirth of a Welsh nation seems to have genuinely taken place, we might find another watchword - "for Wales - see Scotland".

The historic differences between the two nations are as old as the Scots and Welsh themselves. Modern Scotland is the product of an Act of **Union**, between two sovereign states, passed in 1707, less than 300 years ago, which is comparatively recent in the historian's eye of eternity. Modern Wales is the product of an act of **conquest**, imposed on a defeated and fragmented people by Edward I over 400 years earlier. In the thirteenth century, when Prince Llywelyn's last bid for Welsh statehood was crushed by the English, the kingdom of Scotland under Alexander III was recognised as enjoying sovereignty. Alexander was to observe in 1278 "No-one has a right to homage for my kingdom save God alone" (Grant and Stringer 1995: 91). There was a territorial Scotland. For all its acknowledged cultural identity, there was not and never had been, a clearly territorial Wales. "When was Wales?" the late Gwyn Alf Williams memorably asked (Williams 1985). It might be added, where or what was Wales? A bishop of St David's in the later nineteenth century was much abused by Liberals and nonconformists when he referred to Wales as a "geographical expression" (Morgan 1980: 60), as Metternich had so described Italy prior to its unification. But Bishop Basil Jones was not far wrong in so describing at least the outward forms of one of Karl Marx's classic 'unhistoric nations'. In 1282 Edward I mopped up the fractured Welsh kingdoms, exploiting their rivalries and lack of common identity. Wales was assimilated into the English state and legal system thereafter, culminating in the relatively trouble-free passage of the Acts of Union under Henry VIII in 1536 and 1543. One Welsh institution after another was extinguished, culminating in the quiet demise of the once popular Court of Great Sessions (which had allowed the use of the Welsh language in legal proceedings) in 1830 (Ellis Jones 1998). The Edwardian settlement in Wales had done more than construct powerful, if picturesque, castles around the periphery of the principality. It had also created patterns of English or Anglo-Norman infiltration, which indeed were to be confirmed with remarkable exactitude in the polling of the various Welsh counties on 18 September 1997. The one great rebel over the years was Owain Glyndŵr in the early fifteenth century, on whom Rees Davies has recently written a powerful study. But it was his total failure that made him a figure of legend. "No Welsh poet or story teller commemorated his deeds as John Barbour did those of Robert Bruce", Professor Davies tells us (Davies 1995: 340). He never had the subsequent resonance in popular consciousness enjoyed in Scotland by William Wallace or Robert Bruce, let alone Bonnie Prince Charlie. Owain Glyndŵr has never inspired an epic Welsh *Braveheart* - though perhaps that is just as well.

Scotland, for its part, was unified with the English kingdom in 1603 and with the English state in 1707. But there remained no doubt about Scottish separateness. The Scots and the Irish, after all, in their different ways provoked the crisis in the United Kingdom in the late 1630s that led to the civil wars, the execution of the king and an 11-year republic. It is inconceivable that the Welsh, largely docile royalists at the time, could have had a similar impact. Even after the Act of Union, as is universally recognised, the Scots retained crucial forms of institutional and social identity. There were the Scottish Kirk and its established Presbyterian religion, a national banking system and currency, the Scottish educational system at all levels, and perhaps most important of all, a totally distinctive Scottish legal system. The Scottish legal profession became latimers of national identity. In the university world, Glasgow and Aberdeen dated from the fifteenth century, almost challenging Oxford and Cambridge in their antiquity. As recently as the 1990s, I was constantly struck as a vice-chancellor by how much greater authority Scotland's representatives in the Committee of Vice-Chancellors and Principals seemed to enjoy in speaking for their system of higher education than the Welsh did for theirs. Wales, then, had nothing like the Scottish institutional inheritance. Its education, fiscal and legal systems were part of the English. The four Welsh dioceses were part of the province of Canterbury, and no one dreamt of their disestablishment. In Scotland, enduring and powerful institutions and images created a surviving sense of Scottish citizenship. A similar sense of Welsh citizenship prior to 1800 lay in the realms of imagination or fantasy.

In the nineteenth century, powerful global forces of integration and of pluralism transformed the world. Naturally they affected Scotland and Wales in their different ways, and of course Ireland, north and south, as well. Industrialisation, urbanisation, a country-wide financial market, the force of growing literacy, could work in different directions. They could make the United Kingdom more of a homogeneous whole - reinforcing the insular, entrepreneurial, Protestant forms of Britishness of which Linda Colley has written powerfully (Colley 1992). But they could also, perhaps to an extent which she under-estimated, lend a distinctly national focus to the component parts of a formally united kingdom. Glasgow, Cardiff, Belfast were great imperial cities and ports which exported to the world. They were also, or became, powerful *loci* of the self-assertive identity of Scotland, Wales and Ulster. The consequences for Scotland and Wales, at least, proved however to be predictably different. Scottish distinctiveness acquired new robustness in an increasingly wealthy and literate age. The Scottish aristocracy, fading flowers of the forest as they had been, became themselves bearers of a new sense of national identity. Their role in fact and legend was popularised by the wizardry of Sir Walter Scott. The Welsh have produced many remarkable men of letters from Dafydd ap Gwilym to R S Thomas (and latterly a few women, too) but it is a matter of profound historical significance that there has never been a Welsh Walter Scott. It is not surprising, given the character of nineteenth-century Scotland, that it was members of the Scottish aristocracy, the young Lord Rosebery, the Duke of Argyll, the Earl of

Fife, who led the agitation which persuaded Gladstone to set up a revised secretary of state for Scotland in 1885. As Arthur Balfour sagely remarked, "The best salmon river in Scotland will go a long way" (Harvie 1994: 16).

Welsh national consciousness and its revival took a very different form. Interestingly enough, Gladstone played a significant part here, too. The Welsh aristocracy, however lengthy took their antiquity, had long been symbols of Anglicanism and Englishness in speech, outlook and aspirations. The campaign for Welsh identity, therefore, was, unlike Scottish, much more of a case of historical pressure from below. In the 1840s, it took the form of a campaign to protect the proudest and most distinctive feature of the Welsh as a people - their native language, spoken at the time by perhaps 90% of the population. The dismissive contempt shown it by the Blue Books on Education in 1847, known in popular legend thereafter as *Brad y Llyfrau Gleision*, the Treachery of the Blue Books, documents which correctly showed the stark limitations of Welsh educational provision at that time, stung Welsh nationalism awake. The newly emergent Welsh-language press, editors like 'S R', Samuel Roberts of Llanbrynmair, and Gwilym Hiraethog and their middle-class readers, symbols of the power of the word, became instruments of protest that took an increasingly national or nationalist form.

After the passage of the Reform Acts of 1867 and 1885, Welsh identity became much more overtly political (Morgan 1980). Welsh national consciousness in its modern form is a function of mass democracy - of course for men only at this period. A new Liberal ascendancy totally dominated Welsh parliamentary politics and captured virtually all the new county councils as well after 1889. A variety of well-organised national campaigns resulted; indeed the 50 years from the 1860s to the end of the First World War were a decisive crucible of change in Wales - peaceful, constitutional change - which may be why some of the more colourful commentators on the Welsh scene, seeing the Welsh as eternally rioting and demonstrating, knocking down toll-gates or flattening enclosure walls, tend to pass it by. There was a long propaganda campaign for disestablishment of the Church in Wales, for a reform of the system of landed tenure along the lines of that achieved in Ireland, and for a new educational structure which led to the 'county' schools of 1889 and the national federal University of Wales achieved in 1893. There arose a new generation of young nationally-minded radical politicans. Of these, the most beguiling was the philosopher-patriot Tom Ellis, who became Liberal chief whip and died at 40, but the most spectacular talent of all was 'the little Welsh attorney', David Lloyd George, elected to parliament in 1890 on a strongly Welsh national programme at the tender age of 27.

They challenged comparison with Parnell's Irish Nationalist Party at the time, and perhaps they won quite as many victories. Certainly, they won over key English supporters, Gladstone above all. The champion of struggling nationalities abroad - Greeks, Italians and Bulgarians - himself part Scots, he had married a Welsh woman, lived at Hawarden in north-east Wales, and patronised the Eisteddfod. The Welsh Sunday Closing Act was passed with Gladstone's vocal support in 1881 (Morgan 1980: 42). It was the first legislative enactment to apply to Wales (though not yet Monmouthshire) a wholly different set of principles from those obtaining in England. It may seem odd now to regard closing the pubs to the thirsty Welshmen and others on the sabbath as a badge of nationhood, but so it was. Again, the Intermediate Education Act in 1889 created a free, undenominational secondary schools system in Wales, different from and superior to that operating in England. The University of Wales in 1893 was to be a model for the federal National University of Ireland, based on the colleges of Dublin, Cork and Galway, a few years later. Above all, the disestablishment of the Church in Wales (including Monmouthshire this time) in 1920 (something the Scots, with their very different religious complexion never came close to achieving) was in its modest way a remarkable political victory. It was, significantly, passed through parliament while David Lloyd George was in Downing Street - or rather while he was in Versailles signing the peace treaty in 1919, busying himself with extending the principle of nationality among the fallen empires of continental Europe but keeping his own nation on his agenda as well.

But - and it is a crucial 'but' - all these political achievements for the Welsh were far removed from devolution. In Wales, and indeed in Scotland too at this time, there was no demand for any form of separatism on the lines of the Irish. Wales and Scotland sought national equality within the United Kingdom, not exclusion from it. In a worldwide Victorian empire, they wanted, in Bismarck's famous phrase, their own place in the sun. There was no Welsh or Scottish Parnell or de Valera. During the Anglo-Boer war of 1899 to 1902, as I had to remind an audience in Pretoria in August 1998, despite Lloyd George's courageous protests, the majority of the Welsh were staunchly imperialist (Morgan 1995: 46). They cheered the defence of Mafeking and the capture of Pretoria by such alleged Welshmen as Lord Roberts and Baden-Powell. The Welsh members took a very different line from the Irish who actually cheered in the House when the news came through of British army defeats at Colenso and Spion

Kop. While the Irish kept on resolutely pressing for Home Rule down to the Great War, and for republican status thereafter as Sinn Fein supplanted the old Nationalist Party, the Welsh rejected the concept of separatism out of hand. The only attempt at a movement for some form of devolution was the Cymru Fydd (Young Wales) campaign of 1894 to 1896. It was a political catastrophe which almost tore Welsh Liberalism apart; perhaps it had more to do with the personal ambitions of David Lloyd George than with a grass-roots demand for home rule. Even the scenario of the historian/publicist F S Oliver in the imperialist periodical *Round Table*, for 'home rule all round' as part of a federal imperial system, got no support. In the 1890s, as later on, the Welsh language was claimed to be a divisive force politically. It ranged the southern coastal cities and ports - the famous 'Newport Englishmen' who shouted down Lloyd George at the South Wales Liberal Federation in January 1896 (Morgan 1973: 94) - against the Welsh hinterland, rural and industrial. In 1979 that division was still there.

For disestablishment of the Church in Wales, unlike Ireland, was not a precursor of separatism but an alternative to it, sufficient in itself. Movements led by worthy politicians like E T John for a Welsh secretary of state led absolutely nowhere. Lloyd George in 1920, when prime minister, advised his fellow Welsh Liberals to "go for the big thing", that is a secretary of state. But he himself did absolutely nothing to further that objective, then or later; even the greatest Welshman of the age had turned unionist, too. It should be added that the Scottish people, in the late Victorian and Edwardian period, were more unionist still. After all, the Scots, as ship-builders, soldiers, doctors and, especially in Southern Africa, as missionaries, felt themselves to be at the heart of empire, the very model of a virile imperial race. In the 'khaki' general election of October 1900, held at the height of the Anglo-Boer war, the Scots results actually showed a small swing to the Conservative and Unionist Party, the one part of the kingdom so to do.

The twentieth century, from the First World War down to the late 1960s, has been for Scotland and even more for Wales, an age of centralism and of unionism. The Conservatives called themselves the Unionist Party from the crisis over Irish Home Rule in 1886 down to the Irish Free State Treaty in 1922. They continued so to designate themselves in Scotland until well after the Second World War. The emergent Labour Party, which represented a very different class interest and supplanted the Liberals, and came to be dominant in the Celtic nations by 1945, proved in time to be no less unionist. After all, it was essentially a product of the integrative forces of the First World

War, in which the trade unions emerged nationally as vital compo-
nents of a new, if short-lived, corporate order. Until 1918, there had
been many symptoms of Labour favouring devolutionist ideas. The
Independent Labour Party favoured localism and the politics of
community. The Fabian Society endorsed municipal socialism and
experiments in local government. There were forces for industrial as
well as political devolution - witness the quasi-syndicalists in the
Rhondda who produced the tract, *The Miners' Next Step*, published by
the Unofficial Reform Committee at Tonypandy in 1912, and who
wanted workers' control at the point of production not state
nationalisation. Keir Hardie, member of parliament for Merthyr and
Aberdare, championed Welsh and Scottish home rule, as did Ramsay
MacDonald in his youth. He sought to unite the Red Dragon and the
Red Flag. Hardie's aim was to create a more pluralist, locally based,
genuinely democratic Labour movement in Britain in contrast to the
inert bureaucratic Prussian centralism of the German Social Democrats
(Morgan 1975: 209).

But after 1918, social and economic pressures during the depression
years, notably the role of the nationally organised trade unions, made
a working-class Labour Party as unionist as the wealthy Tories.
Solidarity meant the unity of workers in all nations. Arthur
Henderson, as Labour's general secretary, proved to be stoutly
resistant to the quasi-separatist pressures of the comrades in Scotland
and Wales. Socialism and nationalism were clean different. Not until
as late as 1947 did the party create a unified organisation in Wales,
called with due modesty the Regional Council of Labour.

Attempts once favoured by Labour and some Liberals at some kind
of United Kingdom federalism in 1918 to 1919 - an idea backed by
some apostles of imperial federation such as Philip Kerr, now lodged
in Lloyd George's 'garden suburb' of private advisers - attracted no
interest. Not that this seemed anything less than wholly appropriate
during the grim depressed atmosphere of the inter-war years. The
Scottish National Party was minute: its one MP, Dr Robert McIntyre,
elected in the last few months of the Second World War, proved to be
a fleeting phantom. Plaid Genedlaethol Cymru, founded in 1925,
significantly during the Eisteddfod at Pwllheli, was in the main a
pressure group of intellectuals and *littérateurs* campaigning on behalf
of the Welsh language (Butt-Philip 1975: 13). Its early politics were
complicated and compromised by the apparent neo-fascism of its
charismatic first president, the poet and dramatist Saunders Lewis,
and the sympathy for fascist-style corporatism shown by him and
other Roman Catholic leaders of the party. Plaid Cymru was given an
emotional boost by the imprisonment of Saunders Lewis and two

other nationalists after an admitted arson on a RAF base in Llŷn in 1936. But it was fundamentally a pressure group. Down to the 1950s it could hardly be designated as an organised political party at all.

Even in this era of unionism, however, the differences between Scotland and Wales were apparent and persisted right down to 1997 and beyond. The contrast comes out with great clarity during the latter part of the Second World War. In Scotland that famous socialist, Tom Johnston, made the Scottish Office a powerful laboratory of change (Harvie 1994: 32). He did so partly by persuading Churchill that if he did not get his way, an upsurge of the SNP would follow. As a result, Johnson was able to create a Scottish Council of State and a Council of Industry, to get planning powers transferred to the Scottish Office in St Andrew's House and to create in Edinburgh the basis for a powerful impulse towards greater self-government. He gained the support of powerful Scottish establishment figures such as John, Lord Reith and John Boyd-Orr. In Wales, by contrast, there was nothing. The Welsh Council of Reconstruction, established in 1942, in which James Griffiths was a prominent figure, failed to achieve any devolution in central economic planning or decision-making. The Attlee government (1945-51) offered nothing to Welsh sentiment in the running of the nationalised industries (Morgan 1981: 377). There was to be no Welsh secretary of state. Instead of any kind of elected assembly, Herbert Morrison produced a purely nominated and ineffective Council for Wales which limped along until the 1960s. All he and Attlee could offer otherwise as a *douceur* to national sentiment was a Welsh coat of arms (where the location of the leek created problems). Cardiff did not even become a capital city.

The ethos was relentlessly centralist. The Welsh, like others, were instructed, in Douglas Jay's memorable phrase,[1] that "the gentleman from Whitehall really did know best". The Parliament for Wales campaign in the early 1950s, which attracted the support of Welsh-speaking MPs such as Cledwyn Hughes and Goronwy Roberts, was allowed to peter out (Jones 1992). A Welsh Day debate was held in the Commons for the first time in October 1944, but it was not a success. That doughty socialist, Aneurin Bevan, poured scorn on the whole occasion: it was totally unnecessary: Wales and England were inseparable, how did Welsh sheep differ from English sheep? they grazed on the same grass and were subject to the same environmental circumstances (the fall-out from Chernobyl could not be predicted in 1944). Nye Bevan at that time (he modified his stance somewhat in the later 1950s) was no more a nationalist than his Scottish wife, Jennie Lee, was either a nationalist or a feminist. The different political cultures of Scotland and Wales were thus publicly exposed.

The story of devolution or separatism in Scotland and even more in Wales is thus the history of a non-event until well after the Second World War. But since the 1960s, that era of change in modern Britain in matters political and sexual, a major transformation has occurred. Celtic nationalism proved to be an offshoot of the 'permissive society': Welsh nationalist students, clambering up television masts, defacing road signs or blockading post offices, were part of the new rebellious youth culture. The creation of the Welsh Office in 1964, with the veteran James Griffiths as first secretary of state, left a legacy of frustrated expectations. The change since then has been considerable, the era of Margaret Thatcher notwithstanding. Scotland and Wales have responded sharply to wider movements in the British and worldwide experience - the end of empire and the emergence of a united Europe, the rise of a global economy, the erosion of a London-centred, Fabian civic culture, all of which questioned the role or authority of Westminster and Whitehall. As before, it was Scotland that led the way. The Scottish National Party proved to be more widely rooted than was Plaid Cymru. In October 1974 no less than 11 SNP MPs were elected; the party could claim local government strength all over Scotland, from the remote western isles to Cumbernauld new town in the south. With a few articulate exceptions like Tam Dalyell and the young Robin Cook, the Scottish Labour Party became strongly committed to the notion of a Scottish parliament. Welsh nationalism, by contrast, as the five Plaid Cymru seats gained variously between 1966 and 1997 suggested, was securely based only in Welsh-speaking rural areas in the north and west; in these areas it managed to establish a permanent presence in place of either Liberals or Labour.

The Crowther-Kilbrandon royal commission, reporting in 1973, noted the differences (Bogdanor 1979). In particular, it cited the distinctive Scottish legal system as a major reason for discriminating between the two nations (though the election returns must have been an even stronger factor). It proposed a Scottish parliament, which indeed the Scots were to endorse very narrowly in the referendum on 1 March 1979. But a proposed weak Welsh elected assembly was, as noted, thrown out by four to one. It was an emphatic action replay of the Cymru Fydd debacle of 1896, with Welsh politics again riven by divisions over regionalism and the language. In Caernarfon people feared domination by an entrenched south Wales Labour 'taffia'; in anglicised Cardiff by contrast, there were fears of the potential influence of the Welsh speakers of the distant north. Maverick Welsh Labour MPs like Leo Abse in Pontypool fanned the flames with hints that Taffy was a thief, probably resident in the wilds of Gwynedd. So matters seemed to continue throughout the Thatcher years. That period brought several recognitions of Welshness, notably Channel Four - Sianel Pedwar - on television, and funding for Welsh-language primary and secondary schools. These appeared to be enough. The Scots launched an all-party Constitutional Convention in 1989, chaired by Canon Kenyon Wright, to draw up a scheme for devolution (see chapter by McCrone and Lewis in this book). In 1992, the Scottish Labour Party declared itself strongly in favour of a Scottish parliament with tax-raising powers: this inevitably figured in the party manifesto. In Wales, however, devolution seemed to attract scant support other than from small groups of intellectuals and journalists: the man on the Cardiff omnibus was apathetic if not actually hostile. The Labour Party leader, Neil Kinnock, was himself a Welshman traditionally against devolution, as indeed was his Welsh-speaking wife, Glenys.

On the other hand, the very fact that in 1979 the Welsh had even considered the issue of devolution, for the first time in history, left its legacy on the terms of reference of public debate. In addition, the Welsh Office in the 18 years of Conservative rule, even if run by a sequence of Englishmen - Peter Walker, David Hunt (on the party left), John Redwood (from the Thatcherite right) and William Hague - quietly changed the terms in which Welsh issues were considered. Almost by stealth, the Welsh Office's extended role after 1979 reinforced the sense of the territorial identity of Wales (Griffiths 1996).

Since 1992, a major historic transformation of opinion has occurred in Scotland and to a lesser degree in Wales. There are a number of reasons for this, many of them external to the principality. First, the pressure for devolution in Scotland became overwhelming. There was the consensual meeting point of the Scottish Constitutional Convention. Labour figures like John Smith and Robin Cook, previously hostile because of concern for maintaining Scottish Labour representation at Westminster in full, were compelled to change; Gordon Brown, on the other hand, author in 1986 of an excellent biography on Jimmy Maxton of the ILP, seems always to have been a robust devolutionist. The very strength of feeling in Scotland had its impact on Wales too. Second, the advent of Tony Blair and New Labour, with its aversion to centralist state planning and the corporatism of old Labour, has meant a distinct change in Labour ideology towards greater local accountability and a reform of the constitution as a means of both economic modernisation and adjustment to a committed role in a united Europe. Devolution was part of that vision, linked by Tony Blair with the legacy of Jeffersonian democracy in his John Smith memorial lecture (Blair 1996).

Third, in Wales itself, while the active role of the Welsh Office encouraged an emphasis on local identity, other features of Tory rule appeared to be in stark contrast with it. It is difficult to be sure how much popular resentment was really felt about 'the democratic deficit' inherent in quangos appointed by Tory governments for which only a small minority of Welsh electors had voted. But certainly they gave grist to the devolutionists' mill, especially when such fringe figures as the wives of heavily defeated Tory candidates were propelled to the forefront (for example, on NHS trusts) as symbols of Margaret Thatcher's brave new Wales. It may well have added to the air of governmental nepotism, decadence and sleaze that marked the John Major years. A combination of satisfaction with an active Welsh Office and of revulsion at politically unacceptable quangos added to a firmer sense of Welsh identity and perhaps of citizenship.

And finally, and of growing importance, there was the over-shadowing presence of membership of the European Union. This could encourage the attractive notion of a Europe of nations, nourished not only by the SNP but also in such places as the colloquia held at Freudenstadt in Baden-Württemburg, which several Welsh academics and intellectuals attended. In an evolving world, in which ideas of centralised governmental planning, the notion of sovereignty, the relation to Europe, and the contours of the global economy were all in the melting pot, Wales, like Scotland, would inevitably respond.

The outcome, of course, was the events of a year ago which we are commemorating, perhaps even celebrating, in this conference. For the historian of modern Britain, the contrast between 1979 and 1997 is remarkable (see also the chapters by Geoff Evans and Dafydd Trystan, and by Paula Surridge and David McCrone in this volume). In 1979 devolution was reluctantly pushed on to a divided party and an apathetic public by a declining minority government, manifestly at the end of its tether. In 1997, by contrast, devolution was enthusiastically promoted as a legislative priority by a fresh government with an overall majority of 179 seats and the further backing of the Liberal Democrats and the Nationalists. The opposition of the demoralised and derided Tories was in itself a bonus - most of all when Lady Thatcher, of all people, was flown in to Glasgow to lecture the Scots on the merits of an unchanging union. Most attention focused on the massive Scottish majority of over two-thirds both for the principle of self-government and for tax-varying powers. But the Welsh result, albeit achieved on a low turnout, is also not to be derided. That 50.3% of Welsh voters should vote for devolution in itself marked a large swing of public opinion compared with 1979. Not only much of the Welsh-speaking heartland but all the valley constituencies in the south voted 'yes', as also did the important city of Swansea (strongly resistant to Cymru Fydd a century earlier). It is not credible to see the Welsh result as the product of a 'north-south divide' (an east-west divide may be a different matter) (see the chapters by Richard Wyn Jones and Dafydd Trystan and by Geoffrey Evans and Dafydd Trystan).

The implications are immense. For the first time in their history, the Welsh have voted, by however narrow a margin, for some element of power being transferred directly to themselves instead of mediated from afar at Westminster. Quite apart from the fact that Wales, like Scotland, rejected every single Tory candidate at the polls in May 1997, the 'no' campaign was distinctly shadowy as outlined in the chapter by David McCrone and Bethan Lewis. Its major figures included distinctly elderly survivors like Sir Julian Hodge (resident in the Channel Islands as a tax exile) and the aged Lord Tonypandy (who died shortly afterwards). The Conservative Party machine prudently kept its distance.

Since the referendum vote, despite parochial arguments over the Welsh assembly building (which paralleled those over the Welsh opera house and rugby stadium), devolution appears increasingly as an idea whose time has come. Opinion polls show an upsurge of national self-confidence, with demands for a local perspective in social and economic planning - not to mention a buoyant Welsh design industry, a thriving Welsh-language cinema and the youthful appeal of such harbingers of Welsh culture as Catatonia, Stereophonics and the Manic Street Preachers. The old divisiveness created by conflicting views on the Welsh language - the kind of thing that has led to bombings and violence among the Quebecois, the Flemings and the Afrikaaners - has largely disappeared, as Ysgolion Cymraeg (Welsh-medium schools) and Sianel Pedwar (the fourth TV channel in Wales) have taken root. Indeed, it could be suggested that the inability of Plaid Cymru to make inroads beyond the mountainous reaches of north-west Wales in itself helped the devolutionist cause. It could not plausibly be argued in 1997, as Leo Abse and others tried to do in 1979, that a devolutionist Wales would inevitably be a separatist Wales, and bring an end to what Hugh Gaitskell called in another connection 'a thousand years of history'.

Will devolution actually make a difference, or merely impose another ineffective, costly layer of intermediate semi-government upon the backs of the already much over-adminstered people of Wales? In itself, an elected assembly for Wales has very limited powers, and this may well lead to frustration with London control. The potential conflict was foreshadowed in the attempts by Labour's high command at

Millbank to sideline Rhodri Morgan as potential first minister in
favour of the Blairite Alun Michael, following Ron Davies's bizarre
departure as Welsh secretary. The distinction between the far greater
powers of the Scottish parliament and its counterpart in Wales may
well heighten the tension. Another new element since the
referendums, of course, is the elected assembly in Northern Ireland
which introduced yet another local variation, along with the shadowy
role provided for the Council of the Isles, on which the Welsh and
Scottish bodies will be represented. It is not difficult to see prospects of
years of wholesale constitutional and legal confusion to bemuse or
distract the British people. Edinburgh lawyers could enjoy a bonanza
unknown since the Act of Union. The role of the Scottish parliament
may lead to prolonged disputes over such matters as the extent of
Scottish legislative autonomy, local taxing powers, the legal system,
the future of the Lords and even the monarchy. In social policy, local
initiatives may be hard to reconcile with the maintenance of
nationwide standards in such matters as health and education,
adhered to by governments of all political persuasions earlier this
century. Of more immediate importance, the future of any UK Labour
government with reduced Scottish representation must be in serious
doubt, although here Tony Blair no doubt has the long-term potential
weapon of electoral reform and founding his regime in the next
millennium on the kind of broader coalition basis familiar in
continental politics.

But devolution is actually happening. I believe it is more appropriate
here - and more useful in the longer term - to take a positive view, to
regard devolution in Wales as an opportunity not a threat. In my
judgement there are a number of specific advantages which a
reformed system of government in Wales and elsewhere is likely to
bring. In the first place, it is probable that Wales will actually be better
governed - indeed, it is hard to claim, surely, that the present
governmental system attracts mass enthusiasm, especially an
emasculated system of local government for which only a diminishing
minority of electors can be bothered to vote. It will mean the
application of an all-Wales viewpoint at the point of decision-making
for the first time in modern history. In this sense, events will move on
from, say, the work of the Attlee government after 1945 - courageous
pioneers of change in social and economic policy, but remarkably
quiescent in areas of constitutional or governmental change. It is
instructive to recall that Ernest Bevin and his colleagues were anxious
to minimise the role of central government in the newly divided
Germany, to underwrite democracy in the *Länder* and avoid the
revival of any form of totalitarianism, but that they took an almost

exactly opposite approach in the government of the United Kingdom. Not only will the emergence of an all-Wales viewpoint be beneficial in itself in meeting the challenges of the millennium. The power of scrutiny of the administration of Wales in matters great and small by an assembly seen to be representative of the people as whole could be hugely beneficial, and have a democratically educative effect which the role of a largely invisible Welsh ombudsman to inquire into administrative abuses or errors could never achieve.

Let us illustrate the point with one historic, and dreadful, instance from the past. An elected Welsh assembly would not have prevented the catastrophe at Aberfan in which 116 little children died in 1966, smothered to death by tons of coal slurry from nearby tips. But it might well have prevented, or at least vigorously challenged, the disgraceful abuses that followed, and which my Oxford colleague Iain McLean has recently clearly exposed (McLean 1997). One was the power of the National Coal Board to bully the government to avoid a proper investigation of the causes of Aberfan or apportion responsibility among, or take legal action against, Lord Robens (Chairman of the Coal Board) and other officials. Nobody was ever prosecuted. Another was the Board's wilful reluctance to pay proper compensation to bereaved relatives. Yet another was the fact of £150,000 donated by decent, sympathetic people to the Aberfan Disaster Fund being diverted to bail out the money-conscious National Coal Board in meeting the cost of levelling out its own coal tips. (Ron Davies, then secretary of state for Wales in the Blair government, to his great credit reversed this, 30 years on.) Another has been the carelessness in preserving records of the whole affair, which determined scholars, fortunately, have been able to remedy. The aftermath of Aberfan is an appalling instance of local mismanagement which a probing, investigative Welsh assembly would have confronted and maybe exposed.

Apart from the avoidance of governmental errors, an inclusive National Assembly, could draw in individuals and groups from far beyond the somewhat enclosed world of Welsh political culture - women of course (only four of them served as Welsh MPs between 1918 and 1997; there are only four out of 40 now); younger people to revive a society that too often looks like a gerontocracy; ethnic minorities who have played almost no part in our politics hitherto. Within the political world, minority groups would be given a far more positive role, especially Plaid Cymru, among whom able leaders like Dafydd Wigley would relish the prospect of responsibility. An assembly could also revitalise the Welsh Conservatives, born losers for well over 100 years under our present voting system, but offered new hope under the electoral system adopted for the assembly. All this would be for the good, even though the departure of Ron Davies may not have improved prospects of a more inclusive political culture.

As a supplement to this, one can be too defeatist about the limited powers that the Welsh assembly will have at the outset. Of course it is far less powerful, as matters stand, than the Scottish parliament: its remit will not include powers of primary legislation at all (see the Introduction to this volume). However, the powers over secondary legislation could prove more far-reaching than anticipated, not least in the powers over 600 statutory instruments. There must be influence over financial powers as well. I notice that Jonathan Evans, a former Conservative minister now apparently a convert to devolution, has urged that the Welsh assembly should have more than a mere permissive 'concordat' with central government: he has suggested an input over such key matters as rates of interest and the level of sterling, both of central importance to the performance of the Welsh economy and the growth of jobs - which indicates the way that the agenda can move forward (Evans 1998). No doubt there will also be a Welsh view offered in the debates over joining European Monetary Union. I take it as probable that, at some stage, the assembly will acquire financial powers, perhaps substantial ones, of its own. Otherwise, as a body exercising executive power without financial responsibility, the assembly will be on a par with the appointed or nominated quangos of the Tory past. Beyond these matters, any new body will surely acquire a life and personality of its own. At the moment, before it comes into effect, the prospect of an assembly seems less than enticing: perhaps a talking shop for the Welsh chattering classes. But it will want to act, to challenge and question. It will attract publicity and a wider attention in the media. It will have the stimulus of a pro active and probably highly independent Scottish parliament to encourage it.

Above all, it will have the essential legitimacy that arises from being elected. The Council for Wales after 1949 raised major issues and had an inspirational first chairman in Huw T Edwards. But it never got over its origins as Herbert Morrison's Celtic kindergarten. It could advise, encourage or warn, like Walter Bagehot's monarchy, another dignified part of the constitution. But it could never act. Therefore it could never inspire. Edwards resigned in 1958, sadly complaining of the inability of 'Whitehallism' to understand Welsh aspirations (Morgan 1981: 333). The Welsh assembly will by contrast have from the first the power of a popular mandate. Its first secretary will not be a prime ministerial nominee. The people will to an increasing degree be governed by and from Wales, not from Whitehall or Westminster, let alone Wokingham, John Redwood's leafy stronghold in the Thames Valley. Like the constitutional reforms of the Blair government in general, the assembly will have a dynamic all its own.

A quite different, and potentially important, point relates to regionalism. Just as the Scottish parliament is likely to encourage an elected Welsh assembly to be proactive, so the latter may stimulate ideas of local autonomy among the people of England. There is already the precedent pushed through by the Blair government of an elected mayor of London, with the status of his counterparts in, say, Paris or New York to aim for. Attempts to eliminate Ken Livingstone as Labour's candidate do not remove the historic potential of this new departure. Beyond that, surely some at least of the regions of England with a sense of historic identity - the north-east, and Merseyside and the north-west, surely, perhaps East Anglia or the west country - would want to follow the Welsh example. If this were to happen, then among other things, Tam Dalyell's famous West Lothian question - unanswerable as things stand, insoluble even for the mighty intellect of Gladstone at the time of Irish Home Rule over a century ago, when perhaps it appeared as the Mid-Lothian question - would be made redundant. Instead of glowering at the advantages, alleged or real, acquired by the assemblies of Scotland and Wales, the English regions, one after another, would surely be moved not to beat them but to join them. An English nationalist backlash would not occur. The outcome could be more fundamental changes. For instance it could shape the reform of the House of Lords, not on the basis of prime ministerial personal patronage to create a new and greater quango, but on a regional basis of devolved authority and democratic audit. At any rate, devolution, in Wales and Scotland, is not just a structure but a process - part of an on-going range of redefinitions as our constitution adapts belatedly to modern circumstances. Gladstone remarked that there were no bounds to the march of a nation. Perhaps we might substitute or add the term 'region' as well. Or perhaps in a post-modernist society, the difference between the two will simply wither away.

A third giant benefit, in my view, is that it could lead to a new relationship with the European Union, not only for Wales and Scotland, but for the United Kingdom as a whole. The EU is often condemned for a democratic deficit of its own, the bureaucratic centralism of Brussels poised against the comparative ineffectiveness of the European parliament other than as a forum of debate. It is right that the Blair government now should seek to reform its structures and methods of business. The EU reflects the statist constitutional and legal traditions of the central continental powers rather than the (alleged) parliamentary basis of the British constitution. It is not surprising that this should be so. Time after time, from the failure to enter the Schuman coal and steel community in 1950 onwards, British governments missed a series of historic opportunities to join, and thereby influence, the new Common Market (later the European Economic Community). Historic or sentimental attachment to the myths of empire or the sea-faring exploits of an island race, a narrow definition of national sovereignty based on an ancient vision of the crown in parliament, the symbolism of Big Ben chiming out for liberty, proclaimed by Margaret Thatcher in her Bruges speech, a kind of 'Dad's Army' sentimentality dating from Dunkirk and the Battle of Britain, recalling how this happy breed fought alone while defeatist or treacherous continentals surrendered to the dictators - all these have played their part. They have particular resonance for the home counties: the bluebirds and nightingales which Dame Vera Lynn told us hovered over the white cliffs of Dover or Berkeley Square seldom made it to the Rhondda Valley.

But under New Labour it is clear that membership of Europe is central to all aspects of our external policy, with a likely prospect that in the nearish future – perhaps shortly after the next general election – we shall enter the monetary union as well. What matters now is not only that British foreign policy is shaped accordingly, but also that our domestic structures are made appropriate as well. We are already in the process of incorporation into European law. The United Kingdom - or its component nations if Scotland were to break away - now requires political incorporation too.

This is where devolution, Welsh and otherwise, comes in. There are some excellent pointers in this direction offered by Sir John Gray and John Osmond, a distinguished ambassador and a crusading journalist respectively, which indicate the kind of opportunities open to a Welsh assembly even within existing structures (Gray and Osmond 1997). In fact, for all its centralisation at the executive level, the European Union operates in some measure within the localities. It is increasingly a regional/national Europe, not a controlled monolith. The Committee of the Regions is a particular reflection of this. In the various regions of Spain, Italy, Belgium or the Netherlands, emphatically so in the *Länder* of Germany where Baden-Württemburg, for instance, has been a powerful engine of economic growth (even in the difficulties following reunion with the east), decision-making is local, even parochial, rather than centralised. In the shifting world of an inter-meshed global economy, where change, constructive or destructive, can be so rapid and cataclysmic, it is no longer feasible to think simply in terms of the protective shield of central government over the nation-state. The EU operates in practice because its regional or national entities make many of their own decisions over trade, investment and employment, and interact with one another.

In a very modest way, I have been a witness to this myself in seeing the way the so-called Motor Scheme, consisting of Catalonia, Rhônes-Alpes, Lombardy, Baden-Württemburg and (thanks to the initiative of the Welsh Office) Wales, operated on an inter-regional basis. It certainly brought benefit for the University of Wales when I was vice-chancellor, since our institutions of learning have enormous economic and social clout as well. The research money accruing to the six university institutions in my last year, 1994 to 1995, amounted to around £20 million (Welsh Select Committee 1995). Indeed recourse to the EU could be a more straightforward and agreeable matter than trying to prise funding out of funding councils nearer to home. Further I was frequently told in Brussels how beneficial it was that Wales's university was a nationwide, federal institution, since it represented a known territory, with its own culture and historic identity, which made it easy for other Europeans to grasp. It is not the least important argument for a national university.

In this and other ways, devolution will help Wales to progress within the European context that surely is our future. It will offer new choices for us at the Council of Ministers (where the German and Belgian regions are represented), on the Commission and in relations with other member-states. A Europeanised devolved Wales may also find other role models. Instead of being obsessed by England as we have been ever since the time of the Tudors, we may look, for example, across the Irish Sea. Ireland is a remarkable success story within the EU, another largely rural and apparently peripheral nation like Wales, whose rate of growth has made it the tiger economy of Europe, leaving the Germans gasping in admiration and lagging behind. Naturally, the Irish have used the system with much subtlety as befits a people with rare political talent. But they have also seized on the emphasis on supply-side skills and training, the use of information and other technology, the revamping of education and applied research, as now advocated by New Labour in Britain. So the millennium may bring us another novel idea - 'for Wales, see Ireland'.

Devolution in Wales is an important part of a new concept of politics. It reflects a form of political post-modernism in which a more subtle, flexible and contemporary range of relationships will arise between communities: national, regional and local. Even without devolution, the United Kingdom would have had to change. It has been for centuries, at least since Henry VIII, perhaps since William the Conqueror, among the most centralised countries on earth. It has retained, with remarkably little overt change since 1688, a constitution designed for control and conquest. It has not reflected the pluralism of our society. Britain has in the course of the present century transformed itself in fundamental ways, many of them beneficial. It has peacefully shed an empire, it has launched a welfare democracy, it has survived mass depression and world war. Its constitutional structure has remained impervious, but now there is real change here also. The *status quo* is not an option. It may be a rough ride, but to me it is a potentially exciting prospect. For Wales, after its colourful and in many ways unfulfilled history - a story of frequent defeat - the prospects of this imaginatively-designed assembly on the Cardiff waterfront are historically fascinating. Some of us have spent our working lives showing that Wales has a continuous past, the past not of a state but of a living society. But you can have too much obsession with history, too, even if I am hardly the person to say so. Arthur Griffith in 1922 protested against a hopeless view which saw Ireland eternally poised between the dead past and the prophetic future. Was there not to be, he asked the *Dail*, a living Irish nation in the here and now?

Now is the time to say the same for Wales, to ditch the patrician certainties of the 'gentleman from Whitehall' (or the message-maker from Millbank) in favour of what Nye Bevan called the wisdom of ordinary people. It is not inappropriate to recall Bevan today, in the year that marks the fiftieth anniversary of his National Health Service. Nye was an anti-devolutionist who, late on, began to change his mind. He was above all a passionate democrat, who saw in the popular will the agency of historic necessity. He might just be with us now, seeing devolution as the democratic mobilisation of power, saying as he did in his last great speech in 1959, just before cancer destroyed him, that it - and we - represent the future, that the tides of history are flowing in our direction (Foot 1973: 646). "And if we say it and mean it, then we shall lead our people to where they deserve to be led."

Note

1.   In *The Socialist Case* in 1937 (repeated in his postwar edition in 1947: 258).

References

Blair T (1996) 'John Smith Memorial Lecture', London, 7 February.

Bogdanor V (1979) *Devolution*, Oxford: Oxford University Press, new edition 1999.

Butt-Philip A (1975) *The Welsh Question*, Cardiff: University of Wales Press.

Colley L (1992) *Britons: Forging the Nation, 1707-1837*, Newhaven: Yale University Press.

Davies R R (1995) *The Revolt of Owain Glyndŵr*, Oxford: Oxford University Press.

Ellis Jones M (1998) 'An Individious Attempt to Accelerate the Extinction of our Language: Abolition of the Court of Great Sessions and the Welsh Language'; *Welsh History Review* **19**: 226-64.

Evans J (1998) 'The Assembly's Economic Hurdles', *Agenda*, summer: 21-22, Cardiff: Institute of Welsh Affairs.

Foot M (1973) *Aneurin Bevan*, 2: *1945-60*, St Albans: Paladin.

Grant A and Stringer K J (eds) (1995) *Uniting the Kingdom? The Making of British History*, London: Routledge.

Gray Sir J and Osmond J (1997) *Wales in Europe: The Opportunity Presented by a Welsh Assembly*, Cardiff: Institute of Welsh Affairs.

Griffiths D (1996) *Thatcherism and Territorial Politics*, Aldershot: Avebury Press.

Harvie C (1994) *Scotland and Nationalism: Scottish Society and Politics*, 1707-1994 new edition, London: Allen Lane.

Jay D (1937) *The Socialist Case*, London: Faber and Faber.

Jones J G (1992) 'The Parliament for Wales Campaign, 1950-56', *Welsh History Review* **16**: 207-36.

McLean I (1997) 'On Moles and the Habits of Birds: The Unpolitics of Aberfan', *Twentieth Century British History* **8**: 285-309.

Morgan K O (ed) (1973) *Lloyd George: Family Letters c. 1885-1936*, Oxford and Cardiff: Oxford University Press and University of Wales Press.

Morgan K O (1975) *Keir Hardie: Radical and Socialist*, London: Weidenfeld and Nicolson.

Morgan K O (1980 edn) *Wales in British Politics, 1868-1922*, Cardiff: University of Wales Press

Morgan K O (1981) *Rebirth of a Nation: Wales 1880-1980*, Oxford and Cardiff: Oxford University Press and University of Wales Press.

Morgan K O (1995) *Modern Wales. Politics, Places and People*, Cardiff: University of Wales Press.

Welsh Select Committee (1995) *Wales in Europe* (evidence from the University of Wales), London: HMSO.

Williams G A (1985) *When was Wales?* London: Black Raven Press.

10 The Scottish political system revisited

James G Kellas[*]

When my book *The Scottish Political System* first appeared in 1973, its reception in academic circles was mixed.[1] The main point of contention was the use of the term 'political system' to apply to Scotland. Richard Rose preferred to use the word 'subsystem', since Scottish politics was dominated by British government, itself dominated by English politics. In fact, he called his textbook on that subject *Politics in England* (Rose 1965). Michael Keating and Arthur Midwinter espoused the term policy networks to describe Scottish politics, and also stressed the ultimate authority of London over Scotland (Keating and Midwinter 1983: 34, also Midwinter *et al* 1991).

This top-down view of Scottish politics might have made sense in constitutional law, and under Thatcher and Major it applied to the political power wielded by Westminster over a reluctant Scotland. But the lesson which that period taught was how distinct Scottish politics had become from that in the rest of Britain (or rather England), and that the Scottish political system was responsible for that. For it was a bottom-up manifestation of politics, especially that of public opinion in Scotland, which caused the change in Scottish and indeed in time in British politics.

In Scotland, the reaction against the Conservatives was severe, and the demand for devolution rose again in the later 1980s and 1990s. This was not just a question of Scottish electoral behaviour, different as that was. It was also a resurgence of what sociologists in Scotland came to

[*] James Kellas is Professor of Politics at the University of Glasgow.

call Scottish 'civil society' (see the chapter by Lindsay Paterson and Richard Wyn Jones in this volume), acting independently of constitutional and political constraints laid down by the sovereignty of parliament and other centralising conventions of the British political system (this approach dominated Brown *et al* 1998 and Paterson 1994). This civil society provided the dynamic for change in Scottish politics, and was clearly related more to the concept of a Scottish political system operating independently than to the idea of a British governmental system determining the shape of Scottish politics. Lindsay Paterson even asserted that Scotland had long had 'autonomy' in the absence of devolution, federalism or independence, although he accepted that the Thatcher and Major governments had upset that autonomy, so that devolution was now necessary to restore the traditional balance (Paterson 1994).

What was crucial in the development of Scottish politics was the interaction between electoral behaviour, civil society, and institutional structure. This was to lead to the establishment of the Scottish parliament in 1999, and it might yet lead to full Scottish independence.

From 1959, electoral behaviour in Scotland began to diverge from that in England. From near parity in voting patterns between Scotland and England in the general election of 1955, when the Conservatives actually had a small majority (50.1%) in Scotland, and the same (50.4%) in England, 1959 marked the start of a long trend of Conservative decline, which culminated in its all-time low in 1997, when the party lost all its seats and won 17.5% of the vote.

Meanwhile, a most significant change came with the rise of the Scottish National Party (SNP), from almost total obscurity in the 1950s to a peak of 11 MPs and 30.4% of the Scottish vote in the election of October 1974. After a period of decline starting in 1979, the SNP rose again from 1987 to reach 21.5% of the vote in 1992 and 22.1% in 1997. Its total of seats in those elections, however, was very small: three in 1992 and six in 1997. This was the result of the lack of proportionality in the electoral system. The Liberal Democrats with fewer votes in 1997 (13.0%) won 10 seats, concentrated in certain rural constituencies. The Conservatives, with more votes, got no seats at all. Labour, with 45.6%, won 56 seats out of 72 (77.8%). The political result of these electoral trends was to greatly weaken the position of the Unionist Party (the Conservatives) and to strengthen the Nationalists.

The Nationalists were to benefit further from the proposed setting up of a Scottish parliament. Seen by most as the party which best serves Scotland's interests,[2] according to opinion polls in 1997 and 1998 levels of support for the SNP were, not surprisingly, much higher in relation to voting for the Scottish parliament than voting for the Westminster parliament, where Labour maintained its strong lead. In several polls conducted for Scottish newspapers during 1998, which asked about voting intentions for the Scottish parliament, the SNP actually went into the lead over Labour. Some voters appear to be prepared to change their votes between the first and second ballots, of which the electoral system to the Scottish parliament consists, and they tend to give the SNP more support at the second ballot - the party list. This would bring the SNP more seats, as the second ballot is a top-up to bring the number of seats more into line with the number of votes for each party.

The electoral divergence between Scotland and England, which the elections to the Scottish parliament will magnify, has had profound effects on Scottish politics generally, and particularly on the structure of Scottish political institutions. When Scotland and England voted the same way, the UK government could represent both nations. But when Scotland voted differently from England, and did so consistently, then the so-called 'doomsday scenario' emerged.[3] This was the situation in which Scotland felt unrepresented in the UK, since its votes were over-ridden by the other parts of the kingdom. This situation might not have been too serious if Scotland had retained its autonomy, in Lindsay Paterson's terms. But the Conservative governments of Thatcher and Major were in no mood to maintain this autonomy. Their view of the UK was that it constituted one civil and political system, and that the mandate granted by the British voters gave the government the right to govern Scotland as it wished. This made some Scottish Conservatives uneasy, especially those who had supported devolution when Edward Heath had proposed it in 1968, such as Alick Buchanan-Smith, George Younger and Malcolm Rifkind. They continued to support it at the referendum in 1979, but the failure of that vote to meet the 40% rule (see the chapter by Paula Surridge and David McCrone) for a 'yes' decision sapped their enthusiasm, and all the Conservative leaders apart from Buchanan-Smith (who died in 1991) ceased their public support for devolution in the 1980s and 1990s.

After 1987, the Conservatives embarked on a more radical policy agenda, which included the introduction of the community charge (poll tax) in Scotland one year before England and Wales. With a strong Thatcherite, Michael Forsyth, at the Scottish Office from 1987 as a junior minister, and eventually as Scottish secretary of state from 1995, Scotland was governed more as a colony than as an autonomous part of the UK. Nonetheless, Forsyth responded to Scottish nationalism in several ways. For example, he brought the 'Stone of Destiny' back to Scotland. This coronation stone had been taken to

England by Edward I in the thirteenth century; it was 'stolen' by some Scottish nationalists in 1950, and returned to Scotland - temporarily. It had been a grievance of some Scottish nationalists that it was kept at Westminster when its rightful home was Scotland.

More substantively, Forsyth gave the Scottish Grand Committee[4] of the House of Commons more prominence, and it embarked on sittings in various towns in Scotland. This move had a double edge, however, from the Conservative point of view. It gave an opportunity for aggrieved citizens to demonstrate against the government with considerable media attention, and it reinforced the demand for a Scottish parliament. For if the Scottish MPs alone could be entrusted with the work of parliament in the Committee, why not go all the way, and set up a Scottish parliament which would have real powers?

The Conservatives had in fact already conceded that Scotland had the right to independence if its will was clearly expressed. In the White Paper, *Scotland in the Union. A Partnership for Good* (1993), John Major and Ian Lang (then secretary of state for Scotland) stated that "no nation could be held irrevocably in a Union against its will"(1993: 5). While the government was not going to give Scotland the right to vote on the question of independence in a referendum at that point, this statement was a hostage to fortune. At some point in the future, such a referendum might take place, and then Scotland could vote itself out of the Union.

Curiously, in June 1996 Labour pledged itself to a referendum on devolution when previously it had stated that a Labour general election victory was sufficient to endorse devolution. The referendum pledge turned out to be good tactics, since it effectively passed the decision from the Labour Party to the people, and deflected the Conservative attack, especially on the 'tartan tax', which was to be the subject of a separate question.

But Labour's decision to hold a referendum strengthened the SNP's position also, for once the referendum had become the preferred method for determining the will of Scotland, there was little to stop the SNP demanding a referendum on independence. This it has duly done in the run-up to the elections for the Scottish parliament (Salmond 1998). It is curious to see the Labour Party and the Liberal Democrats denying the SNP's demand for an expression of the popular will on the question of independence, although this is of course entirely explicable in terms of Labour Party interest and the desire to establish firmly the devolved government of Scotland, without the devolved system being threatened from its beginning by independence. Yet the SNP could insist upon such a referendum if it were to hold the balance of power in the Scottish parliament, or (less likely) if it were to gain an overall majority.

The Liberal Democrats are just as hostile to a referendum on independence as is Labour, but this could change if the Westminster situation were to become intolerable for the party. There are already some Liberal Democrat activists whose attitude to independence is ambivalent. In a federal European Union, which the Liberal Democrats espouse, a federal United Kingdom, which is also supported by the party, might be part of the evolution of a 'Europe of the Regions'. In such a union, Scotland could be directly represented in the EU as a member, and the role of the UK minimised, and perhaps eliminated. So a quasi-independent Scotland is not feared by at least some Liberal Democrats in this scenario, although it is a different scenario from that which the SNP prefers, which would cut the constitutional link with Britain altogether. There is a snag, however, for these independentist Liberal Democrats. The 1997 Scottish Election Survey showed that Liberal Democrat supporters are distinctly cool on independence; just 11% support it (Brown *et al* 1998: 162). Indeed, of Liberal Democrat supporters who voted in the referendum, 58% voted 'yes' on the first question, compared with 91% of Labour supporters and 99% of SNP supporters. Liberal Democrat supporters are, however, considerably more devolutionist than Conservative supporters, of whom only 20% voted 'yes' (see the chapters by Paula Surridge and David McCrone and by John Curtice in this volume).

While electoral behaviour and party choice has been the crucial agent for constitutional change in Scotland, and has also inspired institutional change short of altering the constitution itself, it has never been easy to separate Scottish from British factors in Scottish voting behaviour. Thus, the result of the 1979 referendum, with its bare majority for the Scotland Act (51.6% on a 63.6% turnout) seemed to owe as much to the unpopularity of the Callaghan government after the 'winter of discontent' as to the feelings of Scots about devolution itself (Bochel *et al* 1981, Mitchell 1996: 163) (see also the chapter by Anthony Heath and Bridget Taylor in this volume). But it was also in a way a false result, in that the 40% rule imposed the requirement that 40% of the registered electorate should vote 'yes' for the Act to be endorsed. No such rule applied in the 1997 referendums; if it had, the Welsh referendum (with 50.3% voting 'yes' on a 50.1% turnout) would have been treated as a negative vote. By the standards of 1997, Scotland should have had an assembly since 1979!

Most commentators have tried to explain devolution and nationalism in Scotland in terms of general changes in Scottish society and politics. But the paradoxes abound here, as well as in the interaction of Scottish and British factors in voting in particular elections and referendums. For just as civil society was serving to distinguish Scotland from England, so political culture was bringing them closer together.[5] Evidence from various surveys conducted in the 1990s points to only minor differences in attitudes between Scotland and England on issues of equality and liberty, public and private enterprise, and the like.

Miller and his colleagues concluded that despite the distinctiveness of Scotland in a wide range of matters from institutions to voting behaviour and national identity, these did not seem to have much of an impact on the attitudes investigated (Miller *et al* 1996). Oddly they state that "any assumption that the culture of a people can be inferred, with any accuracy, from its institutions of government is false" (Miller *et al* 1996: 409). Instead, in their view, Scots shared a commitment to common western values with other Europeans and north Americans. "It was not a peculiarly English culture that dominated the public mind on either side of the border. On the contrary, our evidence was that **neither** the Scots **nor** the English had principles which were consistent with the British constitution" (Miller *et al* 1996: 373, emphasis in original). Although Scotland clearly had a political system and different electoral behaviour from England, it was not a 'distinct society', at least in comparison with Canada, or even more, with Quebec. It was of course Quebec's claim to be a distinct society which was at first accepted in the Meech Lake Accord of 1987, but this was never ratified as part of the Canadian constitution. This remains a strong grievance in Quebec, and has strengthened nationalism and separatism there. But the academic findings on Scotland's distinct society (or lack or it) have not surfaced as a political issue in Scotland, at least as compared to Quebec.

The relevance of these findings to contemporary Scottish politics is not clear. The rise of Scottish nationalism and the devolution question seem to slip through the net in this context, as does the significance of Scottish national identity. Moreover, the increasingly distinctive electoral behaviour is unaccounted for by this thesis of an absence of distinct political culture in Scotland.

Brown and her colleagues, while endorsing the conclusions of the 'one political culture' theory, nonetheless argue that Scotland's civil society remains distinct from England's and that different agendas and discourses now operate north and south of the border (Brown *et al* 1998). The definition of civil society adopted by Brown and her colleagues avoids the political. It is "those areas of social life - the domestic world, the economic sphere, cultural activities and political interaction - which are organised by private and voluntary arrangements between individuals and groups outside the direct control of the state" (Held 1992: 73, Brown *et al* 1998: 30): see the chapter by Lindsay Paterson and Richard Wyn Jones in this volume for discussion of civil society in Scotland and Wales.

This definition leaves the Scottish political system and electoral behaviour to one side. Clearly, on this understanding, the political institutions in Scotland, such as the Scottish Office and local government, are part of the state, and not part of civil society. And yet Scottish civil society both reflects and is deeply enmeshed in the institutions of the state as they have developed in Scotland. It could be argued that without the establishment of the Scottish Office in 1885 it would have been difficult to sustain the demand for devolution and independence. For once the executive had organised itself on a Scottish basis, the case for a legislative branch to underpin it became more credible, and eventually irresistible. And nearly all the features of Scottish civil society are tied into the state, such as education, the arts, and so on.

As far as electoral behaviour in Scotland is concerned, the differences from England were already apparent in the nineteenth century, when the Liberals were in the ascendancy in Scotland. The Conservatives, reduced to eight seats out of 60 in Scotland in 1870, and seven in 1880, revived only when Gladstone split the Liberal Party over Home Rule for Ireland in 1886. The Liberal-Unionists took 16 seats in 1886, and the Conservatives 12. By 1912 the Conservatives had merged with the Liberal-Unionists to form the Unionist Party. This alliance of old-style Conservatives and Liberal-Unionists was still in being in 1955, when it won 36 out of 71 Scottish seats, two seats more than Labour. The disjunction of the Liberals from the Conservatives finally took place in the 1960s under the Liberal leader Jo Grimond, and the Unionists decided to join completely with the Conservatives and change the party name from Unionist to the Scottish Conservative and Unionist Party in 1965. In everyday usage it was the Conservative Party. This effectively cancelled the Liberal vote for the Unionists, and was one reason for the steady decline of Conservative voting in Scotland. The old Liberal-Unionist vote largely dispersed to the Liberals and the SNP in rural areas, and in the lowlands to Labour, which recovered the anti-Irish/Catholic working-class vote from the Unionist Party.

These differences between Scotland and England in voting behaviour owe much to Scottish civil society, especially the religious division between Protestants and Catholics, and the close links with Ireland as a result of immigration and imperial commerce. Only now since 1992, do surveys indicate that distinctive voting patterns according to religion are dying out, as Catholics integrate further into Scottish society (Brown *et al* 1998, Bennie *et al* 1997). Moreover, in Scottish politics 'the Union' is now that between Scotland and England, not between Britain and Ireland. But the electoral repercussions of that have not benefited the Conservatives this time, rather the reverse. The Conservatives have seen their vote slip away, in part because of their resistance to devolution, and their image as the English Party. A new anti-Conservative Party, the SNP, has emerged and has taken the Conservative seats in rural areas which had represented the last stand of the party in Scotland.

Brown and her colleagues argue that "the distinctiveness of Scottish voting is not really a social conflict with England but a political one. Scottish voters dislike the Conservative Party, which until 1997 the majority of the people in the south of England chose to further much the same social and economic goals as the Scots entrust to the parties of the left and centre" (Brown *et al* 1998: 165). That these goals, under Thatcher and Major, really were the same for Conservative voters in the south of England as for non-Conservatives in Scotland is difficult to believe and cannot be deduced from the limited survey evidence provided. As Brown and her colleagues state also (Brown *et al* 1998: 163), support for a Scottish parliament was seen by the voters in the 1997 referendum "as a means to secure economic and social reform", and this was certainly seen as a break away from a Conservative-dominated UK parliament. So the political conflict with England was underpinned by a desire to change the economic and social agenda in Scotland. By that logic, the political conflict was also a social and economic one.

A big divide between Scotland and England exists of course in terms of national identity and nationalism. It is difficult to know whether a sense of Scottish identity has increased in recent years, in line with the rise in support for the SNP and support for devolution. Surveys addressing the subject of national identity date only from the 1970s, and even so the variation in the questions asked makes it difficult to plot a trend over time. From a wider historical perspective, the period from the Union of 1707 to the 1920s was the heyday of Britishness in Scotland. The name North Britain was often used in place of Scotland, and Victorian Scots seem generally to have been proud of their British identity. In the absence of survey evidence, however, it is of course impossible to know whether this was widespread in the population or largely confined to the middle class. The 1997 Scottish Election Survey shows a stronger Scottish identity in the working classes than in the middle classes (Brown *et al* 1998), and it is likely that even in the heyday of North Britain, the working class retained a strong sense of Scottishness. This sense of Scottishness was reinforced by the education system, at least at the elementary school level, and in popular culture. In schools the poems of Robert Burns and the novels of Sir Walter Scott were in daily use, and emphasised Scottish identity and history, often portrayed in conflict with England. While the higher levels of education and culture moved sharply away from this towards British (meaning English) literature and history, the mass of the population probably retained its Scottish identity, culture and nationalism.

The change in national identity then came in the middle to late twentieth century, and is still underway. The middle class gave up North Britain and replaced it with Scotland.[6] The old adjective Scotch was replaced with Scottish, except for whisky and mist. The Labour movement moved in the other direction in the early and mid-twentieth century, with the Scottish Labour Party of Keir Hardie and Ramsay MacDonald integrated into the (British) Labour Party, and the Scottish trade unions, with few exceptions, merged with British ones. A change back to Scottishness began in 1945, when Labour candidates in Scotland at the general election supported home rule (a Scottish parliament). Attlee and his Scottish Office ministers were able to ignore this by strengthening the Scottish Office and the Scottish Grand Committee, although the nationalists gathered around two million signatures for a Scottish Covenant in 1949-50 demanding a parliament. The electoral weakness of the SNP, however, meant that British parties did not have to worry about their seats. The 1960s changed all that, especially after Winnie Ewing won the safe Labour seat of Hamilton for the SNP in 1967. From that moment, devolution was strongly on the agenda once more.

The story of the devolution campaign and its relationship to nationalism cannot be told here (see the chapters by David McCrone and Bethan Lewis, and by Paula Surridge and David McCrone in this volume). The "settled will of the Scottish people" (in the words of the late John Smith MP) was never clear, right up to the time of the referendum of 1997. Not only did the 1979 referendum result reveal a deeply divided nation, albeit narrowly voting 'yes', but the period from 1979 to 1997 was marked by indecision about devolution in all the parties, and apparently lukewarm support in the electorate. The end-result of the Scottish parliament may have come after "a story of an astonishing minor miracles", in Canon Kenyon Wright's words (Wright 1998: 11), but it was also the working out of a general trend, which began in 1959, of disjunction between politics in Scotland and politics in England. By 1997 Scottish national identity had been politicised in a way not seen since the Union of 1707. *A Claim of Right for Scotland*[7] (Wright 1998: 52-3), proclaiming the sovereignty of the Scottish people, was signed by 50 of the 72 Scottish MPs at the inaugural meeting of the Scottish Constitutional Convention on 30 March 1989. Although the Conservatives did not attend, their commitment to Scottish sovereignty seemed to be no less, as in John Major's 1993 statement in the White Paper, referred to earlier.

There was an element of political unreality in all this of course. The Scottish Constitutional Convention could not operationalise Scottish sovereignty on its own. The election of a Labour government of the UK was needed to bring to fruition the desire for a Scottish parliament. When Canon Wright proclaimed in 1989, "What if that other single voice we all know so well [meaning Margaret Thatcher] responds by saying, 'We say No, We are the State,'? Well We say Yes and We are the People" (Wright 1998: 52), he had no constitutional means of realising that popular will. In fact, the option of Scottish independence was ruled out at the start of the Convention, with no possibility of it seeking a referendum on that question. It is little wonder that the SNP boycotted the Convention, although they probably lost electoral support because of that. The Convention did not even propose a referendum on its proposed scheme when it finally reported in November 1995 (Scottish Constitutional Convention 1995). So the sovereignty of the Scottish people was to be expressed by means of a UK general election and the election of a British Labour government. It was an unpleasant surprise to some in the Convention when Tony Blair announced in June 1996 that there would after all be a referendum on Labour's devolution proposals, with a separate question on the tax powers. This prompted the resignation from the Convention of one of its joint Chairs, Lord Harry Ewing, a former Labour minister. (The other Chair, David Steel, stayed on.) So the settled will of the Scottish people and the sovereignty of the Scottish people came down to a two-question referendum on devolution.

Along with the decisive result of the referendum, Scottish nationalism has come back on to the political agenda. As with the study of devolution, the study of Scottish nationalism has occupied much of the literature on Scottish politics. After a brief period of enthusiasm starting with Winnie Ewing's election in 1967 and ending with the referendum of 1979, most analysts were inclined to write off Scottish nationalism as a spent force (Curtice and Steed 1984). While Labour may have intended devolution to 'kill Scottish nationalism stone dead', the electorate apparently thought otherwise. During 1998, the SNP drew level with Labour in voting intentions for the Scottish parliament according to opinion polls, especially when the second (party list) vote is taken into account. Even more surprising, support for independence - in response to poll questions about a hypothetical referendum on independence - has exceeded the 50% mark on several occasions in 1998. More ominously for the future of the Union, a large majority appear to expect that Scottish independence would come in the next 5, 15 or 20 years (the time periods vary in different polls).[8]

Is this at last "the break-up of Britain" predicted (and supported) by Tom Nairn in 1977? Yes, it is certainly on its way this time, for in Nairn's view a Scottish parliament would lead inevitably to "its eventual accompaniment, a Scottish state" (Nairn 1997: 222-23). As it happens, the 'eventual' has looked a lot nearer in 1998, according to the polls. Nairn, writing in the *Independent on Sunday*, on 20 September 1998, saw the referendum result in nationalist terms, as "an abruptly re-politicised national identity and not from 'democratic deficit' and regional economic needs alone." According to Nairn, devolution is not much good in this situation: "it's independence or nothing".

Curiously, 'nationalism' as such has never been so much in disrepute in Europe. Events in the Balkans, the Basque country and Corsica, in particular, have made the old-style nationalists of the SNP and the Social Democratic and Labour Party (SDLP) in Northern Ireland shrink from that label. John Hume, leader of the SDLP, proclaimed that he was a 'post-nationalist', and Alex Salmond, convener of the SNP, repeated that for himself. Interviewed by Stephen Fay in the same issue of the *Independent on Sunday* (20 September 1998: 15), he even said he wanted to drop the word National from the name of the SNP, renaming it the Scottish Independence Party. "It's a much better encapsulation of what we're about. Independence is our idea, and our politics are social democrat. I'm a post-nationalist".

Meanwhile, Cardinal Thomas Winning, the leader of the Catholic Church in Scotland, told a conference of bishops in Brussels that in Scotland there had been a "growing realisation that our future as a nation is European" (*The Scotsman*, 6 October 1998). He described Scottish nationalism as "mature, respectful and international in outlook". He was no doubt aware of the survey result (quoted in note 8) that in a referendum a majority of Catholics say they would vote for independence. Both the SNP and Cardinal Winning had their eyes on the European dimension, which no doubt has different resonances for the SNP and for the Roman Catholic Church. 'Independence in Europe' had been a slogan for the SNP since the late 1980s, apparently banishing the separatist taunt. For the Cardinal, the Scottish presence in Europe would no doubt represent the revival of a Catholic strategy harking back to the Declaration of Arbroath of 1320, which the Scottish bishops sent to the Pope on behalf of a wide range of Scots, asserting Scottish independence from England.

One aspect of Scottish nationalism which has attracted adverse publicity in recent years is anti-English feeling. Always obvious on the football field, by the 1990s this feeling was apparently on the rise, and was associated - at least by some journalists and academics - with the increasing support for the SNP and for devolution. Organisations such as Scottish Watch and Settler Watch opposed the so-called white settlers from England, who were increasingly buying houses, farms and businesses in rural Scotland. Abuse was reported, and one politics lecturer actually received a mock letter-bomb.[9]

The SNP expelled any of their members associated with the two anti-English organisations, which by 1998 had virtually disappeared. Nonetheless, the media continued to publicise the anti-English elements in Scotland, in a variety of broadcasts and in Sunday colour magazines.[10] Some cases came before the race relations bodies or industrial relations courts, alleging discrimination against English people in employment in Scotland. None of these was sustained. (There were also cases in England alleging anti-Scottish discrimination.) Survey evidence on anti-English feeling in Scotland did not support the view that this was strong, and the anecdotal evidence was contradictory, some people supporting and some denying it. For a while in 1998 attention was focused on Scottish attitudes to the England football team in the World Cup, but the political relevance of that was not clear. However, all this pointed to a heightened consciousness of Scottish-English relations as a result of devolution and heightened nationalism.

Conclusion

Since the 1970s, the Scottish political system has changed in fundamental ways. Not only had support for devolution risen dramatically in the 1997 referendum compared with that in 1979, but the implementation of the scheme is underway. There is already a new Scottish political system.

Meanwhile, nationalism is stronger and the prospect of independence is taken more seriously. This is only in part the result of the electoral strength of the SNP (which is still weaker in votes and voting intentions for Westminster than it was in October 1974). Nationalist attitudes and support for independence have spread throughout the population, and across all parties, with perhaps the exception of the Conservatives, who at the end of a long decline since 1959, sank to under one-fifth of the vote and no seats in 1997. Their virtual extinction (perhaps temporary) marks the lowest point of unionism in Scottish electoral history. Support for independence as measured in opinion polls was running at record levels in 1998, with a majority assenting if the question asked was intended vote in a referendum on the subject.

It is more difficult to tell whether the political culture in Scotland has changed, and whether it now diverges more than previously from that in England. Survey evidence points against this, and there is clearly more in common between Scotland and England in social and economic attitudes and interests than between these nations and Wales and Northern Ireland. In the latter two, language and religion respectively are major cleavage lines. Scotland and England share a language, and their Protestant-Catholic relations, while more strained in Scotland than in England, bear no real comparison with the divided communities in Northern Ireland.

Explanations for these changes are highly paradoxical (Miller 1998). As Scotland and England grew closer together in social and economic profiles and attitudes, so Scottish nationalism also grew, particularly the desire for a Scottish parliament. That is because the tensions arising from divergent voting behaviour and the long period of radical right Conservative rule changed attitudes in Scotland towards Westminster government. The Labour Party in the 1980s became far more committed to devolution, and the Scottish Constitutional Convention brought the party into line with the Liberal Democrats on proportional representation for a Scottish parliament and other liberal reforms.

Even as England came more into line with Scotland in voting behaviour in the 1997 election, especially as far as Labour voting is concerned, the SNP remains a distinctive Scottish phenomenon and Scottish nationalism a stronger threat to the union. In a survey in March 1998 62% expected that Scotland would be independent in the next 15 years (see note 8). English nationalism seemed to grow as a reaction to devolution and Scottish nationalism, mainly through the Conservative Party in its Euro-sceptic stance and William Hague's reference at the party's 1998 conference to the possibility of setting up an English parliament.

Expectations of the break-up of the United Kingdom at some point in the near future are stronger than before, but much will depend on how devolution works in Scotland and indeed in Wales. If the Labour government at Westminster were to repeat the mistakes of the Conservatives from 1979 to 1997, and try to rule Scotland (and Wales) in home rule matters - even if indirectly - the impetus for break-up will grow stronger. As before, the future of the United Kingdom depends on a partnership of its nations, not on the sovereignty of the UK crown in parliament.

This partnership is essentially a political one, and it is to polities rather than to 'civil society' and 'political culture' that we should look for clues to the future. Voting patterns in Scotland (including a possible referendum on independence) and political relationships between the Scottish and UK parliaments will determine the future of Scotland and the UK.

Notes

1. For an account of these reviews see the 4th edition of Kellas 1989.
2. In the 1997 Scottish Referendum Survey, 62.3% of respondents said that they trust the SNP to work for Scotland just about always or most of the time, compared with 60.7% Labour, 27.5% the Liberal Democrats, and 10.5% the Conservative Party.
3. The phrase was first used in the magazine *Radical Scotland* 25, Feb./March 1987: 9.
4. The Scottish Grand Committee consists of all the 72 Scottish MPs and has a variety of functions, including debating Scottish bills at the second reading stage, taking a question time for Scottish ministers and holding short debates on matters relating to Scotland. In 1996-97 it even heard non-Scottish Office ministers such as the prime minister and chancellor of the exchequer in debates held in Scotland.
5. Miller *et al* 1996, especially 366-73; Brown *et al* 1999 (1996 edn): 163-5; Curtice 1988, 1992 and 1996.
6. Names such as the North British Railway and North British Hotel started to disappear from the 1920s, although the latter name survived in Edinburgh until the 1980s. It then became the Balmoral Hotel, which could be interpreted as 'crown imperial' as much as Scottish national! The name certainly has a higher tourist potential, since North British has no appeal in tourism.
7. *A Claim of Right for Scotland* asserts the 'sovereign right' of the people of Scotland to determine their form of government. It was signed in 1989 by all but one (Tam Dalyell) of the Scottish Labour MPs and by the Liberal Democrat MPs.
8. System Three in *The Herald*, 6 May 1998, gave the SNP a 5-point lead over Labour, and on 6 July a 14-point lead. ICM in *The Scotsman* showed a closer result at this time, with SNP and Labour more or less level. By August 1998, both System Three and ICM were showing a narrow Labour lead, but in the crucial second vote, which determines the overall party shares, the SNP consistently did better than on the first ballot, even if in later surveys not as well as Labour. Labour believed that voters were being misled into

voting for their second choice at the second vote, and pledged to educate the electorate to cast both votes for the same party.

As for support for independence, ICM from June to September 1998 showed a consistent majority for independence in a two-option referendum (yes/no), but devolution well ahead of independence (48% to 33%) in a three-way choice including no parliament (17%) (*Scotland on Sunday*, 3 May 1998). While young people continued predominantly to support the SNP and independence, as they had done in previous studies as far back as 1974, a more recent change was in Roman Catholic preferences. ICM showed that Catholics backed independence in a two-way referendum at 58%, more than non-Catholics (51%) (*Scotsman*, 28 August 1998). Catholics were more loyal to Labour than non-Catholics when it came to voting at elections for both Westminster and Edinburgh, and were the most loyal supporters of Labour in Scotland.

Expectations that Scotland would go independent in the next 15 years ran at 62%, with only 30% disagreeing, in a MORI poll for the *Mail on Sunday* quoted in *Scotland on Sunday* (29 March 1998). Yet a federal system for Scotland, England and Wales got most support (76% agreed, 21% disagreed) in an ICM poll for *Scotland on Sunday*, 3 May 1998.

9. Malcolm Dickson, then a lecturer in Political Science at Dundee University, now at Strathclyde University, received a mock letter-bomb in 1994. He had written an article on Scottish-English relations in *Scottish Affairs* (Dickson 1994). Using the same British Rights Survey evidence as Miller and colleagues (1996), Dickson concluded that while there was "little evidence to support a wide problem, it may well be the case that localised problems do occur in areas where economic and social infrastructures are more fragile and vulnerable" (Dickson 1994: 131). He added, "the most significant comparisons are in the similarity between the English and Scots born populations. This, added to the fact that in key political attitudes the English in Scotland are significantly different from the English in England, means the overall claims of groups such as Scottish Watch over a widespread and dangerous problem are probably somewhat exaggerated".

10. See for example the *Independent on Sunday*, 20 September 1998, and 'Scotch wrath' in *The Sunday Times Magazine*, 4 October 1998, 16-22.

References

Bennie L, Brand J and Mitchell J (1997) *How Scotland Votes*, Manchester: Manchester University Press: 119.

Bochel J, Denver D and Macartney A (eds) (1981) *The Referendum Experience: Scotland 1979*, Aberdeen: Aberdeen University Press.

Brown A, McCrone D and Paterson L (1998) *Politics and Society in Scotland*, Basingstoke: Macmillan, first published 1996.

Curtice J (1998) 'One nation?' in Jowell R, Witherspoon S and Brooks L (eds), *British Social Attitudes: The Fifth Report*, Aldershot: Gower.

Curtice J (1992) 'The North-South Divide', in *British Social Attitudes Survey: The Ninth Report*, Aldershot: Dartmouth.

Curtice J (1996) 'One Nation Again?' in Jowell R, Curtice J, Park A, Brook L and Thomson K (eds) *British Social Attitudes: The 13th Report*, Aldershot: Gower.

Curtice J and Steed M (1984) 'The Results Analysed' in Butler D and Kavanagh D *The British General Election of 1983*, London: Macmillan.

Dickson M (1994) 'Should Auld Acquaintance be Forgot? A Comparison of the Scots and English in Scotland', *Scottish Affairs* 7: 112-34.

Held D (1992) 'The Development of the Modern States' in Hall S and Gieben B (eds) *Formations of Modernity*, London: Polity Press.

Keating M and Midwinter A (1983) *The Government of Scotland*, Edinburgh: Mainstream.

Kellas J G (1989) *The Scottish Political System*, Cambridge: Cambridge University Press, 4th edition.

Midwinter A, Keating M and Mitchell J (1991) *Government and Public Policy in Scotland*, Basingstoke: Macmillan.

Miller W L (1998) 'The Periphery and its Paradoxes', *West European Politics* 21: 167-96.

Miller W L, Timpson A M and Lessnoff M (1996) *Political Culture in Contemporary Britain. People and Politicians, Principles and Practice*, Oxford: Clarendon Press.

Mitchell J (1996) *Strategies for Self-Government. The Campaigns for a Scottish Parliament*, Edinburgh: Polygon.

Nairn T (1977) *The Break-up of Britain*, London: Verso.

Nairn T (1997) *Faces of Nationalism. Janus Revisited*, London and New York: Verso, 222-3.

Paterson L (1994) *The Autonomy of Modern Scotland*, Edinburgh: Edinburgh University Press.

Radical Scotland (1987) **25** (February/March): 9.

Rose R (1965) *Politics in England*, London: Faber and Faber.

Salmond A (1998) Foreword in *Towards the Scottish Balmoral*, Edinburgh: SNP.

Scottish Constitutional Convention (1995) *Scotland's Parliament. Scotland's Right*, Edinburgh: Scottish Constitutional Convention.

White Paper (1993) *Scotland in the Union. A Partnership for Good*, Edinburgh: HMSO, Cm 2225.

Wright K (1998) *The People Say Yes. The Making of Scotland's Parliament*, Glendaruel: Argyll Publishing.

Appendix I
Technical details of the survey

Katarina Thomson [*]

Background

The 1997 Scottish and Welsh Referendum Studies form part of a larger programme of British Election Studies (BES). Cross-sectional surveys have taken place immediately after every general election since 1964, giving a total of ten so far. There have also been two non-election year surveys (in 1963 and 1969), a postal referendum study in 1975, additional or booster Scottish studies in 1974, 1979, 1992 and 1997, an additional Welsh study in 1979, a Northern Ireland Election Study in 1992, and campaign studies in 1987, 1992 and 1996-7. The 1997 British Election Study also included an ethnic minority booster sample and a qualitative study of electoral volatility. There was a multi-wave British Election Panel Study (BEPS) in the period 1992-97. In addition, the 1997 British Social Attitudes survey carried an election module. Since the 1997 general election, the programme has continued with the Scottish and Welsh Referendum Studies in 1997, a Northern Ireland Referendum and Assembly Election Study in 1998 and a new multi-wave British Election Panel Study (BEPS2) which is designed to run until the next general election.

The BES series was originated by David Butler (Nuffield College Oxford) and Donald Stokes (University of Michigan) who continued to direct the studies up to 1970. The series then passed to Ivor Crewe, Bo

[*] Katarina Thomson is Research Director at SCPR, co-director of the British Social Attitudes survey series and a member of CREST.

Särlvik and James Alt at the University of Essex (later joined by David Robertson) who organised the two 1974 studies and the 1979 study. The 1983, 1987, 1992 and 1997 studies were directed by Anthony Heath (Jesus then Nuffield College Oxford), Roger Jowell (Social and Community Planning Research) and John Curtice (University of Liverpool then University of Strathclyde). Since 1994, this collaboration has taken the form of the Centre for Research into Elections and Social Trends (CREST), an Economic and Social Research Council (ESRC) funded Research Centre, linking SCPR and Nuffield College Oxford. In 1997 the BES team was joined by Pippa Norris (Harvard University). (For publication arising from earlier studies see, for example, Butler and Stokes 1974; Särlvik and Crewe 1983; Heath *et al* 1985; Heath *et al* 1991; Heath *et al* 1994; Miller 1981; Brand *et al* 1983; Bennie *et al* 1997, Brown *et al* 1998, Brown *et al* 1999; Balsom *et al* 1983, Balsom *et al* 1984, Balsom 1985, Evans and Norris 1999, Heath *et al* forthcoming.)

Nuffield College found the bulk of the funds for the fieldwork for the early Butler and Stokes surveys. The ESRC (formerly the Social Science Research Council) then became the major funding agency, wholly supporting the Essex surveys. The 1983 study was funded jointly by the ESRC, Pergamon Press and Jesus College Oxford; the 1987 study by the ESRC, Pergamon Press and the Sainsbury Family Charitable Trusts; and the 1992 and 1997 studies by the ESRC and the Gatsby Charitable Foundation (one of the Sainsbury Family Charitable Trusts).

The 1997 Scottish and Welsh Referendum Studies

The 1997 Scottish and Welsh Referendum Studies were conducted by CREST in co-operation with David McCrone (University of Edinburgh) and Richard Wyn Jones (University of Wales, Aberystwyth). The studies were funded by the ESRC *via* an additional grant to CREST. The research team also included Lindsay Brook, Caroline Bryson, Alison Park and Katarina Thomson at SCPR; Geoffrey Evans and Bridget Taylor at Nuffield College Oxford; Alice Brown and Lindsay Paterson at the University of Edinburgh; and Paula Surridge then at the University of Aberdeen.

The 1997 Scottish and Welsh studies were intended to be comparative, hence the questionnaires were designed to contain largely identical or functionally-equivalent questions. Some sections were added to deal with issues specific to Scotland or Wales, such as the Welsh language. In many cases, the questions were drawn from earlier British Election Studies, to enable comparison over time, especially in Scotland where the 1992 and 1997 studies had included Scottish booster samples and Scottish modules.

In common with the British Election Studies, the data from the 1997 Referendum Studies have been deposited at the Data Archive at the University of Essex together with full documentation. More detailed information about the survey design and fieldwork is presented in Thomson *et al* (1999 forthcoming).

The sample

The sample was designed to be representative of the adult population, eligible to vote in the Scottish and Welsh referendums, that is who were included on the electoral registers in Scotland (including north of the Caledonian Canal) and Wales. However, in practice, the sample was strictly speaking one of adults registered to vote at the address at which they were living at the time of the referendums, and does not include adults registered to vote at another address in Scotland or Wales.

The sample was drawn from the small users Postcode Address File (PAF) using a multi-stage design as follows:

1.   Any postcode sectors with fewer than 500 delivery points (DPs) were grouped together and treated as one sector.

2.   Sectors were then sorted into groups:

       In Scotland: five groups of councils were formed. Within each of the five groups, postcode sectors were listed in order of population density and two cut-off points drawn at approximately one-third and two-thirds (in terms of DPs) down the ordered list to create three roughly equal-sized bands. Within each of the 15 bands thus created, postcode sectors were listed in order of percentage of households with the household head in non-manual occupations (SEGs 1 to 6 and 13).

       In Wales: postcode sectors were sorted by county, giving eight groups. Within each county, sectors were listed in order of percentage of persons speaking Welsh (using 1991 census data). Two cut-off points were drawn approximately one-third and two-thirds (in terms of DPs) down the ordered list to create three roughly equal-sized bands. Within each of the 24 bands thus created, postcode sectors were sorted in order of population density.

3.   37 postcode sectors were thus selected in Scotland and 37 in Wales with a probability proportional to DP count. Thirty-one DPs were sampled systematically throughout each selected sector with probability proportional to the number of occupied units as given by the Multiple Occupancy Indicator (MOI). This resulted in 1,147 **issued addresses** in each of Scotland and Wales.

4.   At each issued address, the interviewer selected at random one or two dwelling units (DUs) for interview as follows:

   •   If there was only one DU at the address, this was selected.

   •   If there were 2 to 5 DUs, **one** DU was selected for interview at random.

   •   If there were 6 or more DUs and MOI was 2 or above, **one** DU was selected for interview at random.

   •   If there were 6 or more DUs and MOI was 1, **two** DUs were selected for interview at random.

The random selection of DUs was done using a Kish grid and random numbers generated separately for each serial number. This resulted in 1,170 selected DUs in Scotland and 1,151 in Wales.

5.   At each (selected) DU, the interviewer established the number of adults normally resident there who were also on the electoral register at that address. This was established through the following sequence of questions:

   FOR EACH PERSON AGED 18+: *Are you/Is he/she* on the electoral register **at this address**? INCLUDE PEOPLE WHO ARE ON LOCAL AUTHORITY ELECTORAL REGISTERS WHETHER ON PARLIAMENTARY REGISTER OR NOT.

   IF DK: Did *you/he/she* vote in the recent referendum?

   IF NO/DK: Did *you/he/she* get a polling card for the recent referendum?

   IF NO/DK: Did *you/he/she* vote from this address in the General Election on May 1st?

> IF NO/DK: Did *you/he/she* receive a polling card at this address for the <u>General Election</u> on May 1st?

> From those recorded as "on the register" or "don't know" as a result of this sequence of questions ('eligible persons'), the interviewer selected one person for interview at random, using a Kish grid and random numbers generated separately for each serial number.

The unequal selection probabilities arising from steps 4. and 5. are taken into account by the weighting (see below).

Data collection and response

A small-scale pilot to test new questions was carried out in August 1997. Respondents were selected by quota sampling methods to include men and women in manual and non-manual jobs across a range of ages. Interviewers were personally debriefed by members of the research team.

Interviewing began in each country immediately after the referendums. Interviews in Scotland were conducted during the period 12 September to 22 October and in Wales during the period 19 September to 30 October.

An advance letter was sent to "the resident" at all selected addresses. It briefly described the purpose of the survey and the coverage of the questionnaire, and asked for co-operation when the interviewer called. In Wales, the letter was double-sided with an English language version on one side and a Welsh language version on the other.

Fieldwork was conducted by interviewers drawn from SCPR's regular panel. They attended one-day briefing conferences, conducted by the researchers, to familiarise them with the selection procedures and questionnaires. In all, 37 interviewers in Scotland and 23 interviewers in Wales undertook assignments.

The face-to-face interview was administered using a traditional paper-and-pencil (PAPI) questionnaire. The average length of interview was 35 minutes in Scotland and 38 minutes in Wales. In addition to the face-to-face questionnaire, respondents were asked to fill in a short self-completion questionnaire which was done either at the end of the interview or collected later by the interviewer. Where this was not possible, a stamped addressed envelope was supplied to the respondent. A total of 97% of those interviewed in Scotland and 92% of those interviewed in Wales returned a self-completion questionnaire.

The Welsh face-to-face questionnaire, showcards and self-completion questionnaire were translated into Welsh. Interviewers in Wales asked whether the respondent preferred to answer the questionnaire in English or Welsh. If the respondents wished to be interviewed in Welsh and if the interviewers were not themselves Welsh-speaking, they left a copy of the showcards and self-completion questionnaire in Welsh with the respondent. The interview was then conducted over telephone by a Welsh-speaking interviewer. Four interviews were conducted in Welsh.

The response was as follows:

Table A.1

Response summary, Scottish and Welsh Referendum Studies

	Scotland		Wales	
	N	%	N	%
Issued address	1147		1147	
Selected dwelling units	1170		1151	
Out of scope	183		209	
Of which 'no electors'	67		68	
In scope	987	100.0	942	100.0
Interview obtained	676	68.5	686	72.8
Of which with self-completion	657	66.6	633	67.2
Interview not obtained	311	31.5	256	27.2
Of which:				
- refusal	195	19.8	169	17.9
- non contact	81	8.2	58	6.2
- other	35	3.5	29	3.1

Notes on the table:

Out of scope = vacant, derelict, no private dwelling, no electors.

Refused = refusal before or after the selection procedure, 'proxy' refusals (on the selected person's behalf), broken appointments after which the respondent could not be recontacted.

Non-contacts = households where no one could be contacted and those where the selected person could not be contacted.

Other interview not obtained = ill or away during survey period, selected person senile or incapacitated, 'partial unproductive' (a few question asked but interview not completed), inadequate English etc.

Weighting

The weighting scheme takes account of differential selection probabilities: in brief, the PAF sample generates addresses with equal probability. However, since only one person was interviewed at each address, people in small households have a larger selection probability than people in large households. The weights also use information about non-responding addresses to counter-balance the effect of non-response bias. The weights have been scaled so that the weighted sample sizes equal the unweighted sample sizes.

Geographical data

The addresses of respondents have been linked *via* postcode to the 1991 Census database held as part of the Manchester Information Datasets and Associated Systems (MIDAS) at the University of Manchester. This has enabled information about county and district council, constituency and ward to be added to the file.

Notes on tables in the book

1. Figures in the tables are from the 1997 Scottish and Welsh Referendum Studies, unless otherwise stated.
2. The data used for the analyses are weighted.
3. In tables, '*' indicates less than 0.5% but greater than zero, and '-' indicates zero.
4. The bases shown in the tables are the **un**weighted bases, unless otherwise stated.

References

Balsom D (1985) 'The Three Wales Model', in Osmond J (ed) *The National Question Again*, Llandysul: Gomer.

Balsom D, Madgwick P J and Van Mechelen D (1983) 'The Red and the Green: Patterns of Partisan Choice in Wales', *British Journal of Political Science* **13**: 299-325.

Balsom D, Madgwick P J and Van Mechelen D (1984) 'The Political Consequences of Welsh Identity', *Ethnic and Racial Studies* **7**: 160-81.

Bennie L, Brand J and Mitchell J (1997) *How Scotland Votes*, Manchester: Manchester University Press.

Brand J, McLean D and Miller W (1983) 'The Birth and Death of the Three-Party System: Scotland in the Seventies' *British Journal of Political Science* **13**: 463-88.

Brown A, McCrone D and Paterson L (1998) *Politics and Society in Scotland*, second edition, London: Macmillan.

Brown A, McCrone D, Paterson L and Surridge P (1999) *The Scottish Electorate* Basingstoke: Macmillan.

Butler D, and Stokes D (1974) *Political Change in Britain: The Evolution of Electoral Choice*, 2nd edition, Basingstoke: Macmillan.

Evans G and Norris P (1999 forthcoming) *Critical Elections: Voters and Parties in Long-term Perspective*, London: Sage.

Heath A, Jowell R and Curtice J with Field J and Levine C (1985) *How Britain Votes*, Oxford: Pergamon Press.

Heath A, Jowell R, Curtice J, Evans G, Field J and Witherspoon S (1991) *Understanding Political Change: The British Voter 1964-1987*, Oxford: Pergamon Press.

Heath A, Jowell R and Curtice J with Taylor B (eds) (1994) *Labour's Last Chance? The 1992 Election and Beyond*, Aldershot: Dartmouth.

Heath A, Jowell R and Curtice J (forthcoming) *New Labour and the Future of the Left*, Oxford: Oxford University Press.

Miller W (1981) *The End of British Politics?*, Oxford: Clarendon Press.

Särlvik B and Crewe I with Day N and Macdermid R (1983) *Decade of Dealignment: The Conservative Victory of 1979 and Electoral Trends in the 1970s*, Cambridge: Cambridge University Press.

Thomson K *et al* (1999 forthcoming) *The Scottish and Welsh Referendum Studies 1997: Technical Report*, London: SCPR.

Appendix II
The questionnaires

The Scottish and Welsh Referendum Studies questionnaires are reproduced in the following pages. The keying codes have been removed and the weighted percentage distribution of answers inserted. Where fewer than 50 people were asked a question, the **number** of people giving each response is shown instead of the percentages. The SPSS variable names have also been inserted in italics above each question. The weighted bases are shown at the top of each page and where the base changes.

Where question wording differed in Scotland and Wales, the two alternative wordings are shown in italics in brackets.

Figures do not necessarily add up to 100% for one or several of the following reasons:

(i)   rounding of weighted figures;
(ii)   some sub-questions are filtered - that is, they are asked only of a proportion of respondents. In these cases the percentages add up to the proportions who were asked the question. Where, however, a **series** of questions is filtered, we have indicated the weighted base at the beginning of the series, and throughout have derived percentages from that base;
(iii)   at a few questions, respondents were invited to give more than one answer and so percentages will add to more than 100%. These are clearly marked by the interviewer instructions on the questionnaire.

Head Office: 35 NORTHAMPTON SQUARE
LONDON EC1V 0AX
Tel: 0171 250 1866 Fax 0171 250 1524

Operations Department: 100 KINGS ROAD
BRENTWOOD, ESSEX CM14 4LX
Tel: 01277 200 600   Fax: 01277 214 117

P.1707   Sept/Oct 1997

SCOTTISH
AND WELSH
REFERENDUM STUDIES

Serial number							
Card	0	5					
Interviewer number							
Time interview started							
O.U.O. Batch code							

1. Please tick <u>one</u> box for <u>each</u> statement below to show how much you agree or disagree with it.

Base S:659

Scotland

*PLEASE TICK **ONE** BOX ON EACH LINE*		Agree strongly	Agree	Neither agree nor disagree	Disagree	Disagree strongly	(DK)	(NA)
	[Wealth1]							
a.	Ordinary working people get their fair share of the nation's wealth	% 5.4	15.7	17.3	49.3	11.9	–	0.4
	[RichLaw]							
b.	There is one law for the rich and one for the poor	% 20.6	44.8	15.8	15.0	3.0	0.1	0.8
	[TradVals]							
c.	Young people today don't have enough respect for traditional values	% 20.7	49.2	20.0	8.8	0.7	0.1	0.4
	[Censor]							
d.	Censorship of films and magazines is necessary to uphold moral standards	% 19.9	52.7	13.4	9.5	4.1	0.3	0.2
	[NoTrUns]							
e.	There is no need for strong trade unions to protect employees' working conditions and wages	% 3.0	13.6	17.9	46.8	18.0	0.1	0.6
	[PrEntBst]							
f.	Private enterprise is the best way to solve the country's economic problems	% 3.5	22.9	39.2	28.1	5.4	0.3	0.6
	[PubOwnSt]							
g.	Major public services and industries ought to be in state ownership	% 11.4	29.1	28.3	26.8	3.5	0.3	0.6

Wales

W:632

*PLEASE TICK **ONE** BOX ON EACH LINE*		Agree strongly	Agree	Neither agree nor disagree	Disagree	Disagree strongly	(DK)	(NA)
	[Wealth1]							
a.	Ordinary working people get their fair share of the nation's wealth	% 5.4	16.1	20.6	46.4	9.9	–	1.5
	[RichLaw]							
b.	There is one law for the rich and one for the poor	% 16.7	46.0	16.9	16.2	3.4	–	0.8
	[TradVals]							
c.	Young people today don't have enough respect for traditional values	% 26.4	48.1	13.4	9.4	1.5	–	1.0
	[Censor]							
d.	Censorship of films and magazines is necessary to uphold moral standards	% 24.8	49.3	13.2	8.6	2.5	–	1.7
	[NoTrUns]							
e.	There is no need for strong trade unions to protect employees' working conditions and wages	% 2.8	13.5	21.3	46.6	14.3	0.5	1.0
	[PrEntBst]							
f.	Private enterprise is the best way to solve the country's economic problems	% 4.7	22.9	39.8	25.4	4.9	0.8	1.7
	[PubOwnSt]							
g.	Major public services and industries ought to be in state ownership	% 10.3	24.8	30.7	26.0	6.7	0.4	1.1

2. | Please tick <u>one</u> box for <u>each</u> statement below to show how much you agree or disagree with it.

Scotland

PLEASE TICK **ONE** BOX ON EACH LINE		Agree strongly	Agree	Neither agree nor disagree	Disagree	Disagree strongly	(DK)	(NA)
[GovJob] a. It is the government's responsibility to provide a job for everyone who wants one	%	14.3	45.6	16.2	22.3	1.5	0.1	-
[ProtMeet] b. People should be allowed to organise public meetings to protest against the government	%	14.7	55.2	20.9	8.0	0.7	-	0.6
[GaySex] c. Homosexual relations are always wrong	%	10.4	16.2	32.0	30.2	10.5	0.2	0.4
[Tolerant] d. People should be more tolerant of those who lead unconventional lives	%	9.0	54.6	26.6	8.1	1.2	0.4	0.2
[BanParty] e. Political parties which wish to overthrow democracy should be allowed to stand in general elections	%	2.4	16.7	27.3	37.3	15.3	0.4	0.7

Wales

PLEASE TICK **ONE** BOX ON EACH LINE		Agree strongly	Agree	Neither agree nor disagree	Disagree	Disagree strongly	(DK)	(NA)
[GovJob] a. It is the government's responsibility to provide a job for everyone who wants one	%	14.8	43.2	17.8	21.8	1.4	-	0.9
[ProtMeet] b. People should be allowed to organise public meetings to protest against the government	%	10.9	54.7	22.9	9.8	0.7	0.2	0.7
[GaySex] c. Homosexual relations are always wrong	%	9.8	13.9	38.7	29.5	7.0	0.1	1.1
[Tolerant] d. People should be more tolerant of those who lead unconventional lives	%	8.8	51.6	30.1	6.8	1.5	-	1.1
[BanParty] e. Political parties which wish to overthrow democracy should be allowed to stand in general elections	%	1.5	12.9	30.6	35.8	17.4	0.7	1.0

3. | Please tick <u>one</u> box for <u>each</u> statement below to show how much you agree or disagree with it.

Base
S:659

Scotland

*PLEASE TICK **ONE** BOX ON EACH LINE*		Agree strongly	Agree	Neither agree nor disagree	Disagree	Disagree strongly	(DK)	(NA)
	[GovNoSay]							
a.	People like me have no say in what the government does	%	11.1	37.1	14.7	33.1	3.2	-	0.9
	[VoteOnly]							
b.	Voting is the only way people like me can have a say about how the government runs things	%	18.3	61.2	8.4	10.4	1.1	-	0.6
	[GovComp]							
c.	Sometimes politics and government seem so complicated that a person like me cannot really understand what is going on	%	10.6	51.3	14.2	20.8	2.4	-	0.6
	[LoseTch]							
d.	Generally speaking, those we elect as MPs lose touch with people pretty quickly	%	11.0	49.2	24.3	13.6	0.8	0.1	1.0
	[VoteIntr]							
e.	Parties are only interested in people's votes, not in their opinions	%	11.9	46.1	19.9	19.6	1.6	-	1.0
	[PtyNtMat]							
f.	It doesn't really matter which party is in power, in the end things go on much the same	%	8.5	31.1	13.8	39.5	6.5	-	0.6

Wales

W:632

*PLEASE TICK **ONE** BOX ON EACH LINE*		Agree strongly	Agree	Neither agree nor disagree	Disagree	Disagree strongly	(DK)	(NA)
	[GovNoSay]							
a.	People like me have no say in what the government does	%	10.8	36.3	18.8	30.4	3.3	0.1	0.4
	[VoteOnly]							
b.	Voting is the only way people like me can have a say about how the government runs things	%	19.7	59.1	11.0	8.8	0.3	0.4	0.7
	[GovComp]							
c.	Sometimes politics and government seem so complicated that a person like me cannot really understand what is going on	%	13.5	49.6	16.0	17.0	3.2	-	0.7
	[LoseTch]							
d.	Generally speaking, those we elect as MPs lose touch with people pretty quickly	%	14.9	46.8	22.8	14.1	0.3	0.2	0.8
	[VoteIntr]							
e.	Parties are only interested in people's votes, not in their opinions	%	16.0	47.2	19.3	15.9	0.7	0.2	0.8
	[PtyNtMat]							
f.	It doesn't really matter which party is in power, in the end things go on much the same	%	7.3	36.3	18.7	32.3	4.9	-	0.6

		Scotland %	Wales %	
4.	**[TaxSoc2]** Suppose the government had to choose between these three options. Which do you think it should choose?			**Base: S:659**
	PLEASE TICK ONE BOX ONLY Reduce taxes and spend less on health, education and social benefits	2.6	3.3	**W:632**
	Keep taxes and spending on these services at the same level	29.8	32.4	
	Increase taxes and spend more on health, education and social benefits	63.2	62.3	
	(DK)	0.7	1.5	
	(NA)	1.2	0.5	

		Scotland %	Wales %
5.	**[EUPolicy]** What do you think Britain's long-term policy about the European Union should be?		
	To leave the European Union	7.6	10.8
	To stay in the EU and try to **reduce** the EU's powers	32.6	35.8
	To leave things as they are	30.2	30.9
	To stay in the EU and try to **increase** the EU's powers	16.0	11.4
	To work for the formation of a single European government	8.7	6.5
	(DK)	2.4	2.3
	(NA)	2.5	2.3

		Scotland %	Wales %
6.	**[EcuView]** And here are three statements about the future of the pound in the European Union. Which **one** comes closest to your view?		
	Replace the pound by a single currency	20.5	17.2
	Use **both** the pound and a new European currency in Britain	19.3	19.0
	Keep the pound as the **only** currency for Britain	57.8	61.2
	(DK)	0.8	1.8
	(NA)	1.6	0.8

		Scotland %	Wales %
7a.	**[PropRep]** How much do you agree or disagree that the UK should introduce proportional representation so that the number of **MPs** each party gets in the House of Commons matches more closely the number of **votes** each party gets?		
	Strongly agree	21.1	14.6
	Agree	45.0	40.1
	Neither agree nor disagree	24.9	35.1
	Disagree	5.2	6.7
	Strongly disagree	1.6	1.5
	(DK)	1.2	1.3
	(NA)	1.0	0.6
b.	**[PropRNat]** And how much do you agree or disagree that the *(Scottish parliament/Welsh assembly)* should be elected using proportional representation?		
	Strongly agree	25.0	16.1
	Agree	47.3	36.2
	Neither agree nor disagree	19.1	35.5
	Disagree	3.4	7.3
	Strongly disagree	0.8	2.2
	(DK)	1.0	1.6
	(NA)	0.8	1.1

Base:
S: 659
W: 632

8a. [UKIntNat]
How much do you trust the UK government to work in *(Scotland's/Wales')* best long-term interests?

	Scotland %	Wales %
Just about always	3.8	7.7
Most of the time	31.0	36.8
Only some of the time	53.4	49.4
Almost never	10.7	5.2
(DK)	0.1	0.7
(NA)	1.0	0.2

**Base:
S:659
W:632**

b. [NatInNat]
And how much would you trust a *(Scottish parliament/Welsh assembly)* to work in *(Scotland's/Wales')* best long-term interests?

Just about always	35.6	24.0
Most of the time	47.9	43.3
Only some of the time	12.4	26.5
Almost never	2.8	4.7
(DK)	0.1	1.4
(NA)	1.2	0.2

c. **SCOTLAND ONLY**
[ScotMPs]
Once a Scottish parliament is set up, do you think that the number of Scottish MPs at the parliament in London should be reduced, stay the same or be increased?

	Scotland %
Should be reduced	43.0
Should stay the same	44.4
Should be increased	11.1
(DK)	0.5
(NA)	0.9

**Base:
S: 659**

ALL   **Base:**
[NatUnemp]   **S: 659**
9a. Thinking now about *(when a Scottish parliament is/if a Welsh assembly was)* set up.   **W: 632**
As a result of this *(parliament/assembly)* do you think that unemployment
will become higher, lower or will it make no difference?

	Scotland	Wales
	%	%
A lot higher	3.0	3.3
A little higher	14.7	9.8
Will make no difference	37.9	60.2
A little lower	38.6	21.7
A lot lower	5.1	3.9
(DK)	0.3	0.6
(NA)	0.5	0.6

[NatTaxes]
b. And as a result of the *(parliament/assembly)*, will taxes in *(Scotland/Wales)*
become higher, lower or will it make no difference?

	Scotland	Wales
	%	%
A lot higher	10.9	8.4
A little higher	64.7	32.4
Will make no difference	19.9	54.5
A little lower	3.0	2.0
A lot lower	0.5	0.2
(DK)	0.8	1.8
(NA)	0.2	0.8

[NatEcony]
c. As a result of the *(parliament/assembly)* will *(Scotland's/Wales')* economy
become better, worse or will it make no difference?

	Scotland	Wales
	%	%
A lot better	17.7	7.7
A little better	46.3	32.9
Would make no difference	23.9	41.0
A little worse	10.1	13.1
A lot worse	1.5	3.0
(DK)	0.4	1.6
(NA)	0.1	0.7

[NatNHS]
d. As a result of the *(parliament/assembly)* will the standard of the
health service in *(Scotland/Wales)* will become better, worse
or will it make no difference?

	Scotland	Wales
	%	%
A lot better	23.4	10.2
A little better	42.0	35.8
Would make no difference	28.1	43.4
A little worse	4.6	6.5
A lot worse	1.2	2.0
(DK)	0.4	1.6
(NA)	0.3	0.6

[NatEduc]		Scotland %	Wales %	Base: S: 659 W: 632
e. As a result of the *(parliament/assembly)* will the quality of education in *(Scotland/Wales)* become better, worse or will it make no difference?				
	A lot better	28.2	11.5	
	A little better	42.2	37.9	
	Would make no difference	25.3	40.9	
	A little worse	3.2	5.6	
	A lot worse	0.5	2.0	
	(DK)	0.3	1.6	
	(NA)	0.3	0.6	

SCOTLAND ONLY

[ScPWelf]		Scotland %	Base: S: 659
f. As a result of the parliament will the standard of social welfare in Scotland become better, worse or will it make no difference?			
	A lot better	12.5	
	A little better	46.2	
	Would make no difference	35.4	
	A little worse	4.3	
	A lot worse	0.9	
	(DK)	0.5	
	(NA)	0.3	

ALL

[NatProsp]		Scotland %	Wales %	Base: S: 659 W: 632
10a. Compared with other parts of Britain, would you say that these days *(Scotland/Wales)* is better off, not so well off or just about the same?				
	Better off	13.9	9.4	
	Not so well off	43.2	52.4	
	Just about the same	41.8	36.5	
	(DK)	0.7	1.0	
	(NA)	0.4	0.6	

b.

[NatPros5]
Compared with other parts of Britain over the last five years
would you say that *(Scotland/Wales)* has been getting more prosperous
than average, stayed about average, or been getting less
prosperous than average?

	Scotland %	Wales %
A lot more prosperous than average	3.4	3.7
A little more prosperous than average	18.0	19.5
Stayed about average	50.5	43.5
A little less prosperous than average	20.9	26.1
A lot less prosperous than average	6.1	5.6
(DK)	0.7	1.2
(NA)	0.4	0.4

11.

[Indepent]
At any time in the next twenty years, do you think it is
likely or unlikely that *(Scotland/Wales)* will become completely
independent from the United Kingdom?

	%	%
Very likely	18.1	5.9
Quite likely	40.5	23.1
Quite unlikely	24.1	34.6
Very unlikely	15.3	34.7
(DK)	1.6	1.2
(NA)	0.5	0.5

12.

[Qtime]
To help us plan better in future, please tell us about how long it
took you to complete this questionnaire.

*PLEASE TICK **ONE** BOX ONLY*

	%	%
Less than 15 minutes	79.1	78.8
Between 15 and 20 minutes	15.5	15.8
Between 21 and 30 minutes	4.4	3.0
Between 31 and 45 minutes	0.6	1.6
Between 46 and 60 minutes	-	0.3
Over one hour	-	0.1
(NA)	0.4	0.3

13.

And on what date did you fill in the questionnaire

*PLEASE **WRITE IN***

DAY ☐☐   MONTH ☐☐   1997

**Thank you very much for your help. Please return the questionnaire to the
interviewer if he or she has arranged to call for it. Otherwise, please post
it <u>as soon as possible</u> in the pre-paid addressed envelope provided.**

Head Office: 35 NORTHAMPTON SQUARE
LONDON EC1V 0AX
Tel: 0171 250 1866 Fax 0171 250 1524

SCPR

Operations Department: 100 KINGS ROAD
BRENTWOOD, ESSEX CM14 4LX
Tel: 01277 200 600   Fax: 01277 214 117

(SCOTTISH/WELSH) REFERENDUM STUDY 1997   **P.1707**

SELF-COMPLETION QUESTIONNAIRE

INTERVIEWER TO ENTER		
2001-2006	☐☐☐☐☐☐	Serial No.
2007-2008	2 | 0	Card No.
2009-2013	☐☐☐☐☐	OUO: Batch No.
2014-2017	☐☐☐☐☐	Interviewer No.

To the selected respondent:

Thank you very much for agreeing to take part in this important study. It consists of this self-completion questionnaire, and the interview you have already completed. The results will be published in a book due out in the next year or so.

Completing the questionnaire:

The questions inside cover a wide range of subjects, but most can be answered simply by placing a tick (√) in one or more of the boxes. No special knowledge is required: we are confident that everyone will be able to take part, not just those with strong views or particular viewpoints. The questionnaire should not take very long to complete, and we hope you will find it interesting and enjoyable. **Only you should fill it in, and not anyone else at your address**. The answers you give will be treated as confidential and anonymous.

Returning the questionnaire:

Your interviewer will arrange with you the most convenient way of returning the questionnaire. If the interviewer has arranged to call back for it, please fill it in and keep it safely until then. If not, please complete it and post it back in the pre-paid, addressed envelope, AS SOON AS YOU POSSIBLY CAN.

THANK YOU AGAIN FOR YOUR HELP.

Social and Community Planning Research is an independent social research institute registered as a charitable trust. Its projects are funded by government departments, local authorities, universities and foundations to provide information on social issues in Britain. The Scottish/Welsh Referendum Study is funded by the Economic and Social Research Council. Please contact us if you would like further information.

		Section 1				

ASK ALL
[ReadPap]

SW1a) Do you regularly read one or more <u>daily</u> morning or evening newspapers?

		Scotland %	Wales %		Base: S: 676 W: 686
Yes		79.5	63.9	**ASK b.**	
No		20.3	36.1	**GO TO Q2**	
(Don't know)		-	-		
(NA)		0.1	-		

IF YES
[WhPaper1] [WhPaper2] [WhPaper3]

SW1b) Which <u>daily</u> morning or evening newspapers do you read regularly? **PROMPT**: Any others?
RECORD UP TO 3. IF MORE THAN 3 GIVEN, ASK: Which (three) do you read most often?

	%	%
The *(Scottish)* Daily Mail	6.3	16.7
The *(Scottish)* Mirror/*(Daily Record)*	47.7	20.5
The Express	5.8	7.6
The Daily Star *(of Scotland)*	1.1	3.3
The Sun	21.5	26.2
The Daily Telegraph	2.3	6.2
The Financial Times	0.5	0.4
The Guardian	0.8	2.7
The Independent	0.6	1.5
The Times	2.4	2.4
The Scotsman	6.8	•
The (Glasgow) Herald	10.5	•
The (Aberdeen) Press and Journal	5.3	•
The (Dundee) Courier	7.8	•
The (Glasgow) Evening Times	6.5	•
The (Edinburgh) Evening News	4.4	•
The Daily Post	•	7.3
South Wales Echo	•	8.8
Western Mail	•	6.8
South Wales Evening Post	•	7.2
South Wales Argus	•	4.4
Evening Leader	•	2.2
Other *(Scottish/Welsh)*/regional/local <u>daily</u> morning or evening newspaper **(WRITE IN)**		
_____	8.6	1.0
Other **(WRITE IN)** _____	0.7	2.1
More than three papers read	1.0	0.3
(Don't know)	-	-
(NA)	0.5	-

Base:
W: 686

ASK ALL IN WALES
CARD
W1c) Which, if any, of these television stations do you watch regularly?
CODE ALL THAT APPLY

		Wales %
[BBC1Wale]	BBC1 (Wales)	70.2
[BBC1Othr]	BBC1 (other)	27.0
[BBC2]	BBC2	54.5
[HTVWales]	HTV Wales	68.4
[ITVOther]	ITV (other)	22.5
[Channel4]	Channel 4	26.0
[S4C]	S4C	33.6
[Channel5]	Channel 5	15.0
[SkyNews]	Sky News	12.9
[OthChanl] Other **(WRITE IN)** _____		7.6
[TVNever]	(Never watches television)	2.6
	(Don't know)	0.5

Base:
S: 676
W: 686

ASK ALL
[RefCare]
SW2. Would you say you cared a good deal about the result of the recent referendum in *(Scotland/Wales)*, or that you didn't care very much?

	Scotland %	Wales %
Cared a good deal	71.7	50.9
Didn't care very much	27.3	43.2
(Don't know)	0.8	5.8
(NA)	0.1	0.1

SW3. How much interest do you generally have in what is going on in politics ... **READ OUT** ...

	%	%
... a great deal,	8.9	7.6
quite a lot,	26.7	24.6
some,	33.8	31.3
not very much,	21.9	26.3
or, none at all?	8.6	9.9
(Don't know)	-	-
(NA)	0.1	0.2

SW4. Talking to people about the recent referendum on the *(Scottish parliament/Welsh assembly)*, we found that a lot of people didn't manage to vote. How about you? Did you manage to vote in the referendum?

Base:
S: 676
W: 686

	Scotland %	Wales %	
Yes, voted	73.7	61.8	**ASK Q5**
No, did not vote	26.3	37.7	
DO NOT PROMPT: Not registered to vote	0.1	0.2	**GO TO Q7**
Refused to say	-	0.3	
(Don't know)			
(NA)	-	0.1	

IF VOTED (CODE 1 AT Q4)
[RefDecid]
CARD A

SW5. How long ago did you decide that you would definitely vote they way you did? Please choose an answer from this card.
CODE FIRST TO APPLY

	%	%
In the week before the referendum	17.4	20.1
In the month before the referendum	11.5	9.9
Between the general election in May and the referendum	15.4	12.0
Before the general election in May	29.2	19.3
(Don't know)	-	0.1
(NA)	-	0.7

[RefVote]
CARD

S6aW6. The question*(s)* asked in the Referendum *(are/is)* set out on this card. How did you vote *(on the first question)*?

	%	%	
I <u>agree</u> there should be a *(Scottish parliament/Welsh assembly)*	55.3	30.7	
I do <u>not</u> agree there should be a *(Scottish parliament/Welsh assembly)*	16.8	30.5	**NOW**
Spoilt paper	-	-	**GO**
Other answer **(WRITE IN)** _____	-	-	**TO**
Refused to say	1.5	0.3	**Q8**
(Don't know)	0.1	-	
(NA)	-	0.5	

ASK ALL IN SCOTLAND
[RefTaxVt]
CARD AGAIN

Base:
S: 676

S6b. And how did you vote on the second question?

	Scotland %	
I <u>agree</u> a Scottish Parliament should have tax-varying powers	47.4	
I do <u>not</u> agree a Scottish Parliament should have tax-varying powers	23.7	
Spoilt paper	0.3	**NOW GO TO Q8**
Other answer **(WRITE IN)** _____	0.2	
Refused to say	1.6	
(Don't know)	1.3	
(NA)	0.3	

IF DID NOT VOTE (CODE 2,3,7,8 AT Q4)
CARD
[NvRefVot]

Base:
S: 676
W: 686

S7aW7. The questions asked in the Referendum are set out on this card. If you had voted, how would you have voted on the first question?

	Scotland %	Wales %
I <u>agree</u> there should be a *(Scottish parliament/Welsh assembly)*	16.6	8.9
I do <u>not</u> agree there should be a *(Scottish parliament/Welsh assembly)*	5.3	15.7
Would spoil paper	-	-
Would not vote	1.6	5.8
Other answer **(WRITE IN)** _____	-	-
Refused to say	-	-
(Don't know)	2.6	7.6
(NA)	0.2	0.1

ASK ALL IN SCOTLAND
[NVRefTax]
CARD AGAIN

Base:
S: 676

S7b. And how would you have voted on the second question?

	Scotland %
I <u>agree</u> a Scottish Parliament should have tax-varying powers	11.8
I do <u>not</u> agree a Scottish Parliament should have tax-varying powers	9.8
Would spoil paper	-
Would not vote	2.2
Other answer **(WRITE IN)** _____	-
Refused to say	0.1
(Don't Know)	2.0
(NA)	0.4

ASK ALL
[VoteRef]

Base:
S: 676
W: 686

SW8. If there had been a general election on the *(11th/18th)* of September which political party do you think you would have voted for, or do you think you would not have voted?

DO NOT PROMPT	Scotland %	Wales %
Conservative	12.4	16.8
Labour	49.9	55.0
Liberal Democrat	7.3	6.8
Scottish National Party	18.7	•
Plaid Cymru	•	10.0
Green Party	-	0.1
Other **(WRITE IN)** _____	0.2	0.4
Would not have voted/not eligible to vote	5.4	4.3
Refused	2.0	1.1
(Don't know)	3.3	5.4
(NA)	0.9	0.1

	[CanvasRf]		Base:

SW9a. Did a canvasser from any party or other organisation call
at your home to talk to you during the referendum campaign?
**ONLY CODE 'YES' IF RESPONDENT ACTUALLY SAW
OR SPOKE TO THEM**

	Scotland %	*Wales* %	
Yes	3.9	4.2	**ASK b.**
No	94.7	94.6	**GO TO**
(Don't know)	1.4	1.1	**Q10**
(NA)	-	0.1	

IF YES (CODE 1 AT a)
b. From which parties or organisations? **PROBE**: Which others?
**IF 'ALL OF THEM', PROBE FOR WHICH.
CODE ALL THAT APPLY.
NOTE: ONLY CODE THOSE THE RESPONDENT ACTUALLY
SAW OR SPOKE TO. IF CANNOT DISTINGUISH, CODE
AS DON'T KNOW**

		%	%
[SctFCanv]	Scotland Forward	-	•
[ThnkCanv]	Think Twice	-	•
[YFWCanv]	Yes For Wales	•	0.5
[JSNoCanv]	Just Say No	•	0.1
[ConCanv]	The Conservative Party	0.5	0.7
[LabCanv]	The Labour Party	0.7	2.2
[LDCanv]	The Liberal Democrats	0.5	0.3
[SNPCanv]	The Scottish National Party	1.2	•
[PCCanv]	Plaid Cymru	•	1.1
[GrnCanv]	The Green Party	-	-
[OthCanv] Other (**WRITE IN**) _____		-	-
[DKCanv]	(Don't know)	0.4	0.8
	(NA)	2.9	1.2

Base:
S: 676
W: 686

ASK ALL
[PhCanvRf]

SW10a. And were you contacted by anyone on the telephone during the referendum campaign asking how you might vote?
ONLY CODE 'YES' IF RESPONDENT ACTUALLY SPOKE TO THEM

	Scotland %	Wales %	
Yes	1.5	5.1	**ASK b.**
No	97.4	94.4	**GO TO**
(Don't know)	1.1	0.4	**Q11**

IF YES (CODE 1 AT a)
b. By which parties or organisations, or did they not say which party or organisation they were from? **PROBE:** Which others?
IF 'ALL OF THEM', PROBE FOR WHICH.
CODE ALL THAT APPLY.
NOTE: ONLY CODE THOSE THE RESPONDENT ACTUALLY SPOKE TO. IF CANNOT DISTINGUISH, CODE AS DON'T KNOW

		%	%
[SctFPhCv]	Scotland Forward	-	•
[ThnkPhCv]	Think Twice	-	•
[YFWPhCv]	Yes For Wales	•	0.6
[JSNoPhCv]	Just Say No	•	-
[ConPhCv]	The Conservative Party	0.1	0.4
[LabPhCv]	The Labour Party	0.4	1.0
[LDPhCv]	The Liberal Democrats	0.1	-
[SNPPhCv]	The Scottish National Party	0.3	•
[PCPhCv]	Plaid Cymru	•	0.7
[GrnPhCv]	The Green Party	-	-
[OthPhCv] Other (**WRITE IN**) _____		0.1	-
[DKPhCv]	(Don't know)	0.4	2.6
	(NA)	1.1	0.6

ASK ALL
[Summary]
SHOW COPY OF SUMMARY DOCUMENT
SW11. Did you read the official summary of the government's proposals sent out by the *(Scottish Office/Welsh Office)*?

	%	%
Yes	42.4	42.0
No	33.2	35.4
Did not receive	22.7	20.0
(Don't know)	1.8	2.6

Base:
S: 676
W: 686

[DfWnGE]
CARD
SW12a. Some people say that it makes no difference which side wins
elections, things go on much the same. How about the last general
election when the Labour Party won? How much difference do you
think that result will make? Please choose your answer from this card.
CODE IN COLUMN a.

[DfWnRf]
CARD AGAIN
b. And what about the recent referendum? How much
difference to *(Scotland/Wales)* do you think the result of that will make?
CODE IN COLUMN b.

	Scotland %	Wales %	Scotland %	Wales %
	a. General Election		b. Referendum	
A great deal	29.9	25.1	30.0	12.3
Quite a lot	34.9	31.6	35.4	22.9
Some	18.3	24.6	16.9	19.5
Not very much	11.4	13.2	8.0	21.8
None at all	2.3	1.6	1.3	6.4
(Don't know)	3.2	3.8	8.5	17.1
(NA)	-	0.1	-	-

CARD
SW13. Please choose a phrase from this card to say how you
feel about the ... **READ OUT** ...

Scotland

		Strongly in favour	In favour	Neither in favour nor against	Against	Strongly against	(Don't know)	(NA)
a)	[LabFeel] ... Labour Party? %	19.4	40.8	26.6	9.3	3.0	0.3	0.6
b)	[ConFeel] ... Conservative Party? %	2.5	9.7	20.8	33.0	33.1	0.4	0.6
c)	[LDFeel] ... Liberal Democrats? %	2.9	16.5	54.3	17.8	3.8	4.0	0.7
d)	[SNPFeel] ...Scottish National Party? %	13.3	24.2	29.8	19.3	10.5	2.4	0.6

Wales

		Strongly in favour	In favour	Neither in favour nor against	Against	Strongly against	(Don't know)	(NA)
a)	[LabFeel] ... Labour Party? %	18.9	44.5	24.2	9.1	2.4	0.8	-
b)	[ConFeel] ... Conservative Party? %	3.2	13.3	26.9	32.6	23.0	0.9	-
c)	[LDFeel] ... Liberal Democrats? %	2.1	22.0	50.7	17.4	2.4	5.4	-
d)	[PCFeel ... Plaid Cymru? %	7.0	16.6	37.5	19.0	12.2	7.8	-

[ConTrust]

CARD

SW14a. Using the answers on this card, how much do you trust the <u>Conservative Party</u> to work in *(Scotland's/Wales')* interests?

Base:
S: 676
W: 686

	Scotland %	Wales %
Just about always	2.3	1.9
Most of the time	8.3	10.3
Only some of the time	31.1	39.0
Almost never	56.1	43.1
(Don't know)	1.8	5.8
(NA)	0.4	-

[LabTrust]

CARD AGAIN

b. And how much do you trust the <u>Labour Party</u> to work in *(Scotland's/Wales')* interests?

	%	%
Just about always	11.4	8.5
Most of the time	49.2	42.4
Only some of the time	32.9	36.4
Almost never	3.6	7.1
(Don't know)	2.6	5.3
(NA)	0.4	0.2

[LDTrust]

CARD AGAIN

c. How much do you trust the <u>Liberal Democrats</u> to work in *(Scotland's/Wales')* interests?

	%	%
Just about always	1.9	1.3
Most of the time	25.7	19.6
Only some of the time	42.2	44.7
Almost never	11.3	12.5
(Don't know)	18.5	21.9
(NA)	0.4	-

ASK ALL IN SCOTLAND

[SNPTrust]

CARD AGAIN

d. And how much do you trust the <u>Scottish National Party</u> to work in Scotland's interests?

Base:
S: 676

	Scotland %
Just about always	28.0
Most of the time	34.3
Only some of the time	19.8
Almost never	10.8
(Don't know)	6.9
(NA)	0.4

ASK ALL IN WALES   Base:
[PCTrust]   W: 686
d. And how much do you trust <u>Plaid Cymru</u>
   to work in Wales' interests?   *Wales*
                                                                              %

                                        Just about always   21.4
                                        Most of the time   29.3
                                     Only some of the time   19.8
                                           Almost never   13.3
                                           (Don't know)   16.2

Section 2

ASK ALL
[LabRcmd]
CARD

SW15a. The question(s) asked in the Referendum are set out on this card.
Which way did you think the <u>Labour party</u> were recommending
you should vote *(on the first question)*, or did they not make a
recommendation?

Base:
S: 676
W: 686

	Scotland %	Wales %
Yes - <u>agree</u> should be a *(Scottish parliament/Welsh assembly)*	90.4	80.4
No - do <u>not</u> agree should be a *(Scottish parliament/ Welsh assembly)*	1.2	2.0
Did not make a recommendation	2.5	4.6
(Don't know)	5.9	13.0

ASK ALL IN SCOTLAND
[LabRcmdT]

S15b. And on the second question?

Base:
S: 676

	%
Yes - <u>agree</u> should have tax varying powers	85.1
No - <u>not</u> agree should have tax varying powers	3.7
Did not make a recommendation	2.9
(Don't know)	8.2

ASK ALL
[ConRcmd]
CARDF AGAIN

SW16a. And which way did you think the <u>Conservative party</u> were recommending
that you vote *(on the first question)*, or did they not make a recommendation?

Base:
S: 676
W: 686

	%	%
Yes - <u>agree</u> should be a *(Scottish parliament/ Welsh assembly)*	2.5	2.3
No - do <u>not</u> agree should be a *(Scottish parliament/ Welsh assembly)*	82.3	71.9
Did not make a recommendation	5.6	5.3
(Don't know)	9.6	20.4

ASK ALL IN SCOTLAND
[ConRcmdT]

S16b. And on the second question?

Base:
S: 676

	%
Yes - <u>agree</u> should have tax varying powers	0.8
No - <u>not</u> agree should have tax varying powers	82.7
Did not make a recommendation	5.4
(Don't know)	11.1

ASK ALL
[LDRcmd]
CARD AGAIN

SW17a. And which way do you think the <u>Liberal Democrats</u> were recommending that you vote *(on the first question)*, or did they not make a recommendation?

Base:
S: 676
W: 686

	Scotland %	*Wales* %
Yes - <u>agree</u> should be a *(Scottish parliament/ Welsh assembly)*	56.9	39.3
No - do <u>not</u> agree should be a *(Scottish parliament/ Welsh assembly)*	4.7	4.3
Did not make a recommendation	6.7	8.7
(Don't know)	31.7	47.7

ASK ALL IN SCOTLAND
[LdRcmdT]

S17b. And on the second question?

Base:
S: 676

	%
Yes - <u>agree</u> should have tax varying powers	51.8
No - <u>not</u> agree should have tax varying powers	7.6
Did not make a recommendation	6.7
(Don't know)	33.7
(NA)	0.1

[SNPRcmd]
CARD AGAIN

SW18a. And which way do you think the <u>Scottish National Party</u> were recommending that you vote on the first question, or did they not make a recommendation?

	%
Yes - <u>agree</u> should be a Scottish parliament	86.2
No - do <u>not</u> agree should be a Scottish parliament	1.2
Did not make a recommendation	2.2
(Don't know)	10.4

[SNPRcmdT]

S18b. And on the second question?

	%
Yes - <u>agree</u> should have tax varying powers	83.6
No - <u>not</u> agree should have tax varying powers	2.3
Did not make a recommendation	2.7
(Don't know)	11.4

ASK ALL IN WALES
[PCRcmd]
CARD AGAIN

W18a. And which way do you think <u>Plaid Cymru</u> were recommending that you vote, or did they not make a recommendation?

Base:
W: 686

	Wales %
Yes - <u>agree</u> should be a Welsh assembly	71.6
No - do <u>not</u> agree should be a Welsh assembly	1.2
Did not make a recommendation	2.5
(Don't know)	24.7

Base:
S: 676
W: 686

ASK ALL
[LabDivdR]
S19a. Thinking again about the referendum campaign.
Would you describe the <u>Labour Party</u> as united or divided on
which way to vote in the referendum? **CODE IN COLUMN a.**

[ConDivdR]
b. And the <u>Conservative Party</u>, was it united or divided on
which way to vote in the referendum? **CODE IN COLUMN b.**

[LDDivdR]
c. And the <u>Liberal Democrats</u>, were they united or divided on
which way to vote in the referendum? **CODE IN COLUMN c.**

ASK ALL SCOTLAND
[SNPDivdR]
d. And <u>the Scottish National Party</u>, was it united or divided on
which way to vote in the referendum? **CODE IN COLUMN d.**

ASK ALL IN WALES
[PCDivdR]
d. And <u>Plaid Cymru</u>, was it united or divided on
which way to vote in the referendum? **CODE IN COLUMN**

	Scotland	Wales	Scotland	Wales	Scotland	Wales	Scotland	Wales
	a. Labour Party		**b.** Conservative Party		**c.** Liberal Democrats		**d.** SNP	**d.** PC
	%	%	%	%	%	%	%	%
United	74.9	43.6	39.4	39.4	49.9	31.9	82.2	67.9
Divided	15.3	35.3	46.4	32.8	14.5	15.1	6.4	3.7
(Neither or both)	1.1	2.0	1.5	2.1	2.3	2.6	0.3	0.6
(Don't know)	8.6	18.9	12.6	25.6	33.2	50.1	11.0	27.5
(NA)	0.1	0.2	0.1	-	0.1	0.3	0.1	0.3

ASK ALL
W20. Now a quick quiz about the government's proposals for a *(Scottish
parliament/Welsh assembly)*. For each thing I say, please tell me if you think it is
true or false. If you don't know, just say so and we'll skip to the
next one. Remember - true, false or don't know:

[ProposPR]
a. The *(parliament/assembly)* will be elected by a
system of proportional representation.

	Scotland %	Wales %
True	66.6	56.0
False	9.0	8.9
Don't know	24.4	35.0
(NA)	-	0.2

[ProposTx]
b. The *(parliament/assembly)* will <u>not</u> be able to change the basic
rate of income tax in *(Scotland/Wales)*.

	Scotland %	Wales %
True	22.1	65.1
False	66.4	16.6
Don't know	11.5	18.1
(NA)	-	0.2

		Scotland %	Wales %	Base: S: 676 W: 686
[ProposPP] c. People will need passports to travel between *(Scotland/Wales)* and England.				
	True	3.1	1.3	
	False	93.7	93.0	
	Don't know	3.6	5.5	
	(NA)	0.2	0.2	
[ProposMP] d. The current plan is eventually to reduce the number of MPs from *(Scotland/Wales)* at the parliament in London.		%	%	
	True	57.7	25.1	
	False	25.3	40.2	
	Don't know	16.9	34.6	
	(NA)	-	0.2	
[ProposDP] e. The *(parliament/assembly)* will have the power to introduce the death penalty in *(Scotland/Wales)*.		%	%	
	True	22.7	3.2	
	False	54.5	81.4	
	Don't know	22.8	15.2	
	(NA)	-	0.2	
[ProposBg] f. The *(Scottish parliament/Welsh assembly)* will control the way in which the *(Scottish Office's/Welsh Office's)* budget is spent.		%	%	
	True	85.3	82.5	
	False	5.3	4.4	
	Don't know	9.4	12.8	
	(NA)	-	0.3	
[ProposDf] g. The UK government, not the *(Scottish parliament/Welsh assembly)*, will make all decisions about defence.		%	%	
	True	75.6	71.8	
	False	9.8	10.4	
	Don't know	14.6	17.5	
	(NA)	-	0.3	

ASK ALL IN SCOTLAND
[SRRefVw1]
CARD
SW21a. Which of these statements comes closest to <u>your</u> view?
CODE IN COLUMN a.

[SRRefVw2]
CARD AGAIN
b. And which would be your second preference?   *Scotland*
CODE IN COLUMN b.

	a. First preference	b. Second preference	Base: S: 676
	%	%	
Scotland should become independent, separate from the UK and the European Union	8.8	9.7	
Scotland should become independent, separate from the UK but part of the European Union	28.2	15.9	
Scotland should remain part of the UK, with its own elected parliament which has **some** taxation powers	31.8	24.1	
Scotland should remain part of the UK, with its own elected parliament which has **no** taxation powers	9.0	22.4	
Scotland should remain part of the UK **without** an elected Parliament	17.2	8.3	
(Don't know)	4.2	17.9	
(NA)	0.7	1.7	

ASK ALL IN WALES
[WRRefVw1]
CARD
SW21a. Which of these statements comes closest to <u>your</u> view?
CODE IN COLUMN a.

[WRRefVw2]
CARD AGAIN
b. And which would be your second preference?   *Wales*
CODE IN COLUMN b.

	a. First preference	b. Second preference	Base: W: 686
	%	%	
Wales should become independent, separate from the UK and the European Union	3.8	2.4	
Wales should become independent, separate from the UK but part of the European Union	9.4	5.5	
Wales should remain part of the UK, with its own elected parliament which has law-making **and** taxation powers	18.3	17.6	
Wales should remain part of the UK with its own elected assembly which has limited law-making powers **only**	25.1	37.2	
Wales should remain part of the UK **without** an elected Parliament	36.9	11.9	
(Don't know)	6.5	24.6	
(NA)	-	0.7	

Base:
S: 676

ASK ALL IN SCOTLAND
[SConRfVw]
CARD G AGAIN
S22a. And which of these statements do you think comes closest
to the view of the <u>Conservative Party</u>? **CODE IN COLUMN a.**

[SLabRfVw]
CARD G AGAIN
b. Which of these statements do you think comes closest to the
view of the <u>Labour Party</u>? **CODE IN COLUMN b.**

[SLDRfVw]
CARD G AGAIN
c. Which of these statements do you think comes closest to the
view of the <u>Liberal Democrats</u>? **CODE IN COLUMN c.**

[SSNPRfVw]
CARD G AGAIN
d. Which of these statements do you think comes closest to the
view of the <u>Scottish National Party</u>? **CODE IN COLUMN d.**

	Scotland			
	a. Conservative	**b.** Labour	**c.** Lib. Dem.	**d.** SNP
	%	%	%	%
Scotland should become independent, separate from the UK and the European Union	1.1	3.3	1.5	27.8
Scotland should become independent, separate from the UK but part of the European Union	1.3	12.8	6.0	46.5
Scotland should remain part of the UK, with its own elected parliament which has **some** taxation powers	3.8	70.4	47.4	12.2
Scotland should remain part of the UK, with its own elected parliament which has **no** taxation powers	7.7	3.6	3.6	0.2
Scotland should remain part of the UK **without** an elected parliament	73.2	0.9	2.2	0.4
(Don't know)	12.7	8.6	39.1	12.7
(NA)	0.2	0.2	0.2	0.2

[SElseVw]
CARD
S23. An issue in <u>Wales</u> is the question of an elected assembly - a special
Parliament for Wales dealing with Welsh affairs. Which of these statements
comes closest to <u>your</u> view?

	%
Wales should become independent, separate from the UK and the European Union	3.9
Wales should become independent, separate from the UK but part of the European Union	12.7
Wales should remain part of the UK, with its own elected Parliament which has law-making **and** taxation powers	21.4
Wales should remain part of the UK, with its own elected assembly which has limited law-making powers **only**	10.0
Wales should remain part of the UK **without** an elected assembly	14.4
(Don't know)	29.2
(NA)	8.5

ASK ALL IN WALES
[WConRfVw]
CARD AGAIN
W22a. And which of these statements do you think comes closest
to the view of the <u>Conservative Party</u>? **CODE IN COLUMN a.**

[WLabRfVw]
CARD AGAIN
b. Which of these statements do you think comes closest to the
view of the <u>Labour Party</u>? **CODE IN COLUMN b.**

[WLDRfVw]
CARD AGAIN
c. Which of these statements do you think comes closest to the
view of the <u>Liberal Democrats</u>? **CODE IN COLUMN c.**

[WPCRfVw]
CARD AGAIN
d. Which of these statements do you think comes closest to the
view of <u>Plaid Cymru</u>? **CODE IN COLUMN d.**

Base:
W: 686

Wales

	a. Conservative	b. Labour	c. Lib. Dem.	d. PC
	%	%	%	%
Wales should become independent, separate from the UK and the European Union	0.5	4.2	2.5	20.3
Wales should become independent, separate from the UK but part of the European Union	2.6	11.6	5.5	25.8
Wales should remain part of the UK, with its own elected Parliament which has law-making **and** taxation powers	2.9	15.9	10.6	17.1
Wales should remain part of the UK, with its own elected assembly which has limited law-making powers **only**	4.8	46.5	24.2	4.8
Wales should remain part of the UK **without** an elected assembly	66.0	1.6	3.0	0.8
(Don't know)	23.2	20.2	53.7	30.7
(NA)	-	-	0.5	0.5

[WElseVw]
CARD
W23. An issue in <u>Scotland</u> is the question of a Scottish Parliament - a special
Parliament for Scotland dealing with Scottish affairs. Which of these statements
comes closest to <u>your</u> view?

	%
Scotland should become independent, separate from the UK and the European Union	7.6
Scotland should become independent, separate from the UK but part of the European Union	15.6
Scotland should remain part of the UK, with its own elected parliament which has **some** taxation powers	30.8
Scotland should remain part of the UK, with its own elected parliament which has **no** taxation powers	9.2
Scotland should remain part of the UK **without** an elected Parliament	15.4
(Don't know)	21.4
(NA)	0.2

Section 3		

Base:
S: 676
W: 686

ASK ALL
[LeaveUk]

SW24a. Which of the following comes closest to your views about a *(Scottish parliament/Welsh assembly)*. A *(Scottish parliament/Welsh assembly)* would
... **READ OUT** ...

	Scotland %	Wales %
... make it more likely that *(Scotland/Wales)* eventually <u>leave</u> the United Kingdom,	42.3	21.1
make it more likely that *(Scotland/Wales)* <u>stay</u> in the United Kingdom,	32.2	28.3
or, would it make no difference?	19.0	44.4
(Don't know)	6.6	6.3

[VoiceUK]

b. And would a *(Scottish parliament/Welsh assembly)* give *(Scotland/Wales)* ... **READ OUT** ...

	%	%
... a <u>stronger</u> voice in the United Kingdom,	70.2	49.9
a <u>weaker</u> voice in the United Kingdom,	9.4	11.7
or, would it make no difference?	16.6	33.4
(Don't know)	3.7	4.9
(NA)	0.1	0.2

[VoiceEU]

c. Would a *(Scottish parliament/Welsh assembly)* give *(Scotland/Wales)* ... **READ OUT** ...

	%	%
... a <u>stronger</u> voice in Europe	60.4	43.9
a <u>weaker</u> voice in Europe,	11.0	10.4
or, would it make no difference?	22.1	38.7
(Don't know)	6.5	6.8
(NA)	-	0.2

[MorPride]

d. And would a *(Scottish parliament/Welsh assembly)* give the *(Scots/Welsh)* ... **READ OUT** ...

	%	%
... <u>more</u> pride in their country,	76.7	53.5
<u>less</u> pride in their country,	1.1	2.3
or, would it make no difference?	19.5	39.4
(Don't know)	2.4	4.6
(NA)	0.3	0.2

[SayInGov]

e. Would a *(Scottish parliament/Welsh assembly)* give ordinary *(Scottish/Welsh)* people ... **READ OUT** ...

	%	%
... <u>more</u> say in how *(Scotland/Wales)* is governed,	79.1	53.9
<u>less</u> say,	2.0	4.4
or, would it make no difference?	16.5	36.4
(Don't know)	2.5	5.3

[IncrsSOL]		Scotland	Wales	
f. Would a *(Scottish parliament/Welsh assembly)* ... **READ OUT** ...		%	%	**Base:** S: 676
... increase the standard of living in *(Scotland/Wales)*,		49.5	28.8	**W: 686**
reduce the standard of living,		13.7	11.9	
or, would it make no difference?		25.5	51.4	
(Don't know)		11.3	7.9	

[ImprvEd]		%	%
g. Would a *(Scottish parliament/Welsh assembly)* ... **READ OUT** ...			
... improve the standard of education in *(Scotland/Wales)*,		71.0	49.8
reduce the standard of education,		3.0	5.0
or, would it make no difference?		19.1	37.0
(Don't know)		6.6	8.1
(NA)		0.3	0.1

[RgImp1st]
CARD
SW25a. This card shows a few things a *(Scottish parliament/ Welsh assembly)* might want to bring about.
Which of these, if any, do you think should be the most important for a *(Scottish parliament/Welsh assembly)* to bring about?
CODE ONE ONLY IN COLUMN a.

[RgImp2nd]
b. And which, if any, should be the second most important?
CODE ONE ONLY IN COLUMN b.

[RgImpNot]
c. And which, if any, should a *(Scottish parliament/Welsh assembly)* not try to bring about? **IF SEVERAL MENTIONED:**
Which is the most important?
CODE ONE ONLY IN COLUMN c.

Base: S: 676

Scotland

	a. Most important	b. Second most important	c. Should not bring about
	%	%	%
Improving education in Scotland	23.0	23.6	0.2
Giving Scotland a stronger voice in the United Kingdom	10.9	13.4	2.5
Giving the Scots more pride in their country	3.6	5.9	1.1
Giving Scotland a stronger voice in Europe	4.1	11.2	1.0
Increasing the standard of living in Scotland	26.9	25.2	0.9
Giving ordinary Scottish people more say in how Scotland is governed	27.6	15.2	0.6
Making it more likely that Scotland eventually leaves the United Kingdom	1.6	1.6	54.5
(None of these)	0.7	0.7	25.7
(Don't know)	1.2	2.5	11.2
(NA)	0.3	0.6	2.5

[RgImp1st] [RgImp2nd] [RgImpNot] continued	Wales			Base:
	a. Most important	b. Second most important	c. Should not bring about	W: 686
	%	%	%	
Improving education in Wales	28.3	19.1	0.1	
Giving Wales a stronger voice in the United Kingdom	14.0	14.5	0.9	
Giving the Welsh more pride in their country	2.9	5.5	1.4	
Giving Wales a stronger voice in Europe	6.8	13.1	1.3	
Increasing the standard of living in Wales	23.9	29.2	0.2	
Giving ordinary Welsh people more say in how Wales is governed	20.8	13.8	0.9	
Making it more likely that Wales eventually leaves the United Kingdom	0.2	0.3	76.1	
(None of these)	1.0	1.8	9.2	
(Don't know)	2.1	2.6	9.8	
(NA)	-	-	0.3	

CARD

SW26. Using this card please say how much you agree or disagree with each of these statements. A *(Scottish parliament/ Welsh assembly)* would ...**READ OUT a. TO d. AND CODE ONE FOR EACH...**

Base: S: 676

Scotland

		Agree strongly	Agree	Neither agree nor disagree	Dis-agree	Disagree strongly	(Don't know)	(NA)
	[LabDomin]							
a.	... be dominated too much by the Labour Party?	% 11.1	33.6	19.4	27.4	2.4	5.9	0.1
	[CntDomin]							
b.	... pay too much attention to the central belt of Scotland?	% 4.7	27.5	17.8	40.5	1.9	7.5	0.1
	[JobPolit]							
c.	... simply mean more jobs for politicians?	% 11.9	34.7	14.8	32.9	1.4	4.2	0.1
	[Cost2Much]							
d.	cost too much to set up and run?	% 10.5	26.5	14.9	35.9	4.3	7.8	0.1

Base: W: 686

Wales

		Agree strongly	Agree	Neither agree nor disagree	Dis-agree	Disagree strongly	(Don't know)	(NA)
	[LabDomin]							
a.	... be dominated too much by the Labour Party?	% 9.0	32.4	22.0	27.6	1.2	7.7	-
	[SthDomin]							
b.	... pay too much attention to South Wales?	% 8.3	31.3	14.0	37.6	2.6	6.1	-
	[JobPolit]							
c.	...simply mean more jobs for politicians?	% 21.0	40.6	11.5	19.7	1.4	5.2	0.5
	[Cost2Much]							
d.	...cost too much to set up and run?	% 23.8	32.7	13.7	21.4	1.8	6.5	0.2
	[WelSpeak]							
e.	...be dominated too much by Welsh speakers?	% 8.1	23.1	20.3	38.0	5.3	5.2	-

ASK ALL IN WALES
[WelQuang]

W26f. And would a Welsh assembly give the Welsh ... **READ OUT** ...

	Wales %
... <u>more</u> control over non-elected bodies or Quangos,	37.6
<u>less</u> control,	6.7
or, would it make no difference?	35.7
(Don't know)	19.9
(NA)	0.1

Base:
W: 686

Section 4

ASK ALL   Base:
[NatBalan]   **S: 676**
CARD   **W: 686**

SW27. Which, if any, of the following best describes how you   *Scotland*   *Wales*
      see yourself?   %   %

	Scotland %	Wales %
(Scottish/Welsh), not British	31.8	16.6
More *(Scottish/ Welsh)* than British	32.1	24.7
Equally *(Scottish/ Welsh)* and British	28.4	33.0
More British than *(Scottish/ Welsh)*	2.9	10.0
British, not *(Scottish/ Welsh)*	2.8	11.9
Other description (**WRITE IN**) _____	1.3	3.7
(None of these)	0.5	0.2
(Don't know)	0.1	-
(NA)	0.1	-

CARD

SW28. How important or unimportant is each of the following
to being truly *(Scottish/Welsh)*?   **Base:**
Firstly ... **READ OUT a. TO** *(c/d)*. **AND CODE**   *Scotland*   **S:676**
ONE FOR EACH ...

		Very important	Fairly important	Not very important	Not at all important	(Don't know)	(NA)
	[NatBorn]						
a.	... to have been born in Scotland?	% 56.6	28.4	10.4	3.8	0.8	-
	[NatLive]						
b.	... to be living in Scotland?	% 38.5	39.2	17.3	4.1	0.7	0.1
	[NatAnces]						
c.	... to have Scottish parents or grandparents?	% 33.6	38.9	19.5	6.3	1.6	0.1

Wales   **Base:**
                                                                                     W:686

		Very important	Fairly important	Not very important	Not at all important	(Don't know)	(NA)
	[NatBorn]						
a.	... to have been born in Wales?	% 48.9	30.7	14.0	5.4	0.8	0.1
	[NatLive]						
b.	... to be living in Wales?	% 31.9	35.8	22.3	8.5	1.2	0.3
	[NatAnces]						
c.	... to have Welsh parents or grandparents?	% 29.0	36.8	25.5	7.6	1.1	-
	[NatSpeak]						
d.	... to speak Welsh?	% 16.8	26.0	36.5	19.8	0.9	-

Base:
S: 676
W: 686

ASK ALL
[SRClass]
SW29a. Do you ever think of yourself as belonging to any particular class? IF YES: Which class is that?

	Scotland %	Wales %	
Yes, middle class	10.4	9.1	**GO TO c.**
Yes, working class	27.6	28.7	**GO TO d.**
Yes, other (**WRITE IN**) _____	0.4	0.8	
No	60.3	60.4	**ASK b.**
(Don't know)	1.3	0.8	
(NA)	-	0.2	

[SRClass2]
IF 'YES, OTHER', 'NO' OR 'DON'T KNOW' (CODES 3, 4, 8 AT a)
b. Most people say they belong either to the middle class or to the working class. If you had to make a choice would you call yourself ... **READ OUT** ...

	%	%	
... middle class,	12.6	10.8	**GO TO c.**
or, working class?	40.6	36.6	**GO TO d.**
(Neither)	7.7	12.7	**GO TO**
(Don't know)	1.1	1.6	**Q30**
(NA)	-	0.5	

IF 'MIDDLE CLASS' (CODE 1 AT Q29a/b)
[NatMidCl]
c. Would you say that you had more in common with middle class English people or with working class *(Scottish/Welsh)* people?

	%	%	
Middle class English	7.0	7.2	
Working class *(Scottish/Welsh)*	11.0	5.3	
(No preference)	3.3	3.5	**NOW GO**
(Depends on the individual)	0.8	2.5	**TO Q30**
(Don't know)	0.8	1.2	
(NA)	-	0.6	

IF 'WORKING CLASS' (CODE 2 AT Q29a/b)
[NatWCl]
d. Would you say that you had more in common with working class English people or with middle class *(Scottish/Welsh)* people?

	%	%
Working class English	17.9	18.6
Middle class *(Scottish/Welsh)*	27.0	16.7
(No Preference)	9.5	19.8
(Depends on the individual)	5.7	5.0
Don't know	7.7	5.3
(NA)	0.5	0.5

ASK ALL
[GBPride]
CARD
SW30a. How proud are you of being British, or do you not see
yourself as British at all? **CODE IN COLUMN a.**

[NatPride]
CARD AGAIN
b. And how proud are you of being *(Scottish/Welsh)*, or do
you not see yourself as *(Scottish/Welsh)* at all?
CODE IN COLUMN b.

Base:
S:676
W:686

	Scotland	*Wales*	*Scotland*	*Wales*
		a.		**b.**
		British		*(Scottish/Welsh)*
	%	%	%	%
Very proud	26.1	42.9	74.5	59.0
Somewhat proud	40.3	38.1	18.8	18.9
Not very proud	12.2	5.7	1.1	1.8
Not at all proud	4.4	3.2	0.4	1.1
(Not British)	15.6	8.7	•	•
(Not *(Scottish/Welsh)*)	•	•	4.2	18.2
(Don't know)	1.3	1.4	-	0.9
(NA)	0.3	-	0.9	0.1

[EngDecid]
SW31. Has it ever made you angry or not that
it is English voters who mainly decide
who runs *(Scotland/Wales)*?
IF 'YES': Is that very angry or somewhat angry?

	Scotland	*Wales*
	%	%
Yes- very angry	40.7	19.7
Yes - somewhat angry	34.7	21.9
No - not angry	24.2	58.0
(NA)	0.4	0.4

CARD
SW32. Here are some things that people sometimes say are
important to *(Scottish/Welsh)* culture. Choosing your answers
from this card, please say how proud, if at all, you feel
of each. Firstly ... **READ OUT a).TO *(f/g)*. AND CODE
ONE FOR EACH** ...

Base:
S: 676

			Scotland					
		Very proud	Somewhat proud	Not very proud	Not at all proud	No feelings either way	(Don't know)	(NA)
[ScSpirit]								
a. ... Scottish community spirit?	%	40.0	43.1	6.6	1.3	7.9	1.0	-
[ScGaelic]								
b. ... the Gaelic language?	%	11.1	32.5	14.1	6.6	34.2	1.4	-
[ScTartan]								
c. ... tartan?	%	39.1	40.1	6.8	5.2	8.3	0.5	-
[ScMusic]								
d. ... Scottish music?	%	39.6	41.8	8.1	3.0	6.9	0.6	-
[ScWallac]								
e. ... William Wallace?	%	40.4	36.7	6.8	3.3	10.7	2.0	0.1
[ScLands]								
f. ... the Scottish landscape?	%	83.6	13.4	0.9	-	1.3	0.6	0.1

			Very proud	Somewhat proud	Not very proud	Not at all proud	No feelings either way	(Don't know)	Base: W: 686 (NA)
					Wales				
a.	[WISpirit] ... Welsh community spirit?	%	44.8	33.9	6.8	2.1	10.9	1.5	-
b.	[WILang] ... the Welsh language?	%	32.4	31.9	9.2	7.5	17.9	1.0	0.1
c.	[WIMaleCh] ... male voice choirs?	%	45.9	32.4	6.3	3.6	10.7	0.9	0.2
d.	[WIEisted] ... the eisteddfod?	%	35.1	33.6	6.1	5.4	18.0	1.7	-
e.	[WIRugbyT] ... the Welsh rugby team?	%	48.6	27.9	6.6	4.4	11.9	0.6	-
f.	[WILands] ... the Welsh landscape?	%	71.6	21.7	1.6	1.0	3.6	0.2	0.3
g.	[WIChapel] ... the Welsh chapels?	%	22.4	33.3	10.8	6.5	25.8	1.1	-

ASK ALL

[EUGood]

SW33. On the whole, do you think the European Union has been
... READ OUT ..

Base: S: 676 W: 686

	Scotland %	Wales %
... good for *(Scotland/Wales)*,	45.0	39.4
or, bad for *(Scotland/Wales)*?	14.0	11.5
(Neither or both)	17.8	25.2
(Don't know)	23.2	23.9

[UKBeneft]

SW34. And on the whole, do you think that England's economy benefits
more from having *(Scotland/Wales)* in the UK, or that *(Scotland's/Wales')*
economy benefits more from being part of the UK, or is it about equal?

	%	%
England benefits more	47.5	16.2
(Scotland/Wales) benefits more	14.1	37.4
About equal	32.0	34.4
(Neither/both lose)	0.4	0.3
(Don't know)	5.8	11.7
(NA)	0.1	-

WELSH LANGUAGE

                                                            Wales   **Base:**
                                                              %   **W: 686**

ASK ALL IN WALES
[RWelshSp]
W35. Can you yourself speak Welsh?
IF YES: Is that fluently or not?

Yes, fluently	16.5	
Yes, but not fluently	12.1	**ASK Q36**
No	71.4	**GO TO Q37**
(NA)	0.1	

[RWelHome]
IF SPEAKS WELSH (CODES 1 OR 2 AT Q35)
W36. Do you normally speak Welsh at home   %
 ... READ OUT ...   ... all or most of the time,   9.9
                                                  occasionally,   6.2
                                         never or hardly ever? 12.1
                                                  (Don 't know)   -
                                                          (NA)   0.4

ASK ALL IN WALES
CARD P
W37. Please tell me who, if any, of the people on this card speak
or spoke Welsh?
FOR EACH 'YES' ANSWER: Is/was that fluently or not?
IF 'NO SPOUSE/PARTNER/CHILDREN' CODE 'DOES NOT APPLY'
PROBE: Which others?
CODE ONE IN EACH ROW

				Yes, fluently	Yes, not fluently	No	Not applicable	(Don't know)	(NA)
a.	*[SpsWelSp]*	Husband/wife/partner	%	9.4	5.9	65.8	18.1	0.3	0.5
b.	*[ChdWelSp]*	Any of your child(ren)	%	12.0	15.1	53.3	19.0	0.3	0.3
c.	*[ParWelSp]*	Either parent	%	25.0	6.1	67.7	0.7	0.1	0.5
d.	*[GprWelSp]*	Any grandparent	%	34.0	3.5	57.8	1.1	2.7	0.8

[WelSchl]
W38. Have you ever sent - or are you considering sending - any
children in your care to a Welsh medium school?   %
PROBE FOR CORRECT CODE

Yes - sent in the past	7.4
Yes - sending now	4.1
Yes - considering	4.5
No	63.9
Never had any children in my care	19.6
(Don't know)	0.1
(NA)	0.3

[WlLivLan]
CARD Q
W39. Using this card, how much do you agree or disagree with the
following statement:
More should be done to preserve Welsh as a living language.

Base:
W: 686

%

Agree strongly	27.3
Agree	37.8
Neither agree nor disagree	20.8
Disagree	9.7
Disagree strongly	2.9
(Don't know)	1.3
(NA)	0.1

	CLASSIFICATION		

ASK ALL
[RSex]
X1. Now some questions about you and your background.
INTERVIEWER: CODE RESPONDENT'S SEX

		Scotland	Wales
		%	%
	Male	45.8	42.7
	Female	54.2	57.3

[RAge]
X2. Can I just check, what was your age last birthday?

		%	%
	18-24	8.6	8.9
	25-34	17.5	17.4
	35-44	22.2	19.7
	45-54	19.3	19.4
	55-59	7.9	7.0
	60-64	5.8	5.3
	65+	18.5	21.9
	DK/Refused/NA	0.3	0.3

[Religion]
X3a) Do you regard yourself as belonging to any particular religion?
IF YES: Which?
DO NOT PROMPT
CODE ONE ONLY

	Scotland	Wales	
	%	%	
No religion	31.6	34.3	
Christian - no denomination	4.5	3.7	
Roman Catholic	15.5	6.9	
Church of England/Anglican/Episcopal	2.6	34.6	
Presbyterian - Church of Scotland	42.2	0.7	
Presbyterian - Welsh Calvinistic Methodists	0.2	2.9	
Free Presbyterian	0.1	0.3	
Methodist (including Wesleyan)	0.1	5.8	
Baptist	0.5	5.5	
United Reform Church (URC)/ Congregational	0.3	1.3	**ASK b.**
Brethren	0.1	0.2	
Other Protestant (**WRITE IN**) _____	0.6	2.8	
Other Christian (**WRITE IN**) _____	0.1	0.3	
Jewish	0.4	0.2	
Hindu	-	-	
Islam/Muslim	0.4	0.2	
Sikh	-	-	
Buddhist	-	-	
Other non-Christian (**WRITE IN**) _____	0.4	0.1	
Refused	0.1	-	**GO TO X5**
(Don't know)	-	0.4	**ASK b.**

ALL EXCEPT 'REFUSED' AT a) (CODES 00 - 18, 98 AT X3a)
[FamRelig]

Base:
S:676
W:686

X3b) In what religion, if any, were you brought up?

PROBE IF NECESSARY: What was your
family's religion?
DO NOT PROMPT
CODE ONE ONLY

	Scotland %	Wales %
No religion	9.3	14.4
Christian - no denomination	2.3	1.9
Roman Catholic	18.2	8.5
Church of England/Anglican/Episcopal	4.1	44.1
Presbyterian - Church of Scotland	57.8	1.1
Presbyterian - Welsh Calvinistic Methodists	0.6	5.8
Free Presbyterian	0.2	1.1
Methodist (including Wesleyan)	0.4	7.9
Baptist	0.9	8.8
United Reform Church (URC)/ Congregational	0.5	1.9
Brethren	0.6	0.2
Other Protestant (**WRITE IN**) _____	0.6	2.5
Other Christian (**WRITE IN**) _____	0.1	0.6
Jewish	0.4	0.2
Hindu	-	-
Islam/Muslim	0.4	0.4
Sikh	-	-
Buddhist	-	-
Other non-Christian (**WRITE IN**) _____	-	-
Refused	-	-
(Don't know)	0.2	0.7
(NA)	3.0	-

IF ANY RELIGION CODED AT X3a/b
(OTHERS GO TO X5)
[ChAttend]

X4. Apart from such special occasions as weddings,
funerals and baptisms and so on, how often
nowadays do you attend services or meetings
connected with your religion?

PROBE AS NECESSARY

	%	%
Once a week or more	16.7	13.1
Less often but at least once in two weeks	4.9	1.5
Less often but at least once a month	7.2	4.2
Less often but at least twice a year	10.3	12.3
Less often but at least once a year	6.3	4.7
Less often	4.6	7.2
Never or practically never	39.3	41.5
Varies too much to say	0.7	0.4
Refused	-	-
(Don't know)	-	-
(NA)	1.3	0.6

Base:
S: 676
W: 686

ASK ALL
[PartySup]
X5a) Generally speaking, do you think of yourself as Conservative,
Labour, Liberal Democrat, *(Nationalist, Plaid Cymru)* or what?

CODE ONE ONLY IN COLUMN a.

IF NONE/DON'T KNOW (CODE 00 OR 98 AT a)
[PartyCls]
b) Do you generally think of yourself as a little closer
to one of the parties than the others?
IF YES: Which party?

CODE ONE ONLY IN COLUMN b.

	Scotland a.	*Wales*	*Scotland* b.	*Wales*
	%	%	%	%
Conservative	15.4	18.9	0.8	1.6
Labour	47.3	51.8	2.1	1.8
Liberal Democrat	7.0	6.6	0.9	0.5
Scottish National Party	18.3	- **GO TO**	1.5	- **ASK**
Plaid Cymru	-	10.2 **c.**	-	0.2 **c.**
Green Party	0.1	0.2	-	-
Other **(WRITE IN) a.** _____	0.9	0.4	-	-
Other **(WRITE IN) b.** _____	-	-	-	-
None/No	8.2	9.4 **ASK**	3.5	4.6 **GO**
Don't know	1.9	2.3 **b.**	0.4	1.1 **TO**
(NA)	0.8	0.1	1.9	2.1 **X6**

IF ANY PARTY CODED AT a) OR b)
[IDStrong]
c) Would you call yourself very strong *(name of party
at a. or b.)*, fairly strong or not very strong?

	Scotland	*Wales*
	%	%
Very strong	20.7	19.9
Fairly strong	47.4	43.7
Not very strong	25.7	27.9
(Don't know)	-	0.2
(NA)	2.7	3.6

Base:
S: 676
W: 686

ASK ALL
CARD
X6a. Please say which, if any, of the words on this card describes
the way you think of yourself. Please choose as many or as
few as apply. **PROBE:** Which others?
CODE ALL THAT APPLY IN COLUMN a)

CARD AGAIN
IF MORE THAN ONE CODE RINGED IN COLUMN a)
b. And if you had to choose, which one **best** describes the
way you think of yourself?
CODE ONE ONLY IN COLUMN b) *(Percentage for b. not shown)*

a.

			Scotland %	Wales %
[NatBrit]		British	53.6	66.9
[NatEng]		English	3.5	13.4
[NatEuro]		European	12.1	12.4
[NatIrish]		Irish	3.3	1.1
[NatNI]		Northern Irish	0.2	0.4
[NatScot]		Scottish	92.1	1.8
[NatWelsh]		Welsh	0.2	73.2
[NatOth]	Other answer (**WRITE IN**) _____		0.6	1.7
[NatNone]		None of these	0.1	0.2
		(NA)	0.1	-

[RaceOri2]
CARD
X7. May I just check, to which of these groups do you consider
you belong?
CODE ONE ONLY

	%	%
Black: of African origin	-	-
Black: of Caribbean origin	-	-
Black: of other origin (**WRITE IN**) _____	-	-
Asian: of Indian origin	-	-
Asian: of Pakistani origin	0.4	0.2
Asian: of Bangladeshi origin	-	-
Asian: of Chinese origin	-	0.1
Asian: of other origin (**WRITE IN**) _____	-	-
White: of any European origin	97.7	98.9
White: of other origin (**WRITE IN**) _____	1.3	0.3
Mixed origin (**WRITE IN**) _____	0.1	0.2
Other (**WRITE IN**) _____	-	-
Refused	0.2	-
(Don't know)	-	-
(NA)	0.2	0.3

Base:
S: 676
W: 686

[RBorn]

X8. Were you born in *(Scotland/Wales)*, in England or somewhere else?
IF 'SOMEWHERE ELSE': Where was that? **(PROBE FOR COUNTRY)**

	Scotland %	Wales %
(Scotland/Wales)	88.3	66.6
England	6.2	21.1
Somewhere else **(WRITE IN)** _____	2.2	4.3
(Don't know)	-	-
(NA)	3.2	8.0

[RLiveEls]

X9. Have you ever lived anywhere other than *(Scotland/Wales)*
for more than a year?
IF YES: Where was that? **PROBE:** Anywhere else?
PROBE FOR COUNTRY
CODE ALL THAT APPLY

	%	%
No - have never lived anywhere else for more than a year	75.0	55.8
Yes - England	14.2	33.8
Yes - somewhere else **(WRITE IN)** _____	8.3	6.8
(Yes - England <u>and</u> elsewhere)	2.3	2.8
(Don't know)	-	0.3
(NA)	0.1	0.4

X10. How long have you lived in this part of *(Scotland/Wales)*?
DO NOT DEFINE 'PART OF *(SCOTLAND/WALES)*' -
LET RESPONDENT DEFINE.
PROBE FOR BEST ESTIMATE.
ENTER <u>TOTAL</u> NUMBER OF YEARS IN AREA.

	%	%
1-10 years	12.4	10.2
11-20 years	10.6	15.9
21-30 years	17.8	20.8
31-40 years	19.5	17.1
41-50 years	16.2	15.8
51+ years	22.9	20.1
(Don't know)	0.1	0.2
(NA)	0.6	0.1
	Years	Years
Median value	35.0	33.0

Base:
S: 676
W: 686

[Tenure]

X11. Does your household own or rent this accommodation?
PROBE IF OWNS: Outright or on a mortgage?
PROBE IF RENTS: From whom?
CODE ONE ONLY

	Scotland %	Wales %
OWNS: Own outright (leasehold or freehold)	21.3	35.5
OWNS: Buying on mortgage (leasehold or freehold)	43.5	41.4
RENTS: Local authority or council	26.3	14.5
RENTS: Housing Association or Housing Trust	2.3	2.1
RENTS: Property company	0.5	-
RENTS: Employer	0.1	0.2
RENTS: Other organisation	0.9	0.7
RENTS: Relative	1.1	0.8
RENTS: Other individual	2.8	3.2
RENTS: Housing Action Trust	-	0.1
Rent free, squatting etc.	1.0	0.7
(Don't know)	-	0.7
(NA)	0.3	0.2

[DadVoted]

X12. Do you remember which party your **father** usually voted for when you were growing up?
DO NOT PROMPT

	%	%
Conservative/National Liberal	18.9	21.4
Labour	50.0	50.4
Liberal/Alliance/SDP/Liberal Democrat	4.1	4.9
Scottish National Party	5.2	•
Plaid Cymru	•	2.3
Other **(WRITE IN)** _____	0.9	0.2
Varied too much to say	0.2	0.1
Not applicable/Not brought up in Britain	0.7	0.6
Refused to disclose voting	2.1	1.3
Don't know/Can't remember	17.9	18.9

[MumVoted]

X13. And do you remember which party your **mother** usually voted for when you were growing up?
DO NOT PROMPT

	%	%
Conservative/National Liberal	19.9	20.1
Labour	45.4	47.8
Liberal/Alliance/SDP/Liberal Democrat	3.8	4.6
Scottish National Party	5.8	•
Plaid Cymru	•	2.6
Other **(WRITE IN)** _____	1.2	0.8
Varied too much to say	0.3	0.2
Not applicable/Not brought up in Britain	0.4	0.6
Refused to disclose voting	2.6	0.7
Don't know/Can't remember	20.6	22.6
(NA)	-	0.1

[REconAct]
CARD Q
X14. Which of these descriptions applies to what you were
doing last week, that is the seven days ending last Sunday?
PROBE: Which others? **CODE ALL THAT APPLY IN COLUMN I.**
IF ONE CODE ONLY AT I, TRANSFER IT TO COLUMN II.
IF MORE THAN ONE CODE AT I, TRANSFER HIGHEST TO COLUMN II.

Base:
S: 676
W: 686

II.

(Percentage for I not shown)

	Scotland %	Wales %	
In full-time education (not paid for by employer, including on vacation)	4.8	2.1	**ASK X15**
On government training/employment programme (for example, Youth Training, Training for Work etc.)	0.6	0.3	
In paid work (or away temporarily) for at least 10 hours in week	53.6	53.2	**GO TO**
Waiting to take up paid job already accepted	0.3	-	**X16**
Unemployed and registered at a benefit office	3.2	3.1	
Unemployed, not registered, but actively looking for a job (of at least 10 hours a week)	0.5	0.6	
Unemployed, wanting a job (of at least 10 hours a week) but not actively looking for a job	1.0	-	**ASK X15**
Permanently sick or disabled	6.3	6.0	
Wholly retired from work	19.5	22.1	
Looking after home or family	10.3	12.3	
Doing something else **(WRITE IN)** _____	-	0.3	

[RLastJob]
IF NOT IN PAID WORK/WAITING TO TAKE UP (CODE 01-02 OR 05-11 AT X14)
X15. How long ago did you last have a paid job of at least 10 hours
a week, excluding holiday jobs?
PROBE FOR CORRECT ANSWER.
NOTE: GOVERNMENT PROGRAMMES OR SCHEMES DO NOT
COUNT AS 'PAID JOBS'.

Base
S: 311
W:321

	%	%	
Within the past 12 months	11.7	5.5	
Over 1, up to five years ago	22.4	21.9	
Over 5, up to ten years ago	22.7	23.4	**ASK**
Over 10, up to twenty years ago	20.1	26.6	**X16**
Over 20 years ago	15.0	12.8	
Never had a paid job of 10 + hours per week	6.9	8.4	**GO TO**
(NA)	1.2	1.4	**X25**

ALL WHO HAVE EVER WORKED (CODES 03-04 ATX14 OR 1-5 AT X15)
X16. **IF RESPONDENT IS IN PAID WORK (CODE 03 AT X14):** ASK ABOUT CURRENT JOB.
   IF RESPONDENT IS WAITING TO TAKE UP WORK (CODE 04 AT X15): ASK ABOUT FUTURE JOB.
   ELSE (CODE 1-5 AT X15): ASK ABOUT MOST RECENT JOB.

a) What (*is/was*) the name or title of your (*current/future/most recent*) job?

b) And what kind of work (*do/did*) you do in that job.
   IF RELEVANT: What kind of materials or machines (*do/did*)
   you use?

c) What training or qualifications (*are/were*) needed for that job?

d) What (*is/was*) the name of the organisation for whom you
   (*work/worked*)?
   WRITE IN FULL NAME

		Scotland	Wales	Base
[Remplyee]		*Scotland*	*Wales*	**S: 655**
X17. Can I just check, (*are/were*) you ... **READ OUT** ...		%	%	**W:659**
	...an employee,	90.6	89.8 **ASK X18**	
	or self-employed?	8.5	9.3 **GO TO X22**	
	(Don't know)	0.3	0.2 **ASK X18**	
	(NA)	0.6	0.7	

				Base:
[RSupMan]				**S:599**
IF EMPLOYEE (CODE 1, 8 AT X17)				**W:598**
X18. (Can I just check), (*are/were*) you ... **READ OUT** ...		%	%	
	... a manager,	14.3	18.6	
	a foreman or supervisor,	15.8	15.4	
	or, not?	68.3	64.9	
	(Don't know)	-	0.2	
	(NA)	1.6	0.9	

[ROcSect2]
CARD R
X19. Which of the types of organisations on this card (*do/did*)
you work for?

	Scotland	Wales
	%	%
PRIVATE SECTOR FIRM OR COMPANY - including limited companies and PLCs	65.3	59.6
NATIONALISED INDUSTRY OR PUBLIC CORPORATION - including the Post Office and the BBC	3.1	4.0
OTHER PUBLIC SECTOR EMPLOYER - including Central Government/ Civil Service/Government Agency/Local authority/Local Education Authority (and 'opted out' schools)/universities/Health Authority/NHS hospitals/ NHS Trusts/GP surgeries/Police/Armed forces	28.9	33.5
CHARITY/VOLUNTARY SECTOR - including charitable companies, churches, trade unions	1.0	0.6
OTHER ORGANISATION **(WRITE IN)** _____	0.2	0.9
(Don't know)	0.1	0.5
(NA)	1.4	0.8

[REmpWkE]

X20. How many people (are/were) employed at the place where you (work/worked)?

PROBE FOR CORRECT PRECODE

	Scotland %	Wales %
Fewer than 10	16.1	17.3
10 - 24	18.2	14.6
25 - 99	22.1	19.3
100 - 499	24.0	27.1
500 plus	16.8	19.5
(Don't know)	1.6	1.5
(NA)	1.1	0.8

Base
S: 599
W: 598

X21. What (does/did) your employer make or do at the place where you usually (work/worked) (from)?
DESCRIBE FULLY. PROBE MANUFACTURING OR PROCESSING OR DISTRIBUTING ETC AND MAIN GOODS PRODUCED, MATERIALS USED, WHOLESALE OR RETAIL. IF FARM, GIVE NUMBER OF ACRES.

GO TO X24

[REmpWkS]
IF SELF-EMPLOYED (CODE 2 AT X18)
X22. (Do/Did) you have any employees?
IF YES: How many?

	%	%
Fewer than 10	90.3	85.9
10 - 24	6.9	2.1
25 - 99	2.0	4.6
100 - 499	-	-
500 plus	-	-
(Don't know)	-	3.7
(NA)	0.9	3.7

Base
S: 56
W: 61

X23. What (do/did) you make or do at the place where you usually (work/worked) (from)?
DESCRIBE FULLY. PROBE MANUFACTURING OR PROCESSING OR DISTRIBUTING ETC AND MAIN GOODS PRODUCED, MATERIALS USED, WHOLESALE OR RETAIL. IF FARM, GIVE NUMBER OF ACRES.

O.U.O RESPONDENT'S
OCCUPATIONAL DETAILS

SOC

ES

SIC92

ASK ALL WHO HAVE EVER WORKED
[RJbHrsi]

X24. How many hours (*do/did*) you normally work
a week in your main job - <u>including</u> any paid or
unpaid overtime.
ROUND TO NEAREST HOUR.
IF RESPONDENT CANNOT ANSWER, ASK ABOUT LAST WEEK.
ACCEPT AN ESTIMATE IF 'DON'T KNOW EXACTLY'

Base:
S: 655
W: 659

	Scotland %	Wales %
10-15 hours	5.3	4.6
16-23 hours	9.9	8.7
24-29 hours	4.2	3.8
30+ hours	75.9	79.8
(Less than 10 hours)	0.6	0.3
(Don't know)	2.4	1.5
(NA)	1.7	1.3

ASK ALL
[UnionSA2]

X25. Are you **now** a member of a trade union or staff association?
PROBE AS NECESSARY AND CODE FIRST TO APPLY.

Base:
S:676
W: 686

	%	%
Yes: trade union	19.3	21.4
Yes: staff association	3.8	3.8
No	76.5	73.7
(Don't know)	0.2	0.5
(NA)	0.2	0.7

[MarStat2]
CARD S

X26. Which of these applies to you at present?
CODE FIRST TO APPLY

	%	%	
Married	60.7	60.3	**ASK**
Living as married	4.2	6.3	**X27**
Separated (after being married)	2.9	1.6	
Divorced	5.1	6.1	**GO TO**
Widowed	9.9	9.2	**X41**
Single (never married)	17.1	16.0	
(NA)	0.1	0.6	

IF MARRIED/LIVING AS MARRIED (CODE 1 OR 2 AT X26)
[SUnioSA2]

X27. Is your (*husband/wife/partner*) **now** a member of a trade
union or staff association?
PROBE AS NECESSARY. CODE FIRST TO APPLY

Base:
S: 440
W: 461

	%	%
Yes: trade union	24.5	23.0
Yes: staff association	5.8	3.0
No	66.7	71.8
(Don't know)	2.0	1.0
(NA)	1.0	1.1

		Base:
[SEconAct]		S: 440
CARD		W: 461

X28. Which of these descriptions applies to what your (*husband/wife partner*) was doing last week, that is the seven days ending last Sunday?
PROBE: Which others? **CODE ALL THAT APPLY IN COLUMN I.**
IF ONE CODE ONLY AT I, TRANSFER IT TO COLUMN II.
IF MORE THAN ONE CODE AT I, TRANSFER HIGHEST TO COLUMN II.
(Percentage for I not shown)

	II.		
	Scotland %	Wales %	
In full-time education (not paid for by employer, including on vacation)	1.2	0.5	**ASK X29**
On government training/employment programme (for example, Youth Training, Training for Work etc.)	-	-	
In paid work (or away temporarily) for at least 10 hours in week	64.0	56.5	**GO TO X30**
Waiting to take up paid job already accepted	0.2	-	
Unemployed and registered at a benefit office	1.8	1.7	
Unemployed, not registered, but actively looking for a job (of at least 10 hours a week)	0.5	0.6	**ASK X29**
Unemployed, wanting a job (of at least 10 hours a week) but not actively looking for a job	-	0.2	
Permanently sick or disabled	4.5	6.0	
Wholly retired from work	16.9	19.1	
Looking after home or family	10.6	14.6	
Doing something else (**WRITE IN**) _____	-	-	
(NA)	0.2	0.9	

ALL WITH PARTNER <u>NOT</u> IN PAID WORK (CODES 01-02, 05-11 AT X28)   Base:
[SLastJob]   S: 157
X29. How long ago did (*he/she*) last have a paid job of at least 10 hours   W: 200
a week, excluding holiday jobs?
PROBE FOR CORRECT ANSWER.
NOTE: GOVERNMENT PROGRAMMES OR SCHEMES DO NOT
COUNT AS 'PAID JOBS'.

	Scotland %	Wales %	
Within the past 12 months	9.1	4.2	
Over 1, up to five years ago	25.9	18.6	
Over 5, up to ten years ago	17.5	21.6	**ASK X30**
Over 10, up to twenty years ago	27.1	32.5	
Over 20 years ago	8.3	10.3	
Never had a paid job of 10 + hours per week	7.8	5.8	**GO TO X41**
(NA)	4.2	7.1	

X30. **INTERVIEWER TO CODE CURRENT ACTIVITY OF**
RESPONDENT (FROM X14 ON PAGE 22):

Respondent in education, training scheme, sick/disabled or 'other' (01, 02, 08 or 11)	1	**ASK X31**
Respondent in work, waiting to take up work, unemployed or retired (03-07, 09-10)	2	**GO TO X41**

X31. **INTERVIEWER TO CODE CURRENT ACTIVITY OF**
SPOUSE/PARTNER (FROM X28 ON PREVIOUS PAGE):

Spouse/partner in work, waiting to take up work, unemployed, retired or looking after family (03-07, 09-10)	1	**ASK X32**
Spouse/partner in education, training scheme, sick/disabled or 'other' (01,02,08 or 11)	2	**GO TO X41**

ALL FOR WHOM SPOUSE'S/PARTNER'S JOB DETAILS ARE BEING COLLECTED (CODE 1 AT X31)
X32. **IF SPOUSE/PARTNER IS IN PAID WORK (CODE 03 AT X28):** ASK ABOUT CURRENT JOB.
IF SPOUSE/PARTNER IS WAITING TO TAKE UP WORK (CODE 04 AT X28): ASK ABOUT FUTURE JOB.
ELSE (CODE 1-5 AT X29): ASK ABOUT MOST RECENT JOB.

a) What (*is/was*) the name or title of (*his/her current/future/most recent*) job?

b) And what kind of work (*does/did*) (*he/she*) do in that job.
IF RELEVANT: What kind of materials or machines (*does/did*)
(*he/she*) use?

c) What training or qualifications are needed for that job?

				Base:
[SEmployee]		*Scotland*	*Wales*	**S: 26**
X33. Can I just check, (*is/was*) (*he/she*) ... **READ OUT** ...		No.[1]	No.	**W: 24**
	...an employee,	15	13	**ASK X34**
	or self-employed?	2	-	**GO TO X38**
	Don't know	-	-	**ASK X34**
	(NA)	8	11	

				Base:
IF EMPLOYEE (CODE 1, 8 AT X33)				**S: 23**
[SSupMan]		No.	No.	**W: 24**
X34. (Can I just check), (*is/was*) (*he/she*) ... **READ OUT** ...				
	... a manager,	1	5	
	a foreman or supervisor,	2	1	
	or, not?	12	7	
	(Don't know)	-	-	
	(NA)	8	11	

---

[1] Where the base is less than 50, absolute numbers are quoted instead of percentages.

[SOcSect2]
CARD U
X35. Which of the types of organisations on this card (*does/did*)
(*he/she*) work for?

	Scotland No.	Wales No.
PRIVATE SECTOR FIRM OR COMPANY - including limited companies and PLCs	10	9
NATIONALISED INDUSTRY OR PUBLIC CORPORATION - including the Post Office and the BBC	-	1
OTHER PUBLIC SECTOR EMPLOYER - including Central Government/ Civil Service/Government Agency/Local authority/Local Education Authority (and 'opted out' schools)/universities/Health Authority/NHS hospitals/ NHS Trusts/GP surgeries/Police/Armed forces	6	3
CHARITY/VOLUNTARY SECTOR - including charitable companies, churches, trade unions	-	-
OTHER ORGANISATION **(WRITE IN)** _____	-	-
(Don't know)	-	-
(NA)	8	11

Base:
S: 23
W: 24

[SEmpWorkE]
X36. How many people (*are/were*) employed at the place
where you (*he/she*) (*work/worked*)?
PROBE FOR CORRECT PRECODE

	No.	No.
Fewer than 10	-	5
10 - 24	2	1
25 - 99	3	2
100 - 499	4	1
500 plus	3	2
(Don't know)	3	2
(NA)	8	11

X37. What (*does/did*) (*his/her*) employer make or do at
the place where (*he/she*) usually (*work/worked*) (from)?
DESCRIBE FULLY. PROBE MANUFACTURING OR
PROCESSING OR DISTRIBUTING ETC AND MAIN
GOODS PRODUCED, MATERIALS USED, WHOLESALE
OR RETAIL. IF FARM, GIVE NUMBER OF ACRES.

GO TO X40

IF SELF-EMPLOYED (CODE 2 AT X33)
[SEmpWkS]
X38. (*Does/Did*) (*he/she*) have any employees?
IF YES: How many?

	No.	No.
Fewer than 10	2	-
25 - 99	-	-
100 - 499	-	-
500 plus	-	-
(Don't know)	-	-
(NA)	8	11

Base:
S: 10
W:11

X39. What (*does/did*) (*he/she*) make or do at the place where
(*he/she*) usually (*work/worked*) (from)?
DESCRIBE FULLY. PROBE MANUFACTURING OR
PROCESSING OR DISTRIBUTING ETC AND MAIN
GOODS PRODUCED, MATERIALS USED, WHOLESALE
OR RETAIL. IF FARM, GIVE NUMBER OF ACRES.

ALL FOR WHOM SPOUSE'S/PARTNER'S JOB DETAILS ARE BEING COLLECTED   **Base:**
[SJbHrsi]   **S: 26**
X40. How many hours (*does/did*) (*he/she*) normally   **W: 24**
work a week in (*his/her*) main job - including any paid
ROUND TO NEAREST HOUR.
IF RESPONDENT CANNOT ANSWER, ASK ABOUT LAST WEEK .   *Scotland*   *Wales*
ACCEPT AN ESTIMATE IF 'DON'T KNOW EXACTLY'   No.   No.

	Scotland No.	Wales No.
10-15 hours	1	1
16-23 hours	-	2
24-29 hours	-	-
30+ hours	13	8
(Less than 10 hours)	1	-
(Don't know)	2	1
(NA)	9	12

ASK ALL   **Base:**
[MainInc]   **S: 676**
CARD   **W: 686**
X41. Which of these is the **main** source of income for you
(and your *husband/wife/partner*) at present?   %   %
CODE ONE ONLY

	%	%
Earnings from employment (own or spouse/partner)	60.6	58.3
Occupational pension(s) - from previous employer(s)	9.0	9.5
State retirement or widow's pension(s)	12.6	13.3
Jobseeker's Allowance or Unemployment Benefit	1.5	1.8
Income Support	7.3	6.1
Family Credit	-	0.3
Invalidity, sickness or disabled pension or benefit(s)	4.2	6.6
Other state benefit (**WRITE IN**) _____	0.4	-
Interest from savings or investments	0.8	0.9
Student grant	1.3	0.8
Dependent on parents/other relatives	1.4	0.5
Other main source (**WRITE IN**) _____	0.4	0.4
Refused to say	0.2	1.4
(Don't know)	-	-
(NA)	0.3	0.2

		Scotland %	Wales %
[HhIncome] **CARD**			
X42. Which of the letters on this card represents the **total** income of your household from **all** sources before tax - including benefits, savings and so on? Please just tell me the letter.			
	Less than £3,999	7.5	6.2
	£4,000-5,999	9.0	9.7
	£6,000-7,999	5.8	7.0
	£8,000-9,999	5.1	6.3
	£10,000-11,999	5.9	5.2
	£12,000-14,999	7.3	8.4
	£15,000-17,999	4.6	6.4
	£18,000-19,999	5.2	4.4
	£20,000-£22,999	4.7	4.5
	£23,000-25,999	5.5	4.5
	£26,000-28,999	4.3	2.9
	£29,000-31,999	4.1	4.1
	£32,000-34,999	2.6	1.9
	£35,000-37,999	2.2	2.6
	£38,000-40,999	2.4	1.6
	£41,000 or more	6.1	6.4
	Refused	10.1	10.2
	(Don't know)	6.4	7.5
	(NA)	1.1	0.1

Base
S: 676
W:686

		%	%
[TEA2]			
X43. How old were you when you finished your continuous full-time education?			
	No schooling received	-	0.2
	15 or under	41.5	34.7
	16	26.8	30.5
	17	7.9	11.4
	18	5.5	8.3
	19 or over	14.5	13.1
	Still in full time education	2.9	1.6
	(NA)	0.9	0.1

		Scotland %	Wales %	Base S: 676 W:686
[SchQual] **CARD** X44a. Have you passed any of the examinations on this card?				
	Yes	57.3	54.6 **ASK b.**	
	No	42.7	45.2 **GO TO X45**	
	(NA)		0.2	

IF 'YES' (CODE 1 at a)
CARD AGAIN
b. Which ones? **PROBE:** Which others?
CODE ALL THAT APPLY

		%	%
	GCSE Grades D-G		
[EdQual1]	CSE Grades 2-5		
	GCE 'O' level Grades D-E or 7-9	11.6	17.5
	Scottish (SCE) Ordinary Bands D-E		
	Scottish Standard Grades 4-7		
	GCSE Grades A-C		
	CSE Grade 1		
	GCE 'O' level Grades A-C or 1-6		
[EdQual2]	School Certificate or matriculation		
	Scottish SCE Ordinary Bands A-C	40.7	44.7
	Scottish Standard Grades 1-3 or 'Pass'		
	Scottish School Leaving Certificate (SLC) Lower Grade		
	SUPE Ordinary		
	Northern Ireland Junior Certificate		
	GCE 'A' level/'S' level/'AS' level		
	Higher School Certificate		
[EdQual3]	Scottish SCE/SLC/SUPE at Higher Grade	25.8	15.3
	Northern Ireland Senior Certificate		
[EdQual4]	Overseas School Leaving Exam/Certificate	0.1	0.2

Base
S: 676
W: 686

ASK ALL
[PSchQual]
CARD

X45. And have you passed any of the examinations or got any
of the qualifications on **this** card?

		Scotland %	Wales %	
	Yes	51.4	48.7	**ASK X46.**
	No	48.3	50.9	**GO TO X47**
	(NA)	0.3	0.4	

IF 'YES' (CODE 1 AT a)
CARD Y AGAIN

X47. Which ones? **PROBE:** Which others?
CODE ALL THAT APPLY

		Scotland %	Wales %
[EdQual5]	Recognised trade apprenticeship completed	9.3	2.8
[EdQual6]	RSA or other clerical or commercial qualification	4.7	8.9
[EdQual22]	City and Guilds Certificate - Part I	5.1	4.8
[EdQual23]	City and Guilds Certificate - Craft/ Intermediate/ Ordinary - Part II	5.2	3.5
[EdQual24]	City and Guilds Certificate - Advanced or Final or Part III	2.3	3.8
[EdQual25]	City and Guilds Certificate - Full technological or Part IV	0.9	1.6
[EdQual10]	BEC/TEC/SCOTBEC/SCOTECH General or Ordinary National Certificate (ONC) or Diploma (OND) or National General Certificate or Diploma	6.4	4.5
[EdQual11]	BEC/TEC/SCOTBEC/SCOTECH Higher/Higher National Certificate (HNC) or Diploma (HND)	8.4	3.8
[EdQual17]	NVQ/SVQ Level 1 or GNVQ Foundation Level	2.2	1.8
[EdQual18]	NVQ/SVQ Level 2 or GNVQ Intermediate Level	2.0	2.0
[EdQual19]	NVQ/SVQ Level 3 or GNVQ Advanced Level	0.9	1.5
[EdQual20]	NVQ/SVQ Level 4	0.2	-
[EdQual21]	NVQ/SVQ Level 5	-	-
[EdQual12]	Teachers training qualification	4.0	5.8
[EdQual13]	Nursing qualification	2.0	4.4
[EdQual15]	University or CNAA degree or diploma, including higher degree	12.4	10.6
[EdQual14]	Other technical or business qualification/certificate	3.6	5.4
[EdQual16]	Other recognised academic or vocational qualification (**WRITE IN**)	4.0	6.6

ASK ALL   Base
[Vote97]   S: 676
X47. Now (may I just check), thinking back to the <u>general election</u>   W: 686
in May of this year - do you remember which party you voted for
then or perhaps you didn't vote in that election?
IF 'YES': Which party was that?
IF NECESSARY, SAY The one where Tony Blair won against   *Scotland*   *Wales*
John Major?   %   %

			Scotland %	Wales %
DO NOT PROMPT	**Yes voted:**	Conservative	12.9	17.6
		Labour	45.6	51.4
		Liberal Democrat	6.8	8.5
		Scottish National Party	18.0	•
		Plaid Cymru	•	9.7
		Green Party	-	-
		Referendum Party	0.4	0.2
Other **(WRITE IN)** _____			0.3	0.1
		Refused to disclose voting	1.0	0.9
		Did not vote/Was not eligible to vote	13.5	10.4
		(Don't know/Can't remember)	1.2	0.7
		(NA)	0.2	0.4

[RGovtNow]
X48. Say there was an election to the Scottish Parliament tomorrow,
which political party do you think you would be most likely to support?
DO NOT PROMPT

		Scotland %	Wales %
	Conservative	11.6	16.5
	Labour	47.0	49.0
	Liberal Democrat	6.9	6.9
	Scottish National Party	21.1	•
	Plaid Cymru	•	11.9
	Green party	0.1	-
Other party **(WRITE IN)** _____		0.4	0.3
Other answer **(WRITE IN)** _____		0.3	0.4
	None/Would not vote	3.6	4.9
	Refused to say	0.9	0.7
	(Don't know)	8.0	9.2
	(NA)	0.2	0.1

			Scotland	Wales	**Base**
	[Phone]		%	%	**S:676**
X49a.	Is there a telephone in (your part of) this accommodation?				
		Yes	94.1	93.7 **ASK b.**	**W:676**
		No	5.9	6.3 **GO TO X50**	

IF YES AT a)
[PhoneBck]

b. A few interviews on any survey are checked by a supervisor to make sure that people are satisfied with the way the interview was carried out. In case my supervisor needs to contact you, it would be helpful if we could have your telephone number.

ADD IF NECESSARY: Your 'phone number will not be passed on to anyone outside SCPR.

IF NUMBER GIVEN, WRITE ON THE ARF

	Scotland	Wales
	%	%
Number given	86.6	86.4
Number refused	7.4	7.3

ASK ALL
[Stable]

X50. We may wish to contact you again some time in the future for a similar interview. Could you give us the address or phone number of someone who knows you well, just in case we have difficulty getting in touch with you?

IF NECESSARY, PROMPT: Perhaps the address of a relative or friend who is unlikely to move?

PROBE FOR FULL DETAILS AND RECORD ON BACK PAGE OF ARF.

	Scotland	Wales
	%	%
Information given	51.8	54.6
Information not given (other than outright code 3)	44.4	41.0
DO NOT PROMPT: Outright refusal ever to take part again	3.7	4.3

[SCXplain]

X51. **INTERVIEWER: THANK RESPONDENT FOR HIS/HER TIME AND EXPLAIN ABOUT THE SELF-COMPLETION.**
IS IT TO BE ...

	Scotland	Wales
	%	%
... filled in immediately in your presence	92.3	83.8
or, left behind to be filled in later	6.5	11.6
or, refused?	1.2	4.5

X52a. TIME INTERVIEW COMPLETED

b. TOTAL LENGTH OF INTERVIEW

minutes

c. INTERVIEWER'S SIGNATURE

d. DATE OF INTERVIEW

Day   Month   Year

9 7

Subject Index

A

Aberdeen, University of 202, 238
Aberfan Disaster Fund 213
Aberystwyth 17, 65, 95,
 169, 239
Abse, Leo 96, 97, 208, 211
Acts of Union, Wales (1536-1543)
 65, 172, 173
Aigner, Nick 30
Alexander III 201
Ancram, Michael 24
Andrews, Leighton 29
Appendix I - Technical details of
 Surveys 237-244
Argyll, Duke of 202
Assembly: see Welsh Assembly
Attlee, Clement 5, 207, 212
Australia, referendums in 1, 4

B

Baden-Powell, Robert 204
Bagehot, Walter 214
Balfour, Arthur 203
Balsom, Denis xxxv, 83, 84, 238
Barbour, John 201
Barnard, Allan 30
BBC Wales xii, 192
Beaufort poll 35
Belfast 6, 202
Benn, Tony 5, 6
Bevan, Aneurin 207, 218
Bevin, Ernest 212

Bismarck, Otto von, Prince 204
Blair, Tony 18-23 *passim*, 27-31
 passim, 105, 119, 151, 182, 183, 209,
 212-215 *passim*, 230
Bogdanor, Vernon 5
Bonnie Prince Charlie 201
Bowen, Betty 32
Boyd-Orr, John 207
Brand, Jack xxxvi
Britain in Europe campaign 7
British Academy lecture, 1998 xxi,
 xxxv
British Election Panel Study (BEPS)
 (1992-1997) viii, 237
British Election Panel Study (BEPS2)
 (1997-2002) viii, 237
British Election Study (BES) 1997
 xxxv, 121, 124, 126, 237, 239
British Social Attitudes survey 237
Brown, Alice xxxv, 238
Brown, Gordon 9, 209
Bruce, Robert 201
Brussels 217
Buchanan-Smith, Alick 223
Burns, Robert 229
Butler, David viii, 6, 12, 20, 135, 150,
 237, 238

C

Cabinet solidarity 6
California, referendums in 1, 14
Callaghan, James 6, 41, 151, 182, 191

Carmarthenshire 119
Canada, referendums in 225
Canadian Constitution 225
Cardiff 11, 30, 32, 34, 37, 65, 90
Cardiff Development Corporation 175
Census Report for Wales 185
Centre for Research into Elections and Social Trends (CREST) viii, xi, xii, xxxv, 238
Churchill, Winston 4, 207
Civil society 169-197 *passim*, 222-227 *passim*
Coalition for Scottish Democracy (1995) 21
Coalition, war-time 5
Colley, Linda 202
Common Cause (Scotland) 21
Common Market (European Economic Community) 3, 5, 6, 10, 216
see also: European Community and European Union
Connery, Sean 26
Constitution Unit 10
Constitutional amendment 2, 4
Constitutional convention: see Scottish Constitutional Convention
Consultative Steering Group 181
Convention of Scottish Local Authorities 20
Cook, Robin 208, 209
Council for Wales, the 207, 214
Council of Ministers 217
Council of the Isles 212
Countryside Council for Wales 175
Court of Great Sessions 201
Crewe, Ivor 237
Crowther-Kilbrandon Royal Commission 96, 208
Cunningham Amendment (also referred to as 40% rule) 7, 10, 13, 20, 22, 42, 223
Cunningham, George 13, 20
Curtice, John viii, 9, 52, 81, 100, 143, 157, 185, 192, 225, 238
Cymru Fydd (Young Wales) 1894-1896 205, 211

D

Daily Express, the 188
Daily Mail, the 188
Daily Mirror, the 29
Daily Post, the 29
Dalyell, Tam 26, 188, 208, 215
Data Archive xxxvi, 239
Davies, Rees 201
Davies, Ron viii, 27-38 *passim*, 90, 132, 166, 183, 212-214

Declaration of Arbroath (1324) 231
Democracy for Scotland 21
Democratic effectiveness 47-49
Denmark, referendums in 2, 4
Denver, David 77
Dewar, Donald 22, 23, 26
Diana, Princess of Wales 26, 35, 119
Dicey, A V 4, 12, 14

E

Economic and Social Research Council (ESRC) (formerly Social Science Research Council) viii, xi, xxi, xxxv, 238
Edinburgh 207, 212
Edinburgh, University of xxxv, 238
Edward I 172, 200, 201, 224
Edwards, Huw T 214
Edwards, O.D 44
Electoral Commission 11
Electoral Reform Society 10
Electoral register 7, 26, 168, 239, 240
Electoral Systems:
additional member system xxi, 37
alternative vote 9
first-past-the-post 13
single-member plurality system 13
see also: Proportional Representation
Ellis, Tom 203
Encyclopaedia Britannica 171, 200
Essex, University of 238
European Community: see Common Market
European Monetary Union 9, 143, 214
European Union 9, 13, 14, 55, 210, 215-217, 225
see also: Common Market
Evans, Geoffrey viii, 8, 36, 70, 119, 129, 130, 137, 151, 191, 210, 211, 328
Evans, Jonathan 214
Ewing, Winnie 229, 230
Expectations
of parliament/assembly 45-47, 54, 55, 139-141
of democractic effectiveness 47-52, 82

F

Farmers Union of Wales 175
Fay, Stephen 218
Fermanagh 12
Fianna Fail 13
Fife, Earl of 202
Finlay, R J 44
First order elections: see Second-order elections

First World War 205
Foot, Michael 6
Forsyth, Michael 19, 20, 22, 42, 223
Forty-percent rule: see Cunningham
  Amendment
Fry, Michael 36

G

Gellner, Ernest 99
Germany 212, 216
Giggs, Ryan 32
Gladstone, William Ewart 203, 204,
  215, 227
Glasgow 26, 202, 210
Glyndŵr, Owain 172, 201
Goldsmith, James (Sir) 9
Good Friday Agreement 7-9
Government of Wales Act, 1998 142
Government of Wales Bill, 1997 38,
  142
Gramsci, Antonio 170, 180, 191
Griffiths, Arthur 218
Griffiths, James 207, 208
Grimmond, Jo 227
Guardian, the 35

H

Hague, William 209
Hain, Peter 29-31
Hands, Gordon 77
Hardie, Keir 206, 229
Hart, Judith 6
Heath, Anthony viii, 9, 62, 102, 124,
  132, 137, 139, 140, 190, 225, 238
Heath, Edward 5, 6, 223
Heffer, Eric 6
Hegel, Frederick 170, 174, 176, 177,
  180
Henderson, Arthur 206
Henry VIII 173, 217
Herald, the 26, 36, 62
Hiraethog, Gwilym 203
Hitler, Adolf 5
Hodge, Julian (Sir) 211
Hodge, Robert 32
Home Rule, Ireland 4, 12
Home rule, Scotland/Wales 19-21,
  26, 27, 170, 187, 188, 193, 205
Hughes, Cledwyn 207
Hume, John 231
Hunt, David 209

I

ICM polls 26, 35, 53, 205, 215, 227
Independent on Sunday, the 231
Independence 18, 25, 27, 37, 38, 42,
  52-54, 59-63 *passim*, 95, 98, 139, 140,
  162, 176, 178, 188, 191-194 *passim*,
  222, 224- 227 *passim*, 230-235 *passim*,
Institute of Welsh Affairs (IWA) xii,
  29
Intermediate Education Act (1889)
  204
Ireland 2, 12-14, 124, 202, 203,
  218
Irish Free State Treaty (1922) 205
Italy, referendums in 2, 4, 216

J

Jay, Douglas 207
Jenkins Commission 9
Jenkins, Roy (Lord) 5, 6
John, E T 205
Johnston, Tom 207
Jones, J Barry 97
Jones, Basil (Bishop) 201
Jones, Jack 6
Jowell, Roger 143, 238
Just Say No campaign, Wales 32, 70

K

Keating, Michael 221
Kellas, James viii, 124
Kiewif, D 44
Kilbrandon Commission: see
  Crowther-Kilbrandon Commission
Kinder, D 44
Kinnock, Neil 96, 97, 209
Kitzinger, Uwe 6
Knowledge of devolution proposals
  (quiz) 71, 80, 81, 110, 156

L

Labour Party: (National Executive
  Committee) NEC 5, 6
Labour Votes No campaign,
  Scotland 7, 8, 17, 20, 24
Lang, Ian 224
Language: see Welsh Language
Lee, Jennie 207
Left-right scale 138, 145
Lewis, Bethan viii, 8, 41, 70, 71, 97,
  114, 166, 176, 209, 211, 229
Lewis, Saunders 206
Lipset, S M 120
Livingstone, Ken 215
Livsey, Richard 34
Lloyd George, David 204-206
Llywelyn, Prince 200
London 30, 31, 211, 215
  referendums in 8
Lynn, Vera (Dame) 216

M

Madgwick, Peter xxxv
Major, John 9, 170, 210, 222-224,
  228, 230
Manchester Information Datasets
  and Associated Systems (MIDAS)
  243
Mandates 12, 23, 38
Mannheimer, Renato 156
Marx, Karl 201
Maudling, Reginald 6
Maxton, Jimmy 209
McAllion, John 19
McAllister, Ian 31, 32,
McCrone, David viii, xxxv, 7, 8, 27,
  38, 41, 70, 73, 74, 81, 97, 114, 119,
  120, 124, 137, 139, 157, 166, 176,
  183, 184, 186, 209-211, 223, 225, 229,
  238
McIntyre, Robert 206
McLean, Iain viii, 20, 150, 213
Meech Lake Accord (1987) 225
Michael, Alun 212
Midwinter, Arthur 221
Millbank, Labour Party
  Headquarters 30, 31
Miller, William xxxvi
Mitchell, James 20
Moreno measure of national identity
  (Moreno scale) 50, 54, 74, 75, 78, 84,
  124, 126-128, 130, 133, 135, 157
Morgan, Kenneth O viii, 7, 8
Morgan, Rhodri 212
Morrison, Herbert 207, 214

N

Nairne Commission, the 10, 11
Nairne, Patrick, (Sir) 10, 12
Nairn, Tom 231
National Assembly for Wales: see
  Welsh Assembly
National Assembly Advisory Group,
  Wales 183
National Coal Board 213
National Health Service 218
National identity 49-52, 54, 63, 66,
  72-90 *passim*, 99-102, 110, 113, 120-
  143 *passim*, 156-158, 170, 174-179,
  183-187, 192, 201-205, 209, 226, 228,
  229, 231
  and age 76-77
  and birth place 75, 88, 100
  and language (Welsh) 78-80, 83, 88,
  89, 100, 101, 122, 134, 135, 211
  knowledge and expectation of
  devolution 80-83
National Museum of Wales, Cardiff
  xi

National University of Ireland 204
Neill Committee on Standards in
  Public Life 8, 10-12, 114
Netherlands, referendums in 217
Non-voting 130-133, 149
  see also: Turnout
Norris, Pippa xxxv, 238
Northern Ireland 212, 231
Northern Ireland Act (1972) 6
Northern Ireland Election Study
  1992 viii, 237
Northern Ireland referendums, in
  5, 8, 237
Norway, referendums in 13
Nuffield College Oxford viii, 238

O

Office of National Statistics (ONS)
  122
Opinion polls 6, 9,38,52-55, 62, 63,
  65, 102, 188, 189, 192, 227
Osmond, John 97, 216

P

Paisley, Ian 6, 8, 9
Parliament for Wales campaign, the
  207
Parliamentary sovereignty 4, 10, 179,
  222
Parties, electors' opinions of 55-59,
  70-73, 102-105, 222
Partisan alignment 43, 66-72 *passim*,
  83-90, 96, 106, 110, 116, 136, 137
Party cue theory 66, 67, 72, 83, 88,
  105, 107, 108
Party identification: see Partisan
  alignment
Party identity: see Partisan
  alignment
Party perceptions 69-72, 104-106
Paterson, Lindsay viii, 80, 90, 114,
  120, 156, 166, 176, 177, 222, 227, 238
Pedley, Phil 71
Pergamon Press 238
Policy Commission, Wales 28
Postcode Address File (PAF) 239,
  243
Powell, Enoch 6
Powell, Ray 32
Prescott, John 27
Pretoria 204
Proportional representation 9, 28, 58,
  80
  see also: also Electoral systems
Public opinion 24-27, 166
Pugh, Carys 32

Q

Quango(s) 97, 175, 178, 191, 210, 214, 215

R

Rational voting 45, 116
Referendum Act, the (1975) 7
Referendum Commission 10
  see also: Constitution Unit
Referendum(s) 1-15, 44, 45, 53, 65, 66, 96, 97, 99, 110, 113, 133-137, 224, 225, 229, 230, 232- 234
  Advisory 4, 10
  Binding 4
  Moral 2, 3
  Nationwide 1, 5
  Non-constitutional 14
  Post-legislative 8, 10
  Pre-legislative 8, 10
  Territorial 2, 3, 12, 13
  As second-order elections 102, 132, 149-168
  Conservative Party 70-71
  Labour Party 70
  Liberal Democrat 72
  Plaid Cymru 71-72
Referendum Party 9
Referendum Studies Scottish and Welsh, 1997 xi, xxi, xix, xxxv, 45, 58, 80, 84, 95, 121, 124, 156, 184, 187-193, 211, 238-244
  data collection and response 241-243
  face to face questionnaires 241
  geographical data 243
  postal 237
  questionnaire 241, 245-301
  sample 239-241
  weighting 243
Reform Acts of 1867 and 1885 203
Regional Council of Labour, the 206
Reif, K 150, 152, 158
Reith, John (Lord) 207
Religion 43, 92, 174, 227, 233
  Catholic 43, 227, 233
  Protestant 227, 233
Research Services Ltd xxxvi
Richard, Henry 174
Rifkind, Malcolm 23
Robert, Samuel (of Llanbrynmair) 203
Roberts, Goronwy 207
Robertson, George 19-23
Rogers, Allan 32
Rose, Richard 221
Rosebery, Duke of 202
Round Table 205

S

Sainsbury Family Charitable Trusts, Gatsby Charitable Foundation xxxv, 238
Salmond, Alex 25, 26, 231
Särlvik, Bo 238
Scanlon, Hugh 6
Schmitt, Hermann 150, 152, 156
Scotland Act (1978) 7, 97
Scotland and Wales Bill, 1977 96
Scotland FORward 24, 26, 27
Scotland on Sunday 20
Scotland's Elections, May 1999 59-61
Scotsman, the 19, 20, 23, 26, 53, 188, 231
Scott, Walter (Sir) 202
Scottish CBI 26
Scottish Chambers of Commerce 26
Scottish Civic Assembly 21
Scottish Constitutional Convention 20, 21, 23, 25, 28, 30, 42, 121, 179-181, 187, 209, 230
Scottish Election Study 1979 xxxv, 44
Scottish Election Study 1997 xxxv, 44, 45, 186, 225, 228, 237, 239
Scottish Grand Committee, the 224, 229
Scottish Office, the 177, 179, 180, 207, 227, 229
Scottish Parliament, the 8, 122, 129, 142, 152, 161, 162, 167, 179, 185, 187, 189, 192, 193, 208, 211, 212, 214, 215, 222, 223, 224, 228-231, 233
Scottish Referendum Study 1997: see Referendum Studies
Scottish Trades Union Congress (STUC) 20, 21, 24
Scottish Watch 232
Scotland United 21
Second-order elections 102-105, 132, 139, 140, 146, 150, 152, 153, 158-160, 167
Second World War 205-208
Settler Watch 232
Shore, Peter 6
Sianel Pedwar 211
Single European Currency: see European Monetary Union
Smith, John 17, 24, 42, 187, 209, 229
Smith, John Memorial Lecture 209
Smith, Llew 32, 33
Smith, Steve viii
Social and Community Planning Research (SCPR) viii, xii, xxxv, 238
Social Surveys (Gallup Poll) Ltd xxxv
South Africa 205
Spain, referendums in 216
Speed, Gary 32

St David, Viscount 71
Steed, Michael 9
Steel, David 230
Stokes, Donald 135, 237, 238
Stormont Parliament 5
Strathclyde, University of xxxvi, 238
Sun, the 29
Surridge, Paula viii, xxxv, 7, 8, 27, 38, 74, 81, 119, 120, 124, 137, 139, 156, 183, 186, 210, 223, 225, 229, 238
Sweden, referendums in 4
Switzerland, referendums in 1, 4
System Three polls 26

T

Tartan tax 19, 42, 224
  see also: Tax-varying powers, Scotland
Tax-varying powers, Scotland 5, 8, 17-27 *passim*, 41, 42, 122, 188-191 *passim*, 200, 209- 212 *passim*, 224
Taylor, Bridget viii, 62, 102, 132, 139, 140, 190, 225, 238
Thatcher, Margaret (Lady) 23, 26, 41, 113, 170, 178, 186, 208, 216, 221-223, 228, 230
Think Twice (Scotland) 24, 26
Thomas, R S 202
Thomson, Katarina viii, 238
Thorpe, Jeremy 6
Tonypandy, Viscount 32, 206, 211
Trades Union Congress (TUC) 174
Trades Union Congress of Wales 182
Treaty of Rome 3
Treaty of Versailles 204
Trystan, Dafydd viii, 8, 36, 70, 97, 100, 105, 110, 119, 122, 124, 126, 129, 130, 135, 151, 156, 185, 191, 192, 210, 214
Turnout 4, 6-10, 20, 26, 35, 78, 96, 106, 108-113, 119, 121, 129- 132, 141, 150, 152-158, 167, 200, 210, 225
  see also: Non-voting
Tyrone 12

U

UK Press Gazette 29
UK, referendums in 4, 6, 7
Ulster 202
Union of 1707, the 176, 179, 200, 201, 212
Unofficial Reform Committee 206

V

Van der Eijk, Cees 150

W

Wales, University of xii, xxxv, 174, 191, 203, 204, 217, 238
Walker, Peter 209
Wallace, Jim 26
Wallace, William 201
Welsh Assembly 8, 65, 66, 69, 78, 80, 113, 114, 123, 129, 142, 151, 152, 160-162, 167, 175, 181, 182, 185, 189, 191-193, 200, 208, 211, 213, 214, 216
Welsh Context xiii
Welsh Council of Reconstruction (1942) 207
Welsh Development Agency 175
Welsh Election Study 1979 xxxv, 96, 237
Welsh language 78, 79, 83, 86, 101, 127, 128, 135, 184, 238, 241
Welsh Local Government Association 30
Welsh Office 30, 97, 175, 208-210, 217
Welsh Referendum Study: see Referendum Studies
Welsh Select Committee 217
Welsh Sunday Closing Act (1881) 204
Western Mail, the 27, 29, 33, 35, 38
West Lothian 26, 215
Wigley, Dafydd 34
William the Conqueror 217
Williams, Glanmor 173
Williams, Raymond 73
Williams, Shirley 6
Wilson, Gordon 25
Wilson, Harold 6, 11
Winning, Thomas (Cardinal) 231
Winter of discontent, the 7, 8, 151, 199
Women's Co-ordination Group (Scotland) 21
Wright, Kenyon (Canon) 209, 229
Wyn Jones, Richard 8, 36, 71, 80, 90, 97, 100, 105, 110, 114, 119, 120, 122, 124, 126, 135, 156, 159, 166, 176, 185, 191, 192, 211, 222, 227, 238

Y

Yes for Wales campaign 29-34
Yes for Wales papers 30
Younger, George 223
Ysgolion Cymraeg (Welsh medium schools) 211

UNIVERSITY OF WOLVERHAMPTON
LEARNING RESOURCES